World Bank Financing of Education

How has the financial power and influence of the World Bank helped to shape education policies around the world?

Based on detailed analysis of thousands of confidential World Bank documents and extensive interviews with key World Bank officials, this book outlines the evolution of World Bank lending policies in education, and assesses the policy impact of the Bank's education projects and programs.

The author demonstrates that the World Bank lies at the center of the major changes in global education of our time. Its financial power and influence have helped shape the economic and social policies of many governments, including policies that affect education. It has been an influential proponent of the rapid expansion of formal education systems around the world, and has financed much of that expansion. It has been instrumental in forging those policies that see education as a precursor to modernization. It has served as a major purveyor of western ideas about how education and the economy are, or should be, related. It has championed human capital perspectives on educational development and the integration of education policies with global economic integration and reform.

Professor Jones' exposition of how all of this has been achieved, and the implications of this achievement, is unique. It will be of enormous value to those studying, or working in, educational policy in developing countries, international organizations and financial institutions, and aid agencies.

Phillip W. Jones is Director of the Research Institute for Humanities and Social Sciences at the University of Sydney, Australia. He is a prominent authority on the education policies and programs of the World Bank and UN agencies. Professor Jones' most recent RoutledgeFalmer title was *The United Nations and Education: Multilateralism, Development and Globalisation* (2005).

World Bank Financing of Education

Education

Lending, learning and development

Second edition

Phillip W. Jones

Routledge
Taylor & Francis Group

LONDON AND NEW YORK

First edition published 1992
by Routledge

This edition published 2007
by Routledge
2 Park Square, Milton Park, Abingdon, Oxon OX14 4RN

Simultaneously published in the USA and Canada
by Routledge
270 Madison Ave, New York, NY 10016

Routledge is an imprint of the Taylor & Francis Group, an informa business

© 1992, 2007 Phillip W. Jones

Typeset in Garamond by
Newgen Imaging Systems (P) Ltd, Chennai, India
Printed and bound in Great Britain by
Biddles Ltd, King's Lynn

British Library Cataloguing in Publication Data
A catalogue record for this book is available
from the British Library

Library of Congress Cataloguing in Publication Data
A catalog record for this book has been requested

ISBN10: 0–415–40476–2 (hbk)
ISBN10: 0–203–96593–0 (ebk)

ISBN13: 978–0–415–40476–1 (hbk)
ISBN13: 978–0–203–96593–1 (ebk)

For Alison, Graham and Janet

Let knowledge grow from more to more,
But more of reverence in us dwell;
That mind and soul, according well,
May make one music as before,

But vaster...

(Alfred Lord Tennyson)

Contents

Tables

Preface to the first edition

The twentieth century will be remembered as the one in which the world embraced formal education. Acceptance of education as a universal right has been translated into rapidly increasing rates of expansion, access, and participation. Given the numbers of people involved, the preferred length of schooling, and its substantial cost, this constitutes an enormous social development, of deep cultural and economic significance.

It was not until the twentieth century that the world saw in formal education both the sign and the means of rapidly entering a modern existence. In the West, the eighteenth and nineteenth centuries had seen processes of agricultural and industrial change precipitate the need for universal schooling. For non-Western societies, by contrast, formal education was seen as a necessary forerunner of technological change and economic growth. This is a significant difference, and ironies abound in those many places where celebration of independence from Western colonial rule was marked by the desire to transform society along lines implied by the Western technological and economic experience. In many non-Western societies it was the Western institution of schooling that was deemed powerful enough to bring about that transformation.

None of which is to deny the growing significance of nonformal education, especially among those of post-school age. Commitments to human rights and equity have resulted in vigorous attempts to foster literacy and basic education among the unschooled, while economic goals have frequently stimulated interest in patterns of worker education and training capable of leading directly to increased productivity and economic expansion. Notions of lifelong education have had important cultural as well as economic justifications. Economic perspectives on educational planning and management have, in fact, gone far in encouraging consonance between formal and nonformal educational provision.

This accelerating provision of educational opportunity has been accompanied by vigorous debates over the ultimate purposes and deeper meaning underlying education. The history of education in the twentieth century has been very much concerned with the need to choose between the moral and the material purposes of education. In particular, analysis has shown the political and cultural functions of education to be unavoidable concerns. Were education's principal effects the unlocking of individual potential or rather the enhancement of social administration? Did education foster liberty or stifle it? Did it promote creativity and entrepreneurship or rather passivity and subservience? Was it a vehicle for the renewal of society or its mere reproduction? If education provided rich evidence for all these interpretations, then was it best promoted in humanistic and moral terms or more precisely and powerfully in economic and material terms? At its heart, education as both a personal and social enterprise is an undertaking that has demanded a choice. A view of education that is both compelling and complete is yet to emerge, one that convincingly binds up its moral and material dimensions, so that questions of human dignity, diversity, equity, and freedom rest easily with meeting those tangible material needs so central to the pursuit of happiness and well-being.

Education – and mass schooling in particular – is a phenomenon that unites the world, in the sense that it is a key aspect of that steady process whereby a global technological civilization is being forged. All around the world, the variety and the dynamics of local culture have collided with the steady transformation of societies along the lines implied by modernization. It is when entering the classroom door that this is most evident – the point at which so much of local culture and custom is discarded in favor of the demands of technological civilization.

Notwithstanding their sovereignty, national governments behave in similar ways when addressing educational policy. This trend is bound up with the ascendancy of those material objectives which have come to characterize late twentieth-century education. The world's schools, their teachers, and their curricula are becoming more and more alike. School systems become organized and managed on increasingly similar lines. The uses of literacy become standardized. Universities strive to be as similar as possible. Textbooks become international commodities. The gulf between culture and education first widens, then narrows, as culture is irrevocably altered to conform to the pressures of standardization, inevitably a process that sees the material dimensions of education at a premium.

It is now possible to speak of an international system of influence powerful enough to bind up the educational destinies of the world's peoples. If such a network of global influence limits the discretion of peoples to shape their own educational destinies and imposes its own solution to the moral–material dilemma facing educational policy, then it is worthy of investigation. If so, an inescapable concern must be the set of international organizations for which education is a dominant concern. The reception accorded my earlier book, which explored these themes with reference to UNESCO, appears to justify a concern to understand how international organizations in education have adopted their respective policy positions (*International Policies for Third World Education: UNESCO, Literacy and Development*, Routledge, 1988). That book and this are dedicated to the possibility that the international community might increase its readiness for peoples to decide and put into effect their own educational futures, and to forge their own integration of the moral and material in education.

The World Bank and education

Many of these themes come together when the educational work of the World Bank is considered. The World Bank lies at the center of the major changes in global education of our time. Its financial power and influence have helped shape the economic and social policies of many governments, including policies that affect education. It has been an influential proponent of the rapid expansion of formal education systems around the world, and has financed much of that expansion. It has been instrumental in forging those policies that see education as a precursor to modernization. It has served as a major purveyor of Western ideas about how education and the economy are, or should be, connected. It has assumed a prominent role in educational research and policy analysis, and exercises a degree of leadership among those international organizations committed to education. All of this was achieved in a relatively brief span of thirty years.

The World Bank – first and foremost – is a bank, and requires analysis as such. Its capacity to lend is a direct product of its capacity to raise capital. Like all banks, it is obliged to protect its credibility in the marketplace, and part of that credibility stems from the wisdom of its own investments, as perceived in international financial markets. Its financing of education is not, and cannot be, immune from the discipline imposed by the realities of its existence as a bank. Its judgments, even when arbitrary, must at least appear to be hardheaded. Here, then, we catch a glimpse of the international financial community's views on education and the economy, or at least a glimpse of views it is prepared to back with finance.

A lifespan of six or seven years is not uncommon for a World Bank education project. All Bank projects are large, costly and complex, and address multiple and intermingled objectives. The lead time needed to meet Bank requirements for project preparation is protracted. Bank requirements for the monitoring of financial disbursements are meticulous, with detailed audits seeking reasonable assurance that funds disbursed have been applied as intended, even if more detailed evaluation of project quality and impact is rare. A single lending operation, then, can readily span fifteen or more years, and within a given country successive education loans frequently overlap in chronology and function. In short, Bank projects are substantial undertakings, and for both Bank and borrower the entire project cycle is a demanding one.

Since the first World Bank education loan was approved in 1962 (to Tunisia for the construction of secondary schools), 129 countries have borrowed $36,567 million for projects (as of FY 2005). The annual level of lending is now greatly in excess of $1 billion, in some years reaching

$2 billion. In FY 2004, 142 education projects were being implemented in eighty-nine countries at a combined cost of nearly $8.5 billion. The World Bank has quickly emerged as the largest single supplier of external finance to education, historically providing up to 20 percent of such assistance.

The financial and policy dominance of the World Bank is hardly free of its critics. When, for example, the Bank announced a significant increase in available Bank finance for basic education in the 1990s, the most vocal and negative of reactions were heard from its intended beneficiaries. A typical complainant was the African Finance Minister who accused the Bank of casual arbitrariness in switching its lending priorities from higher to primary education, while his country remained indebted as a result of the now "discredited" higher education loans. He was joined by other critics who attacked the arrogance of Bank officials in their dealings with borrowers, their failure to consult and to see things from the developing countries' perspective, and their simplistic views on how schools actually function and on how educational change can be achieved and made more relevant to economic growth and equity. The World Bank succeeds in attracting both praise and damnation from all quarters – from all political perspectives and from all parts of the world – and for this reason alone is an intriguing institution worthy of scrutiny.

It is important, perhaps, to indicate what this book is not. Bank education loans number in the hundreds, and each one would merit its own detailed investigation. Several days can be spent merely reading the Bank's documentation on a single project or how its programs have a cumulative effect within individual countries. Although I have done this in many cases, readers hoping for detailed analyses of project experience on the ground might be disappointed, although several chapters present numerous instances of Bank project experience. The focus of the book is an explanation of Bank policies in education, especially those seen in educational financing. The book's themes are institutional and historical – the emergence of Bank views, policies and financing criteria for education, each usually intended for global application. It is hoped, indeed, that this study might stimulate regional and country studies that examine the local impact of Bank investment in education. Many possibilities spring to mind, and a range of international comparisons of experience would be timely.

Central to this study is the Bank's own responses to its project and lending experience. Different schools of thought persist among Bank staff about how to interpret Bank projects and their value. Are projects merely rationalized channels for dispersing foreign exchange to borrowers? Are projects realistic vehicles for encouraging reforms in education? Are World Bank projects so ambitious and complex that very few can expect to be successful? What is the best balance in Bank lending between project loans and program loans for educational reform? Scepticism abounds at Bank headquarters about this most central element in the life and work of the Bank – the project – and Bank perceptions of its project experience are crucial as one stance about financing criteria gives way to another.

Perhaps undeservedly, the Bank's use of training as a tool to promote its program is given short shrift in this study. To use Bank parlance, its focus is on the "education sector," that component of Bank work dedicated to the building up of the developing world's education systems. Deserving of a separate study is the Bank's "training" commitments. In all economic sectors, the Bank has utilized training as a key instrument for policy influence and project effectiveness, not least through its own training arm, the Economic Development Institute (EDI), discussed briefly in Chapter 1.

Researching the World Bank

Given the prominent role being played in educational expansion and development by such agencies as the World Bank, it is surprising that there has been so little independent, scholarly analysis of them. It is all the more surprising given the contact between them and the academic community, with which they have forged intimate working relationships. Perhaps there lies the reason. At the same time, there has emerged down the years a good number of diverse but general studies of the World Bank in operation. Some constitute the reflections of retired Bank officers. Some have been commissioned by the Bank. Others, including the present study, have been initiated and conducted independently of the Bank, and for which distance from the Bank is an important ingredient.

Yet research requires intimacy, and most authors have remarked upon how secretive they have found the World Bank to be, even by Washington standards. They claim more than the usual difficulty in gaining access to large, complex bureaucracies, not least those of an intergovernmental kind. My own approach to the Bank for a study of the present kind was approved, enabling me to spend from 1986 up to the present time several sustained periods at the Bank's headquarters in Washington, DC. I was left to my own devices to find my way about this labyrinthine agency, and can report no attempt to color or shape the study or to influence its findings. A certain pragmatism might have surrounded the decision to let me proceed unfettered, but I cannot be sure of its character. Perhaps to their relief, the Bank officers responsible have now moved on to other things.

All authors given access to the Bank run into the problem of how to handle internal Bank documents, which are invariably labeled "for official use only." I have elected to use less than the ideal amount of direct quotation and referencing in the following chapters. On balance, I consider this to be an acceptable price to pay for unrestrained access to the documentation I needed to see. A second problem arises from the amount of printed documentation consulted – several thousand documents in all. Its sheer volume precludes detailed listing in this book, but it should be recalled that only a small proportion of it is publicly available, even with the new openness of recent years.

Procedurally this study constitutes, on the one hand, an institutional history of how the Bank came to commit itself to educational financing and how it adopted certain criteria over others within its portfolio of educational lending. On the other hand, it presents a policy analysis of two key issues: how project experience in education impacted on subsequent Bank policy in education, and how the Bank came to resolve complex matters facing borrowers in their education systems. In terms of methods adopted, of prominence were analyses of internal Bank documentation, and interviews with present and former Bank officers. I was fortunate in having access to a range of interviews previously recorded under the Bank's oral history program, and in fact was pleased to contribute to that program as an interviewer. Also of importance have been interviews I conducted with a large number of persons on the receiving end of Bank lending, and interviews with knowledgeable persons in a wide range of governmental and international organizations.

Sydney, January 1991

Preface to the second edition

It might seem trite to state that since the first edition of this book was written in 1990, enormous geopolitical changes have engulfed the work of the World Bank. The collapse of the Soviet Union brought into the sphere of the Bank twenty-seven new borrowers who would embark with the Bank on an attempt to transform their economies from a socialist to a market basis. This required of the Bank a new way of thinking about its global role, reach and policy menu. The end of the Cold War provided the opportunity – indeed demanded of the Bank – for it to make more explicit its views of economic and social policy. How would the Bank, in fact, serve the needs of such disparate borrowing states? Its answer – by demanding their integration into a single global capitalist economy – was a time-honored answer for the Bank, but the collapse of the Soviet bloc has made it plain for all to see. Thus, the Bank entered into a new period of its work when it was faced with all the policy and program dilemmas that arise when a single policy framework is embraced for all borrowers, from the very poorest to reasonably successful middle-income economies.

The Bank emerged as a champion of economic globalization, the principles of the free market now explicitly voiced as the basis of its development prescriptions the world over. Through the 1990s, of course, globalization became a catchcry across the social sciences, providing new frameworks, objects and lenses for a wide variety of researchers. Despite the vagueness of globalization as a concept, the stance of the Bank in relation to economic globalization is clearly of considerable significance and deserves close attention, not least in its impact on local decisions about economic and social policy. The Bank's conventional stance – to impose a common policy framework on all its borrowers – has remained intact. If anything, the Bank has become increasingly insistent, even strident, although it has made serious attempts to moderate its language, soften its image and mollify its critics.

The impact of globalization on educational theory, policy and practice has been a primary research concern around the world since 1990, although the impact of globalization on actual classroom practice has not been as great as one might imagine. Very important, however, have been the great catchcries of privatization and decentralization, whose immediate impact on access to education, its quality and its organization has been considerable. Economic globalization has transformed labor markets, upsetting conventional relationships between education systems and the supply of an educated workforce. That transformation has proven itself cataclysmic, and debates abound about the medium-to-long-term effects of neoliberal prescription on educational provision. Since the first edition of this book appeared, the Bank has steadily increased its use of education reform program loans to drive neoliberal policies around the world. Less prominent are free-standing projects, although many traditional project components (such as construction) continue as features of Bank reform lending.

All of this has been of consequence for multilateral cooperation in education and for the world of development assistance and cooperation. My recent RoutledgeFalmer title *The United Nations and Education: Multilateralism, Development and Globalisation* (2005) has examined many of these consequences, and the work of the World Bank has not proceeded separately from them, even if the Bank continues to remain aloof from its obligations as a Specialized Agency of the United Nations. The immediate aftermath of the end of the Cold War, when hopes were high that a "peace dividend" might mean dramatic increases in aid budgets, was marked by contrast with steep declines in aid growth and a leveling off of donor commitments. This affected bilateral and multilateral aid programs alike, and influenced both the capacity of the Bank to lend and of developing countries to borrow. The stagnation of conventional aid, in many ways, was bound up with a crisis of confidence about the effectiveness of traditional approaches, and it was the neoliberals who were most articulate and clear about the way forward. It was not necessarily a period in which the legitimacy of aid (and of the World Bank) was broken, but it was a period in which aid agencies and the Bank behaved as if their mandate and principles of working were in urgent need of repair.

With the turn of the century and the adoption of the UN Millennium Development Goals for 2015 (in which education for all is prominent), evidence was there to suggest that the international community had reaped considerable benefits from a broader, more representative pattern of constructing development cooperation. More dynamic working relationships among bilateral agencies, multilateral organizations, civil society non-governmental organizations (both local and international) and the private sector were in increasing evidence as the turn of the century drew closer, a trend accompanied by a restoration of historical aid levels and even steady increases in real terms in several quarters, especially for programs in the lowest-income nations of sub-Saharan Africa. What complicated matters enormously, of course, were the terrorist attacks on New York City and Washington, DC in 2001. The stridency of response from the United States propelled governments once more to the forefront in the conduct of international relations, and for a time the gains of the late 1990s in constructing broad coalitions appeared to be in jeopardy. Achieving the Millennium Development Goals plummeted in priority for the richest Western governments, and multilateral agencies, not least the World Bank, found that their work could not go on as before.

For the World Bank, a key issue has been the upsurge of debate among economists over pathways to economic growth. The whole edifice of World Bank lending to education rests on certain assumptions (if not evidence) that education is indeed an investment, that it will provide tangible returns both to individuals and to societies. Perhaps it has been a matter of assumption (and of false evidence) all along, but since 1962 the Bank has been prepared to include such an item of "social overhead" spending in its lending portfolio. Neoliberal thinking has always been sceptical, to say the least, about the scale of public spending on such social overheads and, by extension, the scale of Bank lending to governments for that purpose. But to date the World Bank has been able to contain, internally, the fallout from such disputation and clashing evidence about education as a potential contributor to growth. Bank Presidents have been especially important here, successive Presidents clearly more interested in maintaining and increasing the scope of Bank lending operations than proceeding in a theoretically pure fashion. Whether the Bank presidency can continue in this way is open to question. The second edition of this book was finalized not long after the presidency of James Wolfensohn (1995–2005) drew to a close. The attitudes and impact of Paul Wolfowitz toward education as a contributor to growth will be of decisive importance to the future of Bank work in education. Whatever transpires, I hope that this account will provide a platform for analyzing and understanding the decisions the Bank will take about its future education commitments.

I appreciate greatly the responses that greeted the first edition of *World Bank Financing of Education*. The many encouraging reviews that appeared in leading journals, and the use made of the work in many examples of fine research and scholarship, have been more than gratifying. I hope that this updated and expanded edition will make a further contribution to understanding patterns of Bank work in education. As with the first edition, I hope that the work will stimulate and inform researchers investigating the work and impact of the Bank at country level, a concern much more in evidence today than it was in 1992. With these scholars, I hope that we can make a contribution to addressing the profound problems of poverty – and their bearing on education and development – still in such evidence today.

Sydney, June 2006

Acknowledgments

I am grateful to the World Bank for its willingness to have my independent research on the Bank proceed, and for its practical assistance in ensuring that my working conditions inside the Bank have been comfortable and conducive to efficiency. Successive education directors Aklilu Habte, Wadi Haddad, Adriaan Verspoor, Maris O'Rourke, and Ruth Kagia have been of particular assistance in this respect. Many others were generous with their time and insights, including Bank officials who consented to interviews, and those responsible for the Bank's bewildering arrangements for its documentation, informatics, library, archives, and oral history program. I have been fortunate in the time afforded me by many former Bank officers, particularly Duncan Ballantine and Ricardo Diez Hochleitner, the early-1960s pioneers of the Bank's educational work.

This updated and expanded edition has been assisted through the support of the Australian Research Council. I am especially grateful to my ARC-funded Research Associate Dr David Coleman who has made a significant contribution to the research on the Bank in the Wolfensohn period. I am also grateful for the confidence shown in this second edition by RoutledgeFalmer, especially by commissioning editor Alison Foyle, and for the practical assistance provided in her office by Tom Young and Kerry Maciak.

Others have also been generous with their time and insights. I remain fortunate at the University of Sydney to have such stimulating colleagues, and the University continues to provide a superb environment for research. Many persons have responded to my claims on their ideas and have thereby made a major contribution to this study, not least Stephen Ball, Mark Bray, Patricia Broadfoot, Birgit Brock-Utne, Colette Chabbott, Raewyn Connell, Michael Crossley, Roger Dale, Steve Heyneman, Keith Lewin, Angela Little, Karen Mundy, Colin Power, Fazal Rizvi, Susan Robertson, John Smyth, Seth Spaulding, Gita Steiner-Khamsi, and Nelly Stromquist. A major contribution has been made by the students of International and Development Education at the University of Sydney, whose questions and suggestions have played a major part in determining the character of this book. All those who have helped know me well enough to appreciate that I will not hold them responsible for my own lapses. Errors of fact, judgment and style are all my own doing.

It would not be possible to acknowledge adequately the care and support that so many friends have provided me during the preparation of this study. The love of my family is deep, and this book is gratefully dedicated to my sisters and brother. For my partner Jon Sanders, this is another book for which thanks can only be expressed clumsily.

The World Bank's greatest successes have come in contexts deserving of that success. By contrast, the greatest failures associated with its lending can usually be found in those countries whose technical and moral capacities to capitalize on Bank financing are parlous. Ironically, the countries making the best use of Bank financing in education are those that have stood firm against the Bank's arbitrary and gratuitous tendencies and its occasional arrogance. That is a lesson the Bank itself can do well to heed. Its vehemence in pressing universal and even arbitrary policy prescriptions – on complex matters that have been inadequately investigated – has been costly not only to its borrowers, but also to its own reputation and credibility.

One factor among many that helps explain the persistence of global poverty is the structural incapacity of the world's poor to exercise discretion over their affairs. It is proving a difficult lesson for international organizations – and not only the World Bank – to learn how best to enhance that freedom and discretion so central to the ultimate purposes of development and the furthering of human dignity. For me at least, the paradox and fascination of education remains its habit of enhancing the prospects of cultural freedom and material well-being among persons and communities whose schooling seemed destined to thwart such an outcome. Despite the mixed motives, institutional constraints and variable patterns of success associated with the World Bank's commitment to education, it needs to be acknowledged that the world's incremental realization of an adequate education for all owes something, in the past generation, to the Bank's faith in it.

Notes on text

In this book, "Bank" and "World Bank" are normally used to refer to the "World Bank group": IBRD, IDA, and IFC. When particular reference is made to one affiliate, that will be made clear.

The World Bank's financial year runs from July 1 to June 30. "Fiscal Year 1960" or "FY 1960", for example, refers to the twelve months from July 1, 1959 to June 30, 1960.

All dollar amounts refer to US dollars ($US).

Successive Bank education loans and projects in a particular country are referred to sequentially (e.g. Thailand I, Thailand II, Thailand III, and so on). In many cases, there is chronological overlap between them.

Abbreviations

AAA	Analytical and advisory activities
AFR	Africa region (World Bank)
BHN	Basic human needs
CAS	Country assistance strategy
CDF	Comprehensive development framework
CIDA	Canadian International Development Agency
DFID	Department for International Development (UK)
DG	Director General
EAP	East Asia and the Pacific region (World Bank)
EAPE	External Advisory Panel on Education
EAS	Education Advisory Service
ECA	Europe and Central Asia region (World Bank)
ECOSOC	Economic and Social Council
ED	Executive Director
EDI	Economic Development Institute
EFA	Education for all
EFD	Educational Financing Division
EKE	Education for knowledge economies
EKMS	Education Knowledge Management System
EMENA	Europe, Middle East and North Africa region (World Bank)
EPDF	Education Program Development Fund
EPTA	Expanded Program of Technical Assistance
ESB	Education Sector Board
ESL	Education Sector Loan
ESSU	Education Sector Strategy Update
ESW	Education sector work
ESWP	Education Sector Working Paper
EWLP	Experimental World Literacy Program
FAO	Food and Agricultural Organization
FPC	Financial Policy Committee
FTI	Fast-track Initiative
FY	Financial (or fiscal) year
GCE	Global Campaign for Education
HIPC	Highly indebted poor country

HIV–AIDS	Human immuno-deficiency virus – acquired immune deficiency syndrome
IBRD	International Bank for Reconstruction and Development
ICT	Information and communications technologies
IDA	International Development Association
IDB	Inter-American Development Bank
IEG	Independent Evaluation Group
IFC	International Finance Corporation
IIEP	International Institute for Educational Planning
ILO	International Labor Organization
IMF	International Monetary Fund
KM	Knowledge management
LAC	Latin America and the Caribbean region (World Bank)
LCR	Latin America and the Caribbean region (World Bank)
MDG	Millennium Development Goal
MIT	Massachusetts Institute of Technology
MNA	Middle East and North Africa region (World Bank)
NGO	Non-governmental organization
NIEO	New International Economic Order
OAS	Organization of American States
ODA	Official development assistance
OECD	Organization for Economic Co-operation and Development
OED	Operations Evaluation Department
OEEC	Organization for European Economic Co-operation
OPS	Operations Policy Staff
PCR	Project completion report
PER	Public expenditure review
PIU	Project Implementation Unit
PPAR	Project performance audit report
PRSP	Poverty reduction strategy paper
RWG	Redistribution with growth
SAL	Structural adjustment loan
SAP	Structural adjustment program
SAR	South Asia region (World Bank)
SIDA	Swedish International Development Agency
SIL	Specific investment loan
SSA	Sub-Saharan Africa region (World Bank)
SUNFED	Special United Nations Fund for Economic Development
SWAp	Sector-wide approach
TA	Technical Assistance
TFHES	Task Force on Higher Education and Society
TOD	Technical Operations Department
UK	United Kingdom
UN	United Nations
UNDG	United Nations Development Group

UNDP	United Nations Development Program
UNESCO	United Nations Educational, Scientific and Cultural Organization
UNFPA	UN Fund for Population Activities
UNICEF	United Nations Children's Fund
UPC	Universal primary completion
UPE	Universal primary education
US	United States (of America)
USAID	United States Agency for International Development
WBI	World Bank Institute
WCEFA	World Conference on Education for All
WDR	World Development Report
WHO	World Health Organization
WTO	World Trade Organization

1 The Bank at work

Legacies from the 1940s and 1950s

The World Bank lies at the center of major changes underway in global education. The Bank's financial power and influence have helped shape the economic and social policies of many governments, even when the relationships have been acrimonious. The Bank has been an influential proponent of the rapid expansion of formal education systems, and has financed much of that expansion. It has been instrumental in forging policies that see education as a precursor to modernization and as a dimension of the ideal operation of free-market economies, serving as a major purveyor of Western ideas about how education and the economy are, or should be, related.

In the World Bank, a glimpse is provided of how the international financial community regards education, and how it is prepared to back its views with finance. As a key component of the institutions of economic multilateralism, the World Bank provides insight into the operations and impact of the organizations making up the UN, multilateral and international financial systems. This book provides a detailed account of how the Bank, since its establishment in 1946, has approached education, lending for which began in 1963 and which continues through to the present day.

Bank purposes, structure, and style

The World Bank, despite the complexity and diversity of much of its work, needs to be understood primarily as a bank. Its operations in such a sector as education cannot be understood otherwise. In other words, the Bank is not first and foremost a forum for the exchange or promotion of ideas about development, nor is it a traditional aid agency that dispenses aid in grant form. Accordingly, the Bank does not lend itself to comparisons with the general range of development assistance agencies. Neither is it typical of UN agencies, despite the often-neglected fact that it is a UN Specialized Agency. It is as a bank that the institution needs to be understood and assessed.

Although the Bank began its work in 1946, after several years' planning it was not until 1963 that lending in education began. Prior to 1960, in fact, the Bank had strenuously resisted such a development. Yet once it was underway, the new education program could not hope to be innocent of all the purposes, traditions, and arrangements that had been accumulating in the Bank since its establishment. Accordingly, this chapter provides an overview of the Bank as it had developed up to about 1960. The evolution of the Bank's character as an international financial institution and how its work in the 1940s and 1950s helped shape a context congenial to the eventual establishment of an education portfolio are the major themes.

Initial orientation

When the Bank was being planned, it was surrounded by an optimistic climate of opinion that the world's governments would opt to conduct much necessary business through the new international arrangements planned for the postwar period. For several years, the allies had been designing a postwar system of multilateral cooperation that had three overarching aims: the prevention of war, the fostering of economic and social development, and the international acceptance of progressive norms and standards. Each was dedicated to preventing the many kinds of excess that had characterized international life in the 1930s and 1940s. Consistent with this, the embryonic international system provided a means of consolidating emerging balances of power, and of promoting Western, liberal, and democratic views of social life. Peace, progress, and international norms were quickly adopted as the hallmarks of the new multilateralism. For the United Nations in particular, the goal was to attain tangible objectives through practical, functional means of intergovernmental cooperation. In 1946, the new multilateral arrangements were seen as a robust means of ushering in a new international order, an order in which western interests might, incidentally, prevail (for an account, see Kennedy 2006).

Such epithets as "collaborative" and "universal" do not rest as easily with the World Bank as with the UN system as a whole. The reasons for this relate to the Bank's establishment. Unlike much else of the UN system, which can only be understood in the context of the Second World War and the excesses of national socialism, the Bank needs to be appreciated more in light of the great depression of the late 1920s and 1930s. The chaos into which banking systems were thrown at that time was seen no more clearly than at the international level, when international economic and financial relations virtually broke down. Assessments, particularly those made by the governments of the United States and United Kingdom, pointed to the need for international mechanisms to prevent the destabilization of international markets and the widespread defaulting on international borrowings that had characterized the prewar decade.

Accordingly, when representatives of forty-four nations met at Bretton Woods, New Hampshire in July 1944, they met to consider an essentially US initiative for both the short-term and long-term management of the international economy. Of the many US officials involved, perhaps the crucial role was played by Harry White, a key adviser to the US Secretary of the Treasury. In the estimation of Mason and Asher (1973: 15) in their definitive account of the Bank's formation, it was essentially White's proposal that constituted the agenda at Bretton Woods. White wrote in his 1942 *Proposal for a United Nations Stabilization Fund and a Bank for Reconstruction and Development of the United and Associated Nations*:

> No matter how long the war lasts nor how it is won, we shall be faced with three inescapable problems: to prevent the disruption of foreign exchanges and the collapse of monetary and credit systems; to assure the restoration of foreign trade; and to supply the huge volume of capital that will be needed virtually throughout the world for reconstruction, for relief, and for economic recovery. Clearly the task can be handled only through international action.
>
> (cited in Mason and Asher 1973: 15)

The resultant Bretton Woods institutions have long since persisted with the intimacy shared at their establishment. The International Monetary Fund (IMF) – charged with immediate relief for governments' balance-of-payments problems and with short-term exchange rate stabilization – shared premises with the Bank at the beginning, and today is located across the street from the Bank's main building. The Fund, indeed, dominated proceedings at Bretton Woods, being the controversial component of the US proposals. Many delegates complained that time would run out before proper attention was paid to the long-term economic tasks envisaged for the Bank. It was John Maynard Keynes of the UK delegation who played the crucial role as broker between the US delegation and the delegates at large, and Keynes became fired with enthusiasm for the Bank, chairing Commission II which designed the Bank and finalized its charter.

What emerged was a bank whose members were governments, each of which forwarded relatively small capital subscriptions, but whose guarantees were considerable. These guarantees gave the Bank its image of strength and stability, notwithstanding the low levels of capital actually paid-up by members. As a result, its reliance for working, loanable capital rested with the marketplace, and hence the credibility of the Bank in the eyes of private investors was, and remains, critical in its functioning. In short, the Bank's capacity to lend was contingent on its capacity to borrow, and here the Bank needed to project an image of responsibility and caution. Fiscally, the Bank could only be as strong as the marketplace would permit. Governmental guarantees were an important element in its credibility, but only up to a point. A Bank Vice President in the 1950s recalled: "There was a great deal of scepticism as to whether the operation was going to be run on sound business financial lines.... The financial community would have been very reluctant to support the Bank unless it had a basis for feeling it was going to operate on sound lines."

It was the "International Bank for Reconstruction and Development" (IBRD) that opened its doors for business on June 25, 1946. Today, it is commonplace to refer to the World Bank as the "World Bank group," in that the IBRD came to be complemented by two other lending mechanisms, the International Finance Corporation (IFC – 1956) and International Development Association (IDA – 1960). Their characteristics are taken up later, but it should be indicated that usage in this book of the term "Bank" and "World Bank" refers to the *group* in general. When specific reference needs to be made to one of the three – such as the IBRD – that will be made explicit. Of course, prior to 1956 "Bank" can only refer to the IBRD.

The Bank's external relations: the United Nations, United States, and Wall Street

Many observers of the World Bank, including those who are relatively familiar with it, express surprise upon finding it to be a UN Specialized Agency. To this day, but emphatically in its early, tentative days, the distancing by the Bank from the UN system has been a deliberate tactic. Both the UN Charter and the Bank's Articles of Agreement made provision for mutual cooperation and coordination. Such a working relationship would have been in line with those envisaged between the United Nations – through its Economic and Social Council (ECOSOC) – and such other Specialized Agencies as the International Labor Organization (ILO), the Food and Agricultural Organization (FAO), and the United Nations Educational, Scientific and Cultural Organization (UNESCO). The Bank, however, could not accept the kind of coordination and cooperation which the United Nations envisaged, and we can learn something of the Bank's self-image at its establishment in the resolution of the matter. The Bank's view essentially prevailed, to the extent that the Bank's chief negotiator with ECOSOC spoke of the ensuing agreement as a "declaration of independence," a term that entered the common parlance of senior Bank management.

The Bank's concern to distance itself from the United Nations is a reflection of its need to assure Wall Street that political judgments would be eschewed at all levels in Bank operations, and that the Bank could be relied upon to function as an independent international organization. The Treasurer of the Bank recalled: "We feared that the UN, which by its very nature was a political organization, might interfere with the work of the Bank which has to work on sound economic principles and on the principles of good management; an organization which has to get its money from the money market. [We feared] that the UN might force the Bank to make certain loans which the Bank thought was economically wrong – that would make a very bad impression." The Bank accepted that UN agencies might "appropriately make recommendations with respect to the technical aspects of reconstruction or development plans," but for them it would be "sound policy to refrain from making recommendations to the Bank with respect to particular loans or conditions of financing by the Bank." The agreement guaranteed the confidentiality of Bank information, not only that relating directly to lending operations, but also that whose availability in the public domain would "interfere with the orderly conduct of its operations."

At the heart of Bank sensitivities about its relations with the UN system was its desired relations with the international financial community. From the very beginning, the Bank's survival, let alone its strength and effectiveness, depended upon its capacity to sell its bonds and securities on Wall Street. Anything that would damage its credit rating or injure its credibility in the international financial community had to be studiously avoided. The climate surrounding the Bank, as far as Wall Street was concerned, was one that perceived a definite newcomer, one that might too readily allow politics to sway its judgments about borrowings and investments, influence the work of its Executive Directors and its appointment of staff, shape the character of its dealings and relationships with borrowers, and render it hostage to decisions made elsewhere in the UN system, over which it had no control. Excessive politicization, whether or not through the United Nations, was seen as a direct threat to the creditworthiness of the Bank and its capacity to safeguard its capital invested through loans to borrowers. For ten years, the Bank worked carefully to avoid such an image. Yet inconsistencies in its structures, not least the direct political, governmental and representational role of its Executive Directors, were not deemed problematic as long as the principle of voting rights weighted in accordance with subscribed capital was preserved.

The robustness envisaged for the entire range of UN agencies was well evident in the five years to 1947. The United States, in particular, had opted for and committed itself to multilateral means of exerting its influence in post-war reconstruction and development. Its leading role in the establishment of the UN system bears testimony to that enthusiasm, and to this day a major legacy of that commitment are the mandates, constitutions, and articles of agreement of the system's organs. The reasons for the United States' virtual abandonment of multilateralism in 1947 were many and varied, bearing major implications for the future of the entire UN system, not just those directly affected by Marshall Plan decisions of June 1947 to bypass multilateralism in the reconstruction of war-devastated Europe.

The effect has been profound: to this day many UN agencies carry mandates that grossly exceed their budgetary and organizational capacities. This is not to say that the United States abandoned the UN as a means of exerting its influence: rather, it elected to concentrate on bilateral means for the accomplishment of its major international objectives. These goals were far from narrowly confined to the political and economic: a good example of its cultural diplomacy objectives in the postwar period were the attempts to transform European secondary schooling from what it saw as an elitist system into its own democratic, comprehensive and universal model (see Ninkovich 1981). That goal, in fact, was to play a major part in the story of the United States' subsequent influence on World Bank educational policy.

The dominance of the United States in the early history of the Bank is reflected in several areas, some features of which have ongoing significance.

First, the voting rights of member governments are weighted in accordance with paid-up capital. This is a far cry from the pattern adopted elsewhere in the UN system whereby all governments enjoy equal voting power. In 1947, the US voting share on the Board of Directors was 37 percent, falling to 32 percent by 1960. Second, the US capital markets were overwhelmingly the dominant market for Bank securities: 98 percent of borrowings in 1948 were in US dollars, a level that gradually fell to 75 percent by 1960. Further, its location and early staffing patterns reinforced its image as a US-dominated institution. Although the Bank emerged from Bretton Woods as an essentially Western institution and has since attempted with some vigor to throw off this image, it remains as such to this day, with the United States very much its senior member.

Staffing was initially a controversial issue. The heads of most UN agencies are bound, in their appointments of personnel, to aim for a balance of nationalities that reflects the membership. Such countries as India pressed this model for the Bank, but unsuccessfully. The President of the Bank is able to bypass the geographical constraints imposed on his colleagues elsewhere, a capacity that has undoubtedly contributed to the time-honored image of the Bank as an efficient and competent institution. Similarly, the early days saw disputes over the status of the Bank's Executive Directors: were they to be regarded as international civil servants (loyal to the Bank and to the international community) or were they better regarded as persons acting on the instructions of their home governments? Again the US view prevailed, this time against the vehement objections of the United Kingdom as expressed by Keynes at Bretton Woods, primarily because the bulk of paid-up capital was being provided by the United States, whose government insisted that its Executive Director be bound by government instructions.

One highly significant legacy that emerged from the character and style of the early Bank was the prominence in Bank policy and operations of its President, upon whose appointment the White House has an effective mortgage. At the heart of things is the President of the World Bank's capacity to say (to his Board of Governors or Executive Directors) "I raised the Bank's loanable capital and I know best what to do with it." Enormous discretion rests with the President, and he is very much the apex of a pyramidical structure. For reasons traversed earlier, the President is considerably freer of the political bounds that constrain the work of other UN agency heads. In particular, the costs of running the Bank itself (buildings, staffing, country investigations, research, and the like) are met directly from operating profits, and the President is an independent actor in meeting his administrative budget. A former Bank Vice President summarized: "Nothing is possible without the explicit endorsement of the President. I would go even further, and say that most Presidents have been able to stamp on the Bank their personality and authority. The history of the Bank can quite legitimately be organized around a history of its presidencies. And don't underestimate any President's prejudices – they can amount to a great deal."

A Bank style of operation?

At the heart of Bank operations is lending, most frequently for project purposes, although "program lending" for more general purposes has always been part of the Bank's repertoire, rapidly gaining in importance in recent years. Bank operations as a whole are many and varied, and it is impossible to understand fully its work and influence by merely focussing on projects, despite their prominence. The Bank is a busy institution, seeking to promote its purposes and interests variously. Some activities of the Bank resemble those of traditional aid agencies; others invite comparisons with development think-tanks and research institutes. At points, the assertion that the Bank is primarily a bank seems shaky given the importance of so many other functions of a nonbanking type. This variety, furthermore, gives rise to organizational tensions within the Bank, for example, the tension that dates from the early 1950s between the Bank's loans staff and economics staff. That instance – examples of which abound throughout the Bank's history – stems from far more than the overlap of function commonly found in large organizations; nor is it merely a case of boundary disputation. Rather, it is a product of the breadth of Bank operations. Yet what remains as a unifying feature of this complex body, nonetheless, is banking – borrowing and lending. All else, eventually, comes to serve it.

The Bank's fifth Annual Report for fiscal year 1950 contained the first comprehensive public assessment of its major operational policies. The language of that report continues to evoke much of the Bank's image of itself, its attitudes towards its borrowers, and its developmental and financial role. Bank loans, the report began, are for "specific" projects of reconstruction and development, meeting the "priority needs" of governments, supporting projects that are the "most useful and urgent for increasing the productive resources of members." "Safeguards" need to be established for avoiding projects which are "economically or technically unsound," the report noting that "few projects thus far have been presented to the Bank in wholly satisfactory form." The Bank saw an important function for itself in working out "modifications" of projects to reduce their cost, to increase their "technical efficiency . . . or [their] financial or organizational features" (Mason and Asher 1973: 151–3, 183).

The tone thereby adopted sums up much that is significant about the Bank. By adopting the role as guardian of economic and fiscal responsibility, the Bank opted to reduce complex matters of development strategy to rather straightforward assessments of technical soundness, as if what was required to promote this was as clear as day. In estimating what might be "proper," the Bank came to reveal much about itself. Throughout its history, Bank officers have made continuous use of such terms as "sound judgments," "good management," "responsible lending," and the like. Bank officers are intelligent, and know that there are no clear-cut criteria for such epithets. What they constitute are code words for what is assumed to be acceptable on Wall Street. Their effect, however, has been to project an image of arbitrariness that is not always justified – matters of policy are usually the subject of intense, frequently vehement, debate among Bank staff, who publicly are quick to close ranks once policy is in place. An Executive Vice President of the day subsequently reflected on the fifth Annual Report of 1950:

> In the first five years of the Bank's operation...we had to feel our way rather falteringly into reconciling financing specific projects with appraising and working on overall programs of economic development.... The fifth annual report was in my opinion a basic document in formulating the policy of the Bank and in expressing the policy as it had begun to be formulated. It was intended, and it was written in language which implied that it was a formulation of received doctrine, that it was not an expression of new policy but a statement of how things were being done. To a considerable extent this is true, but to some extent it is misleading. It's a statement of how things were done in certain areas and by some people. It was not a statement of how things were always done in all cases by all people in the Bank at the time. It was intended...to serve as a binding basis for the future.

The report, accordingly, is perhaps the first major example of the Bank's tendency to appear to have resolved complex matters, in order to boost its image of soundness. Issues subject to intense disagreement within the Bank frequently come to be aired publicly in more straightforward and one-dimensional terms. Although this is not an uncommon feature of bureaucratic and political organization, the Bank has elevated it in its modes of operation. It should be recalled, however, that the fifth Annual Report was prepared shortly after the start of the presidency of Eugene Black (1949–62), whose dominance of Bank policies, style, and operations was close to absolute. The report, in the words of a future Bank Vice President, was an occasion for Black to project a more assertive Bank, one looking to an enlarged scope of activity, and one that bore the stamp of Black's ideas.

Although there were to be only four European postwar reconstruction loans, their legacy on future Bank operations was substantial. Each was approved in mid-1947, to France, the Netherlands, Denmark, and Luxembourg. Although the Bank was feeling its way, and despite the imminence of the Marshall Plan (whereby considerable sums were to be made available bilaterally by the United States for reconstruction), these early loans helped consolidate management thinking about appropriate rationales for lending. What was already clear was that the Bank would not provide finance for recurrent government expenditures, and that its lending would focus on the foreign exchange costs of projects or programs. Its relations with Wall Street ensured a certain focus on the provision of finance otherwise difficult to procure on favorable terms.

What dominated Bank-financed activities was, of course, "the project": although the possibility of extensive "program lending" was hotly debated in the 1950s, what the Bank became well-known for was financing the foreign exchange components of large-scale, public utility infrastructure projects. This is an important legacy. With an emphasis on free-standing projects, designed in some way to generate an economic return, the Bank in the 1950s freed itself of the burden to investigate in any depth the causes of underdevelopment and the meaning of development. A prominent member of the Bank's economics staff in the early 1950s (Paul Rosenstein-Rodan) reflected on this period: "Where therefore the Bank ought to proceed in a cautious way, establish its goodwill and its credit-worthiness for its bonds . . . it would have had to proceed slowly, hand-in-hand with an educational process [to influence] Wall Street. . . . They didn't attempt to do it. . . . What I consider in the 1950s one of the Bank's failures . . . is that far from being the leader in development thinking . . . the Bank was conspicuously absent. All the leadership came from outside the Bank, ECOSOC, the United Nations . . . or some other development authorities."

The reorganization of Bank structure in October 1952 did little to alter this balance. Earlier, professional staff had essentially divided themselves into the Loans Department and the Economic Department, the former concentrating on the technical and operational aspects of projects, the latter on the creditworthiness of borrowers. Because each Department was required to endorse loan recommendations, there was considerable rivalry and tension between the two. The new structure saw three Area Departments created for the analysis of country and regional economic performance, a high-status Technical Operations Department engaged in project appraisal and supervision (organized sectorally for power, transport, agriculture, and so on), and a down-graded Economic Staff. The head of one of the Area Departments reflected on this period and the friction between loan officers and economic staff: "The gap was filled by the lawyer. It's extraordinary how in the early days the legal department produced broad concepts and ideas and suggestions, and gradually management began to expect the lawyers to have these ideas rather than the economists."

Bank activities in retrospect

The major issue of concern in this book is that of Bank criteria for lending. Such criteria, in effect, constitute Bank policy. The story of the Bank is essentially a story of how its lending criteria have evolved. To be sure, there is much more to be considered, not least the Bank's keenness to influence countries' domestic policies. But that interest stems in some measure from the Bank's desire to protect its investments, a protection which in turn is bound up with its initial selection of lending criteria. In their unrivalled history of the Bank's first quarter-century, Mason and Asher sum up the first years of Bank lending with a statement worth reproducing in full:

> One of the principal self-assigned jobs of a bureaucracy is to prove to itself and others that it is engaged in a rational, professional, genuinely

significant undertaking. Whatever the reasons are that first push an agency into a particular pattern of activity, the bureaucracy can be relied on to give a cosmic twist to the rationale for that activity. The Bank was set up to help complete specific productive projects rather than to make general purpose loans, to finance only the foreign exchange costs of those projects, to secure a guarantee of repayment from the government of the country in which the project was to be located, and to finance only activities for which other financing was believed to be unavailable. These requirements, along with the practical necessity of concerning itself only with projects large enough to justify review and appraisal by a global agency with headquarters in Washington, DC, practically assured a heavy concentration by the Bank on power plants, rail road lines, highway networks, and similar physical facilities. It was the availability of financing for such undertakings that stimulated philosophizing about the vital role of economic infrastructure in the development process, rather than the reverse.

(Mason and Asher 1973: 152)

The significance of this last sentence cannot be overstated. It points, above all else, to a certain arbitrariness on the part of senior Bank staff in the initial appointment of criteria for lending, criteria which admittedly were profoundly shaped by the circumstances surrounding the Bank, its self-image, and interests. Nevertheless, the powerful legacy from Bank project experience in the late 1940s and 1950s, which has so effectively shaped the parameters of all that has subsequently developed in the history of the Bank, can be explained to only a limited extent by appeal to rational, intentional assertions and investigations about the meaning of development. As Rosenstein-Rodan reflected on the early 1950s, "I never quite approved of the distinction made in the Bank's thinking between operators and thinkers.... The distinction between the loan department and the economics department...[was] wrongly conceived...exaggerated." As an economist with a pronounced flair for economic theory, he quite likely felt marginal.

Influencing global policies

There has been a steady increase in Bank interest in raising its status as a development assistance agency, relying on the quality of its thinking as much as on its financial leverage and power to influence and shape governmental and intergovernmental thinking about development issues. One observer placed emphasis on his observation that "many would argue that these activities are the most important activities of the World Bank. They tend to judge the worth of the Bank by the extent to which it performs well its role in the international marketplace of ideas" (Ayres 1983: 20–1).

Of the more general activities of the Bank, it is perhaps research that, with time, has come to stand out. From an extremely limited interest in the 1950s, there has been a steady crescendo, first with economic analysis, and later with supplementary work in economic development studies and sectoral research. Researchers in the Bank, many of whom were consulted during this study on this very point, like to complain that too often the policies of the Bank (notably its criteria for financing) appear to lack a sufficiently rational basis. Major policy decisions, they would claim, continue to be made irrespective of the quality of 'supporting' evidence. Research staff, then, see themselves as potentially key actors in the Bank policy process, being committed to more rational and predictable lending patterns.

Accordingly, many of the Bank's research staff see the Bank itself as their major client, as they attempt to mount evidence for a particular approach or viewpoint about development. They find useful allies in potential borrowers, in a curious twist, and so considerable energy goes into persuading borrowers that the views emanating from Bank research are the correct ones, in the hope that these will be reflected by borrowers in loan negotiations. In a wider sense, it is hoped the international community in general can be influenced by Bank research, international climates of opinion being shadowy but enormously influential determinants of international programming.

The major legacy of the policy–research axis in the Bank has been the search for a single way – a straightforward approach that the Bank as a whole and borrowers are expected to fall into line with. It keeps things neat and tidy at the Bank's end, even if reality is distorted at the other. This would seem to be a quality of policy-oriented research when policies for global consumption are in the bureaucratic order of things, and is a characteristic of international organizations in general, for whom diversity is managerially inconvenient. One regrettable but common feature of Bank experience with research is that evidence from a limited range of instances is used to determine policies for much wider application. As is taken up in considerable detail in subsequent chapters, one of the most comprehensive changes in Bank education policy (which led to the discrediting of many loans for vocationally "diversified" secondary schools) was promoted by research staff who analysed project experience in just two countries, Colombia and Tanzania. Examples abound of where too much was made of too little.

Bank research staff need not look far for their data. Projects themselves provide overwhelming amounts of up-to-the-minute information about general and specific phenomena in client countries. At the same time, Bank culture prevents the publication of highly speculative or particularly creative research – what is found are sober analyses intended to reinforce the Bank's self-image as a key source of technically sound and responsible advice. This colors the character of Bank research – and its researchers – considerably.

In addition to research, much else takes shape at this general level of activity. Policy documents – intended to influence borrowers – address a wide range of themes related to the Bank's work, not least policy papers in the sectors, including education. *Sector Policy Papers*, especially in the 1970s under McNamara, achieved both internal and external prominence. Such papers indicate – perhaps bluntly, perhaps obliquely – what the Bank might entertain in a loan application. They also aim to influence borrower behavior more generally, with the hope that the Bank's view of what is "sound" policy might be taken up, irrespective of impending loan possibilities. Again, despite lip-service paid to the diversity of borrowers, such policy positions usually aim at a fairly common approach to policy resolution around the world. Less prescriptive or more tentative approaches are usually reserved for policy discussion papers of various sorts, or for commentary in such publications as the annual *World Development Report*, or in the various and extensive series of staff working and research papers. In recent years, all of this material is available on the Bank's voluminous website (http://www.worldbank.org).

In short, all of this generalist activity is capable of being channeled through Bank publications. Some might have restricted circulation for a time, but eventually Bank aspirations are to influence policy decision-making around the world. That process of persuasion starts inside the Bank, is extended direct to borrowers, and then usually finds its way into the public domain, through the press, international agencies, and academic discourse. At the same time, Bank publications are many and varied, and it is enormously important – in attempting to understand the Bank as an institution – to distinguish between them. Only a particular kind of publication would purport to declare Bank "policy" on an issue, and even then there can be great variation in precisely what Bank "policy" means and is intended to achieve. Many publications air issues and perhaps even preferred Bank positions, but stop short of being Bank policy pronouncements, while others simply are produced to generate discussion on what the Bank has deemed to be matters of policy significance. Commentators occasionally lapse in failing to make these distinctions. At the same time, those themes or policy issues that are *not* taken up for discussion inside and outside the Bank can also indicate something of Bank thinking, priorities, and style.

Country-level policy influence

At a quite distinct level, Bank operations can next be grouped as those pertaining to Bank–borrower relationships. The Bank frequently makes appeal to the significance of its working relationship with each client and to the "country dialogue" it "enjoys" with each. As early as 1950 in its influential fifth Annual Report the Bank was able to describe this relationship:

> [In addition to project monitoring] the Bank from time to time sends staff missions to visit member countries in order that they may familiarize themselves with the course of events in those countries, through observation and through discussions with government officials and other interested elements of the community.
>
> One objective is, of course, to ensure that the maintenance of service on Bank loans is not jeopardized by the emergence of conditions which might reasonably be prevented. But the Bank also has a broader objective

in view. By keeping closely in touch with the progress of its members, the Bank hopes that it may be able to be of some assistance to them in meeting important economic problems. The member countries, in turn, are able to discuss their plans for investment well in advance and to obtain an early indication of the Bank's opinion.

It is here, in the country dialogue, that the Bank is perhaps at its most influential, for the canvas being worked on is considerably larger than that being prepared for specific project work. Of greatest concern for the Bank is the "soundness" of the economic environments to which it has committed and may yet commit finance:

> It happens not infrequently that the Bank's examination of general economic conditions in the borrowing country reveals the existence of economic or financial practices or policies which so adversely affect the financial and monetary stability of the country that, if continued, they would endanger both the productive purposes and the repayment prospects of any Bank loan. In such cases, it is the policy of the Bank to require, as a condition precedent to Bank financing, that the borrowing country institute measures designed to restore stability to its economy.

This policy (termed "leverage" by the Bank) needs to be understood in historical terms. Leverage has most commonly resulted in the attachment of side-conditions ("covenants") to Bank loans, conditions which usually bear little on the specific character of the loan itself. Accordingly, in seeking to understand the Bank's record of lending to education, it is important to appreciate the existence of leverage (which helps account for the Bank's enormous power and influence), although not always important to investigate the actual covenants attached to education loans.

Leverage is an important aspect of the Bank's perceptions of its close working relationships with borrowers. Along with the IMF, it ensures a continuing and detailed assessment of the economic "performance" of borrowers, monitoring closely the security and stability of borrowers' political, economic, fiscal, and social environments, to the extent that weaknesses in these areas might jeopardize the safety of the Bank's investments. It is the encouragement of such "close working relationships" with borrowers that is, perhaps, more important to grasp in this study than the exercise of particular instances of leverage from loan to loan. In more cases than not, covenants with an educational objective have been merely paid lip-service by consenting governments, and have been weak instruments of Bank policy influence. More influential have been the covenants designed to impinge directly and quickly on government's fiscal policies and developmental priorities.

The most tangible and influential products of the process of country dialogue are country economic reports, which usually appear for each country every 12 to 20 months. They are normally the product of an intensive investigation of the overall economic policies, structures, and performance of borrower countries. Such investigations might have a visiting mission as its focus, but the Bank's economists in its various Regional Divisions have the ongoing task of monitoring trends and perhaps publishing shorter updates or analyses of particular aspects. The reports are usually prepared in cooperation with the IMF, and their influence – inside and outside the Bank – is immense. The drafting process, very frequently, carries enormous political implications, particularly if the Bank is approaching conclusions and recommendations unpalatable to the borrower. Further, the Bank's judgments about the credit-worthiness of a client are highly sought after and respected in the commercial banking field, in aid agencies, in political circles, and in academic institutions. In fact, a great deal of the power and influence of the Bank stems from its country economic reports, particularly through their direct influence on the commercial attitudes of the private banking sector towards developing countries. They are also of critical importance when loans are being extended to borrowers by the Bank. The Executive Directors will only approve a loan in the full knowledge of the latest country report, and will attach covenants to that loan on the basis of that report. Very frequently, the loan approval process at the meetings of the Board sees far more scrutiny of the covenants than of the loan being considered.

Ranking high among traditional Bank concerns in country economic reports are such matters as inflation, interest rate policy, currency valuation, export performance, balance-of-payments, and prospects for growth. Inevitably, the reports take up broader issues of sectoral policy, not least trade policies, policies concerning agricultural and industrial development, and public sector spending. The Bank consistently has promoted the benefits of devaluations, strict limits on imports, tight controls on government spending and services, and movement towards "user pays" principles of public sector financing. It is frequently in these last areas where the Bank collides with the short-term political interests of governments, which can be tempted to spend their way into a favorable political position. A 10 percent cut in government spending might be fiscally responsible, but its immediate effects on public services and quality of life can be severe.

This tension is a living component of the Bank–borrower relationship. It is in the broader area of overall structural reform (e.g. land reform) that the Bank can be placed in a highly ambiguous position: some staffers press for a more militant Bank, especially where they observe gross inequities in borrowing countries, rampant corruption and uncontrolled military spending. Others recognize the real constraints imposed on the Bank by its inter-governmental character, its role as a UN Specialized Agency, its own Articles of Agreement, and the stated intention of the Bank to limit itself to the technical aspects of economic policy. On his retirement from the Bank, Stanley Please deftly captured this tension in the title of his reflections *The Hobbled Giant* (Please 1984).

Technical assistance (TA) is an aspect of the Bank's use of country investigations which has a particular significance in this study of Bank commitments to education. From the 1948 fiscal year when country investigations began, it took only a year or two for the Bank to appreciate the need for technical assistance for its members. The 1950s saw a deep Bank commitment to technical assistance, which continuously highlighted the lacked of trained, skilled, and experienced personnel in borrowing countries. It was not a big leap, in a sense, for the Bank to explore means of addressing these deficiencies. More is said about technical assistance in a later section of this chapter, while the transition to a full program in education is the theme of Chapter 2.

Lending operations

Delegates at the Bretton Woods conference took pains to ensure that the International Bank for Reconstruction and Development would avoid the kind of lending that had proliferated in the 1920s – lending for vague or nonspecified purposes, often in the absence of evidence concerning the creditworthiness of borrowers. Bank lending, by contrast, has traditionally been focussed on specific activities, specific enough to enable the economic benefits of lending to be described, if not precisely calculated. Assessing the capacity of borrowers to repay loans is also a dominant feature of Bank–borrower relations. Particularly over the Bank's first 40 years, the broad distinction between the two types of Bank lending – "project" and "program" lending – there was a pronounced preference for project lending as that which met criteria for specificity, as envisaged in the Bank's Articles of Agreement. Accordingly, "the project" came to be enshrined as the dominant modality of World Bank operations, a project being a specific activity whose technical viability can be assessed and whose contribution to economic development can be gauged. These *specific investment loans* far outweigh all other forms of Bank lending, are free-standing, and bear foreign exchange costs that are readily calculated. In the early days, project lending for power generation and distribution, and for transport and communications, dominated the Bank's loan portfolio. The availability of considerable loan funds for such projects, it was noted earlier, led to some overestimation of the importance of large-scale public sector infrastructure in the development process.

The Bank, in the 1950s and 1960s, seemed somewhat ambivalent about non-project, program lending. It was the theme of hotly contested debates in-house, and inconsistencies between stated policy and actual lending practice. Bank President Eugene Black (1949–62), for example, saw the specified character of project lending as strengthening the Bank's credibility on Wall Street, an almost obsessive, if understandable, concern of his in the early uncertain days. Black is reported to have claimed that non-project "program" lending "really means a loan for a purpose or purposes unknown" (Mason and Asher 1973: 261). However, it is now generally conceded that the four European reconstruction loans were program loans, as was the series of Australian loans in the 1950s. Lending of this type was for broadly specified and wide-ranging purposes, with inputs almost impossible to trace through to identifiable and quantifiable developmental "outputs." As far as developing country borrowers were concerned, the Bank in the 1950s and 1960s was virtually unwilling to initiate the possibility of non-project lending.

It is difficult to overstate the importance of the Bank's concentration on project lending for the initial phases of its work in education, for which operations began in 1963. Specific project lending dominated the education sector thereafter, which placed a premium on the construction and equipping of educational institutions. Education staff in the 1960s and well into the 1970s, for example, consisted almost entirely of architects. It was not until the 1980s that program lending in education became of interest, with its accompanying concerns for the "process" aspects of education, its relevance and quality, which hitherto had tended to be the subject of rather weak covenants.

Program lending, which came into its day at the Bank under the presidency of Tom Clausen (1981–6), enabled the Bank to address in a significant way (through its actual lending rather than loan conditions) the structural problems underlying underdevelopment, through what were termed *structural adjustment loans*. At the same time, it was difficult for the Bank to lift its level of program lending above the somewhat arbitrary level of about 20 percent. The problem, in the words of one Executive Director, is that a higher level of program lending would enable the Bank to "exert a policy influence in borrower countries that few could accept as desirable. Hence the dilemma facing the Bank – how to use its influence to promote responsible and affordable development policies and activities, yet stopping short of being an unwelcome intruder." Hotly contested on the Board, in fact, has been the appropriate balance between project and program lending, and within program lending the appropriate level of lending designed to effect radical adjustments to borrowers' macroeconomic policies. The austerity of many adjustment loans in the 1980s and 1990s prompted unprecedented public and political interest in the Bank, which by 2005 was officially describing all program, reform and structural adjustment lending as *development policy loans*.

Unlike projects which might be implemented over as much as ten years, program loans more typically provide rapid disbursements over one to three years, in order to provide support for macroeconomic reforms, moving more recently to support social policy reforms and improving public sector resources management. When applied to a particular sector (e.g. education) such loans, according to a Bank document, differ from project loans "in that they focus more on policy and institutional objectives and shift responsibility for detailed project design and implementation from the Bank itself to the borrower." Accordingly, they enable the Bank to exert a strong influence on overall country approaches to the sector in question, through its financing of a share of a country's broad sectoral investment program. Such a sector loan for education might see an attempt to overhaul a country's entire system of primary school teacher education, or the introduction of a new syllabus in schools on a national level.

The *structural adjustment loans* (SALs) of the 1980s and 1990s provided scope for an even more interventionist Bank, in that they addressed the need perceived by the Bank for comprehensive economic reform across the board. On the basis of country economic reports, and increasingly in collaboration with the IMF, these loans were designed to ease the burden of economic reform through the provision of relevant foreign exchange. *Sector adjustment loans* have had a similar purpose, but within the confines of a particular sector, such as education, thereby addressing the comprehensive reform of a country's entire education system. It is common for such lending to be found in contexts of acute economic difficulty, and disbursement of loan funds is usually much more speedy than is the Bank norm. The 1980s saw an energetic use of SALs, but held to a ceiling of 10 percent of overall Bank lending.

Through the 1990s and into the twentieth century, combinations of investment and adjustment lending appeared as *hybrid loans*, under the general category of *development policy loans*. Especially in poorer countries, they enabled the development of required infrastructure concurrent with sectoral reform, where normally the time-line from adjustment through to implementation of projects would be considerable, a decade or more. Of particular importance has been encouraging competitive market structures, fostering environments conducive to private sector investment, promoting good governance and civil service reform, and mitigating the short-term effects of adjustment reforms through social protection funds. The weight of their education policy implications has been considerable.

Technical assistance

The question is frequently posed as to why countries should seek IBRD loans (which are extended at close-to-commercial rates of interest) when the private banking sector would seem to have the capacity to meet their financial requirements. The answer is not straightforward, but in its early days the Bank made some attempt to carve out for itself a niche in lending for large-scale public infrastructure construction for which private resourcing was difficult to procure. Yet once the Bank had demonstrated that such lending could be responsibly undertaken, it in fact made it possible for the private banking sector to compete in such areas of lending.

With time, the competitive advantages of the Bank came to lie in its in-house expertise: it was a specialist institution that focussed on development. This meant that, with its increasing numbers of specialist staff, the Bank was able to provide advice far beyond the capacity of the traditional banking sector. Reference has already been made to the Bank–borrower relationship and dialogue, and to the processes of country economic reporting, which in time provided the Bank with unrivalled knowledge of borrower circumstances and a capacity to assist in the future planning of economic and development policies in member countries.

It did not take long for the Bank to recognize and capitalize on these comparative advantages in the marketplace. It quickly placed a premium on its in-house capacity to render technical assistance (TA) to its borrowers. The fifth Annual Report identified in 1950 two levels of such assistance. First, technical assistance:

> ... may take the form of suggesting technical modifications to projects submitted for financing, or advising on marketing or managerial problems, or of assisting with the financial aspects of the undertaking, including the raising of local capital. In a number of cases . . . the Bank has been requested to aid the borrowing country in determining which among various projects in its investment program should initially be selected for Bank financing. The provision of all these types of assistance is an integral part of the Bank's lending function; its essential purpose is to ensure that the Bank's resources will be used with maximum effectiveness.

This last aspect was particularly important in the early days when the Bank's record was unproven, and it needed to project an image of security and conservatism. Yet to this day, the IBRD by virtue of its nature as a bank, needs to be certain of the security of its investments. It needs to assure itself that its funds are being invested in stable and secure environments: to behave otherwise would be fiscally reckless. In time, the Bank came to realize that it was in a strong position to help shape the contexts in which its funds were dispersed, by exerting a policy influence on borrowers. This could be done not only through leverage: technical assistance was another possibility.

In addition to the project-related forms of TA identified earlier, the fifth Annual Report discussed a second, more general, means:

> Although advice on particular aspects of a country's investment activities can be of real value, the Bank is convinced that many of its less developed member countries need assistance of a broader nature . . . [The purpose of such assistance] is to help the country formulate a program of investment which will indicate priorities among the important sectors of the economy and among types of undertakings within each sector; to suggest measures and methods, other than investment, to improve productive efficiency in existing enterprises; and to recommend improvements in the government's economic and financial policies and organization in order to facilitate and encourage further development.

Technical assistance that is directly related to project lending might be applied at any stage in the life of the loan, from the earliest days of formulation through to audit and evaluation. It might be applied to purposes intimately connected with the success of the project itself, or for more general purposes surrounding it. In their early days, projects might rely heavily on foreign nationals for technical and managerial support, but come to involve increasing numbers of local persons once they have received training provided as a TA component of the loan. Accordingly, Bank technical assistance can touch on any aspect of a loan. A steel mill, for example, needs to be conceived, justified, designed, constructed, operated, maintained, and further developed. From the first development loan to Chile in 1948, the Bank has consistently been of the view that, virtually without exception, deficiencies could be expected in the technical capacities of borrowers to exercise full responsibility at all stages of the project cycle. This assumption has meant that technical assistance has been an axiomatic feature not only of project lending and operations but also of the Bank–borrower relationship in general. The line between technical assistance and country economic reporting, for instance, is a fine one, as is the line between technical assistance and Bank supervision and auditing of project operations and expenditures. The Bank in almost every lending operation, conclude Mason and Asher (1973: 334), has sought to contribute "something more than financing. Not all of the 'something more' has been technical assistance, but much of it, including a portion of what borrowers may have regarded as administrative harassment, has been technical assistance."

The 1950s saw, throughout the UN and bilateral aid system, a flowering of technical assistance. The inaugural address of President Truman in January 1949 had contained the now well-known Point Four, which pledged the United States to the provision of technical assistance, in organized programs, in significant amounts, on the international level. Several weeks earlier, the US delegation to the UN General Assembly had successfully generated a commitment to what became known as the UN Expanded Program of Technical Assistance (EPTA), and here can be found two prongs of US international economic strategy – bilateral and multilateral – being developed as key aspects of US foreign policy. The EPTA was sufficiently well-financed to enable TA to become a hallmark of UN economic and social programming in the 1950s. Such agencies as UNESCO flourished under it. It also gave the Bank a point of contact with the rest of the UN system, yet in a way that did not jeopardize its independence or its relations with Wall Street.

A particular feature of the EPTA was its concern for "pre-investment" and "feasibility" studies, whereby developing countries might be assisted to identify development goals, possible projects or other development activities, and undertake detailed planning and preparatory work. This emphasis, in time, gave the United Nations a degree of influence in development strategies that had hitherto been denied it, in favor of the well-resourced Bank. Even well before its merger with the UN Special Fund to form the United Nations Development Program (UNDP) in 1965, the EPTA was making significant resources available at the pre-investment level, and tended to contract out such studies to other UN agencies, including the Bank. Hence there developed precedents for Bank–UN cooperation, as well as Bank concerns for the broader "human resources" aspects of development strategy.

Economic Development Institute

There is one important element in the Bank's provision of technical assistance that will receive undeservedly short shrift here, the work of the Bank's own training arm, the Economic Development Institute (EDI), renamed the World Bank Institute (WBI) in the Wolfensohn years. Initially conceived by Bank senior economist Paul Rosenstein-Rodan, it became operational in 1956 under the guidance of Professor (later Sir) Alec Cairncross, on loan from the Department of Social and Economic Research, University of Glasgow. Although Rosenstein-Rodan's intention was for an institute that concentrated on the fundamentals of development theory and policy, the view came to prevail among senior management that EDI would be more distinctive if it were closely connected with the "day-to-day" problems of development in practice, drawing on the considerable amount of documentation accumulating in the Bank. As outlined earlier, the widespread perception in the Bank of Rosenstein-Rodan was that of a brilliant but rather theoretical economist, whose interests did not readily align themselves with the tangible concerns of banking and finance. Any cause he championed suffered from this perception of the tension between the academic and the practical. Accordingly, it is not surprising that senior management discouraged thinking about a training arm that was too theoretical or research-oriented. At any rate, it is the case that the origins of EDI saw an intermingling of the twin themes of how best to understand generally the development process, and how best to promote specific development activities. In particular, its establishment reflected the tendency during the 1950s for Bank senior management to lean towards the practical aspects of lending operations when resolving in-house tensions about Bank priorities and image.

Cairncross' initial work, in 1954 as an external consultant to Bank President Black, was to consider options for EDI and recommend accordingly. In the words of William Diamond (the first Bank staffer to be transferred to EDI): "The heart of his . . . response to Mr Black was that the one important thing which the Bank had to offer which no other institution had to offer was close and intimate day-to-day contact with the real development problems abroad. He felt that the use, particularly of Bank staff and Bank documentation, would lend a reality to both the research and the training program, which no other institution outside could provide." Cairncross' recommendations to Black of August 19, 1954 clearly emphasized this point, that the Bank's staff is in "intimate touch with the *process* of economic development." The Cairncross report justified the establishment of EDI in these terms:

> . . . one of the major impediments is the lack of trained and stable administration skilled in dealing with problems of economic and financial policy. This has naturally impressed itself strongly on the Bank, which has a responsibility not only for seeing to it that any capital it lends is prudently employed but also for trying to help to promote the more rapid

development of its member countries. There are, inevitably, many other obstacles in the field of management, in the intellectual and social climate, and in the absence of effective means of organizing and communicating information.

Cairncross had consulted widely – within the United States – on the role and work of EDI. Theodore Schultz (University of Chicago), Willard Thorp (Merrill Center for Economics), Dean Rusk (Rockefeller Foundation) and John Howard (Ford Foundation) were all visited by Cairncross in July 1954, and Cairncross' report reveals general, if not warm, support for this diversification of Bank operations. The two foundations, although initially cool, were supportive to the extent of contributing half of EDI's operating budget from 1955 to 1958. Theodore Schultz, very frequently consulted by senior management on Bank policy matters throughout his career, was enthusiastic, and argued that the Bank had emerged as an institution with very great potential to persuade governments to adopt sound economic policies. Schultz, wrote Cairncross, "said that he had heard a number of criticisms of the Bank in South America on the grounds that its attack on the problems of under-developed countries was on too narrow a front.... [But] Schultz took the view that the main things to be taught were extremely simple."

A fascinating conversation was reported by Cairncross with Dag Hammarskjold, Secretary General of the United Nations. Hammarskjold appeared rather hostile to the idea of EDI, being particularly defensive of his own technical assistance domain. "Senior officials" in developing countries, claimed the Secretary General, "were best left undisturbed," and he doubted that economists had much to say to them. "It was always preferable to let them come to their own conclusions on the evidence of experience, rather than to try to force general principles on them." Hammarskjold clearly was concerned that training might become bound up with the Bank's exercise of leverage, and would best be left to the United Nations' own TA effort: "Hammarskjold also emphasized that the Bank had first and foremost to be good at banking... [and should not masquerade] as a kind of academic institution." Cairncross studiously avoided inviting Hammarskjold to defend the relevance and effectiveness of the United Nations' technical assistance and training efforts.

The Bank, through EDI, initiated a means whereby appropriate persons from the developing world could be given a "staff-college" type of training, on timely and relevant issues, for intensive periods of several months' duration. Training dominated, rather than research and publication. Most memorialists concur that the influence of EDI on the Bank itself has been slight, in that the analyses of Bank documentation and experience that underpinned much of EDI's training failed to find its way back to Bank economic and lending officers. This had been a major justification for EDI, as reflected in working documents for the Board of Directors throughout 1954.

The greater significance of EDI in the early history of the Bank lies in another direction. As with technical assistance in general, a Bank commitment to a training arm constituted an acceptance of the notion that prospects for development in many countries were being compromised through deficiencies that could be seen in part to have an educational solution. Cairncross recalled in 1985:

> It was also a very important point in my mind that the Bank had a feeling that what was holding up development in the countries they were lending to was not capital. They could provide the capital. But it was more other difficulties of a managerial character – there were various impediments – and that until they had people adequately trained in the handling of projects, in thinking about how to run an economy, the business that they were trying to engage in – of accelerating development – would not succeed. So I could see the importance of an educational role in a body attached to the Bank.

EDI both reflected and stimulated a recognition in the Bank that the persistence of underdevelopment had, to some extent at least, an educational dimension. The Bank's response in the 1950s was to contain that recognition within the boundaries of TA and, by extension, the EDI. For how much longer it could thus contain its response to educational needs in its client countries is the theme of Chapter 2.

The International Development Association

By the late 1950s, the World Bank was facing the prospect of a diminishing role. Western Europe and Australia were rapidly graduating from eligibility for IBRD finance, and it was clear that Japan would not be a borrower indefinitely. By contrast, the important group of borrowers in South Asia was rapidly becoming so indebted that their interest in conventional IBRD loans was also likely to wane. Even the rapid increase in membership expected with the demise of African colonialism was not expected to provide the Bank with significant numbers of creditworthy clients, at least in the immediate term. Although the IBRD had succeeded in establishing itself and demonstrating its worth both to borrowers and to Wall Street, it faced a limited role in the 1960s and beyond. Were the Bank to extend its lending, on conventional terms, to countries whose creditworthiness was limited, its own credit rating on Wall Street would have plummeted.

Throughout the 1950s, the United Nations had been the arena for wide-ranging consideration of development assistance and financing. The IBRD's role was clearly established, yet there remained an additional need for a channel for substantial funds – either loans or grants – on more generous terms than the Bank's close-to-commercial rates. The progress made in the UN system during the 1950s, while important, was limited, mainly confined to the technical assistance work of the EPTA, and the pre-investment work of the UN Special Fund established in 1958 (these two were to merge as UNDP in 1965).

The scale of these activities was far below that required for a relevant UN role in financing development. As early as May 1951, the UN Economic and Social Council had received a report from its Department of Economic Affairs, *Measures for the Economic Development of Under-Developed Countries*, prepared by a group that included W. Arthur Lewis, Theodore Schultz and George Hakim. The group was critical of Bank operations to the extent that its financing virtually bypassed the pressing needs of the poorest (least creditworthy) countries. Qualitatively, they were more vehement, charging the Bank of ignoring the fact that it was an agency "charged by the United Nations with the duty of promoting economic development." It "attaches excessive importance to the foreign currency aspects of development... [putting] the cart of foreign exchange difficulties before the horse of economic development" (82–3). By 1950, the annual level of IBRD lending was approaching $300 million: the UN experts were recommending the establishment of a concessional grant-in-aid authority whose annual outlays would be ten times that amount.

Throughout the decade, the United Nations considered and debated various options for such an authority, which in time was referred to as SUNFED (Special United Nations Fund for Economic Development). A major issue was whether an existing body could accommodate SUNFED. A second was whether its funds would be disbursed as grants, or as loans on highly concessional ("soft") terms. The Bank was a trenchant critic of both options for disbursement. In March 1951, Black addressed the ECOSOC, and attempted to demolish the soft-loan option:

> ... the very fact that these loans are made on especially easy terms and are still called loans should make us suspicious.... In the end, although some loans will turn out well and be repaid, others will bring in their train, first, severe strain on the economy of the borrower and, finally, default.... The effect of such defaults is to destroy credit generally and to wither the integrity of all orthodox lending. In my opinion, when a country has a choice between making loans or quasi-loans of this kind, it pays in the long run to choose grants.

Black's sentiments, repeated later in the year in his address to the Bank's Board of Governors, says much about the IBRD and senior management attitudes in 1951: they indicate nothing of what was to eventuate, for by the end of the decade it was clear that a soft-loan channel was inevitable, and Black had to work hard to head off the establishment of a rival lending body in the UN system, whose loans would be concessional. In 1961 he was asked whether the Bank would be even more successful than hitherto if it remained the only lending institution, so that a country in difficulty could not be bailed out by other agencies. Black's reply is significant:

> Yes, I think so. The strength of the World Bank is our ability to speak frankly to these countries and to insist upon them carrying out their

proper policies. That's very difficult for the US government to do, or for any large government to do, because then they are under suspicion of a big country trying to interfere in the affairs of a small country, trying to dictate to them what they do.... We haven't got any political axe to grind. As a matter of fact, the World Bank is the only place that anybody can go to get money where there's no selfish motive involved.... Analyze our motive, what is it?... That's why I'm very much in favor of multi-lateral aid. I think someday that will be realized.... I think the big mistake that the United States is making today is to try to sell the foreign aid program by saying that the main reason for it is to combat Communism. Well, now... they're not going to combat Communism if that money isn't properly used.... It doesn't make any difference how much you pour in. Money doesn't do any good... unless that money is well spent. Now, if it's well spent, that will help against Communism, in the respect that it will help that country to improve their economy and to improve the standard of living of the people, and make it less likely for them to be suckers to take up Communism.

Black's efforts to prevent the establishment of a rival provider of development finance was successful, but the price was a total reversal of Bank management attitude to soft loans. In September 1960, the International Development Association (IDA) was established as the World Bank's concessional arm, with an initial fund of $1 billion. The IDA's source of funds is its chief distinguishing feature, in that they are derived from grants made by the Bank's wealthiest members, with a three-year replenishment cycle. In one stroke, Eugene Black politicized the procurement of World Bank financing, in that three-yearly IDA replenishments by member governments could only render the Bank more open to intense public and political scrutiny.

The terms of IDA concessional lending were also the subject of vigorous debate among senior Bank management. A discarded option was that IDA's "soft" funds be reserved for "soft" purposes, notably the financing of such social sectors as health, nutrition, population, and education. What eventuated was the extension of IDA "credits" for purposes *identical* to those served by the IBRD. That is, the IBRD and the IDA were to be indistinguishable as far as lending criteria and policy were concerned, the difference stemming from the creditworthiness of their respective borrowers. Much subsequent financing, in fact, has been a blend of IBRD loans and IDA credits.

What characterizes the IDA is that its credit is reserved for the least creditworthy member countries, and that its terms of repayment allow for a fifty-year maturity period with an initial ten-year grace period. IDA credits would be interest-free, carrying an administration charge of 0.75 percent. Organizationally, IDA was not set up as a separate agency, although its formal status as a discrete international organization would suggest this. Rather, its staff, premises and loan procedures are bound together with those of the IBRD. In this way, IDA followed the precedent of the International Finance

Corporation (IFC), the other affiliate of the Bank which was established in 1956 to extend Bank finance to the private sector.

The establishment of IDA and its effects on the work of the World Bank cannot be overstated. Not only did it secure an expanded role for the World Bank, but it freed it from the danger of a rival in the UN system, thereby preserving its status as the largest provider of development finance in that system. More than that, it secured an expanding range of borrowers for the indefinite future, enabling it to serve a more diverse set of developmental contexts. This in turn led directly to a more intensive concern with the nature of development, and an expanded analytical and research role. More profoundly still, the creation of the new affiliate created an atmosphere that saw the active consideration of "soft" sectors for lending. It is no coincidence that the inclusion of social sectors in IBRD's loan portfolio soon followed the establishment of IDA. IDA brought about much discussion in the Bank about social infrastructure, and although the move towards social sectors remained cautious and controversial, they were firmly on the Bank's agenda. The possibility of blends of IBRD and IDA financing also assisted the diversification of IBRD loan criteria. By the end of 1960, then, the scene was set for a busier Bank, lending in more diverse contexts, for more diverse purposes, and on more diverse terms.

Conclusion

By fiscal year 1960, the Bank had clearly become a dominant provider of development finance. In that year, $659 million was lent through the IBRD in 31 loans to 21 countries, 18 in the developing world (see Table 1.1). Nearly one-third of available finance went each to power (31 percent) and transport (29 percent), followed by mining and pipeline construction (18 percent), agriculture (10 percent), steel (7 percent), and industry (5 percent). The costliest projects were those in the power and transport sectors, the cheapest in agriculture.

Between 1947 and 1960, the cumulative total of IBRD lending reflected a similar pattern (see Table 1.2). By that time, 265 loans had been made to 53 countries. Electric power accounted for 32 percent of the total $5,067.9 million lent, followed by transportation (30 percent), industry (16 percent), European reconstruction (10 percent), agriculture (7 percent), communications (0.5 percent), and 4 percent for general development purposes. The geographical distribution of lending reflected a pattern that was not to endure for much longer: Asia and the Middle East (31 percent), Europe (27 percent), Latin America (21 percent), Africa (15 percent), and Australia (6 percent).

By 1960, then, the World Bank had succeeded in establishing for itself a niche in the international banking community, in the UN system, and in the development assistance industry. The early concerns on Wall Street about its prospects for a responsible lending portfolio had been well overcome, as had the Bank's own concerns about the viability of its role. What had secured its

Table 1.1 World Bank loans approved, FY 1960

Country	Sector	Loan amount ($US m)
Austria	Industry	9.0
Algeria and Sahara	Pipeline	50.0
Belgian Congo	Agriculture	7.0
	Transport (two loans)	33.0
Chile	Power	32.5
Colombia	Power (two loans)	42.6
Costa Rica	Industry	2.0
Honduras	Power	8.8
India	Railways	50.0
	Industry	10.0
Iran	Industry	5.2
	Agriculture, power	42.0
Italy	Nuclear power	40.0
Japan	Steel (two loans)	44.0
	Transport	40.0
Kenya	Agriculture	5.6
Mauritania	Mining	66.0
Nicaragua	Power	12.5
Norway	Power	20.0
Pakistan	Power	2.4
	Industry	10.0
	Transport	12.5
Peru	Power	24.0
	Agriculture	5.0
Rhodesia and Nyasaland	Agriculture	5.6
Sudan	Agriculture	15.5
United Arab Republic	Transport	56.5
Uruguay	Agriculture	7.0
Total		658.7

Source: World Bank Annual Report 1960.

survival in the 1940s and the 1950s was its institutional conservatism; what ensured the Bank's ongoing relevance and growth from 1960 onwards was its capacity to adapt.

At the same time, and despite the diversification of function and influence made possible by IDA, the elemental features of the Bank that derived from the IBRD remained intact. The Bank requires continuing appreciation and assessment as a bank. It might have become a busier bank, with an increased portfolio of lending operations and economic concerns, but its essential characteristics were retained. The legacies of the 1940s and 1950s as they accumulated in the IBRD experience provide a necessary framework for understanding the dramatic changes that affected the World Bank after 1960. The decisions to establish an education portfolio in 1962 need to be

Table 1.2 World Bank loans, by sector, cumulative to June 30, 1960

Loan type	$US million
Development loans	
Electric power	1,604.9
Transportation	1,526.2
Communications	23.9
Agriculture and forestry	375.7
Industry	835.4
General development	205.0
Reconstruction loans	496.8
Total	5,067.9

Source: World Bank Annual Report 1960.

understood both in light of the conservative pressures embodied in the IBRD experience to 1960 and the liberalizing forces that found their most dramatic expression in the establishment of IDA.

Notes

Multilateral organizations since the Second World War: For a range of perspectives, see Ansari (1986), Archer (1983), Bennett (1984), Cox and Jacobson (1973), Farley (1982), Feld and Jordan (1983), Finkelstein (1988), Jacobson (1984), Jones (1988 and 2005), Jordan (1988), Kennedy (2006), Knight (2000), McLaren (1980), Meisler (1995), Pentland (1981), Riggs (1988), Righter (1995), Rosenau (1992), Scott (1982), Taylor and Gordon (1978), Weiss *et al.* (1997), White (2002).

The establishment of the World Bank: The definitive account remains the towering survey of Mason and Asher (1973), commissioned by the Bank but conducted with a reasonable degree of independence. The Bank's half-century also saw the commissioning of a second official history (Kapur *et al.* 1997). For Bretton Woods, see US Department of State, *Proceedings and Documents of the United Nations Monetary and Financial Conference*, Bretton Woods, New Hampshire, July 1–22, 1944, esp. vol. 1. See also *Articles of Agreement of the International Bank For Reconstruction and Development*, as amended, and the *Articles of Agreement of the International Development Association*, as amended.

World Bank annual reports: The *First Annual Report of the Executive Directors* was published on September 27, 1946, and such reports have appeared annually thereafter, incorporating IDA matters from 1960 onwards. Of more general interest is the series of reports of *Proceedings* of the annual meetings of the board of governors.

World Bank oral history program: A source of major importance for Chapter 1 was the series of interviews of current and former Bank senior management personalities conducted between 1961 and 1985. A major difficulty arises in citation from the oral history program, given the variety of conditions under which memorialists were interviewed and made transcripts available to subsequent researchers. Some transcripts are unavailable while memorialists remain alive; others may be perused but not cited; others require Bank approval for use by outside researchers; others are in the public domain. Many interviews were conducted for the Bank by the Columbia University Oral History Research Office in 1973, others by the Brookings Institution (especially Robert Oliver) in 1961. Some later interviews were also conducted by Robert Oliver in 1985 through the California Institute of Technology, and others by the Bank's own archivists. The most significant memorialists for this chapter were: Siem Aldewereld, Director, Technical Operations Department (1961); Gerald Alter, Economic Adviser, Western Hemisphere Department (1961); Eugene Black, President (1961); Sir Alexander Cairncross, former Director, Economic Development Institute (1985); Richard Demuth, Director, Technical Assistance and Liaison Staff (1961 and 1985); Daniel de Iongh, Treasurer (1961); John de Wilde, Acting Director, Economic Staff (1961); William Diamond, Assistant Director, Western Hemisphere Department (1961 and 1985); Robert Garner, President, IFC (1961); Harold Graves, Director, Office of Information (1985); Michael Hoffman, Director, Economic Development Institute (1961); Sir William Iliff, Vice President (1961); Burke Knapp, Vice President (1961); Harold Larsen, Economic Adviser, South Asia and Middle East Department (1961); Hugh Ripman, Technical Operations Department (1961); Leonard Rist, Special Representative for Africa, and former Director, Economic Staff (1961); Martin Rosen, Executive Vice President IFC (1961); Paul Rosenstein-Rodan, former Head, Economic Department (1961); Davidson Sommers, Vice President and General Counsel (1961).

Published works on the World Bank: Observations and commentaries by former staff members of the Bank include De Vries (1987), and Please (1984). Commissioned histories and analyses of experience include Mason and Asher (1973), Baum and Tolbert (1985), and Kapur *et al.* (1997). Independent studies of significance include Ayres (1983), Gilbert and Vines (2000), Feinberg *et al.* (1986), Fox and Brown (1998), Hayter and Watson (1985), Hirschman (1967), Hurni (1980), Le Prestre (1982), Mallaby (2004), Morris (1963), Nelson (1999), Nelson ((1995), Payer (1982), Reid (1973), and Van De Laar (1980).

The *Agreement Between the United Nations and the International Bank for Reconstruction and Development* came into force on November 15, 1947, with the attached *Protocol* describing the chronology of its drafting. Original versions are deposited in the archives of each organization.

2 Getting started in education 1960–3

It would be too easy to argue that evolving Bank criteria for lending have closely reflected mainstream thought and practice concerning economic and social development. Bank lending policy has always been more closely related to the Bank's institutional circumstances than to any theoretical developments surrounding its work. In particular, these institutional circumstances have seen an interplay between those pressures (best seen in individuals) fostering stability and conservatism, and those stimulating innovation and adaptation.

Pressures of the former kind are seen in traditional forms of IBRD financing and project supervision, with Wall Street projecting an implicit preference for conventional lending, lending that must be unambiguously perceived as technically competent and fiscally sober. Similarly, links with the United Nations needed to be down-pedalled: the Bank was emphatically not like the other Specialized Agencies. A hallmark of Bank operations was its declared resistance to external political influence or control, economic criteria being claimed as its sole guiding principle. Another hallmark was the emphasis on free-standing projects, which to a degree obviated the Bank of the need to elucidate detailed, elegant, or comprehensive views of economic and social development, which would have been essential had the emphasis been on program or general purpose loans.

Black's spectacular success in selling the Bank's bonds rendered the Bank one for whom access to loan funds was not a problem. Its challenge was to find adequate numbers of creditworthy borrowers able to implement responsible projects. The Bank's fiscal prominence in turn produced a certain patronizing air to its style of operation and dealings with borrowers, readily according it "that tranquil consciousness of an effortless superiority," to employ Manning Clark's phrase.

The Bank's seventh Annual Report (1953) had noted that a "low standard of education and training were among the obstacles to development," and increasingly in the 1950s the Bank's economic reporting system was indicating among many borrowers severe shortages of adequately and appropriately trained manpower, to the extent that economic growth was perceptibly affected. Political pressure from borrowers first emerged publicly in 1956, not at the Bank's annual Board of Governors meeting, but rather at the ninth session of the General Conference of UNESCO, which adopted a Colombian-sponsored resolution requesting the Bank to consider "the financing through loans of the construction and equipment of schools, colleges and universities."

The Bank's response in March 1957 was firm: the resolution was not in accord "with the Bank's established policy." Further, "as a matter of general policy derived implicitly from the Articles of Agreement, the Bank concentrates its lending on projects designed to make a direct contribution to the productive capacity of its members." While granting the developmental potential of education and training, the response emphasized that Bank lending "can most effectively be applied in the more directly productive sectors of the economy."

At the same time, and with accelerating intensity in the latter half of the 1950s, there could be seen the steady accumulation of forces for change. The growing interest in and commitment to technical assistance and institution-building was increasingly evident in country economic analyses, project appraisal work, and in project preparation, design, and supervision. The Economic Development Institute reflected after 1955 an explicit Bank recognition of education and training deficiencies in borrowing countries. The impetus towards the UN Special Fund, established in 1958, saw a more comprehensive interest by the Bank in its own pre-investment surveys and analyses, in addition to those financed by the Fund and executed on its behalf by the Bank. Last and of profound importance was the manner in which the Bank succeeded in adopting and adapting the proposals for SUNFED: the establishment of IDA in September 1960 grafted onto the IBRD an affiliate which would change it forever. In making the fundamental decision that technical and fiscal standards for IDA project appraisals would not differ from those currently applying to the IBRD, and that there would be no distinction between the purposes for IBRD and IDA lending, Bank senior management and the Board of Directors made a judgment that was as profound in its implications for the IBRD as it was for the new IDA. "Soft" money was not to be reserved for "soft" sectors; therefore, "hard" money might be considered for the previously ineligible social sectors, if the conditions were right.

Options for educational financing

The first public indication that senior Bank management had an education program under active consideration came on April 7, 1960 when Eugene Black presented his eleventh annual address to the UN Economic and Social Council in New York. Having reviewed the previous year's lending profile, Black turned to the future, focussing on the impending establishment of IDA, affectionately referring to IDA's dominant feminine characteristics, an Aphrodite perhaps, or maybe "a lady of easy virtue drawing on herself the pained disapproval of the spinsterish World Bank." Black took pains to tread a cautious path between liberality and prim caution, and insisted that all IDA activities would need to reach the high technical standards established by the IBRD. He returned to one of his favorite themes, that the quality of investment was far more important for borrowers than its quantity, that is, "the amounts that can be effectively absorbed in worthwhile and well-thought-out development activities."

One factor above all gave Black the rationale for an active IDA that would not jeopardize the reputation and credit rating of the IBRD – the demise of colonialism in Africa, with countries achieving independence in 1960 and 1961 virtually on a monthly basis. Black, rightly, was wary about the wholesale application of traditional IBRD-type projects in that context, and by contrast appealed to the initial developmental significance of human resources:

> The basic requirement for the faster development of the new nations in that Continent, I am convinced, is more education and training at all levels – a more generally literate working force, more skilled artisans, more members of the learned professions, more entrepreneurs, more skilled government administrators. Until the human resources of the new African nations are more fully developed – and no huge injection of money can greatly accelerate that process – the opportunities for the wise and effective utilization of foreign investment will necessarily remain limited. And what is true of Africa is true of many of the other less developed nations as well.

It should not be assumed that the embracing of educational lending occurred quickly or uncontroversially. It was not until October 1963, three and a half years after Black's address to ECOSOC, that the Bank finalized its first set of policies on education. All manner of options were considered for an education program, and the period of consideration, 1960–3, illustrates graphically the institutional tensions between conservatism and change in the World Bank. At the same time, they reveal the institution's capacities for flexibility given relatively firm operational parameters.

Education could never have been considered an option for the Bank without the explicit approval of Eugene Black. At the end of the 1950s, with his smooth southern charm, Black was the only senior management advocate of an education portfolio. At the same time, Black's enthusiasm for education should not be overstated – some senior staffers of the day remember him as being cool to lending in "soft" areas of social concern, especially IBRD lending at commercial rates. Morris (1963: 55–61) described Black as a rangy, handsome, charming Southerner, "one of the most persuasive of American investment bankers," and with a wider range of interests than most. Morris seemed particularly struck by two qualities – a penetrating, finely honed attachment to the dramatic works of William Shakespeare, and a capacity for straightforward, jargon-free speaking. "This detached and apparently guileless enthusiasm reflects what seems to me his greatest asset: his gift of apparent simplicity." And for Morris at least, "with clarity goes flexibility." One can only speculate upon why Black remained the Bank's principal advocate for education at this time, but his literary enthusiasms cannot be irrelevant.

Black also enjoyed warm and diverse relations with the universities, although he was a frequent critic of abstract intellectualism among Bank economists. Notes Morris, "He is one of the four or five people in history to have been awarded honorary degrees by Harvard, Yale, and Princeton all in the same week."

Yet the prospects for Bank educational financing could not shake off the scepticism surrounding it. A senior colleague of Black's recalled: "The education thing was so completely different, such a bottomless pit, that even if we just stuck to building construction, it was difficult to know just how we could go on as before. Yes, Black insisted that we look at it, and look at it seriously." Many memorialists in the summer 1961 round of interviews with Robert Oliver mentioned the impending inclusion of education as a significant move. Most reflected a cautious, uncertain attitude, knowing that educational lending could only proceed on a basis quite different from the IBRD norm. Some were antagonistic to the entire proposition, as was a significant body of opinion on the Board, especially among the European Directors. As late in the day as October 15, 1963 a member of senior management wrote: "The World Bank has a firmly established reputation in the financial community.... When the World Bank enters into the field of education I believe that it runs the risk of using up some of the good-will that it has built up with the financial community.... I would urge that we undertake to define our education programs in such a manner as to be most readily understood by the financial community."

Another internal memorandum concluded "Education is normally a non-revenue earning activity, and the financial analysis of such activities differ markedly from that of revenue-earning projects." By contrast, one enterprizing staffer analyzed long-term borrowing patterns for educational purposes on the US financial markets, and found that school systems in fact borrowed heavily. Of average annual open market obligations of $2.5 billion, 90 percent was borrowed for elementary and secondary schools, a factor which led the writer to conclude that education was, after all, a "bankable" activity, given that "the precedent has already been well-established that school systems borrow long-term capital through regular investment banking facilities." Staff jockeying for position on the education issue was intense. Even if the Bank's embracing of education could not be prevented, at least the character of its educational program could be influenced. By late 1962, the best the conservative forces could hope for, given the prospect of a World Bank program in education, was the specific preclusion of IBRD commercial lending to education.

Justification and rationale for educational financing

The late 1950s saw a revolution in how economists interpreted the field of education. An avalanche of articles by leading economic theorists asserted ways in which educational expenditures might properly be regarded as investment opportunities, rather than as debilitating forms of consumption. By 1960, the field of study now known as the economics of education had emerged with credibility, with such personalities as Theodore Schultz, Gary Becker, Arthur Lewis, C. Arnold Anderson, and Fred Harbison quickly achieving prominence, not only in the United States but throughout the academic world. The notions of investing in human capital and of developing human resources quickly came to be seen as legitimate options for economic and social policy in both the industrial and developing worlds (for an overview see Jones 2005: 27–35).

The educational establishment was equally swift to seize on the benediction of the economics profession, and used what it held up as a hardheaded rationale for an unprecedented rise in educational expenditures worldwide. Educational authorities did not pause to consider which particular patterns of educational activity might yield the best returns on investment. For them, all educational work was valuable, and educational expansion on all fronts could only be a good thing. Coupled with the educational aspirations of the newly decolonized nations – which invariably saw in educational expansion both a means and a sign of throwing off the limitations of colonization – the new economic faith in education resulted in a rate of educational expansion unparalleled in human history.

There is no evidence that senior Bank management embraced education because of new ideas about the development of human capital or human resources. The reasons lie in the Bank's own experience of IBRD-style project lending and in the institutional circumstances that accumulated during the 1950s. Any suggestion that the Bank's move towards education came as a result of the economists' discovery of education is unsustainable, even if the two movements were contemporaneous. The World Bank embraced education just as this expansion was beginning to occur, yet by the end of the decade was itself a major promoter of educational expansion. In 1960, we can see a hint of what was to eventuate only in that at the establishment of IDA there was an explicit recognition by the Bank that the substantial social infrastructure needs of decolonizing Africa would inevitably include a considerable expansion of educational provision. Yet even that recognition failed in 1960 to predict the extent of educational expansion that was so quickly to come.

Senior management needed – emphatically – to look outside the Bank for advice on the emerging economic perspectives on education, partly to guide their planning, partly to provide a justification for it. A role of some significance was played by Economic Staff Director Leonard Rist, who moved in December 1960 to gather external input and advice concerning the Bank's potential approach to education, directing staff in his Department to brief him urgently. After the 1952 reorganization Rist – at the time the French alternate Executive Director – had been "mistakenly" appointed to the top Economic Staff post by Black. One prominent staffer recalled, "it was a catastrophe, because Rist was not an economist. Rist was a banker; his *father* was an outstanding economist." Whether or not for this reason, Rist brought a highly practical and applied interest to the position he occupied for a decade. Among the academic advice he received was a synopsis of recent articles by Schultz, Lewis, Harbison, Becker, and Renshaw, as well as various papers from the Organization for European Economic Co-operation. A month later, a colleague wrote to Rist in a somewhat triumphant tone reporting a telephone discussion with Harold Clark of Teachers College, Columbia University. Professor Clark "is a strong advocate of using recently developed and more efficient ways of education and thinks that underdeveloped countries would make a serious mistake if they should copy the traditional systems of the West. I was impressed with his concern for the more efficient use of resources in the educational sector. This must surely be a major consideration from any rational economic point of view." Bank management – intelligent, demanding, innocent – was beginning to discover something of the day's conventional wisdom.

And learn they did, and it is of some significance that Bank officers were quickly in touch with the leading personalities in the field of economics of education. They may all have been US-based, but they were the leading figures nonetheless. Rist himself flew to Geneva in February 1961 to an interorganization meeting on education and training, and reported on the relative distinctiveness and territorial claims of ILO, UNESCO, and the OEED. Such staffers as Kenneth Bohr and J.C. Snaauw prepared lengthy essays for Rist on such topics as investing in education and technical education. Snaauw, in fact, was on the IBRD staff in Paris, and spent time at UNESCO with such education specialists as Ricardo Diez Hochleitner and H.M. Phillips.

On March 14, 1961, Rist forwarded to President Black and Vice Presidents Iliff and Knapp an important memorandum containing some "preliminary thoughts" on educational projects. This paper has the distinction of being the inaugural in-house paper on education considered at this level of management. Rist began on a conservative note: "From the point of view of IBRD–IDA, the economic question which has to be answered concerning an education project is the same as for any other project, namely what effect will it have on economic growth and development or, more precisely, what rating does such a project merit in the scale of relative priority when compared with others in more conventional fields." Rist initially confined his remarks to what he termed the "limited policy issue," that of Bank support for technical education only, being the form most directly related to IBRD project experience to date. Should the Bank receive requests for training in industrial, mining, agricultural, or administrative skills, Rist proposed enquiry on two points: (1) are the needs "well defined, real and urgent" and (2) "could they be met otherwise than by a new investment in local educational facilities," for example, through overseas training? In this way, Rist was faithful to the major reason whereby the Bank had developed concerns for technical assistance, pre-investment studies, and, now, education: deficiencies in borrowers' technical capacities as evidenced in IBRD project preparation and supervision.

Yet Rist went on to discuss the broader issue of general education. He was convinced that the Bank needed to recognize the indirect costs (incurred by borrowers in developing physical infrastructure) of the general education that acted as forerunner to the required technical skills. "One cannot help feeling that technical schools, while they can be quite useful, represent only a fraction of the educational problem of the less developed countries." Rist elegantly summarized the arguments for a basic education for all, citing the experience of Denmark in the nineteenth century, and Japan and the Soviet Union in the twentieth:

> Whether it be for... economic reasons or whether it be out of a human-istic desire to see all men enjoy the same educational opportunities simply because education is an end in itself, the need (or desire) to spread education more widely in the underdeveloped world is very real, and there can be little doubt that the economic progress of future generations would be made easier if literacy was widespread.

Rist concluded by recommending to senior management that although technical schools would constitute a ready and easy option for immediate IBRD and IDA support, UNESCO should be invited to prepare feasibility studies for "appropriate" IDA financing of general education on a broader scale. With UNESCO's new concern for educational planning, noted Rist, it was well-placed to prepare programs of this broader kind. "It would be unfortunate if the present interest toward technical education should detract the UNESCO experts from taking (or keeping) a broader view of the educational problem."

While the Economic Staff had been investigating the economics of education, Siem Aldewereld's Technical Operations Department was not losing out on the opportunity to examine some of the practical aspects of educational banking. TOD Assistant Director Hugh Ripman issued an important memorandum on September 11, 1962 on educational "projects and problems," a well-informed document but less theoretically oriented than Rist's. In it, Ripman revealed a healthy scepticism for manpower planning, "an art and not a science. There are so many variables, so many uncertainties, that to pretend to make an accurate forecast for 15 or 20 years ahead is quite impossible." The paper outlined five major problem areas facing governments, with which the Bank would need to grapple in its lending program: the administration of education; the structure of educational systems; teachers and teaching policy; the financing of education; and the planning of education.

While such a list was arbitrary, with overlapping concerns, it was reasonably prophetic from the point of view of early Bank experience in lending. In particular, Ripman hinted strongly at educational leverage: the Bank would "need to be satisfied that the administration and organization of the educational system were going to be efficient.... We should expect to find arrangements made for exercising a continuing planning function, efficient coordination... and some assurance of continuity in policy." TOD loan officers and project supervisors, in particular, were keen to maintain their reputation for quality control, thereby safeguarding the Bank's external reputation and credit rating. No education program was going to threaten these.

It is not possible to attribute to any particular person or senior management group the origins of the "limited policy" approach to education, whereby Bank finance would be confined to technical education. The approach, nonetheless, clearly reveals the conservative reaction in the Bank to the possibility of an education portfolio. Much opinion weighed against any form of education lending, especially for the IBRD, but given Black's enthusiasm there was little point in resisting education altogether. The conservative's response was to tie education to particular educational needs as identified to that point in conventional IBRD projects. This implied the kind of training required to help design and service large-scale physical infrastructure facilities. It is of significance that such response was *ad hoc*, in that it was related in no way to borrower sentiment, new thinking in the economics of education, or mainstream educational thought. What was becoming dominant in the early 1960s was a concern for educational planning, whereby the attempt was made to integrate formal and nonformal education provision at all levels into a single, coordinated entity. This became important in the economic analysis of education, in that the real costs of education and its benefits could be better estimated. For the Bank, by contrast, reality was above all else the dynamics of a World Bank project.

The terms of educational finance: grants or loans?

The first major policy consideration was, therefore, to reconcile the tensions between the limited policy approach (in favor of technical education), and one that embraced education more broadly. Tightly connected with this were the terms of Bank financing of education. From the start, it was assumed by all that IDA concessional finance – credits – would be available to the poorest countries for purposes that included social infrastructure. That was uncontroversial, given the sources of IDA funds. It was a far different matter to countenance the provision of IBRD "hard" money for social purposes. Conservative opinion among senior management saw a deep reluctance to extend IBRD finance to education, and the possibility was intensively canvassed of extending grants for educational purposes, financed from IBRD profits. Yet again, the central issue at stake was the perception of the Bank's creditworthiness in Wall Street and, increasingly, the European money markets.

In November 1960, senior management went off on one of their periodic "lost weekends," and on this occasion educational financing was raised and discussed. It was agreed that Vice President Sir William Iliff put arrangements in place for policy formulation. His co-Vice President, Burke Knapp, advised him formally on November 29 of his thinking to date:

> I am fully convinced that education is an investment, and that indeed over the long run it may well be one of the most productive investments

in economic development. It also seems to me vastly preferable to support it by way of grants rather than loans.... Within the general education field it would seem desirable for us to concentrate on technical education... and leave general education... to other agencies.... As for the type of expenditures to be financed, I think we should beware of going in too heavily for buildings and equipment just because they look like "capital investment".... Perhaps grants for teacher training would be the answer.

The Bank needed to move quickly on these policy matters, given the fact that potential borrowers were already expressing interest in Bank finance for educational purposes, not only Tunisia but also Pakistan, Afghanistan, Nigeria, Tanganyika, Colombia, Peru, Jordan, the Philippines, and Thailand. The absence of any specialist education staff made the task difficult, and management's procedural remedy was to establish a "Working Party on Educational Projects," which began its work with an intensive series of meetings in the two weeks from August 15, 1961. Its chairman, significantly, was Richard Demuth. Throughout the 1950s, Demuth had been Director of the Bank's Technical Assistance and Planning Staff, and as a matter of course was deeply involved whenever the Bank had major policy initiatives under consideration, or when matters of policy required contact and liaison with external agencies. Although Demuth, a lawyer, was an architect and supporter of the Bank's "declaration of independence" from the United Nations, his responsibilities in the TA arena brought him into close contact with a wide range of external agencies, not a few of which impressed him.

Given the appreciating significance of technical assistance in Bank operations, and the willingness of the Bank to undertake pre-investment studies on behalf of UNDP's predecessors, Demuth was well acquainted with the policy environment in which both IDA and IBRD education financing surfaced. He was joined on the education working party by the Directors of the Area Operational Departments (Cope, Rosen, Rucinski, Schmidt), the Technical Operations Department (Aldewereld), EDI (Hoffman), Economic Staff (Rist), and the Special Representative for Africa. The Area and TOD Directors could be relied upon to emphasize the need to preserve in the education sector the Bank's customary quality control measures in project preparation and supervision. Rist was quickly acquainting himself with the emerging literature on human capital formation, while Hoffman understood the need for an educational link with development.

The terms of reference provided by Vice President Iliff on July 28, 1961 are instructive, in that they indicate clear senior management support for IDA financing of education well before any possibility of IBRD loans. Iliff had posed the following questions for the working party:

1   What sort of projects should be regarded as offering a *prima facie* case for IDA financing (e.g. technical education, vocational training, etc.)?

2   Should IDA be prepared to consider the financing of local expenditures as well as foreign exchange costs?
3   Should IDA financing be restricted to nonrecurring (i.e. capital) expenditures?
4   Should the collaboration of UNESCO (and ILO) be sought? If so, what mechanisms of collaboration might be established?
5   Should arrangements be made for economic, financial, and technical appraisals of these projects by IDA itself? If so, what?

In addition, Demuth proposed a sixth item at the group's first meeting: "whether and how the Bank [i.e. IBRD] could spend up to $10 million a year on technical assistance in the field of education." The first meeting also saw active consideration of the first loan possibility, that to Tunisia. This is significant, in that the Bank did not opt for policy perfection prior to active consideration of project lending. Yet as Demuth reported to Iliff, "in the course of discussing the Tunisian project, the Committee found that it had to consider most of the general issues of policy which had been referred to it." The Tunisia initiative will be taken up in Chapter 3, but it is instructive that at the working group's first meeting there was widespread consternation when it became apparent that the proposed project for technical education was in actuality focussed at the secondary school level. To that point, Bank staff had not countenanced the possibility of technical and vocational education in anything except especially designated technical colleges. It was a giant leap for some to entertain the prospect of World Bank support for secondary schooling, particularly in the inaugural project. Despite this complexity, Demuth's group worked quickly, and had a report on Iliff's desk by August 31. The group provided the following (summarized) answers to Iliff's five questions:

1   IDA should be interested in education only to the extent that it is an important factor in economic development and not simply as a socially or culturally desirable end in itself. Under this test, facilities for vocational and technical training would be clearly appropriate. This is agreed by all members of the Committee. Several members would limit IDA financing to facilities of this kind. A substantial majority, however, believes that IDA should be prepared to finance projects in any field of education – whether at primary, secondary, or university level – so long as the projects appear to satisfy important development needs. These members noted that the value of vocational and technical training depends to a large extent upon the ability of the primary and secondary education programs to produce an adequate supply of students. IDA should not be deterred from financing projects at the primary or secondary school level by the difficulty of quantifying the precise results.
2   Educational projects do not present any special features requiring IDA to follow any different policies with respect to financing local currency expenditures.

3   The Committee believes that IDA financing of educational projects should normally be limited to capital expenditures. However, in some cases of an extraordinary nature the need to employ a group of foreign teachers for a period might well be appropriate.

4   The Committee does not believe that IDA should request UNESCO or ILO to act as its agent in appraising projects proposed. It is likely, however, that many IDA members will request UNESCO to advise on the preparation of projects, and UNESCO's reports in this connection are likely to be very useful.

5   IDA will have to make its own appraisal of each educational project, normally made by a team including, at a minimum, an educational expert and an economist. In the case of an educational project, no attempt should be made to quantify the benefits to the economy as a whole expected to be derived from the project.

These answers to Iliff are not reliable as statements of Bank policy on educational financing – these were to come in October 1963. What they do provide are indications of senior management thinking at the time (August 1961), and examples of how lines of educational thought were emerging and developing within the Bank.

There remained the contentious issue of the terms of IBRD financing – grants or loans? Matters were held in abeyance while staff jockeyed for position. In mid-1962, it appeared that the supporters of grants had won the day, and Black went to the Executive Directors, who on September 6, 1962 agreed to Black's proposal that the IBRD be prepared each year to spend up to $10 million from its earnings, provided suitable educational projects and activities could be identified. The figure approved was neither a target nor a limit, much less an appropriation – rather an indicative planning figure. Although one or two western Directors expressed misgivings, the nod was given.

There was only one concrete proposal at that stage – to match UNESCO's contribution to the proposed International Institute for Educational Planning (IIEP) in Paris – for the training of national and international officials in the planning of educational development, and for the study and analysis of educational planning itself. Both the Bank and UNESCO agreed to provide one-fifth of the proposed IIEP annual budget of $500,000, with an initial Bank commitment for three years. This eventuated, and constituted the first element in an active Bank–UNESCO collaboration in education.

What else to do remained a mystery, and so the Bank's first external consultant in the field of education was appointed – Harvie Branscomb, Chancellor of Vanderbilt University since 1946, a former Alabama Rhodes Scholar to Oxford, and soon to commence a term as Chairman of the US National Commission for UNESCO (1963–5). Black's appointment of Branscomb as "adviser to the Bank on educational matters" had as its major reference point the matter of how the IBRD might appropriately make educational grants. It is not so important here for Branscomb's report and recommendations of

April 10, 1963 to be outlined in detail: his principal conclusion that "an expanded technical assistance program would enable the educational assistance program of the Bank to function with increased scope, flexibility, and initiative" was superseded by events. A hint of what was to come was in fact contained in Branscomb's report, when he juxtaposed the probability of IDA credits and IBRD grants: "it would hardly be acceptable to use the $10 million of grant money for the wealthier countries, while requiring the poorer ones to repay the credits advanced to them." This was very fair comment, but Branscomb dutifully recommended his grants scheme, but one integrated with the work of IDA, enabling "a unified program which will make use of both development credits and technical assistance grants." A Bank official recollected: "then came the idea that some of the Bank profits could be allocated to IDA, and that idea began to take hold. And, in fact, it was the one. So the rug was just – not by anybody's fault – pulled out from under... Branscomb. He didn't take it very kindly, and I don't blame him."

The significance of the Branscomb exercise is better seen in terms of the process of consultation that underpinned it. What Branscomb was able to do was discuss the complexities of IBRD and IDA involvement in education on a wide front, inside and outside the Bank, stimulating reflection, probing for possible courses of action, and seeking justifications and rationales for Bank commitments. This was by no means a wasted effort, and the list of outside agencies and persons consulted by Branscomb (who were therefore briefed on Bank thinking and invited to contribute to it) was a veritable who's who in the field of international development and education. Among them were Paul Hoffman (UN Special Fund), René Maheu (UNESCO), David Morse (ILO), Pierre Dorolle (WHO), Alfred Wolf (IADB), senior staff of the Ford, Rockefeller and Carnegie foundations, Philip Coombs of the Brookings Institution, senior figures in US and UK academe (including Clark Kerr, Grayson Kirk, Frederick Harbison, Adam Curle, Sir Eric Ashby, Sir Douglas Logan, and Roger Wilson), government officials in the United States, United Kingdom, Federal Republic of Germany, Colombia, Chile, Mexico, and Brazil, and many more.

Despite the fact that it shelved his report, the Bank was well served by Branscomb, who with skill and insight enabled the widespread consideration of many useful ideas about Bank involvement in education. Branscomb was also correct in his conviction that the Bank would quickly emerge not only as the prominent provider of external finance for education but also a leader in educational policy formulation and influence. Branscomb was a man of deep humanistic conviction, with wide literary interests and pronounced ethical convictions, whose personal and scholarly qualities imbued both the tone of his formal report to the Bank and, more importantly, the quality of the consultative processes that led to it.

Initial contacts with UNESCO

The history of World Bank activity in education is tightly bound up with its relations with UNESCO, especially in the first twenty years, a theme taken up in Chapter 3. At this point, it is worthy of note that, from the outset, Bank educational financing had to take into account – and accept – UNESCO's status as the UN "lead agency" in education. Like the Bank itself, UNESCO had conducted many pre-investment studies for the UN Special Fund, and had built up a solid reputation. The organization had also flourished through its provision of UN technical assistance programs financed through the EPTA. In 1960, UNESCO's reputation was sound, and deservedly so. Further, UNESCO was as skilled as any other agency in protecting its territory.

At this time, UNESCO was championing an integrated approach to educational planning. It was also promoting ambitious programs of educational expansion, as foreshadowed in the 1960–3 series of regional conferences (Addis Ababa, Karachi, Santiago), and was drafting an eventually aborted plan for the UN General Assembly for universal literacy by the end of the decade. At its 1960 session, the UNESCO General Conference had endorsed education as UNESCO's highest priority, as being "central to economic and social development" (see Jones 2005: 30–1).

UNESCO's Director General, René Maheu, was well aware of the movement towards education in the Bank, and was quick to see both dangers and opportunities for UNESCO therein. On the one side, he needed to protect UNESCO's turf. On the other, he was acutely aware of UNESCO's continuing need to attract "extra-budgetary" funding, given the small size of its regular budget, about that of a medium-sized university. UNESCO was doing well with EPTA and Special Fund financing, and Maheu could see distinct possibilities with the Bank. He was therefore quick to reinforce in the minds of senior Bank management the notions of education as an investment and of UNESCO's special competence in the area. UNESCO staff in Paris took pains to establish contact with Paris-based Bank staff, and there was considerable correspondence between the two organizations from 1961 onwards, especially with Demuth on the Bank side. With Hugh Ripman, Demuth visited UNESCO headquarters in Paris in September 1961, a purpose of which was to seek UNESCO advice on appropriate educational consultants, then a clear Bank concern.

Demuth spent considerable time, in particular, with Malcolm Adiseshiah, whom he had come to know in the 1950s when Adiseshiah was stationed in New York as UNESCO's principal technical assistance official, a position not unlike Demuth's in the Bank. Long before Maheu had achieved political power in the UNESCO secretariat, Adiseshiah had built up a large, almost independent, technical assistance and "extra-budgetary" structure. A former UNESCO staffer recalled, "Maheu was able to bypass Adiseshiah in the early 1960s in the race for the Director Generalship, and Adiseshiah (in a political agreement by Maheu with Adiseshiah's supporters) was given the post as Deputy Director General." As soon as Maheu took over as acting DG in 1961, he quickly set about dismantling Adiseshiah's technical assistance empire, integrating the TA staff with those funded under the regular program. Integral to this process was the courting of the World Bank – in fact, good relations with the Bank (culminating in a relationship profitable for UNESCO) was essential to the success of the Maheu strategy (Jones 1988: 109–10). It meant, for the Bank, a UNESCO whose entire education sector, well versed in pre-investment studies and TA, was available to be involved in the Bank's educational initiative.

Demuth's correspondence with Maheu and Adiseshiah in 1961 and 1962 reveals the acute sensitivity on both sides about each other's territory. UNESCO was indisputably the lead UN agency in education, with a solid reputation, global influence, and a strong network of experts. Yet it was a financially poor organization, hugely dependent on external funding for anything beyond the intellectual. On its side, the Bank understood well the power of the dollar, and rightly assumed that its educational significance would quickly become substantial. But this could not happen immediately, given the Bank's inexperience and total lack of in-house expertise in education. Demuth was instrumental in bringing the two parties together to their mutual advantage, and forged the basis for a working relationship whereby the Bank would entrust to UNESCO much of its sectoral investigation and project-identification work. It would also be the case that the Bank's education staff would be kept deliberately small, in favor of utilizing UNESCO's in-house expertise. It was also to transpire that the Bank's first education chief, Ricardo Diez Hochleitner, would be seconded from UNESCO, and that the Bank and UNESCO would share a leading role in the establishment of the International Institute of Educational Planning (IIEP) in Paris in 1963.

Taking decisions on education

A characteristic of the Bank described in the previous chapter is the capacity of its staff to present a united external front. On complex matters of policy, Bank staff is as capable of holding a range of position as is any other group. Life inside the Bank is marked by the vibrancy with which intelligent and articulate persons debate their various attitudes, values, and viewpoints. Given the influence and power of the Bank, the stakes can be high, not only within the Bank (as bureaucratic winners and losers are identified issue by issue), but also for borrowers and their constituencies for whom many Bank staff have a deep, if sometimes patronizing, concern. Yet once decisions are taken, the Bank renders itself subject to considerable discipline. In its dealings with borrowers, other agencies, the media, and the academic community, the Bank projects its policy position as if its correctness were as clear as day. This characteristic is important in (and perhaps is dictated by) the Bank's relationship with its funding sources. Its various commercial and governmental providers of finance are perceived to be more responsive to and accepting of a Bank that is bold and decisive, one that has sorted out nutty problems, and is thereby deserving of its reputation for technical competence and sobriety.

The result, in actuality, can be one of extreme policy recklessness. Economic and social policy, as with life in general, is marked by dilemma, conflict, and doubt, over issues for which no single solution seems right. Simplistic dogmatism, in public as well as private life, can have unforeseen and questionable consequences. The danger run by the Bank is to deny the diversity seen among and cherished by its borrowers. A reasonable expectation is that the Bank–borrower relationship and dialogue would preserve that diversity. In reality, borrowers are confronted by a process of Bank salesmanship, whereby borrowers are advised of the purposes for which Bank finance might be available, are persuaded of the aptness of the Bank position in their particular setting, and assisted to adjust development plans and loan applications accordingly. This is the reality of the World Bank at work.

The Bank's education program is no exception. The Bank cannot bring itself to accept that higher education might be an absolute priority in one country, diversified secondary schooling in another, adult literacy in a third, and primary education in a fourth. Rather, the four countries are subjected to Bank pronouncements about priorities, and must fall into line should Bank finance be desired. In addition to any possibility that the Bank can get it right must be aired the possibility that such arbitrariness is unjustifiable. This is a constant challenge in international organizations and bureaucratic life in general, as they seek to impose order, keeping things neat and tidy through the discouragement of diversity. This is a major issue of our times.

The Woods factor

Eugene Black's retirement prevented him from inaugurating Bank financing in education. The timing of his departure also prevented him from formulating Bank lending criteria for educational loans and credits. On January 1, 1963, George Woods became Bank President, the fact and timing of which was to have an enormous influence on the nature of Bank involvement in education through to the end of the decade. In sum, Woods forcefully and unambiguously insisted that IBRD "hard" money be available for educational projects. At the same time, the educational purposes condoned by Woods for Bank financing were indisputably narrower than those which Black would have entertained.

Like his predecessor, Woods came from the US banking community, and as Chairman of the First Boston Corporation had a strong record in investment banking. There is no doubt that the major achievement of Woods' presidency was to place considerably more emphasis on the nature and dynamics of development, as opposed to free-standing projects, in the Bank's work. Research and policy analysis took on far greater momentum in the Bank, for the first time exerting a powerful influence in the formulation of Bank policies. As is the norm in the life of the Bank, research staff have their greatest influence on Bank policy when loan funds are tight or members are not borrowing, and the critical shortage of IDA capital towards the end of the decade meant that Bank influence could be more strongly exerted through overall policy influence, separate from lending. Another distinct Woods achievement was seen as he built up diverse and constructive working relations with the rest of the United Nations system.

Former Bank staff consulted on the issue concur that the Woods' presidency began on a decisive, energetic note. The second half, to 1968, was less happy. Woods' health had deteriorated, and his relations with the Board of Directors soured. One former staff member recalled: "Board meetings were acrimonious and unpleasant instead of being the rather relaxed and instructive and pleasant affairs that they had been." The second IDA replenishment, whose protracted negotiations lasted from 1965 to 1968, saw Woods fail to achieve his goal of $1 billion: merely $400 million was raised, and the process was politically disastrous for both Woods and IDA. The mishandling of the replenishment by Woods occasioned a serious shortfall in available IDA funds towards the end of his term.

There is one essential element of Woods' approach to educational financing of which explicit mention must be made. Woods was acutely distrustful of universities and university financial processes. He had been a member of the Rockefeller Foundation Board, and frequently reminded colleagues of his perception that university presidents were crafty characters who could not be trusted to spend grant monies for the purposes approved by donors. One senior colleague recalled: "George translated that into a prohibition against the Bank financing higher education. We concentrated on secondary education, the theory being that primary education had the political support of the country and didn't need the extra support of the Bank while secondary education was being neglected."

Another recollection comes from a senior member of Bank education staff: "Whether [his experience] made him also distrustful of university people I don't know, but he was very clear that while we had supported the agricultural universities, that was in places where the technical, vocational, professional studies were the total work of the university. To put it another way, Woods would have agreed to the financing of a project at MIT, but he would not have agreed to financing engineering at the University of Illinois. This was really a very arbitrary but firm position." On one occasion in the mid-1960s, the education staff had proposed support for secondary schools by way of support for secondary teacher education at university level, still heresy for Woods. Their meeting with Woods was confrontational. One participant recalled: "Woods was getting more and more excited. Dumb me, I just kept on arguing with him, because I thought he was so illogical. At no point did anybody get bitter or nasty, but he sort of ended it by saying, 'You're going to be in the Bank a long time after I'm gone, and you'll do it then but not now.' And he was absolutely right on both counts."

Although these considerations of Woods have preempted the chronology of this account of Bank policy formulation, it nevertheless points to the critical impact of the personality, style, and prejudices of President Woods on initial Bank involvement in education. Again, in the history of the Bank, the figure of the President is a commanding one, and here is a good example.

The result was to put initial Bank education policy into a straightjacket, from which it took a long time to extricate itself.

The early education decisions

It is of some significance that prior to the finalization of educational policies by senior management and the Board, which was to come in October 1963, the Bank had begun its lending program in education. This reflects something important about the formulation of Bank policies – they are tightly bound up with lending criteria. In fact, the Bank's accumulation of loan criteria provides a more accurate picture of Bank policy in practice than do Bank pronouncements on policy.

In April 1961, the government of Tunisia had approached the Bank for assistance to expand the provision of technical education at the secondary school level. The government's initial intention was to seek $14 million for the import of equipment. Successive UNESCO and Bank missions confirmed the importance of technical teaching at this level, especially in terms of anticipated labor-market dynamics: "At any rate of expansion of secondary schools that can plausibly be attained in the next few years, there will be no lack of job opportunities for well-qualified secondary school graduates." Interestingly, Bank missions projected the view that a focus on the technical education curriculum alone was insufficient, given its integral role in overall secondary education, a view that favored general secondary educational expansion. With this in mind, the IBRD extended a technical assistance *grant* of $375,000 to Tunisia, to strengthen educational planning and to promote ways of reducing school construction costs, provided by UNESCO and the Bank respectively. Such technical assistance was made on the assumption that considerable expansion was anticipated in future Bank loans and credits for Tunisian education. Thus in September 1962, the Board of Directors approved an IDA credit of $5 million to assist the construction and equipping of six secondary schools, providing places for 4,000 students, half of whom would be boarders, and including a training college for technical education teachers. Although the Bank and UNESCO concurred that considerable improvements were needed in Tunisia's planning of its school construction program, they deemed the six new schools to be sufficiently urgent for construction to start immediately. The IDA share of total project costs was 54 percent.

The next step of significance came in January 1963 with the establishment of an Education Division within the Technical Operations Department. Its prime function was project appraisal and supervision, coupled with the provision of Bank TA in education and the maintenance of external liaison in education. The question of educational staffing had been especially contentious. Conservative forces within the Bank – retaining their scepticism about Bank (especially IBRD) involvement in education – were insistent that the number of Bank education staff be kept as small as possible. They resisted the notion of a sizable cadre of Bank professionals being built up. Their tactic, successful in the early years, was to entrust UNESCO with a significant share of Bank functions, especially project identification, a theme examined in Chapter 3, an approach that served UNESCO's expansionist strategy of the time. At this point, Ricardo Diez Hochleitner was seconded from his position as Head of UNESCO's Educational Planning Division, to become Director of the Bank's Education Division. Diez Hochleitner – discussed more fully in Chapter 3 – has the distinction of being the World Bank's first professional education staffer. He is the pioneer of Bank programming in education.

One of Diez Hochleitner's first reports to senior management concerned the critical issue of the desirable scope of UNESCO planning mission reports, a report which in February 1963 identified the key issue facing Bank policy to be "what investments in specific education and training projects will contribute most to accelerate the processes of economic development?" To that question, Diez Hochleitner posed a broad answer, one whose breadth the Bank was not to embrace for many years to come. Diez Hochleitner had brought from Paris the contemporary UNESCO approach to educational planning that saw educational systems (and learning opportunities for individuals) as an organic whole, whereby strengths and weaknesses in one subsector vitally affected quality in others. "Thus the scope of enquiry should be very wide indeed. It should not be limited to formal education since informal education programs may have much to contribute to economic development." Although Bank loans and credits were not to reflect such breadth, the scope of many subsequent UNESCO sector reports on education in borrowing countries had, in time, a powerful educative effect on Bank staff.

An important series of meetings on Bank education policy was held by the Executive Directors' Financial Policy Committee between July and September 1963. The context of this consideration was of some significance, in that the President's proposals for education were embedded in a series of major recommendations concerning future formulation of IBRD loans and their repayment terms. IBRD grants, whether direct to members as TA or indirectly as grants to IDA, would carry implications for the size of IBRD reserves, and for future periods of grace and amortization. The possibility of transfers of IBRD operating profits to an "earned surplus" account was a particularly contentious issue on the Board. Extremely variable blends of IBRD loans and IDA credits for projects were being anticipated by the President, who in effect was foreshadowing a considerably busier Bank with enhanced flexibility in credit extension and in more diverse areas of infrastructure. Woods' recommendations of July 18, 1963 (FCP63–8) are worthy of detailed reproduction:

> If the Bank is to continue to be a forceful agent of economic development, [its] adaptability to changing circumstances must be preserved. The situation now facing the Bank is different and in some respects considerably more difficult than it was ten, or even five, years ago. We have many new members, most of them lacking the institutional structure,

and relatively inexperienced in the techniques, necessary to carry forward the development process. To lend money wisely in such countries involves a much greater investment of human skills than in countries with a longer experience of development administration. In other countries in which the Bank has been operating for some time, difficulties of a different character are arising. One is the rapid increase in the external debt service obligations of these countries in relation to the increase in their capacity to repay. Another is the fact that, in a number of countries, many of the more obvious and more easily manageable investment projects – the large power plants, the highway, railroad and port expansion schemes, the big irrigation projects – have already been or are being financed. Moreover, such basic projects cannot be fully productive unless they are accompanied by modernization of agricultural practices, soundly based industrial growth, better and more wide-spread education and training programs, etc. In many countries, development in these latter sectors is not keeping pace.

If, in the face of these difficulties and of a rising volume of repayments on outstanding loans, the Bank is in the future to make as large a net contribution towards meeting its members' development needs as it has in the past – and certainly this should be a minimum target – we will have to add new dimensions to our lending and greatly intensify our technical assistance activities. It is in the fields of agriculture, industry and education, in particular, that this more forward-looking approach by the Bank is needed . . . .

I believe that it would be both appropriate and desirable for the Bank to undertake an extensive program of technical assistance in the field of education . . . . I have concluded that, instead of establishing a program of grants in the field of education at this time, our initial approach should be to supplement IDA credits and Bank loans for educational facilities with the provision of expert services and technical advice in such fields as educational planning, teacher training, modernization of teaching materials and techniques, and improvement of school administration and of school design and construction. Help in these and related matters is certain to be a concomitant of, and often a pre-requisite to, effective capital investment in the educational sector. The Bank and IDA, between them, are likely to become a major source of external capital for educational investment purposes . . . . We should, in my judgment, be prepared to consider grants for a few especially important educational projects where, considered on their merits, there are special and persuasive reasons for Bank support. One example of the kind of project I have in mind is the International Institute for Educational Planning, which the Bank has already agreed to support.

Many Executive Directors made comments on behalf of their governments in response to Woods at successive meetings of the FPC. Few expressed reservations about Woods' intentions to create a more diversified and flexible lending operation. Most differences of opinion concerned Woods' means of moving forward, with much conservative opinion being expressed by the representatives of industrialized countries. Prominent among these were misgivings about sizeable transfers of IBRD profits to IDA and the creation of a "surplus account." Many expressed the view that senior management's desire to enter such fields as education should not dictate the pace and direction of changes to IBRD, education itself being seen as a particular threat to the IBRD's own credit rating. Some preferred UNESCO to remain as the principal source of technical assistance in education, on the assumption that a narrow Bank concern for educational construction could not be contained indefinitely – broader issues of educational quality and processes would surely develop. In the words of one ED: "It might equally be suggested that the Bank should reorganize the health, individual, political, religious, social and other habits in its member countries." Another saw education "far afield" from the building up of economic infrastructure. More typical was the view outlined by the Australian Executive Director who said he:

> ...was not happy about the proposed extension of Bank financing to school buildings. He believed that educational projects which fell properly within the Bank field of lending should be associated very closely with development projects. An agricultural training school or a school set up to service an industrial estate would, in his view, be very much more suitable for Bank lending than school buildings justified merely in terms of the general contribution made to development by improving educational facilities....On the other hand, he would not necessarily object to a cautious and hard-headed advance into education, in close association with the proper functions of the Bank, and in close cooperation with other international agencies concerned.

Of perhaps greater concern was the application of "hard" IBRD funds for "soft" purposes, and its possible impact on the Bank's own credit rating. On this point, Woods was emphatic, as his intervention at the FPC made clear on September 17, when he addressed the question of the IBRD's engaging in "IDA-type" activity. Woods asserted he "did not understand how...the Bank might engage in IDA-type business. IDA-type business was the making of loans on extremely soft terms, nothing else. The Technical Operations Department, in vetting a project, paid no attention to whether it would be financed by the Bank or IDA. It was the foreign exchange situation of the recipient country, not the type of project, which determined whether the financing would come from the Bank or IDA."

The outcome of the Executive Directors' deliberations was a request for a more detailed policy statement to be drafted by senior management. Responsibility for this was given to Richard Demuth, who consulted primarily within the Technical Operations Department on its contents. Demuth completed his draft in time for a senior management "lost weekend" at Williamsburg in mid-October 1963, in time for the final policy to be circulated to Directors on October 31 and discussed on November 26. At Williamsburg, the major issue of contention was staffing: how best would the Bank ensure the quality of all project identification and preparation, and attend to the detail of loan negotiations and project supervision? Opinion was divided over the extent to which the Bank should build up its own expertise, as opposed to relying principally on UNESCO staff.

What emerged was a compromise of sorts, in that UNESCO would be entrusted with sectoral investigations in education and project identification, while a small Bank division would attend to "quality control," loan negotiations, and all aspects of project management. As for the rest, the Williamsburg meeting seemed satisfied with what the President was about to recommend to his Board of Directors. As was customarily the case, once the President had made a formal recommendation to the Directors, dissent was highly unlikely. Vigorous questioning might keep management on its toes, but issues were usually well enough canvassed at an informal level between management and Board to ensure their formal acceptance. The status and influence of the President also made dissent unlikely.

Woods, accordingly, unveiled the first major statement of Bank education policy on October 31, 1963 – *Proposed Bank/IDA Policies in the Field of Education* – seeking and obtaining endorsement from the Financial Policy Committee by year's end. The paper began boldly: "Education is of central importance in the development process." It saw the adequacy of educational provision having a direct bearing on the effectiveness and adequacy of governmental administration, the industrial labor force, the commercial system, and agriculture. The paper conceded that for some countries the educational priority was an expansion of higher education, and for some others correcting inadequacies in primary education provision. The boldest assertion was the most arbitrary and consequential:

> In most developing countries, however, the most urgent need is for (a) an expansion of vocational and technical education and training at various levels, including technical schools, agricultural schools and schools of commerce and business administration; and (b) an expansion of general secondary education, to provide middle-level management for government, industry, commerce and agriculture, more candidates for higher education and for specialized vocational training, and more teachers for the primary schools.

The document reflects admirably the tendency of the Bank to project an assertive and united front in areas of great complexity and controversy. In this case, Woods claimed that the Bank's new interest in education would result in substantially increased interest in education in developing countries, "given the Bank's reputation as a lender only for sound development projects and as an unbiased nonpolitical development adviser," an extraordinary claim to competence given the highly conflicting external advice received on educational priorities, the Bank's extremely limited in-house experience, and the division on these issues still seen among senior management. Thus the first statement of Bank educational financing criteria emerged, with a decidedly definite ring:

> The Bank and IDA should be prepared to consider financing a part of the capital requirements of priority education projects designed to produce, or to serve as a necessary first step in producing, trained manpower of the kinds and in the numbers to forward economic development in the member country concerned. In applying this criterion, the Bank and IDA should concentrate their attention, at least at the present stage, on projects in the fields of (a) vocational and technical education and training at various levels, and (b) general secondary education.... Educational expenditures serve social and cultural, as well as economic, objectives. For purposes of determining whether the Bank/IDA should finance a given project in the education sector, however, I believe that only economic factors should be taken into consideration.

Financing would normally be limited to capital expenditures – buildings and equipment – with occasional provision for such operational expenses as salaries for temporarily engaged expatriate staff early in the life of a project. Lending for recurrent costs, including teachers' salaries and funds for the normal annual expansion of school systems, was not envisaged. Woods was careful to point out that duplication of effort with UNESCO was unlikely, given UNESCO's financial incapacity to provide capital funds, "although its technical assistance program is substantial and valuable." UNESCO was proposed as the Bank's "technical arm" in the education sector, although the Bank would retain the sole right to determine whether finance would be extended, and on what terms. The Bank would "rely heavily on UNESCO personnel and experience and accordingly would not have to build up a large staff of technical experts of its own." Last, the document outlined provision for Bank technical assistance in education, ruling out the possibility of a "foundation-type" grants scheme of the kind investigated by Harvie Branscomb. The last word, however, had to be given to the Executive Directors, although it was unthinkable for them to refuse Woods his policy. On cue, the West German conservative Otto Donner tried to put on the brakes:

> I am afraid we have no other choice than to keep the money volume and number of our educational projects at a very modest level. Education should, as other [Executive Directors] have said, be a fringe activity of Bank/IDA.... We should restrict our assistance to vocational and technical schools. Assistance for general secondary education should be made available only under exceptional circumstances.... We should assume no responsibility for mass education.

Otto Donner was not alone on the Board – most representatives of the industrial West reflected his views, while those from the developing world, naturally enough, pressed for liberal criteria for financing. The conservative view, however, gave to senior management policies the air of benign yet responsible liberality. As far as IDA financing of education was concerned, the lady of easy virtue most certainly did not have her day, but neither did the spinsterish IBRD. A middle way prevailed, imbued with the double air of a ready but arbitrary compromise – neither cautious nor reckless in intent, but capable of either.

Conclusion

The education die was cast and negotiations accelerated with nearly twenty countries. From the outset, the Bank considered itself to be in a position to insist on what borrowers' needs and priorities would be. Prior to any country investigation, the Bank was positioned to release (from the borrowers' perspective) unprecedented levels of finance, but for decidedly limited educational purposes. No Bank official at the time is on record as questioning the distortions in educational planning and development this would contribute to, as many UNESCO staffers of the day were predicting. If a decade later, the Bank could refer to its widening of loan criteria in education as a "liberalization," its policies throughout the 1960s could only fairly be described as generously illiberal. Marble cladding on the walls of the inaugural project's technical secondary schools in Tunisia are a vivid testimony, as was the high unemployment rate of the schools' graduates.

Notes

Chapter 2 relies almost exclusively on unpublished material located in Bank Archives. Some documents employed in the course of the Board of Directors' deliberations may be available through member governments. These include Financial Policy Committee documents FCP63-8, FCP63-11, FCP63-15, and FCP63-16. Otherwise, all other papers are internal memoranda and reports reserved for internal Bank use.

For developments in UNESCO at the time, see Jones (1988) and (2005).

On the emergence of the economics of education, see the highly influential presidential address of Theodore Schultz to the American Economic Association in December 1960, subsequently published as Schultz (1961). For commentary, see Blaug (1968), Arndt (1987), and Fagerlind and Saha (1989).

3 Early project experience in education 1963–8

The early years of World Bank education financing (fiscal years 1963–8) saw 23 countries borrow $162 million, 78 percent of which was obtained on concessional terms from IDA (see Table 3.1). It took 4 years to get the first 13 projects operational, increasing to 25 projects in all by 1968. By FY 1968, education was claiming 12.75 percent of total IDA financing, but only 1.25 percent of the IBRD's, making for a World Bank group educational disbursement of $24.2 million of a total $953.5 million in that year, or 2.5 percent (see Table 3.2). For details of education lending by level and purpose in these years, see Table 3.3.

The twenty-five projects were overwhelmingly for the construction of secondary schools, technical schools, and teacher education colleges. The only projects dedicated to higher education were for agricultural universities in the Philippines and Bangladesh, although some other projects had small higher education components. Industrial vocational training, and to a lesser extent agricultural training, were a feature of many projects, while two projects (in Chile and Thailand) were dedicated to vocational education alone. Nearly every project had multiple objectives, addressing educational expansion and diversification in a range that included secondary, technical, vocational, teacher education, and higher education institutions. Many institutions were financed to construct student residences, and projects normally contained provision for equipment and furniture. Two projects (in Ethiopia and Brazil) were for rather broad developmental purposes, of which education was a project component.

The emphasis on construction and equipment should come as no surprise, nor should the emphasis on technical and vocational education for those of secondary school age. Neither should too much be made of the marble cladding on the schools constructed in the inaugural Tunisian project. In these early years of World Bank education financing, little was known about how to organize education projects in terms of the investment models common to all previous IBRD financing. It was only the availability of IDA finance that rendered a World Bank education program plausible, while it was the discipline associated with IBRD commercial lending that rendered educational financing credible.

Table 3.1 World Bank education financing, by region,
FY 1963–8

Region	$US million	% of lending
Africa	60	37
Asia	26	16
Latin America and Caribbean	38	23
Europe, Middle East, and North Africa	39	24
Total	163	100

Source: World Bank Annual Reports, various years.

Table 3.2 IBRD and IDA financing, by sector, FY 1968
($US m)

Sector	IBRD	IDA	Total
Agriculture	145.3	27.2	172.5
Education	10.6	13.6	24.2
Electric power	254.5	14.0	268.5
Telecommunications	27.0	0.0	27.0
Industry	191.5	0.0	191.5
Project preparation	0.0	0.5	0.5
Transportation	196.1	51.2	247.3
Water supply	22.0	0.0	22.0
Total	847.0	106.5	953.5

Source: World Bank Annual Report 1968.

Note
IDA's second replenishment had run into severe difficulties in
1965, resulting in a relatively low level of IDA credits in FY 1967
and 1968.

Establishing a project cycle in education

A major theme of this book is the manner in which Bank activity over the
years has been dominated by free-standing projects. The size and complexity
of Bank projects cannot be overstated. They are demanding for both Bank
and borrower, both of which have made a sizeable financial commitment. The
timespan for preparation is inevitably protracted, and project life is commonly
six or more years. It is not uncommon for the period from initial project
identification to final auditing to be twelve or more years. Bank supervision
of financial disbursements is meticulous – Bank funds are released only in
stages, and only when the Bank is certain that earlier tranches have
been applied, in full, to the purposes approved. At the same time, projects

Table 3.3 World Bank distribution of
education lending, FY 1963–8
(percentages)

By level	
Primary education	—
Secondary education	84
Higher education	12
Nonformal education	4
Total	100
By curriculum	
General and diversified	44
Technical and commercial	25
Agriculture	19
Teacher education	12
Total	100
By outlay	
Construction	69
Equipment	28
Technical assistance	3
Total	100

Source: World Bank Annual Reports, various
years.

are not easy to modify. Given their complexity and protracted nature, it is difficult for projects to adjust quickly to changing circumstances and requirements.

Throughout its history, the World Bank has attempted to deflect criticism of the dominant role of free-standing projects by making its projects increasingly complex and wide-ranging, thereby attempting some broad sectoral impact. It is typical of most project documents that they reflect inflated and unrealistic expectations about anticipated project impact. Even relatively isolated institutions are expected to exert some regional or even national significance, sometimes for the only reason that they have been partly constructed with Bank funds. A former Bank Vice President remarked that this seemed especially true of education projects. Because their direct economic impact was impossible to gauge, their long-term economic benefits tended to be overstated. He complained, in fact, about the striking similarity of many justifications of education projects at the Board of Directors, and the frequent overstatement of their potential and significance.

The project cycle

The Bank's *Handbook for Implementation of Education Projects* highlights the usual complexity of projects. It is organized around the following implementation "checklist," designed to inform both Bank staff and borrowers of typical project components and Bank requirements:

- project management arrangements
- project implementation programming
- coordination and monitoring of educational activities
- engagement of specialists under technical assistance
- local staff development and fellowship program
- sites for project institutions
- project buildings design
- assignment/engagement of architects
- briefing of architects
- preparation of drawings and construction documents
- determination of instructional equipment and furniture needs
- preparation of equipment and furniture lists
- procurement of building works
- procurement of equipment and furniture
- continuous administrative control of project implementation activities
- financial arrangements and withdrawal of loan proceeds
- periodic project progress reporting to the Bank
- arrangements for routine maintenance of project buildings and equipment
- preparations for the use of new facilities
- evaluation of new facilities
- evaluation and monitoring of educational activities.

Such a list, more or less chronologically arranged, is quite typical of project implementation requirements in all manner of public and private sector capital works. What is distinctive here is the Bank's tight control over disbursements. No other development assistance organization is as strict in this aspect of project supervision as the World Bank. Bank projects are invariably free of the gross corruption and misappropriation seen so frequently in public and private sector life. The weak point concerns formative and summative evaluation of project implementation and impact. Once financial audits are completed, the Bank seems little interested in detailed, qualitative evaluation – loan officers are presumably busy with future loan appraisals and negotiations. It is here that Bank research staff – usually far removed from the detail of loan negotiations and project supervision – see a role for themselves, although their impact on lending is problematic, a theme of some importance in later chapters of this book.

From the point of view of understanding World Bank policy, defined as the accumulation of lending criteria, it is important to see project implementation as only one step in what has become known as the "project cycle." In the words of a former Bank Vice President, each project passes through a cycle that is common to all – identification, preparation, appraisal, negotiation, presentation to the Executive Directors, implementation and supervision, and evaluation. "Each phase leads to the next, and the last phases, in turn, produce new project approaches and ideas and lead to the identification of new projects, making the cycle self-renewing" (Baum 1982: 5).

Project identification is tightly bound up with the ongoing dialogue and relationship between Bank and borrower, frequent Bank and IMF economic surveys, and the periodic sector reviews in which the Bank makes assessments of, say, educational policy and practice in the member country. From these contacts are derived perceptions of the country's creditworthiness (its repayment and hence borrowing capacity) as well as multiyear lending programs used by the Bank to guide its forthcoming activities across all sectors. It is in this stage of the cycle that the power and influence of the Bank are seen, given its potentially strong impact on national economic policy, sectoral development, and specific project possibilities. Much can also be learned by outside observers about domestic economic policy and development priorities, as various government departments, economic authorities, and development planning units jockey for position and influence on priorities for Bank loans and other external and domestic resourcing. Much of the Bank's early sector work in education was conducted through its cooperative arrangement with UNESCO. Maintaining an articulation between its broader economic surveys and sector work undertaken in this manner was an early and ongoing difficulty for the Bank.

Project preparation is the responsibility of the borrower, although the Bank is closely involved and frequently provides technical assistance for the purpose. Feasibility studies, partly to examine a range of technical and institutional options for the project, are one aspect of preparation, which would normally address, in the Bank's words, "the technical, institutional, economic, and financial conditions necessary to achieve project objectives." In education, much project preparation work was assisted by UNESCO, whether or not through its formal agreement with the Bank.

No loan can be approved prior to detailed *appraisal work* by the Bank, to ensure that preparation work and standards meet Bank criteria. Appraisal is solely the Bank's responsibility, is jealously guarded by it, and is never entrusted to external agencies under its cooperative agreements. External consultants might be involved in appraisal, but act for the Bank in all cases.

The content of *loan negotiations* reflects each of the prior steps. Appraisal reports often identify procedural issues that require clarification or improvement, while the earlier stages of identification and preparation provide the Bank with details of policy matters it may wish to influence through the attachment of side-conditions (covenants) to the loan. Loan negotiations, then, can be complex, as they invariably address far wider issues than might the project under consideration. Their timing can be politically delicate, especially if covenants are unpalatable to governments or if there is an urgent need for the foreign exchange which loans will provide. For their part, the Bank's Executive Directors know that no project can proceed without their approval. Two observations are pertinent here. First, no project proposal brought to the Board by the President is likely to be rejected. Second, Executive Directors are customarily more interested in the timing of the loan, its size, and the attached covenants than they are in project detail itself. The Board can reward a government with a swift approval, or punish it through delaying tactics or by arbitrarily cutting the size or scope of a project or loan amount. Some Directors, in fact, see Bank projects as little other than as vehicles or opportunities for the Bank to supply foreign exchange, seeing as paramount the Bank's role as a provider of capital. They are irritated with "project perfectionism," and are often more drawn to broad but diffuse program loans than to fussy project loans.

Notwithstanding the Bank's close supervision, responsibility for *project implementation* rests squarely with the borrowing government, which inevitably has a substantial financial stake in the project, additional to those funds borrowed from the Bank. Projects, properly described, are borrowers' projects rather than World Bank projects. The Bank's supervisory interest stems in large measure from its need to protect its own investments, thereby safeguarding its own credit rating. But it is the borrower who needs to establish appropriate implementation procedures, usually centered upon a "project implementation unit" (PIU) within a ministry of education. PIUs need to be sufficiently discrete to enable the orderly implementation of free-standing and complex projects; at the same time, they need to have a sufficiently intimate connection with the education system for the project to have the wider impact desired. Project quality is inevitably a direct product of PIU effectiveness, and this factor more than any other needs to be assessed when project success or effectiveness is being considered. PIUs reflect the same degrees of competence, integrity, dedication, creativity, and flair as can any other group.

In all cases, borrowers make a considerable *contribution to project* costs – either in local or foreign currency – in addition to any contribution made by a third or fourth party (e.g. a bilateral aid agency) in what is termed "co-financing." PIUs inevitably have many masters to serve, needing to satisfy varying procedural and bureaucratic requirements, styles, standards, and timing. Project implementation is frequently the subject of Bank technical assistance. The Bank's supervision of projects is undertaken by the loan departments and officers responsible for the loan – missions visit PIUs and project sites very frequently, perhaps twice a year for the typical six or seven years of project life. A key term is "end-use supervision," by which the Bank must be assured that project funds and procured items are employed for the intended purposes, and with effect.

The Executive Directors have had, since 1975, their own *evaluative* capacity by way of the Bank's Operations Evaluation Department (OED), organizationally separate from the Bank's lending and operations departments, and reporting direct to the Board (OED was later renamed the Independent Evaluation Group). Bank operations staff prepare project completion reports (PCRs), while OED's reports to the Board – little more than confirmation of PCRs with final audit data – are styled project performance audit reports (PPARs). PCRs and PPARs are summative, and focus squarely on project implementation and financial matters. They provide little by way of qualitative assessments of broader impact. Bank research staff address such features, as does OED with its occasional impact evaluation reports, prepared 5 years or more after project completion. OED also organizes occasional assessments of the Bank's long-term impact on a country's education system, or indeed of the Bank's overall relationship with a member country. It is in the bureaucratic scheme of things that Bank operations staff see OED reporting as contributing little to Bank operations, except irritation, while OED staff see their organizational detachment as a guarantor of objectivity.

Such is the manner in which Bank projects are conceived, financed, and executed. Requirements for project implementation, as well as the complexities of the entire project cycle, highlight the multifaceted character of Bank lending operations, Bank–borrower relations, and relations with cooperating agencies (e.g. UNESCO, ILO, and FAO). Further, each step requires its own specialized and experienced staff, technically competent and attuned to the borrower's economic, cultural, and political circumstances. The extent to which the Bank's staffing profile reflects such capacities is open to question and judgment. By 1980 or so, the Bank's education sector staff had grown in size, function, and diversity to typify arrangements for most other sectors. But this took 15 or more years to evolve, from a baseline of negligible in-house capacity in 1962, and it is instructive to consider the beginnings and evolution of Bank education sector staffing.

Early appointments in education

Reference has been made to the efforts expended between 1960 and 1963 by Bank management to acquaint themselves with the field of education. From the President down, internal papers and memoranda were written and exchanged on a wide range of educational and economic issues. Such senior management personalities as Iliff, Knapp, Aldewereld, Rist, Demuth, and Ripman circulated good quality papers among themselves, and had frequent discussions – at the office and on "lost weekends" – on education. They sought advice from credible sources, in the universities, the foundations, and international organizations. They were aware of UNESCO's competence and experience in education, especially on the technical assistance side, and provided an initial, cautious endorsement of UNESCO's emphasis on broadly conceived educational planning. They quickly embraced the notion of education as an investment, but disagreed over the scope of Bank financing of education and over the usefulness of long-term manpower forecasting and planning. They interacted formally and informally with the Executive Directors, encouraging a more liberal line from such western sceptics as Donner and Lieftinck, and pouring cold water on the enthusiasms of Directors from borrowing countries. All up, Bank management did well to raise its initial awareness of educational policy matters.

At the same time, the Bank remained the Bank, a busy and practical organization, and pressures for educational programming had to be accommodated to this reality. With a line of potential borrowers steadily forming, lending procedures had to be quickly put into place. Given the complexities and customary lead time for Bank project approval, as well as sensitivities over whether education was a safe "bankable" sector, delays in getting started were on the cards, a politically undesirable outcome for a new sector of financing. The issue of staffing was pressing.

The initial solution was to establish a small Education Division within Aldewereld's Technical Operations Department, with a staff of fifteen, most of whom were architects. Much of the work of project identification and preparation was to be passed to UNESCO, an arrangement discussed later in this chapter, although the Bank retained its right to exercise the final judgment on any loan application (i.e. appraisal). To head the Education Division, Ricardo Diez Hochleitner was seconded in late 1962 from his position as Head of UNESCO's Educational Planning Division. As was originally intended, Diez Hochleitner returned to UNESCO in 1964 as Director of the Office of Educational Planning, Administration and Finance.

Ricardo Diez Hochleitner provided the Bank with a broad appreciation of how education systems were structured and how they operated as organic entities. A tall, handsome Spaniard whose German mother endowed his name with a certain cosmopolitanism, Diez Hochleitner's career began in academia, in the field of chemical engineering at the University of Salamanca and the National University of Bogota, where he became Dean. Much of his early career was spent in Colombia, and at the time of the first IBRD economic mission to that country (1953–4), Diez Hochleitner was contracted to prepare for the government an advance document on technical and higher manpower needs, in which he proposed several technical universities for Colombia. Several months in 1955–6 were spent on the planning of technical education in Spain, after which he returned to Colombia as departmental Deputy in the Ministry of Education, where he took responsibility for a five-year education plan. After several months in Washington drafting a Latin American strategy for educational planning for the Organization of American States (OAS), he went to UNESCO, Paris in October 1958 to organize a unit on the techniques of educational planning. Diez Hochleitner, with UNESCO DG Luther Evans' blessing, maintained strong OAS links, and in fact spent fifteen months in 1961–2 commuting between Paris and Washington, as Executive Secretary of the Education Task Force of the OAS.

It was at this time that Eugene Black sent for Diez Hochleitner to discuss the Bank's move towards education, discussions that also involved Burke Knapp and Dick Demuth, among others. This was the time of the Branscomb investigation, and Diez Hochleitner stressed to Black the merits of an IBRD commitment to educational loans rather than grants, conceding the attendant difficulties. Two weeks later, Diez Hochleitner spent several hours with Hugh Ripman, who was working intensively on educational project procedures and issues for his TOD boss Aldewereld. Diez Hochleitner enjoyed good relations with incoming UNESCO DG Maheu. Both could see in the secondment distinct long-term advantages for UNESCO, in its quest to gain as much as possible from any Bank commitment to educational financing.

The Bank's senior management warmed to Diez Hochleitner's capacities and breadth of experience. He was an articulate, thoughtful, and charming man, precocious in the sense of still being short of his thirty-fifth birthday upon arrival at the Bank. He had built up over the years close working relations with the major foundations (especially Ford) and the US State Department, as well as broad-ranging governmental, intergovernmental, and academic connections. This credibility was important, as was his practical orientation towards the field of educational planning. TOD was to benefit enormously, in time, from Diez Hochleitner's insistence on instilling in the Bank an appreciation of the need for any free-standing project to be conceived in broader terms.

Diez Hochleitner's June 1963 internal paper on educational planning made much of this, and went into some detail about how borrowers could be assisted to develop their educational planning capacities. At the same time, there were distinct limits to the breadth the Bank could foster, given the dangers of unduly raising borrower expectations about loan criteria. Woods' insistence on narrow and specific criteria for lending collided to a considerable extent with Diez Hochleitner's view of comprehensive educational development, whereby all subsectors in an educational system had to be conceived and developed as part of an organic and coordinated whole. The Bank's limited criteria, in effect if not by design, worked against this orientation, with its underlying justification that certain subsectors were more economically dynamic than others. At heart and by intellect, Diez Hochleitner was a UNESCO person. He maintained a profound respect for UNESCO's commitment to political and technical consultation, to its collaborative procedures, and to its breadth of outlook on education. In a sense when he left the Bank in 1964, Diez Hochleitner returned home.

Fortunately for all concerned, Diez Hochleitner maintained good working relations with the Bank, particularly with his long-serving successor Duncan Ballantine. Back at UNESCO, Diez Hochleitner exercised responsibility for the UNESCO–World Bank Co-operative Agreement, and the quality of his professional and personal relations with Ballantine, in particular, was important. Both were strong-willed men of deep conviction, and the good relations between the Bank and UNESCO were a partial reflection of their mutual respect and warmth. In 1968, Diez Hochleitner returned to his native Spain as Under-Secretary of the Ministry of Education and Science, and more than twenty years of further involvement in international education ensued.

Memorialists interviewed for this study invariably have much to say about Duncan Ballantine, Diez Hochleitner's successor as Director of Education Projects. Under its various guises and titles, the Bank's Education Department was led by Ballantine until his retirement at the end of 1977. A strong case can be made that the formulation of education policy and practice in the Bank was dominated by Ballantine, to the extent that any one person could. Duncan Ballantine was variously described as a towering man, a lion of a man, forceful and strong-willed. Of a tall, strong, solid build, Ballantine was indisputably a leader, and in no setting was a person to be ignored. Ballantine first studied history at Amherst College (in the company of Philip Coombs, the first director of IIEP) and went on to Harvard for study at the Masters level. A period of secondary school teaching led to a lecturing appointment at the Massachusetts Institute of Technology English and History Department, where (with Walt Rostow) Ballantine taught economic history to junior sophomores. After naval service during the war, a doctorate on the history of naval logistics in the Second World War was completed at Harvard, and after a period back at MIT, Ballantine took up his first college presidency, at Reed College, Portland, Oregon, described by Ballantine as "an unfortunate and unhappy period at a tempestuous place," meaning that he had a difficult Council which "interfered" in his work. More happy for Ballantine were the years (1955–61) spent in Istanbul at Robert College, where as President Ballantine could exert all the influence in the world, turning around the institution's parlous finances, and making use of Ford Foundation support to restore academic standards. Ballantine recalled:

> Then Dean Rusk [of the Rockefeller Foundation], with whom I had an acquaintance during my begging days as college president, offered me a grant to retread my tyres and get back more fully into academic life. I accepted that, and went to Harvard where they readily welcomed me as a research associate since I didn't need any money. And then I came to a conference here in Washington with many of the people who were then involved in the embryonic study of education and development. I met an old Ford Foundation friend, Ken Iverson, who was recruiting somebody to go on a Bank mission to Colombia. I went, although I didn't think I knew anything about education as such. But we had a good mission.

Ballantine was quickly recruited to Diez Hochleitner's Division, and the two got on famously. Ballantine, in no time, had participated in a major economic mission to Mexico, and importantly to Pakistan to prepare an education project – project identification, appraisal, sector investigations, and project preparation "all rolled into one," as Ballantine recalled. "It took a bit of re-writing to satisfy standard Bank practice."

It is interesting, in terms of the Bank's external relations and contacts at the time, and given its urgent need to obtain advice about education specialists, how frequently the same names arise. With its strong US identification, the Bank's informal network centered squarely on the US academic community and on the major US foundations. More politically (or intergovernmentally) oriented agencies, of course, need to conduct their external consultations in a more open, comprehensive, and structured fashion. At the Bank's entry into education, it is not unfair to suggest that the old-boy network was brought into play. Unlike many other such networks, this one was competent, if culturally, linguistically, and politically monochrome.

And there seemed little scope for women. Duncan Ballantine, in his interview for the Bank's oral history program, reflected on early staffing issues:

> There were no roadmaps and there were no people who really had experience in education as part of development. Naturally we had to get people who had educational experience of one sort or another of the normal kind. We needed economists to make us respectable in the Bank and to actually treat this as an economic activity. We needed architects because, although this wasn't realised fully at first, it soon became apparent that most of the money would go into civil works.... We needed equipment specialists, but there were none....My impression, and I could be wrong, is that we had a fairly high turnover in the early days. We used consultants quite a bit because we didn't know how many we were going to need, but ultimately we settled on some very good ones indeed.... From UNESCO, of course, we got some recruits... [including] one of our very best people.

UNESCO–World Bank Co-operative Program

Looking to UNESCO for assistance with ideas and staffing suited the purposes of senior Bank management who differed in their enthusiasm for a Bank education portfolio. In one corner stood the education enthusiasts who regarded UNESCO as a competent agency with highly relevant expertise, and in touch with the educational circumstances of member countries. They saw in UNESCO an expedient means of quickly addressing the line of potential borrowers queing up. Detractors of educational financing, for their part, were adamant that the Bank would not build up a sizeable staff of education specialists, at least not before it was demonstrated that education was in fact "bankable." The UNESCO connection served both groups well.

At the same time, the notion of a close working arrangement with UNESCO was controversial, as with the other UN Specialized Agencies. Senior management personnel of the day interviewed on this point all confirm that it was Woods who pushed the idea along of a cooperative agreement with UNESCO, but differ on where the idea originated. Harold Graves recalled in 1985: "It may or may not have been [Demuth's] idea. At any rate, it was an idea that must have originated pretty close to Dick. It was an idea that appealed to Woods and to virtually nobody else on the staff.... [Demuth] certainly was the person who did the most to promote the idea within the Bank." By contrast, Demuth in 1984 distanced himself from such an interpretation:

> [Woods] had unanimous staff opposition to the suggestion that we should work more closely with UNESCO and FAO, including, I must confess, my own....In the end we figured out what was necessary in order to make these organizations effective in our aspect of their business, which was....to set up an elite group within each of those

organizations....So that instead of relying on the organizations as a whole, we had a co-operative program that really involved a group of people that was an extension of our own...Projects Department. And as it turned out, those groups I think were probably as good as, or maybe even better than, the groups that we had collected....Although we had lots of little troubles, the groups had a real impact on developing projects....These arrangements worked very well.

The UNESCO–World Bank Co-operative Agreement, signed in June 1964, was the product of pragmatism. Its wording reflected nothing high-minded about the benefits of international programming and interagency collaboration. Reference has already been made to UNESCO's circumstances at the time. Throughout the 1950s, a sound reputation had developed as UNESCO provided technical assistance to member countries, especially with broad sectoral planning in education. Since 1960, education for development and educational planning had become UNESCO's highest intellectual and programming priority. Its series of ministerial conferences in Karachi, Addis Ababa, and Santiago had put in place ambitious plans for educational expansion. Early co-operation with the World Bank had led to joint funding of the International Institute for Educational Planning in Paris, under the directorship of Philip Coombs, who had become well-known to Bank staff in his earlier Brookings Institution days.

An unexpected benefit of the UNESCO connection came in the area of educational statistics. A former senior Bank official remarked on the 1960s and 1970s: "The connection with UNESCO...developed when we ourselves got into the more statistical approaches to the development process....We found the statistical branch of UNESCO to be by far the best thing there was. They were excellent. Their material was good. I had a high respect for those people. There wasn't any other agency in the world anywhere that could match the stuff that they put at our disposal."

UNESCO, it has been noted, was ever a poorly resourced agency. Its regular budget permits little more than the documentation and dissemination of the products of its intellectual work. Given its sound reputation for undertaking technical assistance funded through other UN agencies, incoming DG Maheu in 1961–2 was swift to build up the expectation that significant levels of "extra-budgetary" funding was available if UNESCO went after it. Maheu was highly skilled at this, and at all stages of the Bank's deliberations over its possible education portfolio was in regular touch – in person and by letter – with Bank Presidents Black and Woods. His letters warmly encouraged the Bank's move into education, and were often appended with long, technically sound papers about aspects of educational planning, financing, or programming. These papers were read by senior Bank management, and most certainly reinforced the notion of UNESCO's pertinence and usefulness to the Bank.

The cooperative agreement made general provision for the Bank and UNESCO to work together at most points of the project cycle – identification, preparation, appraisal, implementation, end-use supervision, and technical assistance are all specified. Allocation of function was more specialized, with UNESCO having "primary responsibility" for project identification and preparation, and the provision of technical assistance to project implementation, while the Bank remained responsible for appraisal and end-use supervision. For each function, however, formal provision was made for collaboration.

To service the agreement, UNESCO established an Educational Financing Division (EFD) within its Paris secretariat, largely financed by the Bank. Appointment to EFD came to be prized among UNESCO staffers, as levels of appointment were higher, travel appeared more satisfying, and professional activities usually led to large, often significant projects, this last dimension normally absent in the work of UNESCO staffers. After his year and a half with the Bank, Diez Hochleitner returned to UNESCO to head the department in which EFD was located. Given his stake in the Bank's education program, and his excellent working relations with his Bank counterparts Demuth and Ballantine, his appointment at UNESCO was auspicious for the cooperative agreement. The several volumes of Bank files – correspondence, internal memoranda, and formal reports on the functioning of the program – all point to a good beginning, as each side felt its way, each keen to get good education projects up and running as quickly as possible.

The first Bank quarterly report on the agreement (September 1964) high-lighted an understandable difficulty. In it, Ballantine advised Aldewereld that the initial UNESCO mission reports "have not shown great precision" in selecting potential education projects, reflecting UNESCO's attachment to "the entire educational field [rather] than the Bank's concern with economic development." This became, with time, less of a practical issue, as EFD built up its own staff, fully conversant with Bank criteria for education financing. Nevertheless, the underlying institutional tension remained, between the relative breadth and narrowness of the two sides' approaches to education. At every opportunity, Maheu urged a broader Bank approach. A good example was Maheu's luncheon talk to the Executive Directors soon after the September 1965 Teheran Congress on literacy, when he outlined an economic development rationale for adult literacy education, a notion not met with much glee on that or subsequent occasions. Literacy aside, the major issue concerning the cooperative agreement concerned practical operations in the field. A report to Aldewereld concluded in August 1965:

> There may be an organic flaw in the setup of the Program. It is becom-ing apparent that in almost all cases thus far the project identification missions have been premature. Such missions have been sent to countries where little basic planning has been done, where priorities are unclear, where statistical data is not assembled or analyzed, where educational policy needs review, where even general targets have not been set, etc. As a result the mission must act as a planning mission and is unable – for lack of time or because of circumstances – to actually identify projects.

As a result missions take longer than they should, the reports have to be more voluminous, and they do not in fact accomplish their purpose.

When Maheu visited Woods in November 1965, four major elements of the cooperative program can be identified from Bank files as being of current concern: common perceptions of the need for greater use of general "reconnaissance" missions (later termed sector work in education); the Bank's complaints about delays in procuring project-identification reports; the Bank's desire to have more of its own staff at work in the cooperative program; and UNESCO's desire to be consulted about side covenants to education loans (to which Woods gave Maheu an immediate and emphatic "no").

By mid-1966, Bank staff were beginning to comment among themselves about the calibre of some recent appointees to EFD. Delays in project identification and preparation remained a problem, and a certain testiness emerged about this time in Bank correspondence and verbal dealings with UNESCO. By early 1967, the tone for the future had set in. Bank letters to EFD Director Van Vliet were universally of a superior, condescending, even dismissive tone. French lessons for newly appointed EFD staff in Paris were declined by the Bank, for example. No malice was intended, presumably. The tone, rather, reflects what was developing at the institutional level. The Bank's lending in education was beginning to accelerate, and it was acutely aware of the gap between the Bank's own economic determinations of member countries' creditworthiness and the project-identification work done externally. It is not so much that UNESCO reports were invariably delayed. Closer scrutiny reveals the problem to be more one of poor articulation between broad economic surveys (with their resultant multiyear lending projections) and project identification. When confined to the Bank, both functions can be timed to advantage, a result harder to achieve under an interagency agreement.

Also by 1967, Bank staff in education had grown to several dozen, and it was inevitably asked by senior Bank management – privately – why could not EFD's functions be transferred to Washington, especially now that the Bank was meeting their full cost, and the Bank's in-house experience and capacity was clearly evident.

On paper, the agreement was to last another twenty years, but its pertinence steadily dwindled through the 1970s, especially following the major reorganization of Bank structure in 1972. From that time, there ceased to be an all-powerful Education Department – most of its functions were allocated out to Regional Departments, Ballantine remaining to lead a small policy and review unit. As far as the project cycle was concerned, the Regional Departments were at the heart of things, and two casualties were the prominence of Duncan Ballantine and the "core" Education Department, and the relevance of the UNESCO–World Bank Co-operative Agreement, which quickly had become an anachronism to be tolerated. It was natural for Regional Department heads to prefer to select their own consultants for project-identification work, rather than being obliged to spend their budget on UNESCO staff and consultants. With the political crisis that had engulfed UNESCO by the late 1970s, no one in the Bank was prepared to defend UNESCO – either in general terms as the lead UN agency in education, or more specifically in terms of continuing with the formal cooperation agreement, which was abandoned in 1986 but had lapsed for most practical purposes well before.

Initial project and policy issues

The first five years of education financing reflected much that was typical of earlier IBRD experience. These years also saw the emergence of a Bank approach to education that was to remain of significance for some time to come. The early Bank loans and credits for education, then, are worthy of scrutiny, and reflect much of the intense difficulty in interpreting Bank projects generally.

Issues in project design

Several projects reveal clearly a high degree of Bank assertiveness in project design. For reasons to do with its own institutional history, the Bank had declared secondary education, and technical and vocational training at various levels, as the areas eligible for financing. Aldewereld and Demuth summed up lending criteria in a memorandum requested by Woods in January 1966:

> The terms technical and vocational were understood to include industrial, commercial, and agricultural skills, as well as teacher training. Medical education was not included since the Bank did not finance other types of projects in the health field. Primary education was excluded since there are relatively few countries where it can be considered a "crucial gap" and since its impact on economic growth, although recognized, is indirect and deferred. In the field of university level technical education the Bank indicated a preference for assisting institutions of a purely or predominantly technical character rather than supporting technical faculties or departments within general universities.

Such criteria had to be sold to borrowers. No account of Bank financing of education can avoid the persistence with which loan officers have exerted pressure on potential borrowers to fall into line with the Bank's own educational priorities. If governments were to obtain their desired access to foreign exchange, then their statements of educational priority had to match the Bank's. This is not at all uncommon in the history of external aid: agencies normally advise governments of what they can provide, and only then do governments indicate their need for it. But in the Bank's case the size of its loans, their complexity, and the Bank's general capacities for leverage put its policy assertiveness on to a different plane. Further, the career prospects of individual Bank loan officers depended a good deal on their record in having sizeable loans quickly approved, and having project disbursements flowing quickly throughout the life of a project. Loan officers were under particular pressure to sell not only Bank finance but also the thinking that accompanied that finance.

The first credit to Ethiopia, for example, was initially justified on the grounds of very low enrolments at the secondary level. In 1966, primary school attendance levels hovered at about 10 percent, while only 1 percent of 13 to 18 year olds attended secondary schools. Of 1,550 secondary school teachers, only 900 were Ethiopian, and of these 800 were considered by the planning mission to be inadequately prepared for teaching. Project justification rested squarely on the need to increase the numbers and the quality of secondary school graduates. The government and the Bank, however, clashed vehemently over the type of expansion envisaged, the former seeking a significant increase in enrolments in "academic" streams, the Bank encouraging the development of new "diversified" curricula, whereby academic subjects were supplemented with significant levels of vocational training. The Bank insisted on extensive curricular reform, and the costly equipping of schools for purposes deemed low priority by the government. As the Bank President explained to the Executive Directors: "Over and above the purely numerical increase, the standard of secondary school education will considerably improve as a result of revision of the secondary school structure and curriculum and of the new facilities provided for agriculture, industrial arts and commerce." All the government wished to do was build some more secondary schools, but it was faced with Bank insistence on a wholesale restructuring of the secondary school curriculum, the Bank providing little by way of a rationale for the policy or assistance for its implementation.

By 1972, the Bank was conceding ground: "The new comprehensive curriculum remains incomplete, especially due to teacher shortages. This led to some underutilization of facilities, also the product of a lack of student interest (e.g. agriculture, industrial arts)." Student interest remained greatest where there were perceptions of employment opportunity, the PPAR reporting that the Bank could have done considerably more to encourage "a better match between curricula and local socio-economic needs." A Bank mission in 1973 concluded unequivocally that the strengths of the project were in the general expansion of secondary education and teacher training. Its weaknesses revolved around curriculum reform and its relevance. The government's original perceptions were vindicated: project effectiveness was least in those aspects imposed by the Bank at loan negotiations.

A similar issue compounded the dismal story of the first education credit to the Sudan. The project's extremely long gestation period resulted from intractable differences between Bank and borrower over fundamental purposes of the loan, the government seeking to raise secondary school enrolment levels quickly, the Bank insisting on what it termed improvements in "quality," that is curriculum diversification. The Bank won the initial round: "While 2,080 new places for pupils will be provided at the 13 secondary schools, the primary purpose of the project is to develop a better balanced instruction program. The inclusion of commercialized scientific courses will be a first step in the modernization of the educational system, adjusting it to the country's economic needs." This rhetoric better reflects the Bank's wishful thinking than either the government's desire or capacity to introduce such "economically relevant" streams.

It should come as no surprise, then, that the project ran into serious implementation difficulties. The PCR was damning of the borrower's "diligence and efficiency," and accused the government and its PIU of lacking enthusiasm in carrying out the project. The PCR concluded in 1980: "Some of the problems . . . were unpredictable. However, the disagreement on the scope of the project, and the long project generation period must have resulted in a lack of resolve by the Government in carrying out . . . the project. The full commitment by any government is essential to the success of a project and this lesson is now well known among Bank Group Staff." The OED's report concluded that Bank assertiveness in project design had resulted in a project with which the government had little desire to identify: "The project was not based on any long-term planning and was of limited relevance to the pressing issues faced by the education system." In short, the many interlocked aspects leading to the gross deficiencies of this project stem from initial Bank attitudes: the distinct lack of borrower commitment, poor preparatory work and appraisal, poor management, and inflated Bank expectations. The serious construction delays caused the abandonment of most TA components, and few of the fellows trained with loan monies were utilized as planned upon the completion of their studies.

Early Bank education loans to Chile, Malaysia, Tunisia, Kenya, Nicaragua, and Thailand provide further examples of Bank assertiveness during loan negotiations, in many instances over the "general" versus "diversified" curriculum issue. The Tunisian case had its ironies, having been approved in 1962 by senior Bank management prior to the final formulation of Bank policy on education at the end of 1963. The government wished to focus on the expansion and modernization of technical subjects in secondary schools; Demuth, Aldewereld, and Ripman suggested that the Bank assist the secondary school system as a whole – quite the opposite of the narrower Bank approach that quickly developed. In Kenya, the side-letters to the credit imposed on the government certain obligations to bring its secondary school system into "harmony with estimated manpower requirements of the economic development plan as it may be modified from time to time," but the Bank remained aloof from providing relevant assistance. In fact, the Kenyan loan provides a good example of the Bank keeping its head in the sand, insisting on relatively rigid interpretations of original project objectives in spite of the rapidly changing circumstances surrounding it.

Other examples are open to scrutiny in which the Bank had a highly focussed involvement in project design. The first IBRD education loan, for the capital upgrading of the University of the Philippines Agricultural College at Los Baños (UPLB), is a prime example, as is the first Thailand loan, for industry-based and agricultural vocational education. In the case of UPLB, Bank involvement had been preceded by many years of academic assistance provided with Ford and Rockefeller Foundation monies through Cornell University. The Bank, then, was able to focus on the capital requirements, remaining free of the need to appoint itself guardian of educational quality. The PPAR concluded in 1975 that the Bank, in fact, should have involved itself in broader educational considerations, but at the time of appraisal (October 1964) there was clearly no need. What the Bank did elect to do was insist on a range of side-conditions that called for a reorganization of the Philippines' government agricultural services; a further side-letter addressed educational administration in the Philippines, calling for specified changes in staff development practices, teacher salaries and conditions, curricular revision, textbook development, and the expansion of educational research. The PPAR concluded: "Had the Bank placed more emphasis on the fulfillment of loan conditions outside of those pertaining to the construction/equipment project, it might have had a more significant impact on improving the long-term effectiveness of the Program's operating outcomes." The PPAR, however, had little to say about how this might usefully have been undertaken.

Project design, shared in varying ways by borrowers, the Bank, and UNESCO, frequently reflected in the early days an optimism that bordered on the unrealistic. The promise of unprecedented flows of external capital for educational expansion was often accompanied by undue expectations about the capacity of Bank projects to effect qualitative changes. As indicated, side-letters and covenants were normally directed at such changes, but did little of a practical nature to address them. Overdesign and excessive sophistication was also a factor in too many projects, and not only because of limited borrower management capacity.

In the Thailand vocational education project, although this was a generally successful project falling within 3 percent of original budget estimates, "substantial savings could have resulted from use of simpler architectural designs, reduced space standards, and less sophisticated equipment, without hindering the achievement of the project's educational objectives" (PPAR). Undue optimism also surrounded the project's expectations concerning the formation of local "curricula advisory committees" and the employment and retention of adequate numbers of teachers with industrial and agricultural experience. The long-term implications of procuring overly sophisticated equipment were serious, in that the 1984 OED impact evaluation study, in addition to the original audit report, drew attention to the high recurrent costs for schools associated with the project compared with non-project schools. "In the trade schools, these costs were 38 percent higher per student, while at the agricultural schools they were 87 percent higher. The PPAR ... noted that some of the curricular changes and the associated utilization of equipment were too specialized and sophisticated for the targeted middle-level production workers." Compounded with these design issues was the fact that 18 percent of equipment (costed in 1966 at $1.1 million) arrived at project schools damaged.

Inflated expectations also resulted from the mere size of projects. In order to match the customary scale of Bank lending for major capital works of public sector infrastructure, it was common for education loans to provide funds for many educational institutions in a single project. Often, these schools were highly dispersed, yet were frequently supposed to address common qualitative issues, an intention sometimes beyond the capacity of a ministry of education to meet. Further, in education projects the foreign exchange components were relatively low, and this reinforced the tendency for Bank education loans to include too many institutions.

Project implementation

It would not be reasonable to hold the Bank to account for aspects of project implementation over which it had little or no control. Examples abound in which project implementation was hampered by factors well beyond the Bank's formal supervision, whether the 1972 earthquake in Nicaragua (which devastated the project), or extremely low initial project baselines in Tanzania and Ethiopia, frequent changes in government as in the Sudan, or poor standards of PIU management. Further, the generally large-scale and complex nature of Bank education projects, and their ambitious character, built the distinct probability of failure into the general scheme of things. It was rare indeed for a Bank project to be declared a general success.

Not often did the Bank display unqualified praise for project implementation units. More often, they were slammed by visiting Bank supervisory missions. Common difficulties included the appointment of staff unqualified or inexperienced in the implementation of complex capital developments, or staff who saw the status attached to their appointments to PIUs as substitutes for diligence. Often, difficulties in PIU management were traceable to inappropriate location in the bureaucracy, PIUs too frequently being placed on the sidelines to the extent that their capacity to effect systemic change was limited. PIU staff requiring training in order to meet project requirements were often appropriate recipients of Bank TA, yet many remained absent throughout the early, critical stages of project implementation. Many projects suffered from too high a turnover of PIU staff, their status upon appointment to a World Bank project often providing good career prospects, yet before anything much was achieved.

By far the most frequent complaints about implementation concerned delays in construction and procurement, and cost overruns. For each aspect there is a long list of potential causes or combination of causes, but the key point here is the Bank's increasingly firm belief in the effectiveness of its supervision. Early Bank education projects were no more immune from delay, cost overruns, and other difficulties than in any other sector. Classic Bank behavior has been "to take upon itself the role of quality control, mainly to protect its own investments and credit rating," in the words of a former Bank Vice President. Perceptions of strong supervision were perhaps more important than creative, intimate involvement in ensuring project quality. What Bank staff, with their flying supervisory visits of 5 to 10 days, thought they could achieve – either in overall policy or project implementation terms – is hard to imagine. The obtaining of oral assurances would seem to have been about the limit.

Bank staff of the day look back to the first Kenyan project as one that reflected the pitfalls of implementation. The project was typical, in that it embodied a major expansion program involving 42 secondary schools, 9 technical schools, and 18 primary teacher training institutes, with associated equipment, laboratories, and books. Also typical was the Bank's insistence that "the secondary school curriculum ... be broadened by the provision of agricultural, industrial, commercial and home economics instruction" (Appraisal Report). IDA provided a relatively large share (73 percent) of the total project cost of $9.66 million. The Bank's PPAR (1974) is damning of the Bank's intransigence on cost overruns, which led to significant reductions in the quality and pertinence of much of what was eventually provided. Design flaws abounded, and while the Bank was deeply concerned about quality issues it was generally uninvolved in them. The government had attempted to keep the project within budget by reducing the number of institutions constructed, in contrast to the Bank which sought savings across the board, leading to disastrous reductions in project quality:

> The number of classrooms and teacher houses built was only 5% less than forecast, but the number of dormitories and other houses built was less than 50% of forecast and most other items showed shortfalls of 10–30%; sick bays and paved walks were eliminated. Most standards of accommodation were reduced; in particular, libraries and dining halls in most schools, and workshops in some, were reduced to sizes that have proved inconveniently small. The failure to provide special foundations ... resulted in some project buildings at three schools now showing sizeable cracks that need substantial repair. A few two- or three-year old buildings elsewhere already need renovation.... Moreover, despite the use of private architectural firms, there has been too much standardization in building design, with high-altitude schools too cold and lower ones too hot; also the building siting on some school compounds was improperly made, partly because school headmasters were seldom if ever consulted prior to construction (e.g. locating noisy workshops close to classrooms, making it impossible to use them simultaneously).

The PPAR concluded that the Bank was "excessively rigid" about the composition of the project as formally set down in the appraisal report and credit documents. When cost overruns loomed, it failed to discuss with the government the range of options available for redesigning and possibly reducing the scope of the project, and stuck rigidly to the number of schools envisaged in the 1965 appraisal. The Bank thereby offset cost overruns by reductions in standards "that have hampered somewhat the effective operation of the project schools."

Economic impact of projects

The deepest abyss into which project design and justification could sink in the early years was forcing a link between an educational project and a particular economic or labor-market outcome. Because the 1960s were years of unprecedented educational expansion – at all levels – it was difficult for any project to fail to make a contribution to national quantitative targets. Expansion was so rapid and extensive that no project appraised in the 1960s was in danger of causing concern in government circles about oversupply of educated manpower. This was particularly true of IDA-eligible countries and their secondary school systems. In later years, of course, in a range of countries that included many more IBRD borrowers, and countries with more extensive technical and higher education systems, graduate oversupply was to become an acute problem and a symptom of over-expansion. Shortages of schooled and skilled persons in IDA countries in the early 1960s, by contrast, were genuine. It was only at the margins that early Bank projects were in danger of producing an oversupply.

The Thailand vocational education project, for example, met the enrolment and output targets set at appraisal. For the industrial schools, the 1972 output of 2,154 graduates matched the appraisal target of 2,110 for 1971. Outputs from the agricultural schools exceeded the target of 1,425 by only 3 percent. The most serious manpower difficulty concerned school staffing: it proved enormously difficult to retain in the schools teachers who had received industry-based training through the project – they readily found satisfactory employment within industry itself. The project sensibly built in, at the Bank's suggestion, a tracer study of project school graduates, which showed that 57 percent of industrial school graduates were employed more or less as anticipated, but a disturbing 42 percent were proceeding on to higher education. Of the agricultural graduates, 70 percent were employed, but 44 percent were working in nonagricultural sectors, and a further 26 percent were pursuing higher studies. In other words, about one-half of the industrial and one-quarter of the agricultural graduates were employed in terms of the project's original manpower objectives. This was considered serious given the considerably higher operating costs of the vocationally oriented schools. The young people were far from lost to the Thai economy, of course, but perhaps too many were unwilling to contemplate careers with the practical orientation for which they had been expensively trained. The OED impact study concluded in 1984:

> Although the project was meant principally to serve the needs of industry for skilled middle-level manpower, it appears that formal vocational training was widely perceived in Thailand as a method of obtaining secondary and even post-secondary education for those who, while being upwardly mobile, were unable to gain direct admittance to academic schools leading on to universities.... Vocational education appears not to have been perceived as terminal education which would lead directly to employment, but as a more open-ended education opportunity. Further it has provided an avenue to further training for those who, for economic reasons, need to work for a period before re-entering a higher educational institution.

At the same time, it needs to be recalled that demand for entry to the project schools was considerably higher than local demography would have suggested. The schools were popular choices among educationally enthusiastic young people, and their eventual employment destination needs to be assessed in this light.

The first credit to Kenya reflected prior economic appraisal of dubious quality. The Bank's own evaluation concedes a number of critical omissions in this regard. Manpower projections, for example, failed to reflect the impact of government economic policies on the generation of employment opportunities, especially in the more dynamic sectors of the economy. The Bank's own conclusions were candid, and reflected admirably in 1974 the battle-lines then being drawn among Bank economists between advocates of manpower forecasting and advocates of rate-of-return analysis as guides to educational policy formulation:

> Had the Bank investigated the use of rate of return studies in education before 1966, the manpower projections could have been usefully complemented by consideration of the private rate of return to secondary education, the private investment that the high return would induce and the supply of educated manpower that would result from private sources, reducing the need for public system expansion. As a result of the emphasis put by Kenya on general secondary education, insufficient preparation and detailed attention was given to the planned development of the technical and vocational schools and to the availability and training of technical teachers for the vocational schools.

Conclusion

Factors that impinged upon the effectiveness of the early education projects – at least as they were understood by Bank management – were beginning to be understood by 1968, although only two projects had been completed by that time. Issues that dominated Bank management concerns came to focus intensely on project identification, design, and management. It is interesting that issues to do with the economic aspects of lending to education took a back seat, and were not at all systematically explored by Bank education staff. This is in stark contrast to the intensive inquiry into the economics of education and human capital theory that senior economic and TOD staff had initiated in the period 1960–3. By contrast, the newly appointed education staff had projects as their central concern, and did very little from the start to explore systematically the economic dynamics of education systems and reforms. In fact, such a concern was not to become a priority for another decade. It was a wasted opportunity.

Nevertheless, useful perspectives on the education project cycle had emerged. It was proving difficult to mount purely economic justifications for education projects – such could not be expressed with the sharpness that the

Executive Directors had come to expect in loan applications. Linking the Bank's education portfolio with country economic reports and multiyear lending projections was conceptually difficult, and was organizationally compounded by the distance between education projects staff in Washington and EFD staff in Paris. Any benefits that had accrued over previous years from the Bank–borrower relationship were difficult to apply to education, whose loans had to be more or less considered *ab initio*.

It is a myth that the early years of Bank education lending saw an exclusive focus on construction and the provision of equipment. While these were dominant concerns, especially in financial terms, from the very beginning Bank – and especially UNESCO – staff were engaged in dialogue with borrowers over qualitative issues – such as the design and introduction of new curricula and textbooks, the improvement of teacher education, and the reform of educational planning and administration. These are clearly revealed as Bank concerns in loan documents. But the Bank tended to remain aloof from any practical involvement in such qualitative issues. It was forming views about them, and was encouraging them in loan covenants and sideletters, but its lending program failed to confront them squarely. There is a myriad of OED findings from the early loans that testify to the Bank's failure to involve itself in practical and effective means of assisting borrowers to raise the quality of planning and reform. Rather, it merely insisted on quality from the distant sidelines.

Hardly a project escaped cost overruns and delays in implementation. They quickly became part of the scheme of things. Tellingly, delays were most serious in the start-up phase, through deficient design and preparation. Problems swept under the carpet early on were bound to surface later. Bank supervision reports tended to place blame more or less exclusively onto PIUs – notably deficiencies in staffing, salaries, expertise, experience and status, inappropriate location in the bureaucracy, divided administrative authority, lack of clear procedures, and unclear lines of communication and decision-making – all working against the smooth and timely exercise of authority when required. Rarely did Bank supervising staff probe beneath the surface of these problems, except to opine that developing countries tended to display such inadequacies. Rarely did the Bank subject its own preparation and appraisal work to the same critical scrutiny, and explore the pronounced tendency for Bank projects to be technically and administratively too complex.

Many factors contributing to delays, cost overruns, and lapses in quality could not have been envisaged in project design, relating as they did to changes to the external environment. But good project design and management would have made room for them. Contingency planning seems to have been displaced by a Bank that proved far too inflexible in disbursements and supervision.

Comment has also been made on the tension between achieving the immediate goals of a free-standing project, and exercising broader, system-wide influence, for example, through the diffusion of innovations. The Bank did little of practical use in the early years to reduce this tension. It imposed an implementation model that derived from physical infrastructure projects – the PIU – which needed to be organizationally discrete, but not marginalized or remote from centers of governmental authority or influence. Education projects early on tended to be of the "turnkey" kind, whereby a foreign group of advisers flies in to complete – as quickly and "efficiently" as possible – a task the recipient cannot perform. This model had been developed for the design and construction of capital works projects, where it was in everybody's interest to come to project completion as quickly as possible, in order to maximize quick returns, savings, and efficiencies. Training and TA had to be conceived in this framework. But there is something about education projects that requires more to be taken into account. Lasting benefits of education "turnkey" projects are often illusory because little of an educational kind has been left behind.

An important lesson was not learnt at all quickly. This had to do with the technical assistance components of large, multifaceted projects with major capital components. When such projects fell behind schedule or the capital works got into serious difficulty, the vulnerability of the TA components (including training) was starkly exposed. In many of the early education projects, this vulnerability meant that TA components were all too frequently abandoned, delayed, reduced in scope, or were poorly integrated with the rest of the project.

When training was provided, it invariably involved removing project personnel from project sites for overseas training – 193 of 200 persons trained under the Thailand vocational education project went to the United States, for example, although much of this component was funded by USAID. Very frequently, such persons on their return were either promoted out of the project or its associated institutions (although they were not necessarily lost to the economy) or their training was aimed at employment at higher levels not already provided for in government civil service. This becomes important when issues of qualitative educational change are considered: the personnel who matter in processes of educational change – teachers, curriculum designers, evaluators, and testers – tended to have low status in hierarchical systems, and were uninvolved in Bank project identification, design, and supervision. Surprisingly often, their involvement in the qualitative concerns of Bank projects came too late.

Much can be said about the meticulous manner in which Bank officers monitored financial disbursements. This gave Bank projects a "squeaky-clean" image which was deserved. However, financial controls, end-use-supervision, and audits should not be confused with project supervision and evaluation. The Bank does not have a strong record in assisting the quality of project implementation – it has been profoundly more concerned with projecting an image of tight financial control – for reasons to do with its own external relations and sources of finance. This is relevant to the customary need for means to be found for quickly identifying and addressing problems that arise *early* in a project. As noted, the most serious problems were seen to occur early, often because of deficient project design. This impinges directly on the Bank's supervisory role and its use of visiting review teams, which are sent periodically, often every several months. Early experience taught the following lesson, that flexible membership and timing should enable review teams to bear some relation to problems actually being encountered in the field, and have some chance of addressing these problems while the review team is in the country. Review visits that are too short usually encouraged a concentration of field visits to sites closest to the PIU rather than to those with the most pressing difficulties. A borrower, further, may be tempted to disguise problems, especially given the likely fact that it is simultaneously involved in other dealings with the Bank – whether country-level assessments of its economic performance and creditworthiness, or project preparation or negotiation in other sectors. Bank supervision missions can take it for granted that borrowers will be reluctant to reveal too much of their difficulties, yet it is surprising how few supervision reports indicate anything but the most superficial understanding of the circumstances facing the country concerned at the time.

Mason and Asher (1973: 257–9) summed up early project experience across all sectors in a manner directly relevant to the embryonic education sector:

> ...it cannot be said that the Bank has been an outstanding leader in applying new techniques of project appraisal or analysis of development processes....A more common criticism, and one more difficult to dispose of, is that the Bank's practice of supervising construction, as well as the operation of projects in their early years, tends to deprive borrowers of learning opportunities....Is it better to emphasize the learning process at the expense of possible mistakes or to make sure that the operation is well done, even though done by outsiders? There is no single answer to this question, but it is probably true that the Bank, perhaps with excessive zeal for the correct technical solution, has not in its project lending contributed as much to the education of borrowers as it should have done....
>
> Perhaps the most serious criticism of IBRD project lending is its failure to assess adequately the developmental consequences of its loans. End-use supervision falls short of dealing with this question....Yet a careful study of the economic consequences of a selected series of Bank project loans could clearly contribute much both to an understanding of the development process and to an improvement of Bank project lending.

It was another decade before such advice was taken up in the education sector. Yet as early as January 1966 senior management were questioning the narrow criteria for Bank lending to education. In an internal memorandum to President Woods, Aldewereld and Demuth, upon Ballantine's advice, recommended a broadening of eligible fields to include (a) "higher technical education either in institutions of a specifically technical character or in appropriate cases in technical schools or faculties within general universities," and (b) "high priority projects for the expansion and improvement of higher level training in science, mathematics and education," with a view to expanding the pool of trained secondary teachers of science and mathematics. Woods could not embrace moves towards general universities, and such avenues of support had to await his departure in March 1968. Nevertheless, management desire to broaden eligibility for support was a direct product of early experience of the project cycle in education.

Notes

The Bank's country economic reports, reports of project identification and appraisal missions, and project completion reports (PCRs) are all prepared by Bank management, and are normally reserved for internal use. Frequently, however, copies are obtainable through member country sources, or occasionally through cooperating agencies. Evaluations prepared by the Operations Evaluation Department (OED), latterly called the Independent Evaluation Group (IEG), include project performance audit reports (PPARs) and impact studies, and are produced independently of Bank and project management for the Executive Directors, the offices of whom may elect to make them publicly available for approved purposes. This chapter has relied on extensive analysis of identification, appraisal, PCR, and PPAR reports for about half of the twenty-five education projects approved to 1968. Note that since the mid-1990s, the Bank has moved assiduously to open to public scrutiny much information of this kind. Thus, for projects that are more recent than those covered in this chapter, documentation is routinely available on the Bank's website: http://www.worldbank.org

Documentation analysis has been substantially complemented by extended interviews, particularly with Ricardo Diez Hochleitner and Duncan Ballantine, and reference made to Bank Oral History Program interviews with Richard Demuth (1984), Harold Graves (1985), and Burke Knapp (1981).

On early project experience, Mason and Asher (1973) remains a useful source, as is the insightful and independent analysis of eleven projects (none of which was educational) contained in Hirschman (1967). See also Kapur *et al.* (1997). The Bank's EDI produced a useful analysis of appraisal experience of thirty Bank projects in electric power, transport, and industry sectors (King 1967). The Bank's formal view of the project cycle is outlined in Baum (1982). None of these address education sector lending directly, yet contain useful institutional perspectives of an overall kind.

4 Education in the McNamara years 1968–80

The dramatic shift in Bank rhetoric that occurred during the presidency of Robert McNamara can readily be detected in the education sector. This rhetoric – which saw emphasis in Bank policy placed on poverty alleviation – has occasioned much debate, analysed usefully by Ayres (1983), Hurni (1980), Kapur *et al.* (1997), and Van De Laar (1980). Doubts persist over the extent to which any substantial change occurred in Bank thinking about development, and whether its lending in fact contributed to poverty alleviation, especially in rural areas. Sceptics see the shift as partly one of rhetoric and partly as an extension of traditional Bank operations into the larger arena of rural development. To be sure, the McNamara presidency coincided with and reinforced a widening of education lending that saw the elevation of primary education as a factor in development and the countenance of Bank activities in nonformal and adult education. It also saw some useful thinking undertaken concerning education and basic human needs. At the same time, this "liberalization" of educational financing criteria would have occurred without McNamara as President, even if more slowly, less extensively, and without a poverty focus. In no way can it be said to have either precipitated or resulted from a radical assessment of the role of education in development. The Bank's constructs on that issue remained intact, if rendered open to broader application.

Policy, conceptual, and organizational changes

The new focus on poverty alleviation (to be achieved through "redistribution with growth" – RWG) found its fullest rhetorical expression in McNamara's September 1973 address to the Bank's Board of Governors, with more substantial theoretical underpinning found in the influential report *Redistribution with Growth* (1974). In the education sector the new poverty focus led to a revision of stated Bank policy, publicly outlined in the *Education Sector Working Paper* of 1974. However, it is not possible to account for these shifts without consideration of policy, conceptual, and organizational developments in the period immediately preceding. These saw, upon the appointment of McNamara as President in 1968, the first moves towards a more liberal lending policy, some telling shifts in the Bank's conceptual approaches to the economics of education, and highly influential changes in the Bank's organization structure. In the long term, these developments may collectively be more significant than the so-called poverty rhetoric and strategies initiated under McNamara after 1973.

The McNamara presidency in perspective

Many of the changes in the work of the World Bank seen in the McNamara years are unrelated to the poverty focus ushered in by this reforming President. The enormous increase in the scale of lending is a good example. FY 1973 saw 153 IBRD and IDA projects approved for $3,428 million, compared with 62 for $953.5 million in FY 1968. By 1981, 85 percent of all Bank lending had taken place during the McNamara years.

Throughout its life, the Bank has had to be creative in ensuring a continuing range of borrowers and loan opportunities: a successful development bank can all too quickly run out of customers. This was seen in the establishment of IDA in 1960. With many borrowers in the 1950s and 1960s having established extensive physical infrastructure in urban areas, an extension of Bank project operations to rural areas would have guaranteed for the Bank considerably expanded lending opportunities. The same can be said of any "liberalization" of Bank lending criteria: frequently, change comes because keeping loan criteria constant runs the risk of a decline in lending.

The Bank's poverty rhetoric under McNamara, it can be argued, was unrelated to the dramatic increase in its lending in these years, except that funds were available to do more. A larger, busier Bank was more willing and able to become a more diverse Bank. While there was considerable energy expended in outlining new theoretical positions on poverty alleviation and development, it is not clear what impact they had on lending, except to provide a rationale and justification for it after the event. At the same time, it is important that McNamara's immediate success in widening Bank operations be appreciated. In his first five-year term most of the additional loan funds were devoted less to physical infrastructure than to what McNamara saw as the major constraints on development – population increase, malnutrition, and inadequate literacy.

Agricultural lending, for example, did not displace more traditional project activities. Rather, it was grafted on. The $172.5 million approved for agriculture in FY 1968 (or 18 percent of total lending for the year) contrasts starkly with the $3.8 billion (31 percent) approved in FY 1981, but did not replace preexisting levels in other sectors. In education, likewise, primary education and nonformal education counted for virtually nothing before 1968, but by the end of the 1970s took up 21 percent and 25 percent of education sector lending respectively, but not at the expense of traditional areas in dollar terms. The Bank merely provided itself with opportunities and reasons for increasing its lending levels, without any radical shift in its educational financing rationale.

Perhaps the greatest institutional development that occurred under McNamara was the broadening of the Bank's range of activity. For the first time, the Bank sought to put in place detailed and comprehensive views about development, seeking to inform its own lending with these views and seeking to exert unprecedented degrees of influence over borrowers' development policies. Development – its character and its means of attainment – became much less an unstated set of shared understandings among a group of culturally and intellectually homogeneous club members, than a matter of intensive debate and research within a rapidly expanding and diversifying bureaucracy. The October 1972 reorganization enabled establishment of sectoral policy Departments (e.g. Agriculture and Rural Development; Population, Health and Nutrition; and Education), Departments which quickly embraced their research roles, complementing the rapidly increasing research work of the Development Policy Staff. Each of these Departments had to engage in vigorous processes of policy debate with those more directly responsible for Bank lending and project operations.

A major outcome of this expanded research and policy role was a more prominent place for the Bank in international development assistance. Although the considerable size and scope of its lending had already delivered it a role, the Bank became, by intent, a more visible organization, expanding and diversifying its interaction with the public world. Yet at the same time, its essential banking characteristics remained intact, and to no extent were displaced by the newer patterns of activity emerging in these years.

The influence on these developments of Robert McNamara was considerable. Like all his predecessors, McNamara dominated the Bank and stamped his personality, prejudices, and ambitions on it. Many of the great changes in the Bank in the 1970s are not attributable to him, but McNamara excelled in seizing the moment and shaping the Bank in line with his perception of opportunities that came from outside. When McNamara arrived for his first day at the office on April 1, 1968, he found a distinct advantage awaiting him, in that his predecessor George Woods had left the Bank with very few supporters. Woods, whose health, charm, and tolerance had all declined in the second half of his presidency, had also presided over the disastrous replenishment of IDA between 1965 and 1968, which had left IDA incapable of achieving anything near its lending targets. Board meetings had become unpleasant, and staffers of the day knew it was time for Woods to move on. Any personable, capable, and enthusiastic successor would have been embraced with open arms in the President's office that spring day, and McNamara was. This helped one concern to dissolve, that for the first time the Bank had a President with a nonbanking background. As President of the Ford Motor Company and as Lyndon Baines Johnson's Secretary of Defense, McNamara was well enough known as a public figure. What was also known in the Bank was McNamara's frequent public testimony – during the Vietnam War – that peace and stability in the developing world "depended far less on armament levels than on raising the standards of life of the poorer two-thirds of the world" (Clark 1981: 167).

Within ninety days of McNamara's arrival, the IBRD had raised more on the world's capital markets than in any full year of its history. The German and Japanese markets quickly assumed significance as sources of loanable capital. McNamara energetically hounded senior management to become more expansive in their thinking, in stark contrast to Woods' testy caution. The trend to expansion continued, with the total borrowings of the Bank doubling from 1968 to 1973, a period in which only 15 percent of funds was raised on Wall Street. The first of his celebrated annual addresses to the Board of Governors set the tone in September 1968: "I have always regarded the World Bank as something more than a Bank, as a Development Agency." William Clark, whose appointment in 1968 as Vice President for External Relations had led to Demuth's resignation from the Bank, later summed up the early McNamara stances (1981: 169–70):

> The problem as he saw it was to create in the Bank a critical mass of power, both financial and technical, sufficient to accelerate the rate of development in the poorer countries to a high but sustainable level.... And since he was determined that the Bank would operate in nearly every developing country, its overall influence could be immense, certainly far greater than any other development agency....The conventional wisdom was that even the World Bank was still essentially a Bank, and should be prudent, not pioneering. So the new President's keynote sentence was not well received by the many conventional bankers present.

A degree of unanimity prevails among former Bank staff who reflect on McNamara's personality and style, an intelligent man who some said related better to humanity as a whole than to some individuals. Former senior management frequently comment on McNamara's fascination with numbers, and brought to his presidency an insistence that issues be quantified to the extent possible. McNamara was a manager supreme, presiding over a rapidly expanding bureaucracy and its fundamental reorganization, creating a considerably more centralized and hierarchical structure than had prevailed in earlier days.

Policy changes for education lending 1968–73

A major argument of this chapter is that, contrary to popular supposition, the poverty focus promoted by Robert McNamara after 1973 had far less impact on the education sector than is frequently supposed. The poverty thesis, as applied to education, asserts that the redistribution with growth strategy inaugurated a period in which the Bank's education loans were consciously directed at the poor, who were targeted by education loans conceived as part of rural development and urban poverty-alleviation strategies. Primary education, adult literacy, nonformal education, and mass media education are all commonly said to have been major elements of this educational assault on poverty. The evidence points to a different truth. Far from evaluating the theoretical and conceptual underpinnings to its approach to education, the Bank's traditional model of emphasizing the kinds of educational provision that could measurably contribute to increases in worker productivity was merely applied on a wider scale. In particular, prospects for increasing by educational means the productivity of farmers working small-farm holdings were investigated with some vigor. Nevertheless, the prevailing consensus regarding the developmental potential of education remained intact: the Bank would countenance only those patterns of provision which could demonstrate the potential to contribute directly to economic growth.

The McNamara revolution in education had nothing to do with the poverty focus: it occurred between 1969 and 1971 when the arbitrary prejudices and restrictions imposed by George Woods dissipated with his retirement, when Bank policy entertained wider eligibility for education projects deemed capable of increasing productivity, and when (in such areas as secondary education) brakes were applied to uncritical educational expansion in favor of more "qualitative" concerns. The tragedy of the McNamara poverty initiative – that it presented a fine but studiously ignored opportunity for the Bank to reconsider the fundamentals of its approach to development – applied to education as much as to any other sector.

Of considerable importance in the McNamara Bank was the group of people, linked up through Cambridge, Massachusetts, who saw eye-to-eye on many policy issues, and who related to each other throughout their careers, intelligent, academically inclined men who had each moved into positions of economic and developmental influence: Robert McNamara, David Bell, Walt Rostow, Mac Bundy, Champion Ward, Ken Galbraith, Edward Mason, and, later, Henry Kissinger. Of personal importance to McNamara was his extensive links with the Ford Foundation, at the time of his appointment a significant actor in global development. Some of these persons had exerted their influence on the pre-McNamara Bank. Others had recently considered the role of education in development, and had influenced deliberations at a seminal meeting held at Williamsburg, Virginia in October 1967, a meeting that considered Philip Coombs' influential assessment of global policy trends and outcomes, subsequently published as *The World Educational Crisis: A Systems Analysis* (1968).

Professor Edward Mason of Harvard University was selected by McNamara in September 1967, on Siem Aldewereld's initiative, to conduct a wide-ranging policy review of the education sector, analogous to the considerably more influential agriculture sector review conducted by Sir John Crawford. Mason, who at the time was Lamont Professor of Economics at Harvard and a former President of the American Economic Association, was soon to start work with Robert Asher on their monumental commissioned history *The World Bank Since Bretton Woods*. Mason's brief was both narrow and wide. In the narrow sense, he was charged to investigate the UNESCO–Bank arrangements for project identification and preparation, particularly in order to assess the extent to which projects of the highest priority were being identified, and ascertain means of reducing elapsed time between project identification and Board approval. On the wider front, Mason was invited to clarify how the educational lending operations of the Bank might develop in the next several years.

Mason's report, delivered to Aldewereld in February 1968, insisted that project identification was "decidedly haphazard," due as much to insufficient national planning capacities on the borrowers' side as to UNESCO–Bank arrangements on the other. Mason also reflected the growing concern among economists that educators of varying kinds in many contexts had misread the economics of education literature, and that investments in education were becoming too diffuse and too extensive. Rationales and priorities for educational financing, in his view, needed tightening, and education budgets were becoming too large for many countries to afford. At the same time, Mason cautiously pointed to the desirability of a broadening of Bank lending criteria, in contrast to the narrow band countenanced by Woods:

> The emphasis placed by Bank policy on secondary education, and on technical, vocational and teacher training at all levels was justified and is still appropriate but I believe the time has come for a substantially greater latitude for exceptions. At higher levels there are identifiable circumstances in which scientific, technical and teacher training can be better provided at existing universities than in separate technical schools and without danger of diversion of funds. At the primary level there is a case for experimental schools using new teaching methods that give promise of having a multiplier effect over the whole level of primary education. And in the field of adult education a program of functional literacy attached to particular areas of economic activity can have a more immediate effect on productivity than any type of formal education. While 80 per cent of Bank lending should probably continue to follow existing criteria, I should like to see up to 20 per cent channeled into more experimental directions.... A similar point may also be made with respect to the support of new techniques of teaching and learning.

In addition, Mason pointed to the likelihood of expanded Bank lending in such fields as agricultural and rural development, public health and population policy, and urged detailed consideration of their articulation with the Bank's work in education. In many respects Mason's views reflected Ballantine's preferences for expanded lending. This is especially the case with support for general higher education and primary education, as well as for more experimental work in teaching techniques and the organization of learning. To this extent, the Mason report formed part of the firming consensus among senior Bank management that, as soon as Woods retired, the rapidly expanding portfolio of educational lending would be able to accommodate general higher education and primary education projects, as well as some activities that addressed the quality and economic relevance of teaching and learning rather than mere educational expansion. At the same time, Mason reported on "wide disparities in the Area Departments' attitudes towards financing education.... These disparities should be corrected if education projects were to be accorded the same priority as other projects." Often, according to Mason, education was not seen by Area Departments staff as a proper subject for the Bank to finance and hence was not always encouraged in the Bank's lending program.

In terms of the UNESCO–Bank Co-operative Agreement, Mason concluded diplomatically that it had worked well, was likely to get "even better," and that on the whole EFD staff in Paris had been well-selected:

> I formed a good impression of the [EFD] staff. This also seems to be the view of the staff of the Bank's Educational Division. In general they spoke favorably of the competence of their UNESCO colleagues. Both personal and official relations between the UNESCO and the Bank unit seem good. I found nothing of the jurisdictional rivalry and legalism in the interpretation of the charter that bothered Sir John Crawford in his survey of Bank–FAO relationships.

At the same time, Mason found the Bank–UNESCO arrangements capable of being less "cumbersome, time-consuming and costly," achievable by tele-scoping project identification and preparation missions. More than that, Mason was keen to involve Bank staff more fully in project identification, in order to facilitate the kinds of cost-benefit analysis he was recommending as an integral part of the project-identification process, and to streamline the preparation and appraisal process. This, in fact, was a major aspect of his report, and Mason had much to say about means of reducing delays in the stages of the project cycle prior to formal approval. Again, for Mason, the issue was less one of organizational efficiency and articulation, although he had much to say of this sort. Of profounder import was the basis of project planning, and his conviction that despite their complexities cost-benefit analyses would in the longer term provide a sounder basis for more relevant and abiding project rationales than would manpower forecasting.

One staffer of the day saw in the Mason report the attributes of its author – "competent, dull, and unimaginative." To be sure, the report anticipated much of what such senior management personnel as Aldewereld, Demuth, and Ballantine had been looking towards in the post-Woods Bank. To that extent at least, the Mason report was hardly revolutionary, yet confirmed the broadening of lending criteria, the need for ongoing review of the efficiency of all points of the project cycle in education, and the consolidation of opinion in the Bank that favored cost-benefit analyses as a basis for development and project planning. In addition, Mason had identified the need to enlarge the staff and extensively reorganize the Education Projects Division into subunits with greater delegation of authority.

Ballantine's formal response to the report, in an internal memorandum of April 29, 1968, listed the likely new areas for educational financing: higher education, primary education, adult education and training (emphasizing vocational objectives), public health, textbooks and teaching materials, and nonformal education and training. At the same time, little was new concerning the developmental rationale of educational lending: the emphasis was still squarely on securing increases in productivity through educational expansion. At the same time, Ballantine foreshadowed an area of potential lending (nonformal education for the unschooled) that was not to attain full recognition in the Bank for another twenty years:

> I suggest that we might think ... less conventionally. If we consider what are our real objectives – to increase human skills and productivity, to impart knowledge essential to higher standards of living, to expand awareness and increase motivation – and if at the same time we approach the process as in part one of communication, we may see a possibility to do a significant amount for the neglected part of the future working force which will not get schooling in any case .... The new communication media are potentially as revolutionary as Gutenberg's printing. What they have already done in politics, business, military practice, transport, navigation and many other fields they may yet do in education and training.

What Ballantine specifically projected was the possibility of using educational broadcasting and other media to address issues "immediately relevant to the lives of the subsistence sector of the population – sanitation, simple agriculture, health, nutrition, rudimentary economics, family planning and also literacy and general education." Yet this immediately points to one of Ballantine and the World Bank's greatest failures in education – failure to come to grips with adult literacy. Ballantine could countenance work-oriented literacy programs, but no more. In his view, outlined in the April 1968 memorandum, "literacy would be regarded as instrumental rather than as an end objective, which it is still to a large extent in the UNESCO approach." General life skills, by contrast to work skills, could be taught by expensive technologies, but not through literacy programs. Primary education as a vehicle for general education was fine, but not literacy for young people unschooled or inadequately schooled. Much can be said about this persistent blind spot in the Bank's vision of education.

A second report for McNamara also influenced the firming of opinion about a more liberal approach to education, prepared by Office of Information Director Harold Graves on Demuth's initiative, and presented to members of the President's Council in December 1969. This report, more academic in style than Mason's, looked to several emergent trends in the education portfolio: a marked expansion of lending; a stronger emphasis on the rational planning of educational systems; a stronger accent on qualitative improvements in education; more assistance to technical innovation; greater interest in out-of-school training; and increased technical assistance. The Graves report canvassed much contemporary academic opinion, reflecting Graves' efforts to consult widely in the academic and development assistance community, including contacts with such figures as John Vaizey, Michel Debeauvais, Clarence Beeby, Philip Coombs, and Alan Pifer. The report also contained a brief but thoughtful history of Bank involvement in education, and a useful analysis of external assistance to education. While the Graves report had little direct impact on immediate policy shifts, there is no doubt that it formed an important element in the liberalizing climate of opinion among senior Bank management concerning education financing.

A particular feature of the Graves report was its view of the Bank's role in educational development. In short, Graves concluded that a far greater role existed for the Bank in what he termed "muscle-building" in borrowing countries, building into Bank projects provision for strengthening borrower planning and management of education capacities. Further, Graves urged that the Bank "markedly increase its efforts to use loan leverage to play a considerably stronger role in building the right kind of educational systems.... This kind of institution-building, which the Bank has already promoted with considerable success in other sectors of development, might well be the most important contribution it could make to the development of education."

At the time, UNESCO was the executing agent for UNDP commitments to work-oriented literacy projects. In fact, UNESCO had shelved its immediate aspirations to achieve universal literacy in favor of a selective, experimental approach designed to measure the impact of work-oriented literacy on productivity and other developmental factors. The Experimental World Literacy Program (EWLP) from 1966 to 1974 dominated, in fact, the UNESCO education program. Its multiple objectives caused serious implementation difficulties for UNESCO and its image: innovation was confused with experimentation, evaluation was poorly conceived, and recipient governments put enormous pressure on PIUs to achieve the highest possible quantitative results, irrespective of the consequences for the experimental/evaluative core of projects (for an extended analysis, see Jones 1988: 143–211). Despite the eventual achievements of the program, the EWLP procured for UNESCO within UNDP and the World Bank a damaging reputation, at least as far as its commitment to literacy was concerned. This, more than any other single factor, justified the ongoing scepticism in these circles that a "hardheaded" approach to adult literacy was difficult if not impossible – possible only if evidence was irrefutable that work-oriented literacy would lead to measurable increases in worker productivity. In August 1969 Harold Graves reported to Demuth on his visit to UNDP in New York, lamenting the slow progress of the EWLP and the lack of usable results to date. Graves concluded: "All this seems to me to put in jeopardy the hope for a quick entry into functional literacy projects." Similarly, Ballantine's deputy, Mats Hultin, reported in the same week on his discussions with UNDP, concluding that the Bank "should not enter into functional literacy projects for the time being but continue to study the development of the [EWLP] programs." To be sure, Hultin reflected more openness on the literacy issue than did his immediate superior, and in fact visited a range of literacy projects (e.g. Iran in 1971) and actively explored ways of avoiding the common pitfalls in literacy work. Nevertheless, the Bank retained its inconsistent and stubborn attitude to this aspect of educational opportunity for all for a considerable time.

The prospect of Bank financing for primary education was, at first, equally contentious. The issue came up at a meeting of the Board of Directors on April 18, 1967, and Woods was able to rely on his prejudices to outline why such financing was not available from the Bank. He urgently sought a fuller rationale, and received it the following morning from Economics Department Director Andrew Kamark:

> I agree with the reasons [you gave to the Board yesterday], but it seems to me there are also in most cases decisive economic arguments for our not financing primary schools.
>
> In most developing countries, there is a very strong demand for primary schools. This demand is so strong that governments tend to allocate a disproportionate amount of their limited education money to the primary schools; our financing and emphasis on secondary and technical schools consequently helps to get an over-all better use of resources.
>
> Secondly, because of the very strong demand for primary schools it is often possible to establish the policy that if people in any locality want a primary school, they have to put up the school building themselves. As a result, the local people either put a special tax on themselves for this purpose or, in some cases, get together and build the school cooperatively. In this way it is possible to get additional local savings that otherwise would not be made. And, it preserves the country's creditworthiness for other activities that cannot be financed in this way.

This bizarre rationale – in a formal communication from the World Bank's Economics Department Director to the Bank President – reflects the view prevalent throughout the Bank that primary education produced low returns on investment, and was potentially a limitless drain on national budgets. Three years later, this was the view reflected by Western Directors on the Board when the first primary loan (to Spain) was presented for approval by McNamara on June 30, 1970, with archconservatives Lieftinck (Netherlands) and Stone (Australia) taking the rare step of abstaining from approval. The loan, for $12 million to support "fundamental education reform at all levels," led to a lively debate with EDs seeing primary education as a bottomless pit that would drain Bank resources: "unless the Bank committed large sums, its impact would be negligible." A week later a confidential memorandum was circulated among senior management foreshadowing a special meeting of EDs to resolve the policy impasse, and for which a paper outlining management thinking would need to be prepared. "Mr McNamara thought that the policy paper should be a tightly-reasoned document.... Participation of a lawyer in its drafting would be arranged." The document further attempted a summary of the President's wishes: he "personally thought that we should do more at the primary level and for functional literacy than we have been doing at present. He did not see much logic in the Board's accepting the Bank/IDA provision of teachers for the primary schools, but denying construction funds for them on general policy grounds."

The document discussed by the Executive Directors on August 4, 1970 *Lending in Education* (World Bank 1970) is a landmark document. It set the scene for the remainder of the McNamara years, and represents the pinnacle of Duncan Ballantine's policy influence. The paper accepted the abiding pertinence of the President's prior policy statement on education, that of October 1963, McNamara quoting and endorsing the basic criterion for Bank lending in education: "The Bank and IDA should be prepared to consider financing part of the capital requirements of priority education projects designed to produce, or to serve as a necessary step in producing, trained manpower of the kinds and in the numbers needed to forward economic development in the member country concerned." Then McNamara made his dramatic departure from the policy and approach of his predecessor:

> However, in applying this criterion in future we should broaden the scope of projects considered and we should determine priorities and select projects on the basis of a thorough examination of the education system as a whole rather than by *a priori* designated areas of eligibility which may not relate to the particular country. We should continue to emphasize projects which, like vocational training, produce trained manpower directly but we should also consider for financing other types of projects with less direct relation to the short-run training of manpower which would have important long-term significance for economic development.

It would be hard to imagine a more polite, restrained but damning indictment of the limitations and arbitrariness of earlier Bank policies for educational financing. In one decisive move, McNamara capitalized on several years' experience of the project cycle in education which had convinced Ballantine and his colleagues that the Woods formula was unsustainable. To bolster his case, McNamara painted an overly bleak picture of educational realities among borrowers, referring to the general prevalence of serious structural imbalances, irrelevant curricula, outmoded teaching methods, lack of planning, inadequate management techniques, and heavy financial burdens. "Traditional ideas are powerful and change slowly but we are beginning to make progress. We encourage our borrowers to be flexible, adaptive and innovating, and when they respond the Bank should be prepared to support them." This concluding sentence of the President's was a little rich – for years borrowers had been complaining of the Bank's intransigence, stubbornness, and arbitrariness in education lending. It had been the Bank that had been slow to keep pace with credible lending policy. The revised policy made explicit provision for lending in the following areas:

- primary education
- secondary education
- post-secondary education for middle-level employment
- university education
- teacher training
- adult vocational training and nonformal education
- technical assistance
- staff and student housing
- educational technology
- general support (including textbooks, equipment, research, planning, management).

For the first time, Bank education policy was organized around the need to conceive of a country's education system as a whole, to ensure ordered and integrated planning and development. This had been the approach promoted insistently by UNESCO since the very beginning of Bank involvement. Its position appeared vindicated, yet basic Bank thinking about the relationships between education and development was in no way questioned or modified. The broad rationale for Bank involvement in education remained intact: the production of trained manpower capable of raising productivity.

At the same time, McNamara displayed a judicious caution in his policy for the Executive Directors. Primary education, while accepted as the "vital first step," was potentially too vast for the Bank to address in quantitative terms, and he argued for the Bank more of an experimental, innovative, and demonstrative role. In the secondary education arena, he asserted that in many contexts the supply of secondary school graduates had approached the "absorptive capacity of the employment market," with perhaps 90 percent of students at this level receiving an overly academic, university-directed education. McNamara maintained a certain arbitrariness towards university education: "Thus far, Bank assistance to university education has been directed principally to the training of high level personnel in agriculture, engineering and education. In addition to these fields, there is need for more university training in the physical and social sciences and in business administration and economics." As far as nonformal and adult education was concerned, McNamara shrewdly opted to omit any mention of literacy. Thus, in a context of a dramatic liberalization of lending criteria, one that left enormous scope for the Bank to respond to priorities as locally determined, a sense of arbitrariness persisted, in that the more liberal approach promoted by the Bank was intended for *universal* application.

Mention needs to be made of the energy put into Bank policy revision by UNESCO, particularly its Director General René Maheu, for whom

McNamara had a healthy regard. From the first weeks of the McNamara presidency, Maheu was corresponding with McNamara, urging a more balanced approach to educational financing, one that reflected a far greater concern than hitherto for overall strategic planning of borrowers' education systems. Often, Maheu's letters enclosed detailed technical papers prepared in the UNESCO Secretariat for the purpose, papers that tended to be of high technical quality and policy relevance. Judging by his replies to Maheu, McNamara needed little convincing of the potential breadth of Bank education lending activity, although he frequently sought to remind Maheu of limits to the Bank's economic growth rationale for educational financing, limits that contrasted with Maheu's institutional capacity to entertain cultural development and human rights as additional justifications for educational programming.

The major public document that arose from this active period of policy renewal was the *Education Sector Working Paper* of September 1971 (World Bank 1971). Achieving wide circulation, the paper was the first statement of Bank lending criteria and the first public summary of project experience to be published by the Bank, one of a series of sector papers initiated by McNamara. Its contents need not be outlined here, summing up as it did existing policy, but perhaps of note is the fact that it was written in four days in August 1971 by an extremely indignant Ballantine who had been recalled from vacation in Turkey with his family in order to prepare it for the Executive Directors (a needless urgency, as it transpired, and which Ballantine never forgot). By this time, the paper did not need to formulate new policies. Rather, it codified the previous two years of policy shifts, and provided a publicly available rationale for what had been a somewhat chaotic period of policy review amidst rapidly increasing lending activity. The paper led to a considerable flow of correspondence between Ballantine and members of the academic community, including such figures in development education circles as Philip Foster and James Robbins Kidd.

Conceptual developments

The early years of the McNamara presidency saw unprecedented intellectual energy expended in the Bank on, among other issues, the economics of education. The focus was on informing Bank lending criteria through improved project identification and preparation. In Chapter 3, it was seen how early project experience in the education sector had thrown up a myriad of questions for investigation and resolution, and how crucial were the early stages of the project cycle in education. As the Bank expanded and diversified under McNamara, there was considerably more room for policy investigations. As the Bank became more complex in structure and function, tension began to develop between the straightforward application of stated lending criteria in loan negotiations – a process simplified while there continued a single Education Projects Department under Ballantine – and the complicating effects of increasing dialogue with borrowers which were not amenable to such straightforward views of things as suggested by criteria intended for universal application. But even as lending policy widened and became more liberal, overall senses of direction had to be found, and the Bank became the arena for strenuous debate over policy issues in the economics of education. Publicly, as ever, Bank officers projected a united front; in-house, there was much jockeying for position.

There was one aspect of the Mason report that exerted considerable long-term influence. This concerned Mason's position in the debate then well underway between proponents of manpower forecasting and projection as a basis for educational (and project) planning, and proponents of the emergent costs-to-benefits school, Mason clearly coming down on the latter side. Mason had concluded that the Bank could make considerably wider use of cost-benefit techniques, particularly in appraising education projects. To date, he argued, the Bank had relied too heavily on educational expansion as a means of attaining stated manpower requirements, themselves expressed in terms of an overall development strategy. Such an approach, argued Mason, was excessively rigid, and made little allowance for such factors as capital–labor substitution possibilities, labor versatility, and on-the-job training. The report argued for more exhaustive analyses of labor markets, labor supply elasticities, and the effects of technical innovation and capital–labor permutations on manpower requirements. As Mason argued to a meeting of the Loan Committee on April 5, 1968, "the Bank should be able to build up a more sophisticated model of a country's changing manpower structure and from there proceed to a meaningful cost-benefit analysis," or in the words of his formal report:

> Since the educational lending criteria of the Bank emphasize the importance of economic objectives there is a prima facie case for applying the same tests to proposed educational projects as to other projects, i.e. does the prospective ratio of costs to benefit promise an acceptable rate of return on the investment.... [Despite difficulties of calculation] a comparison of social costs with social benefits should constitute the analytical framework within which the evaluation of educational as well as other projects takes place. Research now underway in the Bank and elsewhere promises to reduce to some extent uncertainties in the calculations.

It was not so much the case that there were wide conceptual rifts on the manpower planning versus cost-benefit approaches among Bank education staff: in 1968 there were insufficient economists of education on Bank staff to cause such intellectual excitement, dominated as staff was by architects. Rather, it was in the Bank's Economics Department, in borrowing countries, and in other aid agencies that the proponents of manpower forecasting had enjoyed considerable sway in the 1960s, influenced by such theorists as Frederick Harbison, whose son Ralph was later to join Bank education policy staff. Although unbridled educational expansion was not a necessary consequence of the approach, at the political and policy level the manpower approach facilitated uncritical expansion, with emergent analyses by 1968 pointing to many instances of the failure of manpower forecasting to provide an accurate articulation between education systems and labor-market dynamics. According to its proponents and despite a lack of developed techniques, cost-benefit analysis constituted one conceptual means whereby the Bank could encourage borrower restraint on excessive expansion of enrolments. There was also UNESCO's attachment to educational planning, which too easily rendered itself accessible to proponents of manpower planning, and which found expression in a good deal of UNESCO's project preparation work conducted on behalf of the Bank.

Several attempts were made in the Bank to deflect the negative image of cost-benefit analysis, that it was insufficiently detailed to inform educational policy and project preparation (and to do so briskly). Amid considerable departmental scepticism, Economics Department Director Andrew Kamarck had commissioned in 1967 Professor Mark Blaug of the University of London to prepare a putative guide to Bank education policy, an attempt to counter the project-driven preoccupations of Bank education staff: *A Cost-Benefit Approach to Educational Planning in Developing Countries* (Blaug 1967a). In his preface to the study, Kamarck explained its origins and purpose:

> This study originated from a growing awareness that the methods currently used in planning expenditure for education in developing countries fail to take into account important links between the educational system and the economy. For one thing, current methods take the economic value of more education largely for granted; they do not attempt to measure the benefits of the various types of education in monetary terms, thus precluding systematic economic analysis of the benefits as well as the costs of providing additional education by type and level. As a corollary, little, if any, attention is being paid to the role of earnings in the demand for and supply of educated people in a country.
>
> (Kamarck, in Blaug 1967a: ii)

On cue, the sceptics hit back. In a memorandum to his Director, Economics Department staffer C.P. van Dijk warned:

> It is clear that the results of cost-benefit analysis, if ever used for educational planning and project evaluation, should be interpreted with great care.... A strong objection against the cost-benefit approach is that its operational value is very low because it fails to inform us about the rate of return on future investments; in the absence of marginal rate of return calculations we still do not know how much to invest in one direction before the rate of return would decline so much that it becomes equal to the rate of return on investments at the next lower place in the scale.

Or as Bank President George Woods had succinctly put it: "Little people only think in rates of return" (Kapur *et al.* 1997: 38). The Blaug paper failed to have any immediate policy impact in the Bank, which in fact declined to publish it, although Blaug himself put out a revised version soon after (Blaug 1967b).

What created greater interest among Bank education staff was a case study on Kenya conducted for the Bank by Hans Heinrich Thias and Martin Carnoy in 1968–9, *Cost-Benefit Analysis in Education: A Case Study of Kenya* (Thias and Carnoy 1972). Ballantine, it can be noted, had a strong attraction to Kenya, often referring to it in his professional capacity and taking a keen interest in Bank involvement and educational developments there. The Thias–Carnoy study was intended to bolster the perceived relevance of cost-benefit analysis to educational planning in general and Bank project identification and preparation in particular. The study rested on the assumption that in Kenya wages in the private sector were a reasonable reflection of productivity levels, thereby providing a basis for measuring the economic returns from educational investments. The study argued that in the instance of Kenya labor-market distortions, capable of disturbing wage structures and differentials, were either nonexistent or insignificant. A difficulty encountered in the analysis was a typical one, the rigid and artificially high salary structures in the public sector. Thias and Carnoy discounted this effect, on the grounds that those school leavers entering the civil service were the more able school leavers, their higher wages appropriately reflecting higher ability.

It was not until the appointment of George Psacharopoulos to Bank staff in 1981 that the cost-benefit school emerged triumphant, although much enthusiasm for manpower projections waned during that period of its own accord. In the meantime, much intellectual fervor characterized the internal operations of the Bank education staff, with memoranda on innumerable aspects of education circulating in all directions, each with its particular institutional purpose, each attached to its author's career aspirations, and each reflecting some aspect of the Bank's labyrinthine policy processes. Few staffers had the time – or wished to give the impression that they had the time – to circulate ideas for their own sake. Yet Bank files for this period reveal much greater intellectual activity in the Bank than ever before, and which set the scene for future educational debate, with such staffers as Mats Hultin and John Simmons prominent for their voluminous in-house commentaries on matters of educational policy.

Although many other instances can be identified, an example is the in-house workshop on the economics of education held in October 1973. The lead paper, Simmons' *Investment in Education: Alternative National Strategies* (September 20, 1973), took a dismal view of the developmental impact of education on most developing countries. The paper posited the view that school inputs were usually less significant as determinants of learning than such nonschool factors as nutrition, family environment, peer group interaction, and personality. Case-study evidence suggested that schooling also had limited impact on "attitudinal modernization, political socialization or cultural homogenization." Declining external productivity of education and increasing unemployment were identified, as well as the insignificant impact on productivity levels of the cognitive outcomes of education. The paper, in fact, captured much recent thinking on schooling as a factor in promoting social inequalities, with formal education frequently perceived by employers as a screening device rather than as an addition to the stock of human capital. In short, the workshop examined three ways forward for the Bank given the scenario outlined by Simmons: "damp the social demand for formal education, increase the economic relevance of learning alternatives both in and out of school, and neutralize, or compensate for, the inequality aspects of schooling." A major conclusion drawn by participants was the need to curb the growth of secondary schooling in many countries, and to ensure a "selective" expansion of university enrolments, in line with manpower requirements and population dynamics. Financial constraints, economic relevance, and equity considerations were seen at the workshop to combine to produce a new imperative for Bank lending: obtaining maximum participation of the population in some form of basic education. This example reveals much of the institutional character of the Bank's intellectual and policy role: in-house debates reflect the complexity of education and development issues, while the Bank's publicly stated positions and lending criteria inevitably project a simpler but more forceful view of things, a view intended for universal application.

Reorganization of Bank structure 1972

Prior to the restructuring of the Bank in October 1972, Bank staff in education had been grouped into a single unit, the Education Projects Division inaugurated by Ricardo Diez Hochleitner in late 1962, inherited eighteen months later by Duncan Ballantine, and subsequently upgraded to the Education Projects Department. All policy, project, research, and evaluation worked had centered on the one Department, ruled in Ballantine's case by a strong-willed, energetic, forceful man, flexible on some points, unshakeable on others. At first, it was Bank policy to keep small the number of educational professionals in the Department, with the concentration of expertise maintained in the Educational Financing Division of UNESCO, which took responsibility for much of the project cycle in education. Bank education staff, dominated throughout the 1960s by architects, concerned themselves primarily with project appraisal and end-use supervision. In time, Ballantine and his Deputy Mats Hultin found themselves involved less and less in the detail of project work, having to attend to broader aspects of policy and liaison, as well as the day-to-day supervision of a rapidly growing education projects staff. Nevertheless, Bank structures and the arrangement with UNESCO enabled Ballantine to maintain a firm grip on stated education policy, the articulation of lending criteria, the broad shape of project operations, and external relations.

All of this was to change, irreversibly, with the reorganization of October 1972. Its impact on subsequent Bank policy and lending practice cannot be overstated. No longer was the formulation and application of Bank sector work in education subject to tight control and predictable articulation. In short, the reorganized structure that emerged in 1972 permitted a gulf to develop between stated Bank policies in education (with their accompanying conceptual, research, and evaluation dimensions) and the application of criteria in project lending. What emerged were five Regional Departments responsible for all aspects of loan and project operations, in addition to a central education sector policy department responsible for standards, policy statements, and external liaison. Regional Departments could not only diverge in emphasis from the preferred position of the center, they could also readily differ from each other in the application of project lending criteria. For the observer of the Bank, then, the 1972 reorganization resulted in a Bank the analysis of which became particularly challenging. What was Bank policy? Was it to be found in Bank statements of policy, or in Bank lending practice? The answer has to include both.

The Bank's structure had not changed appreciably for twenty years, despite significant increases in Bank size, scope of activity (not least IDA), and complexity of operations. The 1960s had been of particular significance in this respect, with sizeable increases in major administrative areas recorded: number of loans and credits (31 in FY 1960 increasing to 140 in FY 1972); projects under supervision (150 to 620); administrative budget ($10 million to $95 million); commitments ($660 million to $2,970 million); professional staff (305 to 1,520); and total staff (660 to 3,130).

Changes in program composition by sector had been particularly evident. By 1972, the combined professional staffing of the three major newer sectors – agriculture, education, and population – had already exceeded that in the two prominent traditional sectors of transportation and public utilities by almost 50 percent. Between FY 1962 and FY 1966, 65 percent of all lending operations was in transportation and public utilities, with 20 percent in agriculture, education, and population. The Bank was expecting the proportions to be roughly equal by the late 1970s. Further, as has been noted, the Bank was rapidly diversifying its range of activities, becoming a far busier organization. Changes in the scale and composition of lending was readily matched by changes in the complexity of Bank analytical work, as such multisectoral concerns as unemployment, urbanization issues, rural development, income distribution, social development, and environmental issues began to be addressed.

Two particular organizational needs were addressed in 1972: a closer linkage of country and sectoral policy, and a greater delegation of authority. The McKinsey review of Bank organization led to the following reflections contained in a Bank memorandum to senior staff:

> As long as the Bank functioned with major area/projects problems having ultimately to be addressed at the top level and each projects department

performing work in all areas of the world, there was increasing danger that internal Bank coordination problems would have an inordinate cost in staff effort, operational delay and executive energy . . . . The increasingly important multi-sectoral activities were becoming difficult to coordinate. The vital area/projects interactions in day-to-day project work were becoming more formalized and cumbersome, less spontaneous.

More important, while the Bank's centers of country knowledge and sectoral skills were becoming more remote from each other . . . the need for a closer fusion of country knowledge and sectoral skill was growing. Bank effectiveness – particularly in multi-sector analyses and in the newer "softer" sectors where bricks and mortar have comparatively less importance – would increasingly depend on the ready ability to fuse specialized technical expertise with an understanding of local political, administrative, social, economic and cultural conditions. Moreover, it would be easier to have project conditions spring routinely from broader country and sector objectives if there were a closer association between economic and sector survey work – where the broad objectives and strategies are designed – and project preparation, design and implementation – where the conditions are interpreted and applied . . . .

It also became clear that a central projects staff would be needed to prepare policy guidelines and standards for sector and project work, assure a consistent world-wide level of quality in Bank work, provide professional leadership to specialists in the Regions and retain those specialists who – because of their scarcity or their sector's newness – could not be decentralized to the Regions.

This rationale sums up well the intentions behind the reorganization, and point to many structural obstacles to effective project design and implementation not readily detectable in such other sources of assessment as PCRs and PPARs. At the same time, it should not be assumed that the reorganization was an effective solution to the problems so ruthlessly identified in the McKinsey review. In education, as in other sectors, the reorganization brought its own set of difficulties, many of which persisted beyond the next round of restructuring in 1987. An immediate casualty was the dynamism of the UNESCO–Bank arrangements for project identification and preparation. For some time, the agreement was held to be a prime factor in the excessive start-up time for projects, and by 1971 meetings were being held among senior management actively canvassing that the Bank obtain preliminary studies from agencies additional to UNESCO. The reorganization of 1972, in effect but not by design, dealt a death blow to the exclusive arrangements with UNESCO, in that the five Regional Departments felt constrained in their obligation to obtain, and pay for, preliminary studies from UNESCO. While it took another fifteen years to perform the death rites, the new arrangements for Bank projects, combined with the looming and politically disastrous M'Bow period in UNESCO (1974–87), saw a rapid decline in the utility of the Bank looking exclusively to UNESCO for educational expertise. That particular strategy had passed its point of greatest relevance.

For Ballantine in particular, the reorganization implied a separation of policy from operations. Ballantine's new department was given formal responsibility for "functional control" of projects, but everybody knew that in practice this amounted to nothing. Ballantine reflected in later years: "It meant the right to criticize what had been done, which often came to be felt as carping constantly. It meant that operations sometimes lost sight of policy considerations, and policy considerations in turn were not drawn out of the operational experience as much as they should have been. So I think both the operations and the policies tended to suffer." At the same time, Ballantine was able to concentrate resources on research, although he remained sceptical about much of its relevance and impact: "While there were a couple of studies that I think were very worthwhile, there were at least twice that many that didn't matter at all and on which the Bank was spending money. I won't name anybody. There were some that just really weren't very useful."

By his own admission, Ballantine was a strong and forceful leader, who lost the institutional capacity to rule his empire with the 1972 reorganization. Many former staffers have reflected on major rows between Ballantine and the Regional Department heads over lending policy, not least the celebrated clash with Pennisi over the first education loan to Burundi (which Ballantine saw as flagrantly violating Bank policy in its favored treatment of an ethnic minority that had seized political power and was intending to use the project as a means of putting down its opponents). The five years leading up to Ballantine's retirement in 1977 were not always happy for him, and the reorganized Bank was the prime cause.

A poverty focus in education – fact or fiction?

Redistribution with growth

The first twenty years of World Bank operations were theoretically oriented towards classical notions of productivity-driven economic growth, seen at their most influential in former economic staffer Paul Rosenstein-Rodan's view of the "big push" – the massive concentration of capital investment that is sufficiently focussed to self-start an economy into sustained growth. Rostow's view of the "takeoff" stage was embraced by Bank staff as a useful refinement of the big push, as were later elaborations of the conditions required for takeoff by such theorists as Schumpeter, Lewis, Galenson, and Leibenstein. Of very great significance for the first generation of Bank economists was their dedication to external capital investment as decisive interventions which, if sufficiently large and focussed, could deliver the conditions required for the big push or takeoff. Theoretically, the Bank saw itself as well-placed to act out its role as a "locomotive of growth." Chenery's model of national development planning, which came to have enormous theoretical significance in the McNamara Bank, was solidly erected on this model, linked to which was the conviction that massive investment as the major stimulant to growth would with time benefit all economic sectors, including the poorest, in that accumulations of increased productivity and wealth could only "trickle down" and eventually benefit an economy's less-developed sectors. Chenery had a strong theoretical interest in quantifying the additional investments necessary for increased productivity, including the foreign exchange components required. This approach fitted well with the Bank's overarching faith in capital as the main precursor to development, and in economic growth through productivity enhancement as the path to development.

Running in parallel with these perspectives on growth and investment were models that imposed a need for analysis of distributive factors. Their proponents, former Bank staffers recall, enjoyed increasing influence in the Bank of the 1960s. It was not only the Latin American *dependencia* theorists (e.g. Prebisch, Frank) who were demanding such a concern, nor the exponents of "welfare economics" (e.g. Meade, Viner, Little, Perroux) with their focus on the quality (not quantity) of investment and on the allocation of capital rather than its mere accumulation. Many of the Bank's senior economists, through the 1960s, were becoming attracted to Tinbergen's insistence on deriving measures of accounting for the "shadow prices" necessary for accurate attempts at social cost-benefit analysis. The Kuznets U-shaped curve became almost faddish among some staffers who were concerned at the persistence of poverty despite the meeting of big push and takeoff requirements. Also, the Kuznets curve (while confirming the trickle-down effect to the poor) enjoyed widespread application in the Bank, predicting in most instances that in an expanding economy the trickle down to the poor is protracted and diminishing. Also of some influence were Lambert and Perroux' indices of the social and welfare impact of growth, instruments developed by Gini (e.g. coefficient of income distribution), and the Lorenz curve used to highlight differential income distribution at various population levels. Although it is important to emphasize that such instruments were not used in early Bank attempts to evaluate the impact of its own lending, they were nevertheless exerting their influence on overall country economic analyses, which revealed in a variety of contexts the sluggishness of the trickle-down effect.

Perhaps the greatest theoretical challenge by the early 1970s was to examine possibilities of accommodation between growth and distribution of income. Any such accommodation would have needed explicitly to address questions of chronology and priority. Could a prior redistribution of productive capacities and outputs create conditions necessary for, or conducive to, an overall economic system that provided equity? Should productive outputs perhaps be expanded first in order to permit later redistribution? What should be the relative priority between growth and redistribution? Such commentators as Ayres, Hurni, and Van De Laar concur that the Bank under McNamara rejected outright welfarist policies with their short-term emphasis on transfers of income for additional consumption, as it also rejected an intensification of privileges to investors (such as wage restraint and protection). Such other positions as the displacement theories, which held to the inevitably negative effects on the poor of foreign capital inflows and to the need for self-reliance, self-sufficiency, or even autarky on the part of developing countries, were clearly off-limits for the Bank, despite their theoretical and political appeal elsewhere in the UN and development assistance system. Rather, the path opted for was an eclectic and pragmatic middle way championed by Hollis Chenery, which while attached to the idea of capital investment as an important development factor, nevertheless recognized the growing importance of such "noneconomic" factors as education levels, population dynamics, and human culture and behavior.

Hollis Chenery was at the intellectual forefront of the McNamara Bank. A former professor of economics at Stanford and Harvard and a former assistant administrator of the US Agency for International Development (USAID), he was appointed to the Bank as Economic Advisor to the President (1970–2) and subsequently as Vice President for Development Policy (1972–82). It was under Chenery that the Bank's Development Research Center, together with the University of Sussex Institute of Development Studies, produced a theoretical rationalization for the Bank's technical and political positions on poverty alleviation, economic growth, and equity, *Redistribution with Growth* (1974). While stopping short of a formal expression of Bank policy, RWG nonetheless enjoyed elevated status as the intellectual *apologia* of the McNamara Bank. The eclecticism and pragmatism that characterized much of Chenery's earlier academic work paid handsome dividends in the Bank, as his framework provided a pathway through the political and technical tensions between the traditional functions and activities of the Bank and its new concerns with poverty alleviation. Taken with McNamara's address to the Board of Governors in Nairobi in September 1973, the two documents sum up the fundamental policy stance of the World Bank under McNamara.

It is no accident that in McNamara's address the distinction between "absolute" and "relative" poverty was accorded major prominence:

> Relative poverty means simply that some countries are less affluent than other countries, or that some citizens of a given country have less personal abundance than their neighbours. That has always been the case, and granted the realities . . . will continue to be the case for decades to come.
>
> But absolute poverty is a condition of life so degraded by disease, illiteracy, malnutrition, and squalor as to deny its victims basic human necessities.
>
> (McNamara 1973: 6–7)

The difference between the two is fundamental to understanding the McNamara poverty focus. Attempts were made to devise quantified, universal measures of absolute poverty (e.g. annual per capita income between $50 and $75 in 1971 prices), thereby providing measured yardsticks of the denial of fundamental human rights to basic material well-being. Relative poverty had more to imply about structural inequality than did absolute poverty. The difference might appear subtle at first, but its implications were profound: a concern with absolute rather than relative poverty obviated the Bank of the need to examine carefully the structural causes of income inequalities, between societies and within them. The Bank under McNamara did not consider it urgent to examine income shares across the board: rather, it projected a concern with increasing the productivity and income of the poorest. Ayres takes up this point to argue that under McNamara the World Bank missed the opportunity to generate a perspective or theory on income distribution and social inequalities:

> The World Bank's causal chain was very short. Why were people poor? Because they lacked jobs. Because they were unproductive. Because they produced insufficient output. This explanation bordered on the tautological. Why did they lack jobs? Why was their productivity low? Why didn't they produce enough?
>
> (Ayres 1983: 79–80)

A fundamental tenet of *Redistribution with Growth* was its insistence that both Bank and borrowers could tackle redistribution without undermining that most sacred of Bank economic concerns – growth. The Bank's range of country economic studies included many assessments that premature or overzealous redistribution can have adverse effects on growth, and indeed this had been an identifiable aspect of Bank culture. *Redistribution with Growth* advocated the possibility that any trade-off between growth and redistribution need be only temporary, if it were needed at all. Further, "evidence does not support the view that a high rate of economic growth has an adverse effect upon relative equality . . . objectives of growth and equity may not be in conflict" (Chenery *et al.* 1974: 17). This assertion was a statement of political faith, most certainly unsupported by technical evidence. It was a pragmatic attempt to head off advocates who placed their faith in growth strategies. Chenery was particularly interested in the productivity of farmers with small holdings, and recalled in an interview in 1983:

> Some of the early internal debates were about how rapidly we could move in the direction of supporting small farmers and shifting towards poverty-focused agricultural programs. . . . McNamara pushed hard for a specific set of targets that could be supported. . . . The compromise which was reached was translated into evaluating agricultural projects in terms of what proportion went to the poorer groups. . . . How does one reach small farmers? How does one design research to find out whether small farmers are as efficient as large farmers. . . . On the whole, the results of our research were that under controlled conditions small farmers were as productive as large farmers and . . . that the project designed to reach small farmers has had perfectly adequate, if not outstanding, rates of return.

Chenery and his colleagues identified four major approaches to raising the productive capacities and income levels of the poor: (1) maximizing the growth of GNP; (2) redirecting investment to poverty groups; (3) redistributing income or consumption to poverty groups; and (4) transferring existing assets to poverty groups (Chenery *et al*. 1974: 48). Ayres comments:

> The favored strategy was the second. The first had the problem of "relatively weak linkage between the poverty groups and the rest of the economy" [RWG: 48]. The third had "too high a cost in terms of foregone investment to be viable on a large scale over an extended period" [RWG: 48]. The fourth was considered unfeasible because "political resistance to policies of asset redistribution makes this policy unlikely to succeed on any large scale in most countries" [RWG: 49]. In this respect the essence of the RWG approach was on increasing the productivity, incomes, and output (and through these, the welfare) of the absolute poor. This also coincided with McNamara's annual addresses since 1973.
>
> (Ayres 1983: 79)

Redirecting investment to the poor, then, was the essence of redistribution with growth, the McNamara Bank's framework for poverty alleviation. It sought in no way to address relative inequalities in income or well-being; by contrast, it sought to raise the incomes of the poorest. There was no concern to reallocate resources within an economy or across economies, particularly the redistribution of assets or income; rather, it sought to reallocate the focus of investment (income increments) in favor of the poorest, perhaps the softest redistributive option available. Therefore, the entire RWG strategy had a narrow and controllable focus, the income levels, productivity, and the output of the absolutely poor. Who were the absolute poor? While it suited McNamara to claim they constituted up to 40 percent of developing country populations (McNamara 1973: 7), in fact they were heavily concentrated in the poorest countries, notably in South Asia. Not many Bank borrowers were politically challenged by the Bank's RWG strategies. Ayres, one of the more liberal commentators on the McNamara years at the Bank, summed up RWG as follows:

> The strategy of RWG should be seen for what it was: relatively modest, eminently possibilist, bedevilled by political constraints, highly tenuous, subject to complex and formidable problems of implementation. In neither a national or international sense did it seek fundamentally to change the world in which the poor lived; it sought to improve the terms on which they related to it.... The Bank's preferred approach to poverty-alleviation had much to do with the tenacity of its ideology. RWG was more compatible with that ideology; it did not represent a paradigmatic shift. The concern with the poverty of the poor majority was an addendum, not a substitute, and as such was more comfortably accommodated.
>
> (Ayres 1983: 89–90)

Redistribution with growth, as a strategy for poverty alleviation, saw maintenance of the Bank's commitment to "trickle-down" views of development. It was developed, in theoretical terms, by outsiders brought into the Bank by McNamara for the purpose. Their language, motivation, style, and technical approach were all new to the Bank, but in no fundamental sense did they undercut the broad thrust of the Bank's approach to financing development. The Bank remained the Bank, operating within the same parameters as it had since the establishment of IDA in 1960. What RWG provided, above all, was a rationale for a dramatically expanding loan portfolio, and an image of decisiveness in its poverty-alleviation role.

The RWG strategy also solved two other problems facing McNamara. One had to do with the relatively sudden radicalization of development strategy and rhetoric elsewhere in the UN system, which by May 1974 had formally adopted stances calling for a New International Economic Order (NIEO). NIEO perspectives, rooted in the Latin American theorists' propositions of *dependencia*, could only have been off-limits as policy options for the Bank. Nevertheless, McNamara was faced with a vibrant intergovernmental climate concerning global poverty and inequalities that could not be ignored. With its poverty rhetoric, redistribution with growth provided him with the means to address decisively the NIEO issue. His successive addresses to the Board of Governors, in fact, reveal McNamara's responses to the zenith and nadir of NIEO perspectives in the UN system.

The other problem confronting McNamara concerned the prominence and evident appeal of a policy alternative to RWG. This had to do with the "basic human needs" (BHN) approach to poverty alleviation, which had developed in many other development assistance circles and was generating not insubstantial support within the increasingly liberal atmosphere of the McNamara Bank. It is of fundamental importance that RWG and BHN were policy competitors – not complements – in the Bank from about 1970 to 1973. Too many commentators see them as part of a single Bank poverty alleviation strategy. This is not the case. Advocates of the basic human needs approach, building in particular on perspectives that had developed in the International Labor Organization through the work of such theorists as Dudley Seers, Richard Jolly, and Gus Ranis, could not accept the confined economic and political parameters of RWG. They saw in the narrowness of RWG few, if any, prospects for any genuine impact on poverty, whether or not attempted through Bank activities. For them, basic human needs were not being met in a wide variety of settings, but needed to be met if development were to be sustained.

At a rhetorical level, BHN resembled McNamara's focus on lifting the absolute poor out of absolute poverty, but such a comparison can be misleading. The basic human needs approach cast a far wider social and economic net, and was considerably more profound in its insistence on structural economic change. A memorandum circulated within the Bank pointed to the similarities and differences between the RWG and basic human needs approaches.

Points of contact between the two involved productivity – redirecting investment and public services towards the poor in order to enhance income. Where there was no compatibility was clear to the author of the memorandum, who described some essential features of the approach, bestowing upon it a kiss of death:

> The production of non-essential goods (apart from exports) should be tightly controlled, all incentives and market signals should be modified toward the production of basic-wage goods and services, the state should stand ready for large-scale market intervention if the existing markets are a slave to the interests of the privileged groups. The opponents of basic needs programs fear that such market interventions will often be inefficient, serve only the interests of the ruling elite, and are probably a soft-sell for communism.

What the advocates, within the Bank, of the basic human needs approach failed to achieve was any movement away from the simplest notions of human well-being. The rhetoric associated with their position that made its way into the public arena amounted to little more than general ethical assertions, indisputable in character. Within the Bank, there was little, if any, theoretical or analytical progress towards understanding the variables of relevance to meeting basic human needs and how they interrelate, to form in one Bank staffer's words a "congenial policy and political climate conducive to redistributive policies." One Bank memorandum summed up the intellectual poverty of the basic human needs position as perceived within the Bank: "Little analysis has gone so far into the political, institutional, and administrative framework required to make a successful attack on poverty and to remove obstacles to fulfilling basic human needs" (cited in Ayres 1983: 87). At the heart of any basic human needs strategy was supply management, and the McNamara years at the World Bank reveal starkly the Bank's disinterest and incapacity to take issues of supply management seriously. Even the advocates of the basic human needs approach stopped short of the type of analysis than any observer would have found obvious: what difference has politics made to the impact of redistributive and supply management policies? Can evidence be mustered concerning the political variables of relevance in effective poverty-alleviation strategies? What are the facts about political regime type and the effectiveness of poverty-alleviation policies? Again as Ayres asserts: "The World Bank, however, does not appear to be in the business of conducting this kind of analysis. In this regard the Bank is a nonpolitical institution, as it functions without very much attention to the social and political dimensions of its work. It operates with a very reduced conception of the political" (1983: 88–9). Hollis Chenery recalled in 1983:

> In terms of Bank policy, I would not say that we ever adopted a basic needs approach in our project lending. I think that the majority view was

that within the context of the way the Bank operates, it was perfectly feasible to find good projects either in agriculture or in housing or in education which combined the objectives of meeting basic needs, but did not violate the Bank's insistence on a productive social return to the country concerned .... The basic needs approach is one means of implementing a poverty-oriented policy. There are other means which don't involve direct intervention by providing certain basic commodities which basic needs does and which would be more market-oriented. The Bank generally has tended toward raising the incomes of the poor and letting the poor purchase their own set of commodities.

These considerations collectively impinge on a perennial issue facing the World Bank – the interface between its declared policy stances and its behavior as a lender. Its stated policies have multiple functions, partly designed to influence borrowers' economic policies and performance, partly designed to shape the Bank's own lending criteria. However, the organizational divide in the Bank between policy formulation and lending operations means that each requires separate analysis, and that any connection between the two deserves its own particular consideration. One issue for the Bank that derived from the McNamara poverty focus was never openly discussed: how low-yielding "poverty" lending might be compensated for by traditional high-yielding infrastructure loans. The rapid expansion of lending pursued by McNamara demanded some kind of trade-off, but it did not surface as a policy issue beyond the Board and senior management. Traditionally, both IBRD and IDA financing required evidence of economic returns – short-term or long-term – of at least 10 percent, but it was clear in the early 1970s that evidence was lacking of the rates-of-return from poverty lending, that is, transfers of investment capital (and not consumption or assets) to poverty-afflicted sectors. Institutionally, it was less difficult for the Bank: it had already accumulated a decade of experience in such "soft" sectors as education, without distress being aroused on international financial markets by the absence of hard rate of return measures. Further, McNamara had quickly amassed sizeable increases in both IBRD and IDA loanable capital, and poverty lending seemed an expedient avenue for extending loan activities, without upsetting too many IBRD and IDA traditions. Redistribution with growth, in fact, was sufficiently conservative to placate sceptics in the Bank who preferred evidence of calculable returns.

More challenging was the Bank–borrower relationship. The conditions of success facing redistribution with growth decidedly impinge more greatly on borrowers than on any external agent, despite the persistence of structural inequalities at the international level. External input can only have a marginal effect on such pertinent features of inequality as the urban–rural divide, subsidization policies that favor the industrial sector, distorted pricing systems, the marginal political influence of rural populations, inequities in land ownership, and taxation policy, to name a few. Bank loan officers faced the challenge of generating loan applications for poverty-oriented (especially rural development) projects, in the face of innate political and technical conservatism on the part of borrowing country officials. In this sense, Bank policies of leverage had their point, although in essence the Bank's approach to redistribution with growth, once analyzed by the thoughtful governmental functionary, was hardly revolutionary or disturbing to vested interests, despite the acceleration of McNamara's rhetoric. His reformist messages to borrower governments, again best seen in his series of annual addresses, had by 1978 failed to grapple with the political realities of genuine poverty alleviation. Rather, McNamara began to resort to ethical motivations and constructs, appealing, in his 1978 address to the Board of Governors, for "political will" and "sustained political courage." McNamara had begun to sound like a Director General of UNESCO.

Education, poverty, and basic human needs

Education Director Duncan Ballantine was quick to explore the implications of the poverty focus for the education sector. Free of responsibility for projects – following the 1972 reorganization – Ballantine was able to undertake this with some vigor. At the same time, signs of a gap between Bank policy rhetoric and actual lending performance could be detected. In a December 1973 memorandum to Vice President Warren Baum, Ballantine offered some preliminary comments on educational means of implementing the President's Nairobi speech. In it, Ballantine complained about a "plan of action" that had been drafted for McNamara by Baum and his Vice Presidential colleague Ernest Stern, in that only "passing reference" had been made to education. In particular, Ballantine was keen to avoid "the traditional view about the educational component of rural projects which is usually conceived in terms of providing conventional school facilities in a particular geographic area." The next six months saw intensive drafting in Ballantine's Department of a new education policy, one that captured the McNamara poverty focus. The product, the *Education Sector Working Paper* of December 1974 (World Bank 1974), was a far more wide-ranging and innovative discourse than its 1971 precursor, which had merely summed up existing Bank practices. By contrast, the 1974 discussion speculated on possible strategies for future Bank lending, inviting dialogue with borrowers on the issues raised. It helped project the image of a more flexible, innovative, and yielding Bank. Yet a close reading of the paper reveals the limitations of the redistribution with growth strategy as applied to education. An example was its failure to articulate a precise educational application of RWG principles and strategies. After summarizing the RWG argument, the paper turned to education:

> A broadening of development objectives also implies that significant changes are needed in educational policies and practices. If education is to contribute to the development of the rural and traditional sectors of the economy, it will have to adapt itself to the needs of these sectors.

An important implication of this expanded development strategy is that mass education will be an economic as well as a social necessity. Education and training systems will need to be designed to enable the masses that have been unaffected by the growth of the modern sector to participate in the development process as more productive workers – by being able to play their roles effectively as citizens, family members, leaders and members of groups involved in cooperative community action, and in many other ways. This ultimately means that all parts of the population must receive education and training of some kind as soon as resources permit and to the extent that the course of development requires.... Education cannot be restricted to school-age youths. Other target groups such as adults, and especially women, must be included. Given the diversity of target groups and educational tasks, it would be advisable to make effective use of nonformal and informal education, in addition to the formal school system.

(World Bank 1974: 14–15)

This is a somewhat weak application, although Chenery *et al.*'s *Redistribution with Growth* had almost nothing to say about education, except that it was desirable (Chenery *et al.* 1974: 123). What is clear from Bank files is that Ballantine and Hultin failed to perceive in RWG the deliberate "limited policy" approach that constituted the absolute political imperative for the Bank. Rather, they saw the basic human needs approach as complementary to RWG, rather than as a policy competitor in the Bank, and grafted on to their formulation of education sector policy much that had been produced as part of the basic human needs argument, an argument that had much more to imply for educational strategies. Simply, it permitted an expansion of education sector lending without upsetting Bank views on poverty and development.

In particular, Ballantine had been heavily influenced by a study conducted for the Bank through the International Council for Educational Development by Philip Coombs and Manzoor Ahmed, *Attacking Rural Poverty: How Nonformal Education Can Help* (Coombs with Manzoor 1974), which had useful points to make about farmer education. Coombs and Manzoor had put forward the hypothesis that rural development is the product of a dynamic interaction of many forces, of which education is one, and outlined four educational needs for rural education – general basic education, family improvement education, community improvement education, and occupational education. The study centered on occupational education, with surveys of some twenty-five national case studies, identifying three important target groups – persons directly engaged in agriculture, those in off-farm commercial activities, and those providing general services to rural communities. Not surprisingly, rural areas generally were seen to have poor educational resources, especially when compared with urban areas. Those sparse educational resources that did exist failed to reach the groups Coombs and Manzoor deemed most needy, out-of-school youth and the economically deprived. Ballantine warmed to the study's conclusions about the potential of rural education programs to raise agricultural productivity levels and thereby fuel economic growth, and the ways in which formal, nonformal, and informal education could interact to this end. The study's focus on integration, decentralization, and equity, therefore, provided Ballantine with a detailed rationale (and useful case study evidence) for much he was wanting to project into the 1974 ESWP, yet firmly contained within an overall framework of increased worker productivity.

The 1974 *Education Sector Working Paper* focussed on five basic issues seen to have policy interest for both Bank and borrowers: skill development and its potential for productivity increases; mass participation in education and development; education and equity; increasing the efficiency of education; and improving educational planning and management. Such issues remain at the heart of Bank policy concerns to this day. What the paper had to say about equity was weak:

> Educational systems and policies have a regressive character which favors urban populations and middle- and upper-income groups. These groups, therefore, have a definite advantage in terms of access to, and promotion within, the systems.
>
> Equalizing opportunities for access to education is a necessary, but not sufficient, condition to ensure social mobility through education. Providing equal chances for achievement, both in and after school, is a more difficult objective, as factors which cannot be affected by educational policies play a significant role . . . . As a whole, however, equity through education can be achieved only within the context of broader social policies.
>
> (World Bank 1974: 5)

In outlining anticipated Bank lending objectives in education, the sector paper pointed to four goals in particular, goals which summed up the conventional thinking of the day, reflected in many other international documents and statements, not least UNESCO's Faure Report, *Learning to Be* (Faure 1972), a study which went far in promoting the idea of lifelong learning. First, the paper expressed a commitment to a "minimum basic education for all as fully and as soon as available resources permit and the course of development requires" – a goal whose tempering by qualification was more indicative of Bank priorities than the essential goal itself. Second, the paper argued for a selective provision of further education and training beyond basic education "for the performance of economic, social and other developmental roles." Third, and significantly: "a national system of education should be viewed as a comprehensive learning system embracing formal, nonformal and informal education and working with maximum possible internal and external efficiency." Last was outlined, on equity grounds, a commitment to the equalization of learning opportunities (World Bank 1974: 52).

It is of considerable interest that such a formulation of Bank strategy was seen as revolutionary, constituting a decisive break with the constraints of the past. Rhetorically, the notions of a basic education for all – with a rural development emphasis at the forefront – was virtually identical in content to UNESCO's concept and program of "fundamental education," which in the 1940s and 1950s had brought considerable credit and prestige to that organization (for a full account, see Jones 1988: 47–87). Borrowers, too, had been articulating much along similar lines. The major difference was UNESCO's articulation of fundamental education as a vehicle for democracy, enabling the articulation of concerns for land reform and rural cooperatives, items well off-limits for the Bank. Yet in practice it remained to be seen how the Bank's actual lending patterns would be altered as a result of the new rhetoric.

The adult literacy blind spot continued, despite UNESCO's retrieval of the Experimental World Literacy Program and its clear success in generating methodologies of adult literacy teaching with the kinds of developmental and productivity-related returns demanded by UNDP. Adult literacy provision made its way into only the merest handful of Bank loans. Another of Ballantine's blind spots – despite the rhetoric about flexibility and equity – concerned Bank support for community libraries. The following edict was despatched to the regional Division Chiefs from Ballantine's office on September 24, 1975:

> In a number of mission reports there have been increasing references to Bank support for two types of items, namely, libraries and pre-school facilities.... Support of libraries has generally been restricted to facilities which are an integral part of an education or training institution.... Occasional exceptions have been made for mobile libraries.... Although the Bank's expanding interest in adult education and training programs, sometimes including literacy components, might suggest expanding support to general purpose, independent libraries, this as yet has not become accepted policy and should not be treated so.... Similarly, except in special cases, it has not been accepted policy to finance or support pre-school programs.

In short, redistribution with growth was insufficiently powerful as a vehicle for poverty alleviation, and inadequate as a springboard for radical reformulations of educational theory, policy, and practice in developing countries. The real educational revolution under McNamara occurred earlier, with the widening of lending criteria, which permitted the grafting on of new types of lending (not least primary education) to conventional areas. Such expressions of policy as the 1974 ESWP merely enabled the process to continue, and provided the Bank with some external relations window-dressing opportunities. One of the Bank education sector's major lapses was failing to capture the poverty focus and instil it with new educational content. The institutional, political, and conceptual parameters within which the Bank operated placed limits on such a move, but in no absolute sense. The celebrated clash between Ballantine and Peter Williams of the University of London (through the columns of the UNESCO journal *Prospects*) missed this point, Williams being more intent on revealing the Bank's apparent claims to omniscience and the ESWP's overly pessimistic view of educational progress in the developing world (Williams 1975; Ballantine 1976).

Education project experience under McNamara

What the World Bank is prepared to lend for profoundly influences the character and content of its projects, although not absolutely. Assertive and articulate borrowers can to some extent steer project content away from the current fashion in the Bank. An understanding of the impact of Bank projects must begin with what they set out to achieve. Only then is a broader assessment possible of project effectiveness, impact, and outcomes both planned and unplanned.

Project purposes

The McNamara years saw a pronounced shift away from education projects with an almost exclusive focus on quantitative expansion (the provision of additional places through physical construction) towards projects that also addressed qualitative change and experimentation. Of most significance in this respect were projects designed to provide better physical plant in order to enhance the teaching of science and the technologies, especially through the increased exposure of students to practical work in laboratories and workshops and through the design of programs related to future employment. A majority of projects contained provision for curriculum development, and improved teaching and examination. A relatively small number of nevertheless important projects either provided for entirely new kinds of schools or training centers, or attempted major restructuring of a borrower's school system. The McNamara years saw an increasing number of projects incorporate tracer studies to follow subsequent education and employment experience of graduates from Bank-supported institutions, while about one-third included provision for the establishment of school advisory committees for the purpose of better relating school programs to the needs of employers. Many projects had an explicit concern to raise the quality of teaching, while a few addressed issues of the status of teachers and their salaries. Other qualitative concerns that increased in the McNamara years focussed on the need for more economical delivery of education and achieving the maximum reach of educational systems. Many projects saw such innovations as multipurpose institutions (e.g. teacher education, civil service training, and agricultural training combined), double shift schools, the sharing by several schools of a central administration facility, and the use of school buildings in the evening for adult education. Surprisingly, few projects reflected the rhetoric promoted by Ballantine for the extensive use of (or experimentation with) new technologies in education. Textbook supply, also, was surprisingly rare until the late 1970s.

In the McNamara years physical construction in the education sector absorbed 84 percent of available finance, down from 98 percent between 1963 and 1968. By the same token, the application of finance for technical assistance and fellowship training rose from 1.5 percent (1963–8) to 10 percent in the McNamara years. Trends of significance are apparent when education subsectors are analysed for the same two periods, 1963–8 and 1969–80: sub-professional training (technical, vocational, and agricultural education) rose slightly from 26 percent to 32 percent; secondary and higher education declined from 70 percent to 31 percent; and primary, basic, and teacher education rose from 5 percent to 37 percent.

There can be no doubt that in very many projects the Bank's thinking about educational change failed to match that of its borrowers. Progressives would say that the Bank, as a pacesetter of reform, was merely ahead of its clients, trying to drag them along with it. Sceptics would say that the Bank was imposing its will on reluctant borrowers, both through project content and loan conditions. On occasions, projects were premature or overly ambitious as agents of reform. In several instances, loan negotiations saw a diminution of the reforms proposed by the Bank for want of enthusiastic government endorsement. Good examples are the first two education loans to Senegal (1971 and 1975), the third to Colombia (1974), and the third to Tunisia (1976), where final appraisal missions (prior to negotiations and approval) scaled down proposed reform. Fair comment would be that many of the intended qualitative reforms had such goals as the greater exposure of students to practical work, the use of libraries for investigations and problem-solving, changes in school organization, and the introduction of new teaching styles and attitudes – all areas of considerable challenge and complexity in any traditional setting, all requiring bold and sensitive leadership. At the same time, it must be noted that Bank education lending in the McNamara years was rarely oriented towards system-wide reform and the strengthening of education ministries. Few addressed the development of national adminis-trative, planning, or research capacities, or programs requiring sustained external support for a considerable period of time. There were some excep-tions, not least support for the Institute of Education (Kenya III – 1976), the Institute of Education and the educational planning unit in Sierra Leone II (1976), and the adult education service in Indonesia VI (1978).

A project that had an important "muscle-building" component and which was well-regarded within the Bank was Ethiopia II (1971), seen as a good example of building the enhancement of educational planning capabilities into Bank lending operations. Included in this $9.5 million loan was provi-sion of $120,000 for technical assistance to help the Government carry out a comprehensive education review for the country.

The significance of what transpired is that the education sector review was primarily conducted by Ethiopian nationals. The dialogue between the Government and the Bank that led up to the review had begun during the formulation of the second education loan, when the Bank declined to finance the construction of as many secondary schools as the Government wished because of a lack of agreement as to how the development plans at this level of education reflected the country's longer-term educational development needs and financial resources. In discussions with the Education Minister, it was agreed that funds would be included for a review of both the internal and external efficiency of the Ethiopian school system. At this point, a traditional survey could have been anticipated, designed and carried out by foreign consultants. Instead, it was agreed at the outset that the review would be the responsibility of, and be primarily conducted by, the Government, with an Ethiopian Director coordinating a team of local and foreign advisers. A key part of the approach was a symposium held in Ethiopia early in the study, which provided a forum for a wide variety of Ethiopians (from both public and private sectors) and some foreigners to express their points of view on educational needs in the presence of the Minister of Education and other policy-makers. This provided the opportunity to frame the study around needs identified by the Ethiopians themselves, but in the company of such foreign interests as the Bank, other aid agencies, and technical specialists, and with Bank-financed technical assistance when required.

Issues in project preparation

As in the 1963–8 period considered in Chapter 3, the problem of extremely long project gestation continued to plague World Bank activity in education, and was the subject of intense and persistent complaints by borrowers. A confidential Bank document concluded: "In some cases countries have deliberately withheld items from inclusion in proposed projects because they were needed earlier than the normal pace of project processing would have permitted." Among the sectors financed by the Bank, the education sector was by far the slowest in terms of project generation. In the McNamara years, the average elapsed time from project identification to effectiveness was thirty months.

In the first decade of Bank education financing, project generation typically consisted of three distinct stages: identification and preparation (by UNESCO) and appraisal (by the Bank). The 1970s saw a declining use of UNESCO, with the Bank making greater use of its own preparation/appraisal and pre-appraisal missions, and some borrowers relying less on UNESCO for identification work. Increases in Bank education staff were also of relevance to its role in project generation – 7 professional staff in 1964, 20 in 1969, 48 in 1972, and 95 in 1978. With the reorganization of the Bank in 1972, greater scope existed for more continuous dialogue between Bank and borrowers, and formal borrower loan applications tended to fall into disuse. Detailed working papers, often prepared by Bank staff, became the key project papers.

These developments forced a review of the UNESCO–Bank Co-operative Agreement in 1976, a joint task force recommending a declining role for

UNESCO, what it diplomatically termed "a minimization of inter-agency overlap." UNESCO would merely assist the Bank in appraisal, supervision, and completion work, leaving identification and definition of lending strategies largely to the Bank. Further, UNESCO was to provide initial project preparation assistance to borrowers rather than undertaking full-scale preparation work itself through visiting missions. These were major changes.

A frequent complaint of borrowers concerned the seemingly arbitrary demands made by individual experts, whether from UNESCO or the Bank, during project preparation, imposing their individual viewpoints on projects at successive stages, wasting previous efforts through project deletions or causing delay through additions. More generally, project composition frequently changed at each stage of the cycle. Radical reductions in project scope were often required after appraisal where the prepared project had been too large, or where preparation had been based on unsatisfactory cost estimates or on mistaken expectations on loan or credit amounts.

Some attempts to speed up project preparation were disastrous. In both Korea I (1969) and Cameroon I (1970), overlapping UNESCO identification and preparation missions were used by the Bank, with just one Bank official visiting the borrowers towards the end of the identification mission to secure Bank/UNESCO/borrower agreement on project objectives and content. In each case, the arbitrariness of the Bank official substituted itself for careful planning, and in the words of a Bank evaluation "both projects experienced significant additional changes in content during processing as well as problems during implementation, which reflected these inadequacies of project preparation." Another experiment – the use of brief Bank reconnaissance missions instead of the usual stages of the project cycle – also fared badly. In the case of Senegal I (generated from 1967 to 1971), the Bank began with reconnaissance missions (1967, 1968, 1969), but in the end resorted to traditional identification (1969) and preparation (1970). In generating Tanzania II, three weeklong reconnaissance missions were used. The first agreed with the government on a secondary school project; the second added some agricultural schools; the third, recognizing that the agricultural school component would take too long to be prepared for financing, deleted it. At appraisal, fundamental policy changes were still being recommended to the Government about the level at which institutions should operate; at negotiations, some schools were deleted and, soon after loan approval, the project was reappraised and amended in the light of Government decisions on the appraisal mission's recommendations (which the Bank was not aware the Government was considering). The borrower in this instance was dissatisfied about the number of Bank missions prior to project implementation and the resultant delays prior to implementation.

In general, the McNamara years saw the Bank's role in project generation remain extensive. In many instances, the role of individual Bank mission members in determining project content was widely perceived by borrowers to have been excessive, with insufficient consultation and dialogue, making the

Bank appear inflexible and unresponsive, exercising excessive leverage, and displaying insufficient sensitivity to local circumstances and borrower preferences. A confidential Bank memorandum addressed the issue of the Bank's role in project generation in 1978, and concluded that the search for more efficient mission sequences "might have been more fruitful had more attention been given at the same time to developing the borrowing countries' own capabilities and role in project identification and preparation, to ensure stability in project content through the cycle and guarantee the borrowers' commitment to the project." As a whole, the Bank's role in the generation of education projects appears to have been overly assertive.

The period under consideration also saw a marked increase in the use of covenants in loan agreements, generally becoming more detailed and regulatory, frequently provoking complaints from borrowers. In some instances, such conditions appeared to act as a substitute for official commitments to certain education policy objectives, or as a substitute for realistic and practicable implementation of agreed-upon actions. Some covenants were ludicrous and unenforceable. For example, the following was attached to Colombia III: "Before introducing any new diversified curriculum or making any modification in an existing diversified curriculum the borrower shall inform the Bank of the proposed modification or curriculum, and the arguments supporting such proposal, and shall afford the Bank a reasonable opportunity to comment thereon." As the Bank itself was to comment several years later: "If applied seriously, this covenant would have resulted in Bank staff becoming swamped with materials on every proposed modification, and complicated and retarded the normal process of continuous curriculum revision which should be taking place in the country." A more limited covenant in Tanzania III, that all syllabuses of the Agricultural Training Institutes be sent to the Bank for review, was later regarded by the project completion mission as exceeding the Bank's staffing resources available for project supervision.

Issues in project implementation

Virtually without exception, World Bank projects in education are modified in some form during implementation, and experience time overruns. About half of the projects implemented during the 1970s had overruns of 70 percent (of the scheduled completion rate estimated at appraisal). The planned four-year average, giving way to the actual seven-year average, caused major cost overruns in many cases, and caused projects to be implemented in changing social and sectoral circumstances. Most projects thus afflicted tended to be reduced in scope towards the end, so that the imputed time overrun was actually higher. The average overrun rate of 70 percent can be reduced to 60 percent if those projects are excluded which suffered from extensive civil unrest and natural disasters during the period of implementation, not least Bangladesh, Chile, Nigeria, and Pakistan. As in the 1963–8 period discussed in Chapter 3, the most serious delays were experienced in the first eighteen months or so of implementation.

A frequently employed Bank stratagem to avoid such delays was to opt for more detailed and lengthy project preparation, which from the borrowers' point of view did nothing to speed up the project cycle as a whole.

Throughout the 1970s, the Bank maintained its preference for project implementation through semiautonomous project implementation units (PIUs) as distinct from strengthening overall institutional management capacities. Interestingly, the first seven projects in education made use of existing services, and by 1980 the mood was swinging back in favor of such an approach. In the 1970s, 80 percent of projects utilized PIUs, and the difficulties encountered in the 1960s persisted, particularly their local image as a transitory special purpose creation providing no long-term career opportunities for staff. The benefits of PIUs were also clear, being able to focus virtually full-time on project implementation and, as beneficiaries of Bank technical assistance and supervision, generally able to bring projects to completion even in a weak national or sectoral administrative context. In not a few cases, successful PIUs were given responsibility for other national programs, cases which marked encouraging movement away from the expensive and rather alienating original Bank concept of a separate cell devoted exclusively to one project. The challenge, however, was to ensure that PIUs were not too distant from existing governmental structures. In particular, substantial benefits could accrue to government departments upon project completion from the experience built up within PIUs.

As indicated, 84 percent of education loan monies in the McNamara period were applied to the construction and equipping of physical plant. A remarkable achievement of the McNamara Bank is that nearly all of the buildings originally planned were in fact constructed. Much useful work was done on principles of school architecture, and many successful designs were applied to follow-up projects. More disappointing was the Bank's lack of success in achieving radical breakthroughs in new and more economical design and construction of educational buildings, with continuing emphasis on overly standardized designs and too little emphasis on their adaptation to the climate and topography of individual sites. In general, UNESCO and Bank project preparation teams underestimated the capacities of local architects, and in perhaps far too many instances the Bank required the use of foreign architectural firms, with success in some cases (e.g. Guyana I and West Pakistan I) and less so in others (e.g. East Pakistan I and II, Senegal II, and Cameroon I). Actual construction, by contrast, was undertaken in nearly every project by local firms. An issue of major and continuing concern for both Bank and borrower was maintenance. Despite the standard use of covenants requiring adequate maintenance for project buildings, inadequate budgets and management weaknesses usually led to unsatisfactory arrangements, a good example of the irrelevance – in actuality – of many project covenants. Morocco II was the only project in this period that adopted the sensible tack of addressing the issue through the provision of Bank technical assistance to improve the borrower's maintenance capacity.

The provision of equipment constituted one of the largest single educational investments of the McNamara Bank, providing over $500 million for this purpose alone. Obviously, equipment had to be educationally relevant, in good operating order, and actually on-site if the expenditure was to be worthwhile. Even small percentage losses would have been large in absolute terms. The Bank, during the 1970s, was slow to perceive problems in the procurement of instructional equipment, and even slower to address the problems it knew existed. A special task force on the subject analyzed 117 projects and reported in October 1976 that the way forward was a liberalization of Bank procedures and requirements, rather than their further tightening. The report noted the particular challenges of lending operations in remote and poorly serviced rural areas, and argued for greater flexibility in Bank procedures. A second report in 1978 was damning: "Cases abound of unusable, sub-standard or mis-matched equipment items, over-supply or under-supply of equipment, over-sophisticated items, confused distribution, uninstalled and unrepaired equipment, failure to make insurance claims in time and lengthy implementation delays." If school construction was one of the more successful aspects of education projects during this period, the procurement of equipment was one of the most wasteful and poorly supervised.

In Chapter 1 it was argued that the initial reputation of the IBRD rested in part on the meticulous supervision and auditing undertaken by the Bank. Bank projects invariably have a "squeaky-clean" image, and the Executive Directors and their governments may usually rest easy that funds released by the Bank have been expended for the approved purposes. In an important sense, end-use supervision is more straightforward for physical construction projects. Even such complex undertakings as dams, power stations, steel mills, and railway lines are amenable to relatively cursory inspection, to enable confidence about proper end-use. This is not necessarily the case in such sectors as education. Some projects, for instance, aimed at changing staff attitudes in borrowers' education systems. School principals not always grasped the point of vocationally oriented and "diversified" secondary school curricula, thereby thwarting much of their potential. Where none existed previously, libraries demanded an attitudinal shift for their effective use, as did such specialized facilities as science and language laboratories. In the Bank's view, some projects were particularly successful in involving teachers and principals in achieving such goals, particularly through training (but not in project design), for example, Chile III, El Salvador I, Indonesia II, and Philippines II.

There are two main aspects of Bank supervision of education projects – physical and educational. Perhaps understandably if not acceptably, supervision in the 1963–8 period focussed on the problems of constructing and procuring physical plant, and education specialists were not generally considered essential for project supervision. As a result, developments and policy changes in borrowers' education systems frequently proceeded without particular reference to the Bank. With the growing concern in Bank projects for educational change, as distinct from expansion, it became clear that project supervision could address issues of software use as well as the adaptation of projects to evolving educational policies and circumstances. Throughout the McNamara period, however, educational supervision by the Bank was weakened by a common range of factors, not least the relatively brief duration of supervisors' "flying visits," their frequent incapacity to take decisions on the spot to generate project improvements, discontinuity of supervising personnel, Bank delays and inflexibility in considering project amendments, a tendency for missions to visit project sites nearest to PIUs, methodological problems in reporting (e.g. findings based on blends of hearsay and observation), and an alarmingly frequent tendency for mission reports to contain exact quotations from previous reports, with dates changed.

A February 1976 Bank study on project supervision in the education sector highlighted the tension between conducting supervision from headquarters and more directly from the field:

> The advantages of conducting supervision from the field are primarily country-related (physical/intellectual proximity to borrowers, faster decisions, greater responsiveness, more open and direct exchange, etc.) whereas the disadvantages are principally Bank-related (lack of adequate knowledge at Headquarters about field-supervised projects, lack of "critical mass," possibility of staff "going native," lack of management supervision . . . professional isolation, reentry problems, etc.).

Needless to say, the centralist argument as phrased here could only prevail. Control appeared as the prime criterion, closely followed by a keen interest in the attitudinal reliability of field staff. Such is the view of the world from Washington.

Although not a part of project lending, the Bank's commitment to educational research grew steadily in the McNamara years, particularly in the second half. In 1975 an internal paper had been jointly prepared by the Education Department and the Development Economics Department which projected six priority issues for Bank investigation:

- the process of learning
- education and employment
- education and rural development
- equity
- cost and finance
- evaluation, planning, and management.

Four criteria were adopted by the Bank in selecting and approving particular studies:

- the importance of the issue to policy-makers;
- possible contribution to new policy options;

- ultimate contribution to improved resource allocation and income distribution;
- probability of acquiring results within a reasonable time and at reasonable cost.

One staffer, actively promoting the research work of the Bank, wrote to Education Department Deputy Mats Hultin on August 12, 1975 with a blistering attack on the 1974 *Education Sector Working Paper* as a guide for policy or project development. His argument was typical of subsequent researchers in the Bank, that detailed investigation was needed on a country-by-country basis in order to arrive at "the relative importance of investments in education" within countries and to determine "which parts of an education system deserve priority" within particular countries. Bank research staff, in fact, frequently echo the concerns of borrowers, as on this occasion:

> One reason ... for a more detailed evaluation of country problems is to ensure that project priorities are kept straight at a country level and to avoid a propensity to impose the Bank's own global priorities in cases where another ordering may be appropriate. For example, while attention needed to be drawn to in the Bank's sector policy paper on equity and rural development, it is probably useful to start cautioning against the risk of uniformity of education projects across regions.... Some of them may represent a diversion of resources from more important uses (with higher payoffs) such as the development of high and middle level manpower. Research which leads to greater specificity in the application of Bank policy would appear to be in order.

Sadly, it was not to be. Despite the enormous increase in Bank educational research commitments, especially in the 1980s, localized research findings tended to be used to construct (or more commonly rationalize and justify) policies for global application. In the McNamara period, most research on education was contracted to universities, two-thirds in developing countries, on such topics as educational finance and income distribution, the cost-effectiveness of alternative teaching technologies, the Coombs and Manzoor survey of rural nonformal education, occupational structures of industries, the economics of educational radio, the retention of literacy among school leavers, textbook availability and quality, and education and farmer productivity. Methodologically, most studies sought to identify correlations of phenomena – in the North American tradition – and few shed light on those causal relationships that had some chance of enhancing policy. Most, perhaps not surprisingly, had to do with economics. About one-third were "desk studies" – reviews of literature, the establishment of analytical approaches – and thus did not involve field work. The more prominent studies were those subsequently published, and in general were the most competent and operationally useful (Coombs with Manzoor 1974; Manzoor and Coombs 1975; Botti *et al.* 1978; Jamison and McAnany 1978).

A major policy issue confronted the Bank's commitment to research from the outset: was research primarily intended to inform one-off country policies and lending operations, or was it intended to accumulate sufficient case-study evidence to enable the Bank credibly to construct policies for global application? The Bank's answer has been, and continues to be, the latter. Yet a Bank paper on research achievements in the late 1970s pointed to a third, middle way, sadly neglected in subsequent research strategies:

> Two exercises which reflect creditably on the research initiative of Bank staff merit attention. The Project Evaluation Methodology study, conducted jointly by [UNESCO's] International Institute for Educational Planning and the Tanzanian Government with financing provided by the Bank . . . has been so far an enthusiastically received effort to discover relevant evaluation methods which can be permanently built into the education systems . . . . The second initiative related to West Africa where, for some years, the Bank has been concerned about feasible alternatives to regular formal primary schooling in the low income Sahel countries. With Bank financing, and under the auspices of the UNESCO Institute of Education in Hamburg, a study was conducted . . . . The strong points in these two approaches were that they (a) addressed a problem area of concern in several countries; (b) involved the countries intimately in the process; (c) had a direct bearing on educational development generally; (d) made maximum use of the international character of the Bank in bringing several countries together; and (e) tapped the resources of appropriate international agencies.

Dissemination of research findings was a low priority in the 1970s. Some staff published work in the Bank's own *Staff Working Paper* series, while a handful of commissioned studies enjoyed commercial publication. A glaring deficiency was evident by the late 1970s: many developing country planners and officials were clearly unaware of the existence and findings of the Bank's research program. An instance was the key group of Kenyan planners and policy formulators who in 1978 were found to be unaware of the Bank's report on the Thias and Carnoy study, *Cost-Benefit Analysis in Education – A Case Study of Kenya* (1972).

The establishment of the Bank's Operations Evaluation Department (OED) in 1975 – organizationally independent of Bank administration and reporting direct to the Executive Directors – enabled the initiation of a concern for evaluation, as opposed to financial auditing and end-use supervision. Its work was of limited use in the remaining McNamara years, in that much of its project-related work amounted to little more than restatements of previously concluded assessments. The major exception was a major review of the education sector as a whole, completed in December 1978, and discussed in the following chapter.

Conclusion

Tables 4.1 to 4.6 indicate the enormous quantitative and qualitative changes in Bank education lending in the McNamara years. Despite dramatic shifts in Bank rhetoric, the poverty focus failed either to address economic and political fundamentals or to enjoy satisfactory educational application. The key to understanding the McNamara period is expanded lending: the larger and busier Bank was more readily a diversifying Bank. For education, its economic purposes and rationale remained intact: contributing to growth through increased worker and farmer productivity. What was new was the expanded arena for pursuing this fundamental objective, ensuring adequate educational coverage of groups previously neglected, not least primary school pupils, the urban poor, rural populations, females, and adult workers. Embracing them provided the McNamara Bank with a reputation for addressing poverty and inequality, but in a manner which avoided any penetrating consideration of their root causes.

Table 4.1 World Bank distribution of education lending, FY 1963–78 (percentages)

	1963–9	1970–4	1975–8
By level			
Primary education	—	5	14
Secondary education	84	50	43
Higher education	12	40	26
Nonformal education	4	5	17
Total	100	100	100
By curricula			
General and diversified	44	42	34
Technical and commercial	25	30	41
Agriculture	19	15	11
Teacher education	12	12	12
Management	—	—	1
Health and population	—	1	1
Total	100	100	100
By outlay			
Construction	69	49	48
Equipment	28	43	39
Technical assistance	3	8	13
Total	100	100	100

Source: World Bank Annual Reports, various years.

Table 4.2 World Bank education financing, by region, FY 1963–79

	Amount ($US m)	Percentage of lending
Africa		
1963–9	89	37
1970–4	240	29
1975–9	380	23
Asia		
1963–9	40	17
1970–4	221	27
1975–9	455	27
Latin America and Caribbean		
1963–9	55	23
1970–4	120	15
1975–9	228	14
Europe, Middle East and North Africa		
1963–9	59	24
1970–4	234	29
1975–9	617	37

Source: World Bank Education Sector.

Table 4.3 Distribution of project investments, by education subsector, FY 1963–76

	Amount ($US m)	Percentage of lending
General education	963.4	42.5
Primary	133.5	5.9
Secondary	460.5	20.3
Non-formal (literacy)	29.6	1.3
Post-secondary	88.5	3.9
Teacher education	251.3	11.1
Vocational education and training	1,150.1	50.8
Secondary	511.1	22.6
Post-secondary	367.4	16.2
Non-formal	248.5	11.0
Teacher education	23.1	1.0
Non-allocated	152.6	6.7
Total project costs	2,266.1	100.0
World Bank share of total project costs	1,580.1	54.5

Source: World Bank Education Sector.

Table 4.4 Number of World Bank education projects and total lent, by region, FY 1963–78

Region	Number of borrowing countries	Number of projects	Amount of lending ($US m)
East Africa	16	39	392.9
West Africa	16	29	255.6
Asia	12	36	561.3
Europe, Middle East, and North Africa	18	33	674.2
Latin America and Caribbean	18	37	360.3
Total	80	174	2,244.3

Source: World Bank Education Sector.

Table 4.5 World Bank distribution of education lending, by region, FY 1977 and 1978

Region		Total lending ($US m)	Number of projects	Average amount ($US m)
East Africa	1977	37.3	3	12.4
	1978	57.7	5	11.5
West Africa	1977	14.8	2	7.4
	1978	23.8	3	77.9
Asia	1977	98.0	5	19.6
	1978	45.7	4	11.4
Europe, Middle East, and North Africa	1977	79.5	3	26.5
	1978	191.0	4	47.8
Latin America and Caribbean	1977	59.0	3	19.6
	1978	33.7	4	8.4
Totals	1977	288.6	16	18.0
	1978	351.9	20	17.6

Source: World Bank Education Sector.

Table 4.6 World Bank distribution of education lending, by per capita Gross National Product, FY 1976–8 (percentages)

	1976	1977	1978
Up to $US 200	23.8	15.6	15.6
$US 200–499	49.6	37.3	16.5
$US 500–999	26.6	36.0	42.1
Over $US 1,000	—	11.1	25.8
Total	100.0	100.0	100.0

Source: World Bank Education Sector.

Notes

Published sources on the McNamara years: The Bank's half-century official history devotes considerable space to the McNamara years (Kapur *et al.* 1997). Of particular significance for the perspectives adopted here are the analyses by Ayres (1983), Hurni (1980), and Van De Laar (1980), particularly in connection with the character of the Bank's poverty focus under McNamara. *Redistribution with Growth* (Chenery *et al.* 1974) was accorded semiofficial status in the Bank as a theoretical assessment of the Bank's poverty focus under McNamara. Robert McNamara's annual addresses to the Bank's Board of Governors are a useful introduction to his policy stances, each being published by the Bank at the time of delivery, and subsequently published as a complete set: *The McNamara Years at the World Bank: Major Policy Addresses of Robert S. McNamara 1968–1981* (World Bank 1981). An interesting but noncritical survey of these addresses was published by the Bank itself (Maddux 1981). See also Clark (1981) and McKitterick (1986) for contrasting assessments of McNamara as President.

Education policy: The major published sources of Bank education policy are *Education Sector Working Paper* (December 1971) and *Education Sector Working Paper* (December 1974). For a critique of the latter, see University of London, Institute of Education *Report of Proceedings of a Workshop Held on 19 May 1975* by Peter Williams. See also Williams (1975) and Ballantine (1976).

Internal Bank policy documents on education: Of particular significance are the reports by Edward Mason (February 15, 1968) and Harold Graves (November 5, 1969), which were followed by the definitive policy memorandum from the President to the Executive Directors, *Lending in Education* (R70-147), dated July 23, 1970. On the 1972 reorganization, see the internal guide for staff, *The World Bank Reorganization: a Preliminary Guide to Changes in Structure, Process, Management Style* (October 1, 1972) prepared by the Organization Planning Department. For later policy changes in education, see the statement to the Executive Directors by Ballantine, *Education Systems in Developing Countries* (SecM73-391) of June 27, 1973. The major operational documents for Bank staff that followed the 1974 *Education Sector Working Paper* were the August 19, 1975 revision of *Guidelines for Education Sector Reviews and Project Identification*, and the November 19, 1975 *Implementation of Education Projects: Guidelines*.

The second half of the 1970s saw numerous assessments of education financing. These include: *Review of the Education Lending Program FY75–79* (April 1975); *Education and Economic Development: A Perspective on Bank Experience* (undated, but late 1975); *Study of Supervision in Education Sector* (February 19, 1976); *Procurement Practice and Problems in Education Projects* (July 9, 1976); and *Report by Education Equipment Task Force* (November 5, 1976).

World Bank Oral History Program: Of particular significance for Chapter 4 were interviews with the following memorialists, all former members of senior Bank management: Hollis Chenery, William Clark, Richard Demuth, Harold Graves, Mahbub Al Haq, Burke Knapp, and Ernest Stern, in addition to the author's interview under the Oral History Program with Duncan Ballantine.

5 From development to reform

Education policies in the 1980s

If the World Bank in the 1970s was confronted by unprecedented opportunity for expansion and diversification, the 1980s and 1990s were years of crisis and adjustment, produced by the economic deterioration of many developing countries, particularly through protracted recession and deepening indebtedness. The Bank as a purveyor of development policies put itself under considerable pressure to formulate alternatives to conventional approaches devised in contexts of sustained growth. The Bank as a lender found itself caught up in the dilemmas of debt, with many of its borrowers proving so uncreditworthy that, yet again, to stay in business the Bank had to discover new avenues of lending. In particular, the presidency of A.W. (Tom) Clausen (1980–6) saw an emergence of program lending, particularly structural adjustment lending, as a means of addressing fundamental long-term weaknesses in borrowing countries, often conceived in the context of shorter-term austerity measures devised by the International Monetary Fund. With time, tension became apparent between short-term austerity measures, and those designed to stimulate immediate and long-term economic growth.

Further, these years saw a new climate of opinion that put under considerable strain the poverty focus ushered in by McNamara. Opinion both within the Bank and that expressed in dominant political circles in major donor countries saw emphasis shift away from international welfarism to ensuring that national economies themselves were on a "sound" footing. New patterns of lending for "structural adjustment" saw a revival of program loans (although for a time strict ceilings were in place) as the Bank sought to exert a policy influence far greater and more intense than is possible through free-standing projects. Yet at the same time, ceilings were placed on program lending, guaranteeing a continuing and central role for conventional project lending.

Early in the decade, it was assumed that education as a sector of lending would figure in the resolution of the dilemmas of debt and recession in only a minor way – education remained on the margins of those radical considerations put forward for economic renewal in the developing world. Further, education's overall share of lending in the 1980s remained modest, and without the emergence of China as a major education borrower, its share would have been small indeed.

The other side of the coin was that structural adjustment had major educational implications for many borrowers, given the high proportion of government expenditures on education. Heavy curtailments could only have a serious impact on the quality and extent of schooling, and this was especially so in the case of basic education. With time, Bank education specialists became increasingly confident that they could make contributions of some significance to the challenges of debt and recession. The second half of the 1980s saw an energetic and partly successful education campaign to advocate within the Bank and among borrowers the economic potential of education – and of basic education in particular – to address the dire economic circumstances facing the world's poorest countries, and the particular threat of rapidly declining educational quality in debt-ridden countries. It amounted to nothing less than a crusade, and the seeds were put in place in the first half of the 1980s.

Policy assessments in education

Towards the end of the McNamara presidency came another seminal year for Bank education policy – 1978. Duncan Ballantine had retired at the end of 1977, and the first half of 1978 saw a flurry of activity as the vacuum left by Ballantine was the object of much internal jockeying for education policy influence in the Bank. His successor, Aklilu Habte, arrived in August 1977 with a keen sense of borrower sentiment and a broad notion of priorities for the Bank's education sector program. Late in 1977, the Operations Evaluation Department had begun a major review of Bank operations in education, under the leadership of the reflective and quietly assertive staffer Ralph Romain, a review which on many issues was to side with borrower perspectives on Bank shortcomings. Also appointed in late 1977 – on Aklilu's initiative and with Vice President Warren Baum's blessing – was a second education review, the External Advisory Panel on Education (EAPE), that served in some measure to head off the OED review. Ironically, it was the External Panel – consisting of persons from outside the Bank – which was the easier for Bank education staff to influence: the OED review was conducted independently of Bank management and reported direct to the Executive Directors, unlike the External Panel which reported to senior management and was heavily dependent on Bank education staff for data and advice. To a large extent, these three elements set the scene for the 1980s, particularly concerning Bank priorities in education and to some extent its style. Not foreseen in 1977, however, was the depth of developing country debt and recession, which demanded of the Bank a boldness and assertiveness which to some extent worked against the sensitivity towards borrower sentiment it was beginning to display at the end of the 1970s.

Internal organizational matters

Bank files from this period clearly reveal intense staff concern about matters of educational staffing and organization. Staff members were keenly attempting to exert influence on Aklilu and the two reviews, thereby seeking to influence future Bank policy and processes in education. One matter had to do with the divide, by that time firmly entrenched, between central policy staff in education and the Regional Divisions with their operational responsibilities. In effect, it was the Division Chiefs for each region (directly responsible for overall Bank lending in a particular region) who were determining how many Bank loans would be made in education and of what kind. There were extreme differences between them in their attitude towards lending in education, an example being the South Asia chief who virtually ignored education. Regional staff complained that their policy colleagues had too little operational or developing country experience, appeared pontifical or arrogant in their communications, and were little more than irritants in loan operations. Some regional staffers failed to see the operational significance of central staff research papers, despite their acknowledged intellectual interest. By contrast, many central policy staff were complaining that too much of their time was being spent in direct operational support, and not enough for exploring policy options, approaches, and techniques. This viewpoint saw their contribution to operations ideally limited to sector work in education (i.e. broad country policy reviews and needs assessments) and to the initial aspects of project generation.

Bank staff were also raising other concerns at this time. All seemed keenly aware of the serious threats to the quality of Bank projects in education, especially problems of project generation and implementation, as outlined in Chapter 4. Also frequently aired in staff memoranda was the issue of how best the Bank might exert policy influence on borrowers, it being generally conceded that the standard practice of unfunded covenants had led nowhere and should be curtailed as far as possible. Two general issues seemed prominent in staff minds: raising the prominence in lending operations of borrower planning and management capacities, and strengthening the Bank's research work in education with a view to influencing both Bank and borrower education policy. Yet even this was organizationally troublesome: central policy staff embodied its own tensions between policy work and research work, each being claimed by its executors to be reflective activity designed to exert influence over lending operations. Policy and research work remained as much divorced from lending operations as they were divorced from each other. How to identify Bank policy positions in education had become a particular challenge for borrowing country officials, for whom the content of policy messages from the Bank depended a good deal upon which messenger was being consulted.

Aklilu Habte became Director of the Bank's central Education Policy Department upon Duncan Ballantine's retirement, and the contrast between the two was telling. Ballantine, a physically strong, tall, assertive man, was of forceful character, not afraid of quarrels in the Bank, especially with the regional Division Chiefs he invariably had offside. Aklilu, by contrast, was a diminutive and quiet man, prone to understatement and patient diplomacy, capable of elevating consultation to an art form, asserting his own convictions skilfully but subtly. Having completed his PhD in educational administration at Ohio State University in 1957 Aklilu returned to Ethiopia, and remained until 1974 at University College (later the Haillie Selassie I University) working his way up from lecturer to university President. This period saw him engaged broadly in international contacts, through both UNESCO and World Bank projects. A period on UNESCO's Executive Board (1968–74) had seen some canvassing for him to become UNESCO Director General, but crucial Organization of African Unity bloc support was skilfully sewn up by Amadou-Mahtar M'Bow of Senegal, then serving as UNESCO's Assistant DG for education. At this time Aklilu had considered becoming head of the UN University, but rather became Ethiopia's Minister for Culture, Sports and Youth Affairs (1974–7). His appointment to the Bank was a personal initiative of McNamara's, the two having met at the Haillie Selassie I University.

Several things stand out in Aklilu's approach to education sector lending. Perhaps of prominence was the matter of style, whereby Aklilu attempted to personify, with his quiet, consultative manner, those characteristics he saw lacking in the Bank. As a former developing country cabinet minister, he also brought a realistic sense of the capacities and limitations of developing countries to participate in the project cycle, Aklilu placing some emphasis on their rights and abilities to formulate their own priorities and objectives, and recognising their general need for Bank assistance in implementing them. As an "outsider," he also brought to the Bank a language that saw economic analysis as a tool rather than as a prescriptor of policy, an approach embedded with a well-articulated humanism:

> The purpose of the Bank – for any of its sectors – is to change people's lives for the better. As a bank we must weight [*sic*] the economic alternatives of how to do this, and for the most part our analyses, by virtue of the nature of the institution, are confined by the concept of what is most economic. But economics itself is an instrument; it is no more and no less than a scientific measure of the options nations have to select from. What they actually want is a wider scope for choice.
>
> (Aklilu 1983: 69–70)

Intimately linked with this desire for informed choice was Aklilu's acceptance of the dilemmas facing developing countries, especially over the best relationship between education for technological change and education for cultural continuity:

> These two purposes of educational investment may not always be congruent; the need to preserve culture sometimes conflicts with the requirement to enhance scientific and analytic capacity. This problem is universal .... But a country's success in meeting either goal uniformly rests upon the degree to which it is able to educate its citizens .... This statement, one

should notice, emphasizes people – what they know, and the freedom they are given to put their knowledge to productive purposes.

(Aklilu 1983: 70)

From this came a well-articulated view on the role and style of international assistance to educational development, with its emphasis upon people as the object and the means of development. "It is not uncommon to even hear that the purpose of a project is to construct such-and-such a facility rather than to change people's lives *through* the construction of this facility. The difference is subtle but critical." Aklilu's stature enabled the Bank to tolerate such rhetoric, which it could too easily have dismissed as more appropriate for a UNESCO Director General, but his appointment by McNamara came at a time when important assessments of Bank lending in education were to point to a need for a Bank less aggressive in its external relations. Aklilu played the part to perfection, if at some cost to the extent to which education was promoted inside the Bank.

OED review of Bank operations in the education sector

In 1975, the Executive Directors had established the Bank's Operations Evaluation Department (OED) which, with its own Vice President and its bureaucratic separation from all other Bank operations, aimed at providing as independent an evaluative arm as was structurally possible. OED reports, for instance, are forwarded direct to the Executive Directors, although Bank staff normally may comment on drafts, with the President able to react to OED findings as Chairman of the Executive Directors. OED evaluations of projects (PPARs) are little more than confirmed project completion reports (PCRs, prepared by Bank operations staff). In particular, PCRs are dominated by concerns about the pace of project disbursements (i.e. the rate at which successive tranches of project monies are released during the life of a project), it being assumed that the more successful projects display a faster rate. For OED, evaluation means little more than auditing, and OED's separation from Bank operations staff renders formative evaluation (designed to improve project quality during the life of a project) as impossible. In time, OED began a richer set of reporting, analysing such issues as project completion rates, problems in procurement, the economic impact of projects – all drawing on lessons learned from many Bank projects. In 1976, the idea was formed to initiate a series of sector performance studies, by which the quality of Bank operations sector by sector would be gauged. It is a sign of education's relative weakness in the Bank's structure, its relative newness, and the impending departure of Ballantine, that education was selected by senior management as the first sector for scrutiny. The report, *Review of Bank Operations in the Education Sector*, went to the Executive Directors in December 1978. By the end of FY 1977, the Bank had approved a total of 154 education projects, at a cost of $1,892 million. The OED sample for the education study was 55 projects, which had provided about 470,000 new places, 250,000 of which were in secondary schools.

The OED study, conducted by a team of eight OED staffers under the independently minded staffer Ralph Romain from Trinidad, focussed squarely on those matters for which the Bank itself could be held responsible – the quality of Bank performance at various points in the project cycle. For this reason, the report's conclusions seem excessively harsh, but two points require noting. First, the study made little attempt to analyze the quality and impact of projects as entities, merely the quality of Bank inputs. It stopped short of assessing borrower inputs, or the influence on projects of factors beyond the reach of both Bank and borrower. Neither borrower lapses nor theoretical inadequacies in the field of educational development were built in as factors shaping the study's conclusions. Second, being the first OED sector evaluation, the study highlighted serious deficiencies in Bank project work subsequently revealed to be common to most if not all other sectors – design flaws, extensive delays at all stages of the project cycle, poor communications with borrowers, and so on. At first reading, the report makes education appear – quite inappropriately – as a particularly troublesome and inefficient sector. In time, OED was to discover that education was no worse a sector than any other, with the clear exception of the unduly protracted start-up phase characteristic of education projects.

Nevertheless, the report was a damning one. The kinds of inadequacy in project work discussed in this book in Chapters 3 and 4 were taken up in some measure in the review. Two major deficiencies were highlighted. First was the "insufficient emphasis on effective borrower participation in identifying and preparing projects." Second was the Bank's insufficient concern to build up borrower capacities "to plan, manage, research and develop their education systems," although it was noted that some of the more recent projects were beginning to address such institution-building matters (World Bank 1978: iv).

The overall findings of the OED review confirm the view that, for an external aid agency, educational lending is not an easy sector in which to operate. Even school construction differs from such other capital infrastructure as power stations given the social and cultural contexts of schooling. The nature of Bank involvement and the time horizon in which results can be realistically sought are equally divergent from other sectors. Movement into "software lending" adds a further complicating factor. The report noted that there are countries in which Bank financing accounts for by far the major part of investment in education, and others in which it is a major provider of external finance. "In either case, its lending for education in absolute terms is not insignificant; since Bank involvement also acts as a catalyst for other external and domestic investment, its potential for influencing development in the sector is considerable" (World Bank 1978: viii).

The report covered the usual ground, that concerning project generation, implementation, and impact. It was most severe at the point of project generation:

> This has been slower than in any other sector of Bank operations, requiring an average of two and one-half years between project identification and loan or credit effectiveness. Attempts to improve the situation have only compounded the weakness.... On occasion, projects have been generated in the absence of an agreed government development strategy, resulting in relatively weak borrower support for project items during implementation. The negotiations process is designed to finally align the Bank and the borrower on project content and conditions; in many of the cases reviewed, this process was not grounded in full prior understanding between the Bank and the borrower.... What the above conclusions reveal is a dilemma central to Bank operations in a peculiarly sensitive sector. The Bank seeks to achieve results. This is a laudable objective but becomes self-defeating if it erodes borrower involvement in project identification and preparation, causes alienation and results in reduced borrower commitment to the project – a complaint frequently voiced by the Bank. A larger Bank role in project generation, especially if repeated over time, discourages the development of local capability and leaves a trail of resentment and frustration of the kind expressed by a large number of borrowers to OED missions in the course of this study.
>
> (World Bank 1978: vi)

Project implementation problems were dominated by time and cost overruns, initial errors in project design, reductions in project scope, and sudden changes in borrower policies or priorities. In some cases, project alterations (usually reductions in scope) were themselves poorly designed. On average, project implementation took seven years instead of the estimated four, with reductions in scope implying an even longer overrun. Delays were primarily attributable to inadequate preparation, borrowers' difficulties with Bank procurement procedures, and to particular country problems of funding, social or political instability, and natural disasters. The procurement of instructional equipment was shown to be deeply problem-ridden. Technical assistance was frequently underutilized; by contrast, fellowship training tended to be fully utilized, with little loss of the personnel trained (World Bank 1978: 33–45).

By far the most important recommendation contained in the OED report was for the Bank to play a less prominent role in designing borrower education systems and, even, borrower projects. Rather, the appropriate role for the Bank was as institution builder, enhancing borrower capacities to develop, manage, research, and evaluate their national education and training systems. "The Bank has always had an interest in institutional development; what is suggested is that this concern be designed, over time, to systematically address the broader needs of the education systems rather than those of the project, and that this concern be moved to the center of the Bank's strategy for educational lending" (World Bank 1978: ix).

In-house staff reaction to the OED review was predictable. Operations staff were outraged. One loan officer, who ten years later was to move into a prominent education policy position in the Bank, wrote to his Division Chief in November 1978: "I find the revised version of the OED report as shocking as the original one. Maybe the wording has been toned down here and there but the report remains unbalanced. It places the blame for the bulk of the implementation problems in education projects directly on Bank staff, who are accused of being insensitive to borrowers' needs and forcing unwanted projects on borrowers." His Division Chief passed the following ambivalent reaction to his superior: "[The report] gives the impression of a generally unsatisfactory lending performance largely because of weaknesses in the Bank. A journalist of even average calibre could launch a devastating attack on Bank policies and procedures with this document as his source of material. On the other hand, it is so detailed, so worldwide in its coverage and filled with so many practical lessons for Bank staff that it should certainly be required reading for new staff members." Another operations staffer objected to the language of the report, citing such phrases as "Bank staff *insisted* on very narrow interpretations of guidelines," "technical assistance experts *being foisted upon* a country," "the Bank's *blind* application of rules," and "*imposition* of the Bank's norms and standards."

The voluminous comments on the report forwarded by operations staff were defensive in tone. In particular, the OED team was criticized for its "uncritical adoption of borrowers' perspectives" and its failure to test borrower misgivings about Bank practices with operational staff. A frequently made point concerned the acute dilemma between designing more comprehensive "education reform" projects serving balanced educational development (the kind of project clearly revealed in the OED report to have protracted start-up and pronounced implementation difficulties) and projects with simpler, more modest objectives, for which borrowers have the appropriate implementation capacities and in which less can go awry. A staff architect wrote: "One of the preventative measures for combatting implementation problems most consistently agreed on by participants at successive Problem Projects Reviews has been a simplification of projects."

Education policy staff, by contrast, had less to lose, in that they were a large step removed from direct operational responsibility. Not surprisingly, they tended to endorse OED's call for more detailed research and policy evaluation work, especially that type capable of enhancing project identification and design. Also, some central policy staff by this time (notably Wadi Haddad) were beginning to assemble evidence in support of their disavowal of "diversified" secondary schooling, questioning the educational and labor-market advantages of a curriculum that combined general education and vocational training at the secondary level. They found OED's confirmation of the diversified curriculum approach puzzling and worthy of detailed investigation. Of particular importance was the keenly understood fact that the review had led to a virtual breakdown of confidence between OED and education staff (both operations and central policy staff). This did not augur well for future evaluation work in education, and Aklilu in particular surmized that the more operationally useful evaluative work would need in future to be undertaken by his central policy staffers.

External Advisory Panel on Education

Unlike its OED counterpart, the External Advisory Panel on Education's report (October 31, 1978) was produced under the direct influence of Bank education sector policy staff, notably Aklilu, notwithstanding the Panel's formal status as a body of experts providing independent advice. The Panel, unlike the OED team, was less concerned with Bank shortcomings as with future policy positions, having been asked to (1) review the current status of education around the world in terms of its impact on development and meeting basic human needs, (2) evaluate the Bank's track record in education lending, sector work, and policy and research, and (3) recommend future Bank operations in the sector (EAPE 1978: 1). In small groups (usually of one or two) Panel members visited seven borrowers – Brazil, Colombia, Indonesia, the Ivory Coast, Mali, the Philippines, and Tanzania, a far more restricted review of operations than undertaken by OED. More prominent were discussions with Bank education staff, UNESCO, UNDP, and major western bilateral aid agencies. The Panel, known in the Bank as the Bell Advisory Panel, comprised David Bell, Chairman (Executive Vice President, Ford Foundation); Mary Jean Bowman (University of Chicago, USA); Paulo Dutra de Castro (Volkswagen do Brazil); Louis Emmerij (Institute of Social Studies, the Netherlands); Lameck Goma (Minister for Education, Zambia); G.L. Monekosso (University of Yaounde, Cameroon); D.P. Singh (Rajendra Agricultural University, India); and Sippanondha Ketudat (National Education Commission, Thailand).

The Panel's report began with a statement on the Bank's role in development, and how that role should accommodate an education sector commitment. In a brief but elegant statement, the Panel qualified the centrality in development strategies of capital investment and technical progress, by deeming capital and technology to be "inert without human knowledge and effort. In this sense, human learning is central to development" (EAPE 1978: 4). Such assertions as this were expected, but in this instance relate more to internal Bank structures and funding priorities than to borrower policy. From its opening page, the Panel was quietly seeking to consolidate within the Bank the status of education and training, its understated manner a good reflection of Aklilu's own style. The Panel had much to say, at first, about training as a component of Bank projects in all sectors, but quickly turned its prime attention to education sector policy, but not before making a fundamental point about the interplay between general education and specific skill training:

> General education is at least as important to development objectives as specific skill training and is, in fact, a necessary complement to the latter. The point can be illustrated by the results of recent research showing a positive three-way relationship among farm productivity, agricultural extension, and primary education: new agricultural technology is adopted more rapidly and effectively among farm populations with at least four years of primary education than among those with less schooling. More broadly...a combination of general education and skill training is necessary to qualify persons to be able to adapt to change and to take part in it usefully.
>
> (EAPE 1978: 5)

The Panel reflected the wisdom of the day in asserting a broader view of development processes than those that focussed on economic growth through increased productivity. Its own range of ancillary concerns included the role of the broad population in development, environmental protection, and enhancement, concern for the buffetings of traditional culture in the course of rapid social change, and the desire of developing countries to secure full status in the international community. It exerted a pronounced concern for education and equity, and put forward a construct that echoed Ballantine's of 1974 and which still remains intact in Bank parlance:

> In the case of education, equity and national economic development goals are to a considerable extent mutually consistent. Two examples command special notice. First, more education in rural areas would serve equity objectives, but it would also contribute to more rapid adoption of improved agricultural methods, the development of rural industries, and higher incomes in rural areas. Second, greater equity would be served by increasing educational access for females. The equity implications of doing so are both direct, in the sharing of education, and indirect, in the potential effects on the position of women in developing societies. National development is also fostered by a better qualified female population – through changes in the nature of labor-force participation and through gains in family welfare, family planning, and the health and capabilities of succeeding generations.
>
> (EAPE 1978: 6)

At the same time, the Panel was at pains to emphasize international variation in how equity might be defined, applied in context, and translated into economic and social programming. For example, "this could mean that a pattern of allocation of education funds that could be seen to be inequitable in an individualistic culture could be seen as equitable in a culture where the social unit is given greater importance." It appealed for the Bank to depart from its customary tendency to seek a single, correct way in its policy formulation and advice. The panel rejected as too simple the view that, in the absence of radical social change, education serves only as an instrument for social control by ruling elites. "On the contrary, we consider that educational activities may be one of the means for modifying a structural situation." Somewhat obliquely, the Panel concluded: "we agree that education will have its most substantial impact in settings in which several interrelated processes or programs fostering social change and economic betterment are simultaneously at work," and that somehow this conclusion should "influence strongly" the education program of the Bank (EAPE 1978: 6–8).

The Panel members were in no doubt that borrower demand for Bank education financing would remain strong. In particular, they were impressed by borrower sentiments which indicated the Bank to be more ready to provide assistance for general primary and secondary education – on a large scale – than bilateral and other international agencies, preferring "an international to a bilateral agency in this field because education is a politically sensitive subject" (EAPE 1978: 9).

Although a continuing Bank role in education seemed assured, the Panel was unambiguous in its view that education "is a difficult field for the Bank to handle successfully, and the Bank's record so far while creditable in our opinion has not been outstanding." First, the Bank had failed to tailor its education program to the requirements of local settings. Second, it had failed to examine critically the actual experiences of developing countries, and had failed to approach the process of designing improvements in education in an evolutionary, step-by-step manner. The Bank had taken too little opportunity to learn from its own experience. Third, the Panel found it both desirable and practicable for the Bank to improve the quality of the analysis it employed in taking educational decisions. It found the Bank to be applying weak analytical constructs to project design and justification, and found few attempts to make cost-effectiveness a fundamental criterion of effectiveness. Cost analysis was "too rarely used in decisions on which projects to support." A significant exception was described, the growth in the Bank of cost-effective analysis of the internal efficiency of experimental programs in education. Fourth, the Panel found clear "incompatibilities" between the traditional style of Bank operations and requirements for an effective education sector commitment. Fifth, the Bank was seen to be in special need of stronger professional competence in education, not all of which could be accommodated in the Bank's profile of full-time staff. The Panel argued for staffing profiles to recognize two very different sets of traits – "on the one hand reflective, research-oriented, emphasizing step-by-step testing and evaluation, and on the other hand brisk, confident, intent on reaching quickly for large-scale operational results."

The Panel was able to identify four embryonic trends which it endorsed for more general application in Bank operations:

- toward projects which are aimed at building human capacities and institutions, with physical facilities playing a smaller – sometimes even a minor – role;
- toward projects which begin with an experimental and developmental stage . . . thought of in two or three phases totalling a decade or more in time;
- toward projects which cannot be divided neatly into "project preparation" and "project execution" phases, but instead by their nature require reassessment and revision during their course;
- toward projects in which the Bank supports, in addition to capital costs, a part of the recurrent costs during an initial period of operation.

(EAPE 1978: 12)

When considering the Bank's priorities for educational lending, the Panel broke new ground for the Bank, in recommending no particular subsectoral emphasis (on primary education, for example, or on technical education). Rather, it saw the formulation of such priorities as a matter for the Bank–borrower dialogue, on a case by case basis, undertaken in the context of explicit Bank objectives for each subsector, notably efficiency, quality, and equity. While this was to be a hallmark of the early Aklilu period, that Bank priorities were those negotiated in each case with individual borrowers, by the end of the 1980s much firmer Bank prescriptions were in place. At the same time, the Panel exerted its view that the Bank should not resile from formulating its own views of educational development:

Here we may comment briefly on the view that borrowing countries ought to have priorities for educational loans but the Bank should not. Although we shall propose later that the Bank should give the highest priority to helping countries strengthen their own capacities to analyze, design, and manage their educational development, we also think that an international agency like the Bank, committed to the optimal use of funds for development and active in a wide variety of national and regional settings, should bring to its negotiations with borrowing countries its own views of the state of education. . . . Having stated our view . . . we would [also] urge that, whatever its general priorities are at a given time, the Bank should always be mindful of the great variation in circumstances among borrowing countries. What in most countries would be the least promising next step to take may be in at least one country the best thing to do.

(EAPE 1978: 14–15)

The Panel was adamant that, should the Bank accept its views of educational development requirements and of appropriate Bank responses to them, the Bank would be badly placed to respond, in terms of its "institutional habits, procedures, organization and staffing." Panel members "felt strongly" that one of the most significant improvements needed in Bank education loans is for the increased application of introductory phases, in order to determine cost factors, adapt curricula, assess staff development requirements, and improve project design prior to large-scale replication. The Panel was damning of the protracted and repeated failure of the Bank in the 1960s and 1970s to learn this lesson.

> What is called for, in our judgment, is sufficient introductory testing and experimentation to provide reasonable assurance that a large-scale second phase is unlikely to result in major mistakes. In our view, in half or more of the projects observed or discussed in our field visits, substantial changes had been introduced too quickly or on too large a scale – changes which in retrospect turned out to have been seriously flawed by mistakes in project design which could have been rectified if smaller, exploratory stages had been introduced as first phases of the project.
>
> (EAPE 1978: 25)

Coupled with this failure was the Bank's propensity to provide finance for large projects only, tempting borrowers to start big simply because the necessary finance was available, and discriminating to an extent against smaller countries incapable of or uninterested in mounting large projects.

Borrower sentiment tapped by the panel frequently criticized the Bank for its concentration on "bricks and mortar" lending in education, although the Panel rightly defended the Bank on the point, given the Bank's accelerating concern with the quality and efficiency of educational processes through the 1970s. Nevertheless, borrowers criticized Bank evaluations as being excessively preoccupied with physical completion and end-use of capital construction components, and as insufficiently oriented towards formative evaluations of projects as they proceeded. The Panel also reported on the "plainly warranted" criticism of borrowers that Bank standards for construction and equipment were too frequently overly elaborate and expensive.

Panel members were surprised that, for an organization committing several hundred million dollars a year to the expansion and improvement of education, the average annual allocation to research was three staff years and $250,000. The Panel was influential in recommending a substantial increase in the Bank's commitment to educational research, and the strengthening of its linkages with Bank policy formulation and lending practice. However, the Panel failed to appreciate the internal and external complexities concerning research. First, it did not understand the internal, structural ambiguities confronting operational, policy, and research processes in the Bank, and how each contributed to lending. Second, should the Bank's researchers even be able to answer the many questions complicating educational development at the time, the Panel assumed that borrowers would fall in line with their findings. The option of strengthening borrower research capacities – to ask as well as answer their own questions – did not seem to occur to the Panel. Rather, it aligned itself with Bank traditions: discarding the tendency of the 1960s and 1970s for the Bank to assume borrower planning and management responsibilities, the Panel nevertheless permitted the Bank to take on for itself borrower responsibilities for policy-oriented research.

Bank files of the day reflect a generally favorable management reaction to the Bell Panel's report and recommendations. Its criticisms of project experience were no surprise, and its moves towards a larger and more systematic Bank education commitment were welcomed by education staff, providing Aklilu with a seemingly independent rationale to back up his own aspirations for the sector. The operational Divisions were most sceptical about Panel attitudes concerning the role of research in the Bank, and its bearings upon their project lending orientation, seeing a confusion of that research best directed at borrower education policy formulation and that directed at improving Bank operations. Further, operational staff revealed their innate scepticism concerning anything that central policy staff would do to enhance their operational effectiveness.

An interesting written response was provided to Aklilu by his predecessor. Duncan Ballantine welcomed the Panel's conclusions despite his not being consulted during its work, reserving his major criticisms for the report's failure to "bite the bullet" on the UNESCO–Bank cooperative arrangements and on the gulf between Bank policy and operations. Ballantine's major comment was perceptive, stemming from the use by the panel of F. Champion Ward of the Ford Foundation as its senior consultant. Ballantine saw Ward projecting onto the Panel's work "Ford Foundation solutions to World Bank problems":

> I agree 100 per cent with its suggestions for moving into large-scale "impact" projects more deliberately and knowingly through pilot efforts, closer rapport with, knowledge of and reliance on the country.... But in the end I think the recommendations are restricted too exclusively to things which prepare for the big thrust (Ford approach) but barely hint at the challenge of the big thrust itself, which for many countries is the essence of the Bank's mission and mandate.

When the Executive Directors discussed the OED and Bell Panel reports at their "education seminar" on April 23, 1979, the discussion was surprisingly low-key given the serious problems laid before them. As usual, many Executive Directors displayed a distinct lack of interest in project-related matters, revealing the view frequently represented on the Board that projects were mere channels for the disbursement of foreign exchange to borrowers. Others opted to react in only a general way, declaring their intention to await the drafting later in 1979 of a new education policy document, the *Education Sector Policy Paper* published in 1980. Executive Directors representing borrowers tended to plead for some expansion of educational financing, but not at the expense of other sectors, and were generally cool about any significant Bank initiative into extensive policy-oriented research should it encroach on borrower independence in loan negotiations. Western EDs tended to reflect the conventional wisdom of the 1960s, placing emphasis on project-related training, technical education, and vocational education. Of the eleven speakers at the seminar, it was the last (representing Australia *et al.*) who summed up senior management aspirations for the sector, firmly defending the Bank's involvement in primary education, and making an eloquent plea for general rather than vocational education at the school level, reminding seminar members "of their choices of educational paths as youths."

1980 Education Sector Policy Paper

The reviews of the OED and Bell teams, coupled with Aklilu's personal style and policy aspirations for the education sector, all combined in their influence on the 1980 *Education Sector Policy Paper* (World Bank 1980a). It is a paper that can only be understood in terms of the evolving institutional character of the Bank, a factor lost sight of in various discussions in the literature (for example, Heyneman 1983). To only a limited extent was the paper a decisive policy prescription driven by an explicit theoretical understanding of educational development and financing. In fact, very few of its contents are of a policy nature at all, much of the paper being a textbook style discussion of the role of education in development. A reader would complete it perhaps better informed about education needs in developing countries, but would lack insight into Bank lending policies, especially as revealed in lending operations. It was not a prescription to drive Bank lending forward with vigor and purpose.

The major reason for this was Aklilu's insistence that the Bank needed to soften its tendency to prescribe the future of education in borrowing countries. Aklilu, highly respected among developing world education ministers, was acutely aware of and sensitive to borrower charges of Bank arrogance and policy dictation. Aklilu's response was to foster a Bank that would respond to borrowers' own formulations of priority. This was reflected well in the paper:

> The educational needs among developing countries are diverse and the policies and strategies depend on local conditions. Such a situation necessitates a continuing dialogue between the Bank and its member countries, as well as greater collaboration between the Bank and professional institutions and experts in the developing countries.... It is hoped that this collaborative relationship will evolve in such a way that the role of the borrower will increase gradually during the project cycle in activities where the leading part has usually been played by the Bank or other

external agencies.... At the same time, the Bank will continue to approach lending for education and training in an experimental posture and with an open mind, and will systematically analyze experiences derived from projects to enrich its dialogue with borrowers and to strengthen the analytical basis for the evolution of its policy of lending to education.

(World Bank 1980a: 97)

Such was a fair summary of Bank aspirations at the time. Nevertheless, it must be emphasized that the conditions and constraints under which the Bank performed its lending functions had not changed. What were new were a milder rhetoric and a genuine desire to avoid the disappointments of the first two decades of project lending in education. In a sense, then, the Bank emerged in 1980 without a comprehensive policy for education. Rather, it announced a general set of principles to guide its relationships and dialogue with borrowers, characterized above all by a shift in style, whose more collaborative tone matched the softness of Aklilu's own personality. This policy vagueness, however, could not last, given the rapidly deteriorating economic situation in much of the developing world – the legacy of deepening debt and recession – whose severity demanded a bold and assertive, even aggressive, Bank response, considered later in this and the following chapter.

The policy paper reinforced many of the principles outlined in its 1974 predecessor, displaying a degree of continuity following the rapid expansion of education systems in the 1960s and 1970s and the "second generational" issues then being identified by many borrowers:

1 Basic education should be provided for all children and adults as soon as the available resources and conditions permit. In the long term, a comprehensive system of formal and nonformal education should be developed at all levels.
2 To increase productivity and promote social equity, efforts should be made to provide education opportunities, without distinction of sex, ethnic background, or social and economic status.
3 Education systems should strive to achieve maximum internal efficiency through the management, allocation, and use of resources available for increasing the quantity and improving the quality of education.
4 Education should be effectively related to work and environment in order to improve, quantitatively and qualitatively, the knowledge and skills necessary for performing economic, social, and other development functions.
5 To satisfy these objectives, developing countries will need to build and maintain their institutional capacities to design, analyze, manage, and evaluate programs for education and training.

(World Bank 1980a: 10)

Each of the five are of fundamental importance to understanding Bank approaches to education since 1980, despite their generality and looseness. Although the 1980s saw a widening economic gap between low-income countries and others, this policy framework remained intact as a general guide, although the deepening recession required a more interventionist Bank by the mid-1980s. Yet Bank interventions came to be shaped to a very considerable extent by them, despite the intention that they be loosely and flexibly applied.

Hints of this tension were revealed when the Executive Directors discussed, at a long meeting, the *Education Sector Policy Paper* on October 23, 1979. Earlier that week, the Nobel Prize in Economic Science had been awarded to Theodore Schultz and Arthur Lewis, and Aklilu shrewdly introduced the paper by paying homage to these pioneers of human capital perspectives on economic growth. It set the tone for a meeting which was possibly the most enthusiastic consideration of education policy conducted by the Executive Directors. Most certainly, none resorted to questioning education as an appropriate sector for Bank activity, and appeared generally aware of the unique issues facing the sector raised in the wake of the frank OED report discussed a year earlier. Their concerns mirrored many expressed by staff in the previous months of preparation, notably the relative lack of prescription and the emphasis on primary education. For example, in June 1979, a meeting of sector staff with the Bank's Policy Review Committee revealed a dominant mood that the paper was too noncommittal, failing to give adequate attention to the potential trade-offs between alternative education strategies, in particular the trade-off between expanding basic education and meeting specific skill requirements. This was a theme explored by the Executive Directors, although only the Canadian and Austrian directors queried the emphasis on primary education. Importantly, strong support for the basic education emphasis was expressed by the United States, United Kingdom, many western Europeans, and all developing country speakers (with notable qualifications aired by India). A major discussion on the Board concerned the organizational implications of country-specific priorities in education sector lending. Directors were concerned that this might imply decentralization of Bank education staff to the country level, which would cut against long-standing and frequently reviewed Bank policy, McNamara concluding by indicating that cultural and national sensitivity in planning Bank lending operations did not necessarily imply extensive use of field offices. McNamara, it can be noted, declared the paper to be "extraordinarily good," the best sector paper produced by the Bank "in the past several years." Perhaps this was a tribute to its blandness.

Although the *Education Sector Policy Paper* was an important means for Aklilu to put his stamp on the Bank's education program, reference needs also to be made to the staffer most closely involved with its drafting and the associated processes of consultation. Wadi Haddad carried this responsibility, and shared with Aklilu much in terms of style and conviction. Prior to his appointment to the Bank in August 1976, Haddad had spent four years as

Director General of the Center for Educational Research and Development in the Ministry of National Education, Lebanon. A graduate in Physics of the American University of Beirut, Haddad proceeded to a Master of Arts degree in Physics and Education from the same institution (1964), gaining his doctorate in Science Education from the University of Wisconsin in 1966, returning to the American University of Beirut as Professor of Science Education (1966–72). Haddad's first period with the Bank (1976–82) saw him serve as a loan officer for education projects in the West Africa division, building up a sceptical research interest in diversified secondary schooling – a major orthodoxy of Bank education strategy in the 1960s and 1970s – as well as assisting Aklilu with the 1980 sector policy paper.

These contributions were important enough, but a second period with the Bank from January 1987 was of far greater significance. In December 1982 Haddad returned to Lebanon to take up appointment as Adviser to the President of Lebanon for national affairs, a highly sensitive and strategic position. A year in the Center for Strategic and International Studies at Georgetown University followed, as did a period in the private sector. The reorganization of the Bank in 1987 led to the abolition and fragmentation of Aklilu's Education and Training Department, Aklilu moving to become the Bank's Special Adviser on Africa. The reorganization saw education effectively down-graded in institutional prominence, with education researchers and training staff scattered throughout the Bank, and education sector policy located within a broad-based Population and Human Resources Department, headed by Ann Hamilton. It was to this Department that Haddad returned in 1987, as chief of its Education and Employment Division, a smaller and more focussed policy analysis and research unit than that led by Aklilu. Yet Haddad had a firm idea of what he wished to achieve in policy terms, and he presided over a crucial series of initiatives that led to Bank President Conable embracing education as a major element in the development process (although lending levels remained relatively low), and to the "education for all" initiative of 1989 and 1990. This constitutes Haddad's major legacy in the Bank, seen structurally in his management of the World Conference on Education For All (Thailand, 1990) convened jointly by UNDP, UNESCO, UNICEF, and the Bank. In the early 1990s, the Bank was poised to increase markedly its lending for basic education, especially primary schooling. The personal commitments to this shift in priority maintained by both Aklilu Habte and Wadi Haddad shaped more than any other factor the educational policy orientation of the Bank in the 1980s and early 1990s. However, this is to anticipate policy developments somewhat, given the critical significance in the years leading up to this new emphasis of the sharp economic deterioration experienced by many borrowers after 1980.

Adjusting to debt and recession

The approaches to education adopted by the Bank later in the 1980s can only be understood in light of the rapidly deteriorating prospects for growth and sustained development seen in many borrower countries, especially in sub-Saharan Africa, South Asia, and Latin America. The Bank's education staff was not able to pursue policy and lending operations independently of the Bank's overall responses to this deterioration. In particular, it needed to ensure that its approach to education was in line with Bank and IMF austerity measures and structural adjustment policies. A widely variable approach was required, sufficiently flexible to address the divergent economic contexts of which education formed only a part. Varying contexts required not only varying answers to their problems, but also a varying set of prior questions. This was an institutional challenge for the Bank, used as it was to formulating viewpoints about education in contexts of sustained growth and designed, by and large, for universal application. Through its research and policy analysis work in the 1980s, the Bank attempted to evoke generalizable approaches to the challenges facing borrowers. As universal policy prescriptions, they could only be useful as they were flexible. Yet the Bank conformed to its traditions, seeking to keep things conceptually streamlined and straightforward in Washington, thereby enhancing its preferred image of boldness and decisiveness in contexts of policy confusion, doubt, and complexity.

Educational stagnation in the 1980s

The Bank's World Development Report 1990 painted a grim picture as it surveyed the poverty-alleviation record of the 1980s. Sub-Saharan Africa saw a sharp drop of 2.2 percent in real per capita GDP, while Latin America also recorded a fall (0.6 percent). Of particular concern was how severely the overall economic decline in these regions impacted upon the poorest segments of the population, which on nearly every indicator was worse off in 1990 than in 1980 and for whom many levels of public expenditure for services had fallen (World Bank 1990e: 7–38).

Pronounced stagnation of educational development was evident in many countries during the 1980s. In low-income countries, the steadily increasing shortfall in finance available for educational investment meant far more than a temporary setback for immediate goals: it seriously jeopardized long-range development prospects. By 1985, the Bank had estimated that over 100 million school-aged children were denied access to school, of whom 30 percent were from sub-Saharan Africa, and of whom 70 percent were from the lowest-income countries. In the same year, enrolment rates in secondary schools in the lowest-income countries were stagnating at about 19 percent, and at 2 percent at the tertiary level. At the primary and secondary levels in particular, a clear majority of nonattenders were girls. Even given the better enrolment rates apparent in middle-income countries, developing countries in general were seeing in the decade a widening gap between their enrolment ratios and those of industrialized countries. Further, the Bank was assembling evidence of comparative lengths of time in attaining completion to a baseline level of acceptable grade five standards: nine years or more in low-income countries

(10 years in Malawi, Bangladesh, Cameroon, and Brazil), compared with 5.4 years in high-income countries. This, according to Bank assessments, provided evidence of alarming problems concerning the internal efficiency of education, where the enrolment growth that had occurred had stretched all available financial, managerial, and professional resources. Public expenditures on education as a percentage of gross national product were 2.9 percent in low-income countries through the decade, compared with 5.1 percent in high-income countries which were spending fifty times more per student than low-income developing countries. In many of the poorest countries, much of the financial burden of education, by default, was being passed to households. Public primary education was only able to proceed in many countries through cash contributions from families for school construction, maintenance, sometimes to supplement teacher salaries, in addition to the traditional costs of fees, materials, transport, uniforms, and foregone labor and income (a fuller analysis is Inter-Agency Commission, WCEFA 1990: 1–31). An internal Bank memorandum summed up the bleak picture:

> In sum, despite the huge expansion in school enrollments throughout the developing world in the sixties and seventies, the outlook for the future of education is bleak. Access to schooling has resulted in a meaningful education for only a minority of children in the developing world. In many low-income countries, repetition and drop-out rates remain high and the number of school-age children out of school is increasing. Furthermore, the levels of learning achievement of those students who eventually graduate are much below those of students in the developed world. Of particular concern is the lag in female schooling ....
>
> The combination of poor quality education and increased demands on parents to contribute to the cost of schooling may well jeopardize the future of public education, particularly in the poorest countries. Both poor and rich parents might consider withdrawing their children from the public schools: low-income parents to put their children to work...and middle-class parents to enroll their children in private schools. [Some reports] indicate that this might be happening...
>
> The inability of education systems in developing countries to educate students to an acceptable level of achievement has limited the contribution of these systems to national economic development, which, in turn, has weakened education's claim on national resources. Many low-income countries must make difficult decisions in light of the changed economic environment to avoid jeopardizing their long-term social and economic development prospects.

Bank analysts became more assertive in their claims of a "convergence of disadvantage," whereby the lowest-income countries were not only poor but displayed a range of structural obstacles to growth, with the result that many failed to achieve positive levels of growth in the 1980s. The Bank projected a doubling in the 1990s of the numbers of out-of-school children of primary age, of whom 60 percent would be girls and 70 percent from the poorest countries. It became insistent that linear rates of enrolment growth in schools would be far from sufficient to address the world crisis in basic education.

New patterns of program lending

More so than at any time since the establishment of the World Bank, the 1980s saw the global economic environment surrounding its work as particularly adverse. Historically low primary commodity prices and reduced export revenue contributed to widespread recession in the developing world, aggravated in many cases by excessively protectionist policies. Prices of imports, by contrast, tended to remain high for developing countries, while the flow of aid and concessionary finance stagnated and even reversed. In broad terms, the deteriorating economic position of many borrowers set the tone of the term of office of Bank President A.W. (Tom) Clausen (1981–6), who reflected at the end of his period at the Bank: "I would hope that the historians would note that [during my term] the Bank moved more into policy dialogue, to broaden it, to have an impact and influence on the economic and social framework of developing countries" (Drattell 1986: 5).

By 1980, it was abundantly clear that many borrowers were in need of wide-ranging domestic policy reforms, especially the kind that addressed deteriorating terms of trade, changing international relative pricing, and marked falls in the real (net) inflow of foreign capital. As outlined in some detail in Chapter 1, the Bank in its relationships with borrowers has always worked to influence the overall efficiency and productivity of the economic environment. It can suggest ways of achieving this in its ongoing "dialogue" with borrowers, and can insist on them in loan negotiations. Yet with its long-range concerns, with the protracted nature of traditional loan generation, and with the demonstrated weakness of loan covenants and other side-conditions, the Bank had relatively weak instruments of policy influence at its disposal, contrary to much popular belief. Stanley Please suggested upon his retirement from the Bank:

> Bank project operations have never been weak on conditionality. On the contrary, it could be argued that they have had too many conditions attached to them. These are conditions spanning the whole spectrum from detailed technical, administrative, and financial issues relating to the project, through sub-sectoral policy and institutional issues, and, finally, broad issues of sectoral and macro policy. Such a range of conditionality dilutes its effectiveness.... Among other reasons, this loss of strength and credibility arises because the Bank loan is made to a project implementing agency [while] ministries and agencies responsible for policy-making are typically not given appropriate representation at any stage of the project cycle.
>
> (Please 1984: 32)

Of much greater potential to effect immediate change were the short-term austerity measures available to the International Monetary Fund, whose impact proved to be generally severe. A major concern of the Bank in the early 1980s was to effect a consistency between short, medium, and long-term policy requirements, which frequently caused the Bank to part company with the Fund in its view of appropriate adjustment policies (Please 1984: 21; see also David 1985: 110–18). The solution for the Bank was to increase the incidence of program lending in the 1980s, lending which addressed an entire economy or sector (e.g. transport, energy, education) in a single loan. Of the several patterns of program lending, the most radical came to be that designed to give effect to fundamental changes ("adjustments") in national economic policy and performance. The World Development Report 1980 summed up this approach, that of lending for "structural adjustment," for which a cautious start was made in the last two years of McNamara's term, but which came into its own under Clausen:

> Although lending for structural adjustment is a new form of Bank assistance, such assistance is a natural evolution in the traditional program assistance that has always been (and continues to be) a part of the Bank's lending operations. Previous program lending, however, has generally been designed to meet the immediate consequences of crises.... As a result, the programs supported were concentrated on measures dealing with immediate difficulties rather than on finding solutions to a country's underlying, long-term structural problems. Structural adjustment lending, on the other hand, envisages the probability of multiyear programs being worked out and supported by a succession of loans. Because such lending will be developed with long-term objectives in mind, it is expected to have more enduring effects than crisis-oriented operations that were characteristic of the Bank's program lending in the past.
>
> (World Bank 1980b: 68)

In essence, structural adjustment lending is aimed at providing, much more quickly than conventional project lending, finance to assist the enhancement of a favorable and sustainable balance-of-payments position. Its overall aim is to increase the production of exportable goods and commodities through improved resource mobilization and improved allocation policies, objectives not easily attained through the sudden and drastic austerity measures popularly associated with the IMF, but more through sustained changes in such areas as trade liberalization, the removal of subsidies, and the introduction of user charges for public services. This last point is of critical importance in education, given the relatively high share of public revenues devoted to education in the poorest countries. Again, universal prescriptions are tempting for the Bank, especially as the initiative for adjustment lending tends to reside with it rather than the borrower. Some evidence points to the early success of structural adjustment policies in (a) middle-income countries and (b) countries whose own capacities for negotiation and policy analysis were adequate. In poorer, weaker countries, notably those of sub-Saharan Africa, structural adjustment lending has tended to focus upon Bank prescriptions, with less variation from country to country than might appear advisable (Cassen *et al*. 1986: 81ff.; for implications for the poverty focus developed under McNamara, see Annis 1986; Demery and Addison 1987; a later and significant assessment is Stiglitz 2002). A particular difficulty for the Bank has been the tension between its long-range concerns and the more immediate policy prescriptions devised by the IMF, subject as the IMF is to repeated charges of applying the universal prescriptions of "devaluation, deflation and deregulation" in a wide variety of settings. Further, with time and the lessons obtained from early structural adjustment lending, it has become clear that the time horizon for effective adjustment policies to take hold needs to be extended, especially if local objectives and experience are to be built into the scheme of things.

By 1985, Bank sector loans had overtaken structural adjustment lending. In FY 1985, thirteen sector adjustment loans took up over 10 percent of total Bank commitments, compared with three structural adjustment loans (for 3 percent of total loan funds, down from the average of 8 percent since 1980). As far as the education sector is concerned, structural adjustment loans were of significance mainly to the extent that they determined the context in which education systems functioned. In particular, IMF and Bank interventions tended to bear heavy implications for public sector activity, both its scope and its extent. Given the reluctance of many military-based governments in borrowing countries to reduce capital and recurrent military expenditures, the vulnerability of public sector social spending is readily apparent. Given the prominence of education in government social sector spending, it is not surprising that education fared particularly badly in many countries in the 1980s, along with public health. Structural adjustment lending, then, can be seen as both a sign of deteriorating conditions working against educational development as well as an instrument which, at least in the short-term, makes educational development extremely difficult to put into effect.

Not all sector lending in education, however, needs to be interpreted in the context of structural adjustment and the implementation of austerity measures. Sector lending in education has had a wider rationale, in line with the recommendations of the OED and Bell reviews in 1978 and as foreshadowed in the 1980 *Education Sector Policy Paper*, whereby the Bank was searching for new ways to exert system-wide policy influence, traditional project lending regarded as being an ineffective means of achieving this. Often, this becomes a matter of degree, lending falling along a continuum with discrete project (or "enclave") activity at one end, and more diffuse, sector-wide activity at the other. Such an approach mirrored the mounting climate of opinion in the Bank that education lending needed to strengthen its impact in precisely this direction. Accordingly, the Bank's staff operational manual for education lending emphasized the potential of sector loans to encompass "the whole investment program of a sector rather than dealing with discrete elements of it," to strengthen "local capabilities to plan and manage sector investment programs," and to focus both Bank and borrower "on key policy issues necessary to achieve sectoral objectives." In this way, the overriding objectives of sector loans are the achievement of policy changes in borrowing countries, accompanied by requisite institutional development to make such changes operational. Unlike conventional projects, Bank sector lending frequently sees the delegation of decisions about the use of loan funds and project supervision to intermediary institutions in borrowing countries, within the context of agreed-upon criteria and procedures. This radical departure from conventional lending was seen as best suited to those borrowers with sufficient local planning and implementation infrastructure to take on themselves some of the Bank's traditional functions in project work. It also had the distinct advantage – in theory – of speeding up disbursements of loan monies.

The first published assessment of Bank experience, prepared by Aklilu's Deputy Richard Johanson, revealed disappointing progress through the medium of education sector loans:

> ESLs have proved to be more complex to develop than standard projects. This complexity shows up in the length of time required to develop ESLs [... which] generally have taken 50–90% longer (though not appreciably more staff time) to develop than their conventional counterparts. This reflects greater borrower participation and the costs of trial and error in a new form of lending. Second, some ESLs have run into implementation difficulties. Each of the ESLs has started slowly. The disbursement profile of ESLs has been disappointing in the first years of implementation.... This is partly attributable to a lack of a sufficient number of approved subprojects ready for implementation at the time of Board approval.... [Some operations] have encountered major administrative problems in implementation.
>
> These experiences raise questions about whether sector lending constitutes an effective and efficient mode of operation for the education sector that can be applied in more than a few highly advanced countries.
>
> (Johanson 1985: 3)

According to Johanson (1985: 12), the determination of borrower eligibility for sector loans hinged upon capacities in five key areas: (1) decision-making power, as vested in a ministry or agency; (2) capacity to implement policy reforms; (3) capacity to undertake major administrative reforms; (4) technical capacity to prepare plans and programs, appraise subprojects, and evaluate performance; and (5) capability to administer the program through auditing, financing, legal procedures, and personnel action.

Ironically, Johanson concluded that the best evidence of a borrower's administrative capability "is successful performance in implementing previous reforms and education projects," again strengthening the argument that sector lending best suited those borrowers least in need of it. "If the minimum capacity does not exist, efforts should be made through traditional investments to build up the capacity" (Johanson 1985: 12). In addition to the disadvantages of long gestation, the Johanson assessment warned the Bank of other potential disadvantages of sector lending. These included a greater risk of fund misallocation "due to loss of immediate control by Bank over allocation decisions," greater Bank involvement in policy matters "which may be regarded as unwanted interference," and less Bank involvement in allocations "which may subject authorities to greater political pressures for subloan funds." Again, such potential hazards reinforced the tendency for future sector lending to concentrate on borrowers with well-developed capacities:

> The administrative capability of the borrower and intermediary chosen is vitally important to the overall success of the operation. The Bank has not analyzed well the institutional capacity of the intermediary in any of the ESLs thus far. Institutional capacity has been defined too narrowly, concentrating on capacity to implement an investment program. Capacity to carry out administrative and policy reforms has been neglected. Moreover, Bank staff lack a systematic set of criteria by which to evaluate institutional capacity.
>
> (Johanson 1985: 22)

This raises the issue of any implicit Bank viewpoint on key matters of educational change and management: the nature of educational policy processes and decision-making in borrower countries, the links between educational management and educational change, and factors pertaining to successful change in education systems. In each, evidence suggests an overly simplistic Bank view. Policy formulation, for example, seems to the Bank to be chiefly a matter of ministerial or official decision-making, divorced from the kind of decision-making required for effective implementation. It is almost as if Bank staff expected borrowing country institutions to resemble the Bank itself, with its hierarchical structure based on clear lines of authority and decision-making.

Very real limits can be identified to the relevance and impact for education in developing countries of Bank financing for structural adjustment and sectoral reform, especially in the short-to-medium term. The borrowers most deeply in economic difficulty proved, through the 1980s, to be those least able to benefit from such patterns of lending. Further, the extent of their indebtedness cast major constraints on the relevance for them of conventional Bank loans and credits. In particular, conventional Bank activity had evolved through periods of sustained economic growth, and the implicit Bank approach to education was one that reflected an ideal perspective on education in such a context. Just as the education specialists in the Bank failed in the McNamara period to design new educational approaches to poverty alleviation, so in the end they failed in the 1980s to adjust to a sufficient extent their theoretical understandings of education and development, grounded as they were in assumptions of an already expanding economy.

Educational renewal in sub-Saharan Africa

Nowhere were the problems of debt and recession more acute than in Africa south of the Sahara. The twenty-nine countries of that region displayed on most indicators a steadily worsening economic and development picture through the 1980s. Low-income Africa was poorer in 1985 than it was in 1960, with falls in per capita output in the 1980s wiping out the gains made in the 1960s and 1970s. In many countries between 1980 and 1985, per capita income fell 10 percent, and up to 30 percent in such countries as Chad, Niger, Togo, and Tanzania. Across the subcontinent, improvements made since independence in health, education, and public infrastructure were in real danger of being eradicated. Investment levels were rapidly falling, to an extent that prevented further development or even the maintenance and rehabilitation of existing capacity. Debt service payments compounded, increasing for the region as a whole between 1980 and 1984 from 18 percent of export earnings to 26 percent, or 38 percent without reschedulings (for a general survey see World Bank 1986a as well as the Bank's annual World Development Reports during this period).

For the first time in its history, the World Bank was witnessing a whole region suffer economic and social retrogression over a generation. For a Bank more used to guiding economic growth, and taking partial credit for it, responding to protracted recession was an institutional challenge. The fact that the Bank's response to this crisis was detailed and deliberate affords the opportunity to examine more deeply the Bank's evolving approaches to poverty alleviation – away from the welfarist emphasis stressing redistribution of investment income under McNamara, towards the overall structural reforms promoted under Clausen.

The Education Department under Aklilu, especially its policy (rather than research) staff, was quick to seize the initiative in promoting the ascendant view of Bank priorities for education. Somewhat skilfully, Aklilu used the African "worst-case" scenario to bolster education sector arguments across the board, arguments that put at a premium basic (especially primary) education, privatization of educational services, rigorous measures of educational efficiency, and pronounced concern for equity in educational access. A team, led by education staffer Peter Moock, published in 1988 a report of no small influence – *Education in Sub-Saharan Africa: Policies for Adjustment, Revitalization, and Expansion* (World Bank 1988) – and in greater consultation with borrowers and other agencies than was customary for the Bank. Because of the seriousness and urgency of the African situation, the report displayed with stark clarity Bank priorities for global education, summing up as it did overall Bank perspectives on educational development, which usually were expressed both subtly in public and forcefully in the relative privacy of loan negotiations.

The report acknowledged the spectacular growth in African education since independence. From 1960 to the mid-1980s, there was a five-fold expansion in educational provision, to about 63 million places, with the primary school gross enrolment ratio rising from 36 percent in 1960 to 75 percent in 1983. Tertiary enrolments rose in that period from 21,000 to 437,000. In a "median" country, adult literacy rose from about 9 percent to 42 percent, while the estimated educational attainment of working age men and women increased from less than half a year to more than three years.

The report's major point was that such advances were now seriously threatened. Population growth, coupled with intense pressure on public sector budgets, combined to jeopardize access to education, its quality, relevance, and cost-effectiveness. The report put forward a policy framework designed for urgent adoption by borrowing countries and the international donor community, and despite the usual caveats about the need for adaptation by country, focussed on three overarching dimensions: adjustment, revitalization, and selective expansion.

The need for education sector and overall structural adjustment was expressed in the context of the Bank's well-developed framework for such policies. At the core of the African problem was declining public sector finance, which fell from $10 billion in 1980 to $8.9 billion in 1983. Adjustment, then, was essentially a process of diversifying sources of finance, achievable through increased cost-sharing in public education and through privatization, the Bank preferring the phrase "increased toleration and encouragement of nongovernmental suppliers of educational services" (World Bank 1988: xi). The difficulty was the overall incapacity of African economies to diversify educational financing along such lines. In particular, the report acknowledged that, for most, "the scope for further cost sharing in primary education is negligible or nonexistent." The major policy initiative of promise, claimed the Bank, was to address the extravagant manner in which most African countries financed higher education students, enabling some shift of public resources to primary education, where it claimed a higher rate of social return:

> In postsecondary education, the immediate priority is to reduce the public costs per student. In sub-Saharan Africa, the annual public cost of higher education amounts to almost $3,000 per student. That is eight times higher than the cost of higher education in Asia and almost double its cost in Latin America. The costs are high for several reasons. Student–teacher ratios are only seven to one, compared with twelve or fifteen to one in Europe and the United States. Non-teaching costs and student subsidies are also high: a recent survey of twenty-four African countries showed that twenty-two provide free tuition, twenty-one cover board and lodging for most students, and sixteen provide additional cash allowances. Governments can reduce these public costs in several ways....

They should institute tuition charges and provide fewer subsidized services and student stipends.

(World Bank 1986a: 30)

In addition, the report saw scope for reducing in all subsectors of education the unit costs of education. It saw as most promising the "better utilization" of teachers, revised construction standards, and reductions in school dropout and repetition rates. In particular, the report criticized the use of large numbers of "ghost" and ancillary teachers, as well as the large numbers of non-teaching staff on education sector payrolls. It explored and endorsed other less palatable options, not least reductions of teacher salary scales, reduction of the minimum entry qualifications required for teaching, and more intensive use of teachers. Reductions in the numbers of university students were seen as viable for most countries in the region (World Bank 1988: 133–6).

The second major policy prescription was less alarming – the restoration of educational quality through "revitalization." This had to do with a renewed focus on such fundamentals of educational provision as academic standards, instructional materials, and the maintenance of equipment and physical plant. In many countries the Bank was critical of unclear and unenforced academic standards, at all educational levels. It prescribed the exposition of explicit and unambiguous curriculum goals, and examination procedures carefully designed to assist teachers and students attain these goals: "by providing signals on performance to which teachers, students, and parents can respond, the examination system is a powerful measurement-cum-incentive device that should be used explicitly for raising academic standards" (World Bank 1988: 138). The report was damning of the extent to which physical plant in African education systems had been allowed to erode, with more and more institutions displaying unusable facilities for lack of water, electricity, functioning equipment, spare parts, and consumable supplies. Recurrent budget support for that plant and equipment in actual working order was seen by the Bank to be fragile, again contributing to deterioration in educational standards.

Third, the Bank called for selective expansion of sub-Saharan education, and placed emphasis on four measures:

- Renewed progress toward the long-term goal of universal primary education should remain a high priority for most African countries. To maintain the high economic and social returns that have accrued to this investment in the past, however, parallel efforts are required to combat the incidence of disease and malnutrition among young children.
- To expand access at the secondary and tertiary level, most countries will need to make greater use of distance education programs. Now is the time to begin planning such programs and developing the correspondence materials, radio programs, examination systems and other support that will be needed.

- Training for those who have entered the labor force must be increased. This training should be designed to ensure that individuals can acquire the necessary job-related skills and renew these skills during their working lifetime in response to changing market conditions.
- Expansion of Africa's capacity to produce its own intellectual talent to fill the highest scientific and technical jobs is a critical matter. Economies of scale are important and these will be difficult to achieve within a national context except, perhaps, in a few of Africa's largest and wealthiest countries. The pressing need is for Africa to develop, probably with the support of the international donor community, regional and sub-regional approaches to expanding research and postgraduate education.

(World Bank 1988: 138–42)

A particular challenge in the context of expansion was the maintenance of educational standards across the board, especially the enhancement of instructional quality, a matter concerning teachers and a range of instructional materials used by them. To some extent, the report argued, a trade-off might be called for between the rate of expansion and the qualitative improvement of education, an issue the Bank acknowledged needed resolution at the country level.

It would be facile to reject the Africa policy paper merely on the grounds that its prescription was one of painful reform. Further, the report made it clear that, in the Bank's view, successful educational reform in sub-Saharan Africa could not proceed independently of comprehensive economic, structural and administrative changes. In fact the report, emanating as it did from a UN Specialized Agency, maintained a polite posture toward national governments excessively dedicated to short-term political advantage and long-term military extravagance. One commentator on the report made this point clear:

Africa's present difficulties are not primarily due to shortages of educated manpower nor, indeed, to deficiencies in educational quality, substantial though these may be. Nor are they overwhelmingly the result of recent natural catastrophes, rising oil prices, or the self-serving interests of the developed world. They are often the consequence of self-defeating policies pursued largely for short-term political reasons. These policies, which have favored existing and largely urban elites at the expense of rural masses, have included inefficient "big push" strategies involving a degree of centralized planning far beyond the capacity of governments to implement them, the maintenance of unrealistic exchange rates, the control of food prices that benefit politically volatile urban minorities rather than the rural majority, and a consistent favoring of the public over a market-driven private sector.

(Foster 1989: 106)

Of particular significance is the extent to which the report promoted the partial transfer of financial responsibility for education to private sources. This, as noted earlier, was in line with Bank education policies across the board, and the Africa report was only one of many vehicles for promoting the policy of privatization. The deep-seated and protracted recession in Africa south of the Sahara was such that the Bank's Africa report presented its policy prescriptions starkly, privatization being a good example. In many other parts of the developing world, private resources would seem to be sufficiently available to make such transfers of financial responsibility feasible, but critics of the report frequently referred to the perceived incapacity of African economies to undertake such transfers. The Bank, perhaps, promoted the policy too vigorously, giving this dimension of the report an air of unreality, perhaps jeopardizing the chances of its other aspects having a successful impact on both policy and practice.

In addition to the Bank and African borrowers, the report was directed at the general range of aid agencies, both multilateral and bilateral, and is evidence of the accelerating view within the Bank (first seen in the McNamara years) that it was in a position to exercise leadership in international development cooperation. Accordingly, several measures are available for assessing, in time, the impact of the report, not least changed national policies for education in the region, shifting patterns of World Bank lending as argued in the report, and its impact on external aid to education in the region. The importance of external aid was a prominent feature of the report, which argued that even the most radical adjustment policies were unlikely to generate the level of resources required for educational revitalization and expansion. External aid was likely, in the Bank's view, to be the determining factor for the pace of reform. Accordingly, the report saw policy reform as the major object of external aid, although its description of avenues was curiously vague:

- seed money to cover both the local and foreign costs of developing policies and improving management;
- ready access to the on-going experience of other countries in formulating and implementing policy reform. Intensive collaboration among countries, so that they share their accumulated experience widely, should pay high dividends as countries grapple with common issues;
- establishment of a source of high-quality, specialized expertise without direct financial or political ties to any government or international donor. African governments could call on this expertise for help in formulating policies and in monitoring, evaluating, and correcting policies as they are implemented.

(summarized from World Bank 1988: xvii)

It is pertinent that UNESCO's parallel report (*Education and Training Policies in Sub-Saharan Africa: Problems, Guidelines and Prospects*) was stronger on this last point, perhaps reflecting that organization's considerably greater experience in promoting international cooperation in education. Being poorly resourced itself, this was a skill it had always needed, unlike the Bank, whose past interest in cooperation was often limited to attempts to coordinate – overbearingly – the work of others. Interestingly, this swiftly began to change once the momentum generated by the Africa report accelerated into a more comprehensive initiative to promote education for all (UNESCO 1987).

For the Bank, a useful measure of the report's impact would be its effect on Bank lending to Africa, south of the Sahara. Within two years of the report's release, an important series of loans and credits – allied to the report's objectives – had been extended to the region. In 1988, $209.2 million was extended by the Bank to Burundi (education sector development, $37.5 million), Cape Verde (primary education upgrading, $5.3 million), Central African Republic (educational rehabilitation and development, $20.7 million), Ethiopia (technical and teacher education, $95.2 million), Guinea Bissau (primary education, $4.7 million), Mozambique (education and manpower development, $17.9 million), and Nigeria (technical education, $27.9 million). The objectives of the report were reflected even more clearly in the 1989 lending pattern, if to a smaller number of countries: Chad (educational rehabilitation, $25.2 million), Mali (education sector consolidation, $56.2 million), Mauritania (education sector restructuring, $37.5 million), and Uganda (primary education, $27.9 million), a total for the year of $146.8 million (World Bank 1990d: 35–6).

The report also served in subsequent years to shape Bank sector studies for the region. Sector work, it has been noted, contributes to the Bank's overall understanding of borrowing country education systems and policies, providing a basis for dialogue with borrowers on education, and making a contribution to identifying possible projects. In FY 1990, for example, six of the twelve Africa sector studies in education were directly related to *Education Policies in Sub-Saharan Africa*, in addition to a range of regional sector studies on such themes as the use of examinations in fourteen countries in the region; science, education, and development in the region; an educational plan of action for the Sahel; and strengthening capacities for human resources development. Each report is a clear reflection of the approach adopted in the parent study.

The content of Bank projects for sub-Saharan Africa has been profoundly shaped by the lines suggested in the report. The percentage of projects involved with increased privatization of education and cost-sharing rose from 33 percent in FY 1980 to 100 percent in FY 1990. Preferred approaches in FY 1990 included reducing subsidies for secondary and tertiary students (67 percent of projects), raising tuition fees (56 percent), and eliciting community resources to defray school construction costs (67 percent). Some 56 percent of projects contained covenants to encourage governments to support private education initiatives, while 33 percent looked to student loan schemes. The decade also saw a marked increase in projects aimed at reducing recurrent costs in education (33 percent in FY 1980 to 78 percent in FY 1990), restoring academic standards (17 to 56 percent), increasing preventive maintenance (17 to 78 percent), and improved management (50 to 100 percent). Also of significance was the declining emphasis on the expansion of secondary and tertiary institutions during the decade (50 to 11 percent), with 78 percent of projects approved in FY 1990 calling for increases at the primary school level. Last, all FY 1990 projects contained support to enhance national policy, planning, management, design, statistical, and evaluative work. Some policies were taken up in projects for the first time in 1990. These included "increasing official tolerance and encouragement" for private education, making students and families more responsible for living expenses, introducing or raising tuition fees, and introducing such alternative methods of financing as student loan schemes. Also appearing in 1990 were measures to increase teacher loads, increasing instructional time, reducing numbers of nonteaching staff, and deleting from civil works programs such low-priority items as student dormitories and sports facilities.

Undoubtedly, the report is a major landmark in the history of African education, especially in the detail concerning the prevailing situation, which had never before been so thoroughly, competently, and starkly documented. This will be a major legacy of the report and those responsible for it. It also powerfully informed the inter-Agency "education for all" initiative and the WCEFA. For the analyst of Bank policies in education, the report's chief interest remains its stark revelation of Bank priorities and the thinking behind them. The devastation facing African education required nothing short of clear policy prescriptions, and the report in effect pushed the Bank towards more direct language and the unambiguous declaration of policy alternatives.

Conclusion

Tables 5.1 to 5.6 present data on Bank education financing for the 1980s along with cumulative figures for the period since FY 1963, which together

Table 5.1 World Bank lending to education as percentage of total external aid to education, 1980–6

	World Bank lending to education ($US m)	Total external aid to education ($US m)	World Bank percentage of total
1980	440.1	4,091.6	16.8
1981	747.9	3,640.2	20.6
1982	526.4	3,537.1	14.9
1983	547.9	3,802.5	14.4
1984	701.9	4,246.8	16.5
1985	936.8	4,125.5	14.9
1986	839.5	4,702.9	20.2

Source: World Bank Education Sector.

Table 5.2 World Bank education financing, by region, FY 1963–89

Region		Amount ($US m)	Overall (1963–89)	Percentage of lending	Average (1963–89)
Africa	1963–9	89		37	
	1970–4	240		29	
	1975–9	380		23	
	1980–4	510		17	
	1985–9	624		15	
			1,843		19
Asia	1963–9	40		17	
	1970–4	221		27	
	1975–9	455		27	
	1980–4	1,504		51	
	1985–9	1,788		44	
			4,058		41
Latin America	1963–9	55		23	
and Caribbean	1970–4	120		15	
	1975–9	228		14	
	1980–4	355		12	
	1985–9	519		13	
			1,277		13
Europe, Middle	1963–9	59		24	
East and	1970–4	234		29	
North Africa	1975–9	617		37	
	1980–4	582		20	
	1985–9	1,113		28	
			2,605		27
Total			9,786		100

Source: World Bank Education Sector.

provide overall quantitative perspectives on the history of Bank lending in the sector.

The challenges presented by the 1980s were, in many ways, new and required fresh and innovative thinking by the Bank. These challenges also pushed into clear perspective many long-standing characteristics of the institution. New patterns of lending, not least program lending – and a growing number of "hybrid" loans combining elements of both project and program lending – gave to the Bank an undeserved air of decisiveness and innovativeness. More important to the Bank than new thinking about development was staying in business, and the 1980s saw a struggle to keep lending volume at acceptable levels. As far as fundamental issues of development policy were concerned, the tensions between the Bank (with its mid- to long-term perspectives on development) and the short-term austerity measures imposed by the IMF

Table 5.3 Distribution of project investments, by education subsector, FY 1963–90 ($US m)

	1963–76	1977–86	1987	1988	1989	1990
General education	963	6,171	341	767	990	1,222
Primary	134	2,580	263	128	509	456
Secondary	461	1,176	26	68	253	163
Non-formal (literacy)	30	48	—	—	—	—
Post-secondary	89	1,615	23	456	61	323
Teacher education	251	752	29	115	167	280
Vocational education and training	1,150	5,220	226	419	408	489
Secondary	511	706	4	1	27	69
Post-secondary	367	2,810	4	45	11	302
Non-formal	249	1,579	217	327	352	45
Teacher education	23	124	1	46	17	73
Non-allocated	153	368	13	77	165	207
Total project costs	2,266	11,759	580	1,263	1,563	1,918
World Bank share of total project costs	1,580	5,869	440	864	964	1,487

Source: World Bank Education Sector.

Table 5.4 World Bank education financing, by broad category, FY 1963–90 (percentages)

	1963–76	1977–86	1987–90
General education	42	53	60
Vocational education	52	44	36
Unallocated	6	3	4
Total	100	100	100

Source: World Bank Education Sector.

failed to result in particularly creative thinking by the Bank. On balance, what eventuated through the 1980s was a Bank that retained its conventional view of the long-term likelihood of development through growth, but which grafted on IMF-like concerns for austerity, adjustment, and reform. Once these latter needs were addressed, assumed the Bank, so could conventional approaches to development resume. In responding to the circumstances and requirements of individual countries (which as a whole displayed considerable diversity) the Bank initially opted merely to adjust the relative emphases it placed on reform versus growth. That was to prove an unsustainable position.

Table 5.5 IBRD/IDA shares of World Bank education financing, FY 1980–90

	1980–4	1985–9	1990
IBRD education loans ($US m)	1,951	2,436	531
IDA education credits ($US m)	1,000	1,608	957
IBRD as % of World Bank total	75	79	73
IDA as % of World Bank total	25	21	27
IBRD as % of education total	66	60	36
IDA as % of education total	34	40	64
IBRD education loans as % of IBRD	3.9	3.5	3.6
IDA education credits as % of IDA	5.9	8.4	17.4
Average IBRD education loan ($US m)	39	55	66
Average IBRD loan all sectors ($US m)	71	78	125
Average IDA education credit ($US m)	22	34	68
Average IDA credit all sectors ($US m)	33	27	45

Source: World Bank Annual Reports, various years.

Table 5.6 World Bank distribution of education financing, by category, FY 1979–90 (percentages)

	1979–83	1984–6	1987–9	1990
Construction	55	44	32	29
Equipment and furniture	29	31	33	37
Technical assistance	7	10	19	23
Other expenditures	9	15	16	11

Source: World Bank Education Sector.

Notes

Prominent among the sources for this chapter are Bank reports, most of which have been published, the trend towards public access to key Bank documents accelerating during the 1980s. Important, however, is the process of debate and drafting within the Bank, and in all cases it was possible to interview those who produced the reports and in many cases read successive versions of their drafts, affording some illumination of Bank thinking behind them. Interviews with Aklilu Habte, George Psacharopoulos, Wadi Haddad, Adrian Verspoor, Ralph Romain, Dean Jamison, Ralph Harbison, Warren Baum, and Sven Burmester were of particular significance for this period.

Major unpublished Bank reports of significance for the period include: *Report of the External Advisory Panel on Education to the World Bank* (October 31, 1978); OED *Review of Bank Operations in the Education Sector* (December 29, 1978); *Verbatim Record of the Executive Directors' Meeting held on 23 October 1979; Education Sector Support Strategy Paper* (September 1980); *Summary Proceedings* of a meeting of representatives of donor agencies to discuss the implications for donors of "Education in Sub-Saharan Africa: Adjustment, Revitalization, and Expansion," Paris, January 25–27, 1988; *African Education and Socioeconomic Indicators* (October 3, 1986).

6 The triumph of educational fundamentalism 1986–95

Throughout the 1980s and into the 1990s, the World Bank's education sector could not remain innocent of the Bank's overall responses to the twin crises of debt and recession. Bank and IMF austerity measures frequently targeted the government sector as that component of national economies most amenable to rapid alterations in policy, within the longer-term context of price reform and the liberalization of markets. For developing countries, IMF and World Bank strategies for economic reform and adjustment were challenging, not only in terms of the austerity measures put forward, but more fundamentally because they raised profound political questions, not least of the relationship between the public and private sectors. With developing countries' education sector budgets accounting for 10 to 30 percent of public sector outlays, the educational implications of austerity measures and reduced public spending were obvious. The Bank's education sector needed to devise ways, in particular, of responding to the educational challenges of declining public budgets for education and IMF and Bank preferences for user charges in the public arena.

Alternative policies for financing education

Aklilu Habte's Education and Training Department could not ignore the imperative to forge an approach to educational policy that took declining government education budgets into account and, more actively, fostered user charges in education. Coming at a time when the Department was publishing increasing numbers of analyses demonstrating the dynamic links between educational expenditures and development, the need was a painful and difficult one for those staffers who firmly believed in education as a factor in development. Aklilu, in particular, needed to muster reserves of political and technical skill to handle the policy dilemma facing his sector. Aklilu's success was to combine these policy imperatives with other educational priorities then emerging on his agenda, not least the push towards primary education, the fostering of equity in education, and the Bank's emerging interest in the efficiency and quality of education. The institutional challenge was to combine all these interests and policy objectives.

The result was a highly influential policy note issued in January 1986, published in expanded but blander form as *Financing Education in Developing Countries: An Exploration of Policy Options* (World Bank 1986b). It is of significance that the published version stopped one step short of being a formal expression of Bank policy, its contents being too controversial to permit it. Nevertheless, the contents of the parent policy note have subsequently been strongly adhered to in loan negotiations, reflected in many loan covenants since 1986, with a strong emphasis on privatization.

The policy note was based on the assumption that education constituted a productive investment. However, with declining governmental capacity to expand or even maintain educational expenditures, underinvestment in education was common, thereby reversing many past achievements gained through the development of education, and jeopardizing future progress. The authors (George Psacharopoulos, Jee-Peng Tan, and Emmanuel Jimenez) proceeded from such an analysis to build a policy that rested on three major assumptions: (1) governments "do not tap the willingness of households to contribute resources directly to education"; (2) "current financing arrangements also result in the misallocation of public spending on education," with heavy subsidization of higher education at the expense of primary education; and (3) "in schools resources are not being used as efficiently as they might be, [a] problem reinforced by the lack of competition between schools." As usual, the Bank assumed that these policy assumptions applied universally, although with variable force, and proposed a uniform package of policy prescriptions, with the usual rider that some country-by-country variation was required. The package contained three elements:

1   recovering the public cost of higher education and reallocating government spending on education towards the level with the highest social returns;
2   developing a credit market for education, together with selective scholarships, especially in higher education;
3   decentralizing the management of public education, and encouraging the expansion of nongovernment and community-supported schools.

The paper was at its most constructive at those points furthest removed from overriding Bank policies. In particular, it put forward a commanding case for assessing the balance of public sector investments in education, and exposed the grossly inequitable support for higher education students in many countries. It was not a difficult argument to put forward, but not an easy one to sell to governments. The proposed plan for phasing-in the paper's recommendations began, in fact, with reductions in living allowances and other benefits for higher education students. Especially in low-income countries, these students could generally be expected to be well-linked to sources of political power, and the Bank may have overstated the inclination of elite groups to give up such aspects of privilege. Yet the report was clear about such difficulties:

> [Its] implementation will not be easy, at least in some countries. There are three main reasons for this difficulty. First, the suggested policies go against a long-established tradition of free education. Second, some of the policies may conflict with a country's political regime – such as encouraging the private sector in a socialist country. Third, the institutional capacity in a country may mean that administering some of the proposed policies, such as launching a student loan scheme, would be very complex.

The second half of the 1980s saw a vigorous attempt by the Bank to encourage what it had described as the first phase of its new financing policy – reducing higher education student allowances, introducing higher education fees, and supporting the establishment of private, community, and church schools. This first phase was designed, advisedly, to release finance for less resourced but developmentally dynamic parts of the education system, notably primary education in lower-income countries, secondary education in the higher-income countries of Asia and Latin America. Of considerable importance for Aklilu was avoiding the indiscriminate use of public sector cuts in education, regardless of their educational consequences. For example, the policy saw as particularly vulnerable those relatively inexpensive contributors to effective teaching and learning as textbooks and classroom materials, items which for political and other reasons are "more susceptible to cuts than, say, spending on teachers' salaries." Yet there were real limits to which the Bank's education specialists could push such an argument. Low-income countries and middle-income countries alike were facing the prospects of severe reductions in educational expenditures, and there was no way for quality to be preserved, given, in particular, the large numbers of teachers being retrenched.

The financing policy, despite Aklilu's best efforts to contain them, embodied all manners of contradictions and distortions. On one level, Aklilu and his colleagues had been attempting to establish a Bank concern with quality in education, especially of teaching and learning. Yet the banking character of the institution forced an emphasis on tangibles, not least textbooks, equipment, and materials, as well as teacher salaries and conditions. These were, in short, the "bankable" aspects of educational quality, those that could be addressed directly by the Bank with the only tangible resource at its disposal – finance. In addressing matters of educational quality, the Bank by default was limited to addressing such variables as these. Yet these were the ones most vulnerable to economic cutbacks, and Bank education policy simultaneously fostered their development and presided over their decline.

A similar difficulty arose with privatization policies. Monitoring the quality and developmental relevance of education provided through private institutions was especially important in those countries least in a position to undertake such monitoring, for reasons to do with the acute financial and managerial constraints facing them at the time. The Bank's education staff would be the first to criticize any trend to private schools that led to resources – whether private or public – being employed inefficiently and ineffectively. The maintenance of quality and of education's developmental potential was paramount to the success of the privatization push, but too many governments lacked the capacity to ensure them. For low-income countries in particular, the Bank's policies of privatization and of quality enhancement in education were incompatible and contradictory. They rested on the elegant assumption that overinvestment in private education was unlikely, given the rationality of families' economic decisions, an assumption clearly disproven by the excessive overcapitalization – and hence wastage – of private education common in Asia. Again, the education sector of the Bank reflected wider divisions in the Bank over the extent to which development was a process that required careful government planning and regulation, or required sufficient deregulation for market forces to hold sway.

The policy assumed much else, that in many instances teachers were being paid salaries "above market levels," and that public education systems failed to be subject to appropriate accountability and systems of financial incentives. It hinted strongly that unit costs in public education were higher than in private education, and that decentralization of educational decision-making was conducive to incentive, competition, and increased quality in education. It assumed, especially for low-income countries, that significant levels of private finance were available for transfer to the education system. It also assumed that privatization, quality, economic relevance, and equity could be relied upon to walk hand in hand, whereas public sector commitments to education were marked by inefficiencies, declining quality, and waste.

The result, in terms of Bank lending for education in the late 1980s and into the 1990s, was a focus on the structural adjustment of education along these lines. Loan conditions – especially covenants – assumed a new urgency and were applied with an intensity not seen for over a decade. In the words of the Bank policy note on financing of education:

> *Policy conditionality.* In countries where Bank lending for education is substantial, it must be ensured that cost-recovery policies in the subsector are consistent with this policy note – and, minimally, that they are implemented in Bank-supported institutions.

It is worthy of note that the published version of the policy note, *Financing Education in Developing Countries*, omitted this last sentence and, indeed, the section to do with the impact of the financing policy on Bank lending operations. The published paper, while exploring the issues more thoroughly and palatably than the internal policy note, made more of the policy as a set of options (World Bank 1986b). What this implied was that the universal threefold prescription for educational financing reform could be flexibly applied.

By contrast, the internal policy note sought to ensure that loans contained as little room as possible for governments to deviate. The options, as far as Bank lending and conditionality were concerned, were answers.

The policy paper caused a degree of controversy and difficulty within the Bank, but not so much in terms of its broad objectives (determined as they were by overriding Bank strategies for public sector rationalization and privatization). The regional operations (lending) Divisions were more concerned with how the principles might be best applied in those countries under their aegis. The West Africa Division Chief argued, for example, against an immediate transfer of savings from higher education to primary education:

> ... redistribution of education costs and benefits is politically sensitive in any country, even more so in West Africa where it represents a source of political vulnerability for tremulous governments.... We are not advocating ... a reallocation of budgetary funds from higher education to primary education. Rather, we think we are realists in recognizing that this strategy can only be implemented over time by freezing or slowing the growth of the budget allocations to post-secondary education.

The policy paper had used Mali as an example where there was considerable scope to increase cost-recovery in primary education, by raising fees already in place and encouraging user charges for equipment and books. Again, the West Africa Division Chief took issue with the paper, indicating the general incapacity of families to share a larger financial burden in education, especially in the rural areas of Mali. It is not as important to determine which perspective was right as to appreciate the divisions within the Bank on the issue. The acting Chief of the East Asia and Pacific Division pulled no punches in responding to the policy note:

> The major problem with the paper from the analytical perspective is the organization of [its] arguments. The policy options are user charges, subsidies, control of entry, and loan schemes. Each has its advantages and disadvantages which makes it useful to recommend a balanced package rather than a simple piecemeal approach. User charges, and their mirror images, subsidies, can be used to both get the level of investment in education right and to encourage internal efficiency....
>
> The issue of privatization is not as clearly analyzed.... The presumption is made that the lack of privately-funded education is generally the result of controls on the provision of education by the private sector. It seems at least as likely that the provision of free public education simply spoils a good part of the market for private education.... There needs to be more discussion of the drawbacks or problems arising from subsidization of private education. What factors must be considered to determine the appropriate degree of subsidization of private education rather than the expansion of public education? Secondly, there needs to be more

realism about whether the availability of private education will improve the efficiency of public education. Availability of private schools in fact may reduce the pressure of public schools to provide higher quality education and may also release pressure to improve internal efficiency.... Other incentive schemes for improving internal efficiency in public primary education are not discussed. Third, there seems to be too little attention given to the possibility that private education will increase inequities in the provision of education.

The extent of controversy within the Bank over educational financing policies should not be overstated. There was general institution-wide agreement over the broad goals projected and their relationship with Bank and IMF strategies for structural adjustment and reform. Differences surfaced over their precise application within borrowing countries, and here the various regional lending Divisions had room to manoeuvre. Nevertheless, fewer and fewer Bank loans by the end of the 1980s were free of the obligations imposed by loan conditionality to promote the privatization of education through the building up of systems of private institutions and the expansion of user charges in the public sector. Bank-promoted subsidization of private schools increased to disastrous points when it was in clear danger of jeopardizing public commitments to educational quality, in both public and private institutions.

The research–policy nexus

A major outcome of the operational reviews at the end of the 1970s, seen very clearly in the 1980 *Education Sector Policy Paper*, was a more explicit concern with educational research. In terms of its declared policy, this pushed the Bank in two directions – building up its own research capacities in education, and providing assistance to borrowers to do the same. At no point was any intention expressed for the Bank to take on for itself the kind of policy-driven research best left to governments and national institutions – such a possibility was contrary to the principles espoused by Aklilu. Yet this is precisely what occurred. The 1980s saw the development of a sizeable, energetic, and intelligent if not wise research team, whose work (by default if not by design) was used by the Bank as an alternative to building up local research capacities, and whose findings were imposed uncompromisingly by the Bank in later years, especially on low-income borrowers. To be sure, some collaborative work was done with researchers from borrowing countries, but the emphasis throughout was on the generation of research findings from a small number of settings applied on an enormously wider scale. Further, the very topics and themes of educational research reflected a Bank-wide agenda, for example, the studies of educational financing and privatization designed in the context of wider Bank policies to promote user charges for public services. The Bank as a whole, and the education researchers in particular, failed in the task of strengthening national research capabilities, especially those of the kind able to inform and enhance local decision-making about educational policies and priorities.

It would be possible to devote a book to analyzing Bank research in education between 1980 and 1995. It was a major and well-funded commitment, especially prior to the Bank reorganization of 1987, with findings widely disseminated in Bank publications and in the academic literature. The World Bank undoubtedly emerged as a major contributor to research into educational development. Its commitment and achievements receive undeservedly short shrift here, where the intention merely is to locate the period's research effort in the general history traversed in this book. It should be remembered that Bank research staff were free of operational responsibility for projects, were free of education sector investigative work, were located in an institution in which data literally poured in from borrowing countries, worked in a well-financed and well-equipped environment, and enjoyed the benefits of an in-house publication's capacity. Unlike their friends in academe, Bank researchers were free of teaching and supervision responsibilities. It should not be a cause of comment that they were so productive. Rather, it is worthy of comment that more of higher quality and deeper insight was not forthcoming. To anticipate subsequent developments, it is noteworthy that after 1995 Bank research and analytical work in education fell into rapid decline. Partly responsible was yet another internal reorganization, in 1995. More importantly, the Bank's reform agenda in education were securely in place, there being little internal need to generate additional research findings to justify its policy stances. Highly experienced and by now senior Bank researchers were transferred to other parts of the Bank, the smaller number of replacements being relatively inexperienced researchers with little capacity to influence either Bank or borrower behavior.

As noted in the previous chapter, the reviews of the education sector at the end of the 1970s had been critical of the Bank's research program in education. The OED review had found the program to be "underfinanced, unfocused, substantially isolated from Borrowers and not directly tied into the Bank's operational work," while the Bell Panel concluded that "the Bank's record is weak... [and] for an organization committing several hundred million dollars a year [to education]...the scale is clearly inadequate."

One option for the Bank was to intensify the role of research as a component of project lending, and in December 1982 Jee-Peng Tan completed a review of research components in education projects. Although his findings were predictable, and although Tan had no stake in seeing the Bank's research orientation swing towards projects as the focus of effort, the review highlighted the acute vulnerability of research as a component of projects. The traditional shortcomings of Bank education projects combined to work against the integrity and quality of research that was dependent upon the smooth and predictable implementation of projects. Tan found that only half of the research components of Bank projects had been attempted or completed. Tracer studies in particular were vulnerable, with only eleven studies completed from an approved and funded total of seventy-two. Of all research studies completed in English, Tan could identify only four he could regard as meeting "at least a minimum standard of quality." One further finding is worthy of reproduction, highlighting as it does something of broader significance about the World Bank:

> To assess the actual within-Bank availability and accessibility of results from project-related studies we requested staff in the [Bank's] regional Information Centers and Record Center to search for documents which were listed as "available in files." The search was only partially successful. For example, in the Latin America and Caribbean Region, 20 documents were searched for, but none could be located.... Although the missing documents could possibly be miscatalogued, the fact that professional staff at the centers could not find them indicate [*sic*] that once research documents are "sent to files" it is usually hard to retrieve them again.

It is not surprising, then, that the Bank dispensed with the option of intensifying its research work in education at the project level. Yet if the alternative was the establishment and/or strengthening of existing policy and analysis groups within the Bank, the problem remained: where? As described at various points in preceding chapters, the gulf between Bank operations staff and policy staff has always been both wide and untrusting, revealed best perhaps in the reactions to the OED review. The answer came in 1982, when a limited-scale Bank reorganization resulted in the creation of the Operations Policy Staff (OPS), into which was located the Bank's Education Department under Aklilu. Departments in OPS were to provide support to the Regional Divisions undertaking Bank projects, but did not have responsibility for them. Accordingly, OPS staff "assisted" with sector analyses in education, project identification, monitoring, and impact assessments, all designed to influence – above all – the general shape and character of Bank lending rather than its immediate detail. Thus in August 1981 was created a five-person Research Unit, soon to be located within the OPS Education Department. Although there were several other places within the Bank where educational research would continue to be conducted (usually by individuals rather than teams), here was the unit responsible for the overall commitment, charged with exerting an influence on Bank operations in education as a whole.

A troublesome legacy persisted, nevertheless, in that the gulf between Bank operations and "reflection" was not bridged. More than that, the Education Department under Aklilu now had two parts – policy and research. The distinction was far from absolute, the policy analysts claiming that they too were engaged in research, even if their links with operations were somewhat stronger.

Thus the overall institutional picture of how the Bank came to put into place its education policies for lending had become particularly complex by 1982. First, the education sector as a whole could not be innocent of the overall character of the Bank, especially the tensions built into the scheme of things between the Bank as a financial institution and as a development assistance agency. Second, there persisted the divide between operational expediency and policy reflection, loan officers in the Regional Divisions being acutely aware that their careers in the Bank depended a good deal on their success in high volume lending and quick project disbursements – they did not want their personal success jeopardized by troublesome or irritating research findings. Third, there were ambiguities within the Education Department over how Bank lending operations might be supported through research and policy analysis; in addition, there were the complexities within the Department as to how separate units for policy and research might relate. Fourth, there persisted the issue of Bank–borrower relationships, and how research might play a role in ongoing dialogue over long-term borrower policies for development as well as in individual loan negotiations. Last, there was the issue of how the Bank's multifaceted research work could relate to policy development undertaken elsewhere in the international community and development assistance industry, and to educational research conducted around the world in universities and other specialized institutions.

Given the complexities that surrounded, if not engulfed, the Bank's research work in education, what was required in organizational terms was decisive research leadership which displayed clear objectives, an explicit theoretical and methodological approach, a precise articulation of the policy objectives driving research commitments forward, and a capacity to focus on a few, important priority matters. Otherwise, as before, effort would be drowned in a sea of institutional and bureaucratic verbiage.

It was George Psacharopoulos, appointed to head the Education Department's Research Unit established in August 1981, who gave the Bank's research effort in education precisely the organizational characteristics required. It would be facile to criticize Psacharopoulos' research leadership as too focussed, too bound to Bank requirements, insufficiently open-ended and insufficiently free-ranging, as it would be to criticize the highly repetitive nature of his publications (an *apologia* is Psacharopoulos 2006). The Bank is uninterested, as are all operational organizations with precise mandates, in curiosity research. Research needs to be driven by operational requirements and must reflect organizational values, aspirations, and objectives. What becomes an issue is when researchers working in such contexts deny the institutional parameters that shape and dictate their work, and claim their research to be objective, untrammelled by institutional requirements. Some of Psacharopoulos' staff, interviewed for this book on precisely this point, have displayed an astonishing and unpardonable ignorance of the history of the Bank, its character as a lending institution, and the boundaries that define the limits to Bank policies and research. It is one thing to wittingly conduct research in such a prescribed context (and the Bank pays its researchers well). It is another thing for intelligent and educated persons to remain blind to the institutional dynamics that determine the character of their daily professional work, and to remain persistently indifferent to its wider meaning.

George Psacharopoulos brought to the Bank – or at least developed within it – the sharp focus in educational research that was organizationally necessary for research to have some influence on the character and quality of its lending.

He was also committed to the kind of research that would influence educational policies and priorities in borrowing countries. These twin objectives were closely linked in Psacharopoulos' mind, in that exerting a policy influence on the Bank by way of a prior influence on borrower sentiments was a realistic sequence for him. Coming to the Bank from the London School of Economics and Political Science, Psacharopoulos was perhaps the leading academic figure in championing cost-benefit and rate-of-return analysis of education. For him, cost-benefit analysis was far from a dry academic exercise. It had, he argued incessantly, profound policy implications, given his view of the disastrous planning errors and wasted expenditures occurring as a result of "fanciful" manpower planning in the 1960s and 1970s (see Psacharopoulos 1973, 1981, 1985b; on his time at the Bank see Psacharopoulos 2006). Soon after his arrival, he energetically circularized all education staff on the technical and political advantages of cost-benefit analysis, explaining how it could be simply (if not simplistically) undertaken in appraising education projects.

Psacharopoulos tackled head-on such proponents within the Bank of manpower forecasting as Manuel Zymelman, whose institutional influence seemed to evaporate soon afterwards, despite the production of some extended analyses (Zymelman 1977, 1980). Yet Psacharopoulos brought to the Bank not only a clearly defined methodological orientation and a strong commitment (shared by most other staff, in fact) to human capital theory, he was also able to devise a research program which both reflected policy concerns exercising the Bank as a whole, and which concentrated education research on a few policy matters deemed to be of key significance, reflected in his all too tidy reduction in 1987 of critical issues in world education to five (Psacharopoulos 1987; see also his somewhat tongue-in-cheek view of educational policy issues in Psacharopoulos 1990). By 1990, Psacharopoulos' threefold research agenda for the Bank had borne fruit, clearly evidenced in Bank bibliographies of educational research publications (e.g. Kollodge and Horn 1986; Copple 1990).

First, Psacharopoulos identified the "efficiency issue" as a priority area for Bank education research, highlighting both internal and external efficiency matters, not least such within-school events as: student repetition and dropout; relative costs of alternative teaching methods; determinants of learning achievement; and integration of school leavers and graduates into the labor market. In this context, he identified a range of priority research areas, including: cost-benefit analysis of different types of curricula (in post-compulsory schooling); cost-effectiveness analysis of alternative teaching methods; the economic role of the educated in the nonwage, informal sector of the economy; and cost-benefit analysis of school quality improvements.

Second, Psacharopoulos reflected a dominant Bank-wide concern in identifying finance and cost-recovery in education as a research priority, conceived partly in a context of Bank-driven pressures on borrowers to investigate user charges for public services. Here was devised research on documenting discrepancies between private and social benefit-cost ratios; estimates of the price elasticities of the private demand for education; assessments of parental willingness to pay for education; and the feasibility of student loan schemes.

Third was the matter of equity, which Psacharopoulos deemed "notoriously difficult to research," starting from the separation of "normative from positive" elements. Here were pursued three questions: access to particular school types related to the students' sex, socioeconomic background, and regional characteristics; poverty alleviation and income distribution effects of educational provision; and documentation of possible trade-offs between equity and efficiency of given educational policies.

By the time of the major reorganization of the Bank in 1987, when the Education Department's Research Division was disassembled (some researchers staying in a central Education and Employment Division, others like Psacharopoulos joining regional Bank operational Divisions, resulting in a marked institutional fragmentation of the research capacity Psacharopoulos had built up) Psacharopoulos had assembled a group of researchers who by that time had completed projects in the following broad areas:

- linkages between education and development
- pricing in the social sectors
- financing education: privatization and cost-recovery issues
- education and self-employment
- the quality of education
- the economics of vocational training
- vocational versus general education
- participation in education
- determinants of student achievement
- aspects of female education
- improving the quality of educational management
- the quantity–quality trade-off in education.

There can be no doubt as to the quality of much of the Bank's research output in the 1980s, evidenced by the number of articles by Bank staff gaining acceptance in leading academic journals. What is open to question, however, are three matters. One concerns the frequent tendency – again displayed by Bank researchers interviewed on this point – to feel the need themselves to shoulder developing country research burdens. Bank education researchers display little solidarity with building up research capabilities in developing countries, despite their engagement of research collaborators from borrowing countries. This is intimately bound up with a second issue, the tendency for Bank research to find application in a very wide variety of contexts, despite its derivation from one or two. A great deal of global significance is frequently made of evidence from just one country, or a few. Disclaimers about careless application of findings abound, naturally enough, but the overall picture remains one of research findings reinforcing the traditional Bank tendency to find prescriptions for universal application, denying that diversity which policy-makers should both recognize and promote in educational settings. Third is the profound lack of interest by the Bank's researchers in education in anything except a "North American" approach to research. With the major exception of Psacharopoulos himself, the 1980s research team consisted almost exclusively of US citizens. They were not interested in a more universal approach to educational research, and when they did look abroad for collaborators it was usually to Psacharopoulos' former base at the London School of Economics and Political Science. What this meant, in practical terms, was an almost exclusive interest in quantified correlational studies (not least cost-benefit analysis) as means of understanding educational phenomena. Such studies might have thrown up evidence of phenomena existing side by side, but were spectacularly unhelpful in giving depth to the process issues (e.g. student and parental motivation, quality of teaching and learning, barriers to equity, the interaction between education and culture) so central to a true understanding of education. If anything, the cultural style of its research in education reinforced the Bank's tendency to pontificate on educational policy in grandiose, assertive but simplistic terms, partly because the style of research almost exclusively employed was incapable of reinforcing any approach that was more subtle in character. The omniscient Bank has tended to be a simplistic Bank.

It was the reorganization of Bank structure in 1987 that dealt a severe blow to the focus and intensity of Bank research into educational development. That reorganization saw the institutional downgrading and fragmentation of the education sector as a whole. Aklilu's Education and Training Department was abolished, with a small policy analysis and research Education and Employment Division under Wadi Haddad replacing it, as part of a larger, more diffuse Population and Human Resources Department under Ann Hamilton. Most specialist researchers, not least Psacharopoulos, were assigned to the regional operations Divisions, their research intended to play a more direct role than perceived hitherto in influencing lending. Structurally and in theory, the new arrangements presented some possibilities for integrating the Bank's broad human resources strategies. In reality, the various sectors related to human resources (health, population, employment, education) appeared, from 1987, to be rather isolated, with education itself emerging as a highly fragmented sector. Any critical mass it enjoyed under Ballantine and Aklilu was gone, with a general dispersal of many experienced education staff and a lower "education dynamic" in the Bank, except perhaps with the Bank's preparations for the WCEFA in 1989 and 1990.

At the same time, it is important that the policy influence, creativity, depth of insight, and quality of Bank research in education not be overstated. In particular, the period 1980–95 saw a research effort that reflected prior policy decisions rather than anticipating them. Psacharopoulos' major contribution was to provide justifications for policy stances taken on less-informed and perhaps more pragmatic grounds. Such a research strategy could only impose limits on the extent to which Bank research over this period was driven by the desire to explore the unknown. Most research projects, by contrast, were set up with the desired findings already firmly in sight. Bank research findings in education do not explain why the Bank adopted certain policies; rather, they serve as signposts to policies previously put in place on other grounds.

The basics of policy reform

This period of World Bank education policy formation had seen considerable institutional successes on the part of Aklilu, Haddad, and Psacharopoulos. Together they had embarked on nothing less than a crusade to drive the Bank's education sector work. Frequently at odds with the Regional Divisions responsible for loan negotiations with borrowers, they nevertheless ensured that there was never any ambiguity about the Bank's preferred policies for educational reform. Also of priority was the need to take the crusade well beyond the Bank itself, to convince borrowers, aid agencies, and other relevant constituencies of their policy package.

The collapse of the Soviet Union in 1989 and the establishment of a large number of new independent republics brought to the World Bank opportunity to address economic and social policy on a truly global scale. For the Bank, only the OECD membership and a handful of oil-rich states now lay outside its lending aspirations. Decisions to set up in 1991 a London-based European Bank for Reconstruction and Development were only an initial setback for a Bank determined to gain universal recognition for global leadership and relevance. Yet the Bank, with two dozen new "transition" economies to assist, needed to consider the extent to which its 1980s crisis rhetoric and prescriptions – designed with sub-Saharan Africa and Latin America chiefly in mind – could resonate for the large group of new borrowers in Eastern and Central Europe and Central Asia. Despite the time-honored lip-service to country-by-country flexibility and variation, the Bank celebrated the end of the Cold War not in terms of encouraging further diversity but rather by making explicit its adherence to a "one size fits all" prescription for economic policy and management. Although in a sense nothing fundamental had changed, the new global circumstances forced the Bank to make clear its agenda for economic globalization, the integration of national economies into a single economy operating according to the principles of free-market capitalism. Thus in the five years from 1990 the Bank, in addressing for its new members the transition from socialism to capitalism and in comprehensively addressing more generally global economic futures, evoked nothing other than the principles espoused so forcefully through the 1980s crisis years of debt and recession. Its prescriptions for reform were precisely those for the establishment of a globalized world economy.

Of special significance was the way in which the Bank sought to influence the World Conference on Education for All (WCEFA), held in March 1990 in Jomtien (Thailand). At the time of the Bank reorganization of 1987, when

Wadi Haddad assumed leadership of the Education and Employment Division, considerable pressures were accumulating to the extent that Bank equity commitments were in jeopardy. Structural reform and adjustment, moves in favor of privatization and user charges, declining prospects for public sector expansion in education, and increasing concerns for efficiency were all combining to push equity concerns to the background. Ominously for the Bank, education sector lending was in danger of a sustained decline. FY 1987, for instance, had seen a mere 2.5 percent of Bank lending allocated to education projects, down sharply from the 4.5 percent average for FY 1979–86 (see Table 6.1). Only 1.2 percent of IBRD funds of that year were for education, about one-third of previous levels.

This pattern of stagnation in lending levels was only a symptom of a more general malaise confronting educational development, and national governments across the developing world needed no reminding of the impact of debt and recession on the public provision of education. Aid agencies generally were acutely aware of that impact, but there was little evidence of fresh thinking about the future. Generally speaking, governments and aid agencies reflected the view that economic growth would resume in time, and that with it would come a return to historic levels of public support for education. This, of course, was a view flatly rejected by the Bank, wanting to make explicit its conviction that its prescriptions for structural adjustment were no mere temporary measures but rather a permanent framework for global economic and social policy.

Education for all and the WCEFA

Concerns about educational stagnation were mounting elsewhere in the UN system. It will be recalled that the United Nation's lead agency in education, UNESCO, was in deep crisis through the second half of the 1980s, reflected

Table 6.1 World Bank education financing, FY 1980–90

	$US m	Percentage of Bank lending
1980–4	2,951	4.4
1985–9	4,044	4.5
1985	937	6.5
1986	840	5.1
1987	440	2.5
1988	864	4.5
1989	964	4.5
1990	1,487	7.3

Source: World Bank Education Sector.

in the departure of the United States and United Kingdom, reducing not only its claims to universality, legitimacy, and leadership, but also its operational budget. For the World Bank, the UNESCO crisis was a convenient context in which to wind up its working relationships with the organization, and to promote the Bank's own self-image as the global pacesetter in educational development. However, another agency was in the wings, UNICEF, the United Nations Children's Fund, one of the United Nation's "funds and programs" responsible to the General Assembly through the Economic and Social Council. UNICEF staffers of the day recall UNICEF's Executive Director Jim Grant being given something of a green light by UN Secretary General Javier Pérez de Cuéllar to address the gap in UN educational leadership arising from the UNESCO crisis. At several points during the 1980s, Grant had been in touch with UNESCO Director General Amadou-Mahtar M'Bow about increasing global support for educational development, apparently without tangible success. Grant turned his thinking, rather, to a kind of educational offensive along the lines of UNICEF's "health for all" initiative, dominated in several key respects by a mass child immunization campaign in the late 1980s for which Grant had successfully mobilized considerable political and financial support. In short, Grant had adopted the position that a similar global effort in education could halt the prevailing educational decline, especially in the poorest countries (for accounts see Jones 2005; Chabbott 2003).

Grant's achievement was to secure widespread political support for a global campaign to promote basic education for all. The eventuating WCEFA was a massive affair, the tip of the organizational iceberg being the five principal sponsoring agencies, all drawn from the United Nations. Of these, two had come in as sponsors relatively late in the day and had little impact on developments – the United Nations Development Program (UNDP) and the UN Fund for Population Activities (UNFPA). The major players were UNESCO, UNICEF, and the World Bank, and the three vied energetically for political and policy dominance in the preparations, conduct, and aftermath of the WCEFA. This competitiveness was important, in that the Conference ended up involving most national governments, the full spectrum of bilateral and multilateral agencies involved in education, and a carefully managed but influential range of non-governmental organizations working in education.

Where Grant had been successful was his convincing of the other UN agency heads to cosponsor the Jomtien conference and thus to align themselves with his vision for a global campaign for basic education for all. UNESCO's involvement could only be symbolic, although the normative dimension of EFA commitments demanded UNESCO's imprimatur. Several years earlier, the UN General Assembly had endorsed UNESCO proposals that 1990 be designated International Literacy Year, a happy but only coincidental concurrence with the WCEFA. Yet any notion of a global campaign for universal education and literacy was entirely consistent with UNESCO rhetoric and style, its history replete with such aspirational planning. In general terms,

UNESCO's institutional interest in the WCEFA was to ensure no erosion in its time-honored standing as the United Nation's lead agency in education, and as things turned out diplomatic sensibilities required this protocol to be observed: UNESCO was designated at Jomtien as the "lead agency" for monitoring subsequent progress in attaining conference objectives. All of this suited UNESCO's Director General Federico Mayor, who had succeeded M'Bow in 1987 and was keen to make the "UNESCO crisis" a thing of the past, UNESCO's financial constraints notwithstanding.

The Bank's position in this set of multilateral relationships differed markedly from UNESCO's. Although financial capacity was of paramount importance here, it was not the only factor. At about the same time as Grant had embarked on his political offensive (i.e. from early 1988) Wadi Haddad as the new Bank Education Director had begun planning what can only be described as an offensive – both inside and outside the Bank – to restore Bank lending in education to their historical levels, to ensure widespread adherence to the Bank's now explicit policy framework for education, and to promote more vigorously the equity dimensions of that framework. That Haddad could place uncompromising emphasis on the absolute priority of primary education in government spending on education served these purposes well.

What Haddad conceived of was a program of "accelerated educational development" which quickly became subsumed under the WCEFA framework and which enjoyed considerable personal backing from Bank President Barber Conable. Haddad saw in Grant's WCEFA proposals the opportunity for the Bank to take the lead in a politically significant global initiative, provided that the driving principles were in accordance with prevailing Bank educational policies. In other words, it was going to be difficult for the Bank to stay aloof from the WCEFA process. With its overwhelmingly superior resource base compared with any other agency of relevance, the Bank set out to merge its own crusade for educational reform (as designed by Aklilu, Haddad, and Psacharopoulos) with the Jomtien initiative. At the heart of Bank concerns was to persuade all other participants that Bank education policy prescriptions were of direct relevance to EFA objectives. The Bank would go to Jomtien arguing that low-to-middle-income countries were generally underinvesting in basic education, and that many had overestimated the social returns from investments in higher education. More than this, the Bank would ensure that the complex planning and conceptual preparation of the WCEFA would reflect Bank thinking and priorities. The argument was a natural product of a decade's intense reflection on the part of the entire education sector of the Bank, as it was a cause for several past orthodoxies embraced by the Bank to be challenged and discredited.

To achieve this outcome, Haddad himself was seconded out of the Bank as Executive Secretary of the initiative's Inter-Agency Commission, physically based in UNICEF's headquarters in New York. Haddad quickly gained a high profile around the world, especially through the complex set of regional meetings and interagency consultations that intensified as the WCEFA drew nearer. Although most observers at the time saw Haddad's leadership essentially a matter of driving the logistics, for him and the Bank it was much more a matter of selling the Bank's convictions about the push for education for all.

There was a key issue over which major differences of opinion emerged among the UN sponsoring agencies. It had to do with the precise meaning of "a basic education for all." As far as "basic education" was concerned, there was not too much difficulty, and curriculum content came to be described in terms that evoked the UNESCO "fundamental education" literature of the 1950s (Jones 1988: 47–87), although there were vigorous behind-the-scenes debates about how best to measure and monitor basic learning achievement. More fundamental were the initial differences over the term "education for all." At their heart was the contrast between the Bank's commitment to universal primary education (UPE) as the optimum pathway to education for all and UNESCO's simultaneous support for UPE with basic education for adults and young people. It says a great deal about the World Bank that its preferred strategy for universal education is one that looks to the primary school as its engine. Given time as well as increases in efficiency, primary schooling will emerge as the guarantor of universal literacy and basic education. Not so, according to UNESCO, which saw no society achieving universal literacy through primary schooling alone, all societies requiring additional means to consolidate (and to make up the deficiencies of) primary education. It was UNESCO's Assistant Director General for Education, Colin Power, who ensured that it was the UNESCO view of "education for all" that was formally embraced at Jomtien. Accordingly, the WCEFA, its background technical papers and subsequent plan of action embraced adults and young people as worthy recipients of basic education programs in addition to those of primary school age (see Jones 1990b; Inter-Agency Commission, WCEFA 1990). The Bank never sat easily with the outcome, and this highlights its persistent and essentially arbitrary neglect of adult literacy.

If the clash between the narrow and the broad approaches to education for all gained considerable visibility in the lead-up to and during the WCEFA, much less apparent was the essential incompatibility of Grant's and the Bank's views of achieving education for all. For Grant, it was akin to mass immunization, a drive that depended above all else on political will. Although described by Grant as a one-off need, it was nevertheless a Keynesian view that placed governments at the heart of educational futures. Although the Bank agreed that primary education was a public responsibility, the pace of achieving UPE would depend, first, on the speed with which governments could transfer their education spending from higher levels of education (especially higher education and technical education) and, second, with the general rate of economic growth. UPE was in itself not an absolute priority for the Bank; UPE could only be achieved when societies could afford it, and that time was some way off. As things turned out, after Jomtien the key sponsoring agencies returned more or less to business as usual. Neither basic education nor primary education assumed much by way of greater priority in lending and in aid programs, an outcome that was most pronounced in the poorest countries.

The construction of policy 1990–5

A series of internal Bank reorganizations in 1987, 1992, and 1995 had the cumulative effect of flattening out Bank structures, reducing the size and influence of the variously named central education policy department, and speeding up loan negotiation and approval processes by placing greater emphasis on the discretion of the Bank's regional lending and operational Divisions. In 1987, Aklilu Habte was appointed the President's Special Adviser on Africa, to leave the Bank in 1990 to become UNICEF's inaugural Education Chief. His replacement, Wadi Haddad, persisted vigorously with the education reform agenda, a process he himself saw culminating in his departure from the Bank in 1989 to head the WCEFA Inter-Agency Commission. Very importantly, the 1987 reorganization saw the fragmentation of Psacharopoulos' influential and highly productive research team, Psacharopoulos himself moving to the Latin America and Caribbean regional operations Division for a time. The steadily declining central Education Policy Department, with its even more steadily declining research and analytical capacity, was led between 1989 and 1995 by Adriaan Verspoor, Peter Moock, and Marlaine Lockheed, each of whom were long-standing education research and analysis staffers with robust understandings (as participants) in the reform policy processes spearheaded by Aklilu, Haddad, and Psacharopoulos. Overall, these were years during which successive Bank Presidents were under intense pressure, especially from the US Congress, to reduce the administrative costs of running the Bank, in favor of devoting a greater share of its operating profits back into lending. With the large group of new transition borrowers, that in itself was sufficient justification.

By design or by default, the fundamental drivers and descriptions of Bank education policy that were in place by the mid-1980s remained as such for the next two decades. It was an extraordinary outcome, given the rapid and pronounced shifts in Bank education policy the two decades previously, and given the extreme geopolitical changes that were to unfold. It was not a matter, however, of the Bank's succeeding – internally and externally – of convincing education constituencies of the merits of its policy prescriptions. Rather, the simplicities of human capital theory and their ultimate construction as a matter of faith rather than evidence helped preserve the status quo. More than this, the collapse in the education sector's intellectual capacity over the two decades from the mid-1980s meant that prospects for fundamental policy change from within the education sector were slim.

In a memorable phrase employed after his departure, Bank staffer Stephen Heyneman referred to the set of policy prescriptions for education as the 'short policy menu' (Heyneman 2003). The usefulness of the phrase requires some explanation, given the compounding complexities facing the World Bank's policy and financial commitments in education through the 1980s,

1990s, and beyond. Conventional project lending was seen to be of declining relevance as an instrument for effecting qualitative and lasting educational reforms, and was customarily organized around projects that were too large and expensive for many borrowers. The economic situation facing borrowers was not only becoming generally more serious, but more complex, with an increasingly diverse set of factors upsetting traditional approaches to the economics of education and development. Internal divisions and inconsistencies served to limit the efficiency with which the Bank interacted with education borrowers, not least because of intensifying differences between its lending operations, sector policy work and research, in addition to tensions between project and program lending.

If anything, the education sector was faced with the need for a flexible and context-driven dialogue with each borrower. The Bank in its public pronouncements will state that this was encouraged and achieved. The reality is that the Bank failed to respect borrower differences (with the exception of some loan officers in the Regional Divisions), mounting a drive for worldwide educational renewal in the 1980s and 1990s that, while not prescriptive, nevertheless projected vigorously a narrow set of policy options and recommendations. This is seen no better than in Psacharopoulos' tidy reduction of critical issues facing world education to five: how to increase primary school coverage, what type of education to provide, how to enhance school quality, how to finance educational expansion, and how to improve distributional equity (Psacharopoulos 1987: 5–11).

The two decades since the mid-1980s have seen a clear, careful, and constant delineation of the Bank's preferred lending strategy for education. The weaker a borrower's economy, the less it has been in a position to resist Bank formulations. East Asian borrowers appeared most able to offer resistance. Again, the Bank has been careful to cover itself by declaring that its policy positions in education were neither prescriptive nor incapable of contextual interpretation and variation. Beyond that, the general style of the Bank–borrower "dialogue" differed little from that of earlier, more absolutely prescriptive periods.

A series of subsectoral policy papers published between 1990 and 1994 repeated the demands of the short policy menu. Research teams produced variants of the short policy menu as they applied to primary education (1990), technical and vocational education (1991), and higher education (1994). Conspicuous by its absence was secondary education. To only a limited extent were the papers based on careful examination of country experience or even Bank project experience. Much more prominent were the demands of the short policy menu, backed up by carefully crafted research designed to support the policy position. The inaugural paper, on primary education, was an uncompromising statement of the short policy menu, prepared in time for the World Conference on Education for All in March 1990.

The Bank's accumulating experience in primary education was only one factor shaping the major statement of policy that appeared in *Primary Education: A World Bank Policy Paper* (World Bank 1990b). Of equal and direct significance were the various moves towards structural adjustment and increased efficiency in education (not least those reflected in *Financing Education in Developing Countries* and *Education Policies for Sub-Saharan Education*), as well as the arguments underpinning the WCEFA. In many respects, *Primary Education* was a natural product of these various but interrelated forces of change (an extended associated volume containing considerably more country-related data is Lockheed *et al*. 1991).

Primary Education was a policy prescription that saw issues of efficiency and quality as congruous. Thus while much of the policy's content had to do with the quality of teaching and learning, this concern was deeply embedded in the context of the structural reform of education systems along the lines implied by the austerity and adjustment measures seen most starkly in the policy prescriptions for low-income African borrowers. The policy paper cannot be understood otherwise, a point made with emphasis by India's Secretary General of Education, Anil Bordia, at Bank President Conable's shaky and controversial launch of the preceding policy options' review study at the WCEFA. Traversing the Bank's well-documented ground concerning the developmental potential of primary education, and calling for greater national and international support for primary education, *Primary Education* made much of measures designed to enhance the learning environment. In particular, it expressed concern at the educational effects of such adverse conditions for learning. The rationale for these concerns was unambiguous:

> Limited educational effectiveness in developing countries results from the failure to provide the minimum inputs necessary for successful learning. In high-income countries a typical primary school student goes to a modern, well-equipped school, has 900 hours of learning time and $52 worth of noncapital material inputs per year, studies a well-conceived curriculum, has a teacher with at least sixteen years of education, and enjoys a student–teacher ratio of 20:1. In contrast, students in many low-income countries attend shelterless schools or ones that are poorly constructed and ill-equipped. There are typically only 500 hours of actual learning time annually, $1.70 worth of material inputs per student, and a poorly designed curriculum. Teachers are likely to have less that ten years of education, and classes may consist of more than 50 children, many of whom are chronically undernourished, parasite-ridden, and hungry.
> (World Bank 1990b: 14)

What was more controversial was the extent to which the Bank's "worst-case" scenario should determine global policies for restructuring many aspects of primary education systems, including their financing, teachers' pay, working hours and conditions, the management and monitoring of schools, and the balance between public and private systems. While no one could dispute the urgency and depth of need in the lowest-income countries, the Bank's prescriptions for reform were fully open to question, not least the extent to which they were needed in middle-income countries, by which is raised the possibility that the primary school reforms were part of a broader adjustment offensive driven more by ideology than technical requirements either economic or pedagogical.

The *Primary Education* policy paper differed from its African reform policy predecessor in arguing vigorously for a transfer of public sector finance in favor of primary education, and within public sector education budgets for a shift in the same direction, to increase efficiency, enhance learning, and reduce student dropout and repetition. At the same time, the effect of such transfers, whether in low- or middle-income countries, could only be to increase the need in nonprimary school subsectors for the radical adjustment policies argued for more generally by the Bank and IMF, not least privatization. As it stood, the primary education policy was too self-contained, and tended to policy options too extreme for middle-income countries, which partly explains its limited take-up rate in subsequent years of lending.

The precision with which the Bank sought to promote its policies for the principal education subsectors was helped by the dominance of primary education. Once the case was in place for primary schooling to become the absolute priority for government expenditures (and borrowings) in education, then clarity was achieved for secondary, technical, and higher education. For vocation and technical education (both formal and nonformal) in 1991, and for higher education in 1994, policy papers that ran in parallel with *Primary Education* of 1990 were issued. What was stark was the education sector's incapacity to address secondary education similarly. The problem stemmed from the structural ambiguity of secondary education in schooling systems. Was the secondary school essentially an extension of the primary school, there to raise general educational and cultural levels in society and economy, the pace of its growth dictated by the ease with which government budgets could afford as a public responsibility? Or was secondary education better seen as a precursor to further education, preparing students for entry to vocational, technical, and higher education, and for which an element of private household cost-sharing could be justified? This ambiguity was not felt by the Bank alone: it was at the heart of profound policy dilemmas facing secondary education right through the twentieth century as mass education systems grew, the issue not so stark in contexts where secondary schooling was overtly and exclusively an entry to further education.

It suited the Bank – in its promotion of a small set of policy imperatives focussing on public primary education – to relegate secondary education's status as an area worthy of detailed policy assertiveness. Rather, the Bank opted to keep the ambiguities surrounding secondary education in play. Thus, for middle- and high-income countries that could afford it, the expansion of public secondary education might be justified. This could not be so for low-income countries and others struggling to make UPE a reality. However, troublesome evidence was accumulating. An important study conducted by

Bank education researcher Jandhyala Tilak presented conclusions that flatly contradicted Bank assertions and policy:

> While primary education was found to have had a significant effect on income distribution earlier, now we find that it is the secondary level of education that has a more significant effect, and that primary education may not be adequate to produce any recognizable significant effect.
>
> (Tilak 1989: 88)

Were such a conclusion to have any impact on World Bank education policy, it would require the dismantling of a decade's zealous and strenuous campaigning on the part of the powerful leadership group of Aklilu, Haddad, and Psacharopoulos. It was not in the scheme of things that in the years to 1995 such a dismantling was possible. Indeed, it is telling that in an interview with the author in 1997, Psacharopoulos declined to confirm the existence of the Tilak findings.

More straightforward for the Bank, but troublesome for borrowers, was the policy paper published in 1991, *Vocational and Technical Education and Training* (World Bank 1991), prepared by a team led by education staffer John Middleton. Middleton and his group worked squarely within the boundaries set by the leadership group, amassing a considerable amount of data drawn principally from project records, much of it published (as with *Primary Education*) in a commercial companion volume (Middleton *et al.* 1993). Project experience from such countries as Bangladesh, Botswana, Brazil, Cameroon, Chile, Colombia, Egypt, Korea, Mexico, Peru, and Togo was used to construct a vehement critique of earlier Bank–borrower practices that included vocational and technical education as a priority public subsector. That an extensive pattern of Bank lending for technical education and training had accumulated since 1963 was hardly surprising, given the confidence with which the Bank had embarked on education lending. Its quest, after all, had been to assist governments ensure the ready availability of suitably trained technicians and professionals for productive employment in areas directly relevant to employment and growth. The 1991 policy paper, indeed, opened with a celebration of the contribution that suitably skilled technical workers would make to productivity and growth:

> A competent and flexible workforce, one that can acquire new skills as economies change, is a necessary prerequisite for economic and social development. Society benefits in the form of higher productivity and the capacity to adapt to changing economic circumstances and opportunities. Individuals benefit through higher earnings and enhanced mobility in seeking better employment opportunities. In the modern wage sector, skilled workers and technicians enhance the efficiency and quality of production and maintenance, facilitate the adaptation and use of new technologies, and supervise and train workers with lesser skills.
>
> (World Bank 1991: 19)

The policy placed considerable emphasis on labor-market dynamics in a range of countries, painting a picture of public technical education institutions producing unemployable or inadequately trained persons, frequently with dated or irrelevant skills. It was a picture that had also been painted by Haddad in his critique of the diversified secondary school curriculum, with its combination of general and vocational content (Haddad 1987). The basic point of the new paper was to foster no less than as rapid a decline as possible of government support for vocational and technical education. Rather, governments were encouraged to support private provision, on the grounds that not only would funds be freed up for primary schooling but the training provided would be more relevant and efficient. The policy paper presented something of a caricature of public technical education, depicting rigid planning and management, weak links to employers and their requirements, inappropriate training objectives, and inappropriate financing patterns (excessive expenditure on weak curriculum and inadequate finance available for the appropriate kinds).

These features helped propel the education sector towards a policy position that placed emphasis on three dimensions: shifting the focus of publicly financed education away from technical and higher education to primary education, encouraging a shift in favor of private sector training, and improving the effectiveness of public sector training. In a policy context urging privatization and the down-sizing of government, the vocational education and training sector was a natural context for encouraging both learners and employers to take on the bulk of financial obligations. Where government had a role, it would focus on "policy, planning, and quality control," as well as "skills strategic to growth strategies. This support will often be limited, and governments should seek to diversify sources of financing for training" (World Bank 1991: 54). Although such a prescription was entirely consistent with the Bank's overall position on education, it could not be expected to sit easily with a considerable number of borrowers. Many, of course, were unwilling to focus on UPE, including those for whom it was no longer a challenge. Others had limited experience in stimulating employer interest in training, and perhaps did not relish the prospect of embarking on such a course. Perhaps with prescience, the paper underscored possibilities for creating incentives and compensatory measures for employers (a later discussion of the policy paper is Bennell and Segerstrom 1998).

Delayed until 1994, *Higher Education: The Lessons of Experience* (World Bank 1994) had a more troubled and protracted gestation period when compared with the primary and vocational education policy papers. Led by Jamil Salmi, the production team quickly found itself at odds with sentiment among many borrowers not a little unsettled by the overall emphasis on primary education since Jomtien, as well as with sentiment among many Bank operations staff seeing in higher education a means of gaining reasonably quick loan approvals and disbursements.

The crux of the matter was the lack of care in separating out issues of financing from issues of overall education sector planning. The Bank's crusade to render primary education the absolute top priority for government financing of education all too frequently was misconstrued by borrowers (and the donor community as well) as a message to downplay the role of higher education in society and in development. For most middle-income countries, including the formerly socialist "transition" economies, attaining UPE was no longer a problem, and for them issues of overall education system balance and performance were of key importance.

To be sure, the 1994 policy paper on higher education gave recognition to the high social rates of return that could be obtained through higher education. What was significant, however, was that such references were cursory and had no strong connection with the major arguments of the paper. For example:

> Higher education is of paramount importance for economic and social development. Institutions of higher education have the main responsibility for equipping individuals with the advanced knowledge and skills required for positions of responsibility in government, business, and the professions.... In most countries, higher education institutions also play important social roles by forging the national identity of the country and offering a forum for pluralistic debate.... Estimated social rates of return of 10 percent or more in many developing countries also indicate that investments in higher education contribute to increases in labor productivity and to higher long-term economic growth, which are essential for poverty alleviation.
>
> (World Bank 1994: 1)

The core paper itself neglected to take up the matter of social rates of return from higher education, although a vaguer acknowledgment of the social "benefits" was included (such as external benefits accruing from research and technology transfer). Rather, the weight of the paper was given over to a "crisis" diagnosis of the global situation concerning higher education. At the heart of matters was the collapsing capacity of governments worldwide to sustain their historical levels of support for higher education, whether for institutions or for students. Psacharopoulos and his colleagues had consistently presented rates-of-return data that saw the highest returns stemming from primary and general secondary education, and this was the essential policy message of the paper:

> Within the education sector, however, there is evidence that higher education investments have lower social rates of return than investments in primary and secondary education and that investments in basic education can also have a more direct impact on poverty reduction, because they tend to improve income inequality.... [Primary] and secondary education will continue to be the highest-priority sub-sectors in the Bank's lending to countries that have not yet achieved universal literacy and adequate access, equity, and quality at the primary and secondary levels. In these countries, the Bank's involvement in higher education will continue

to be mainly to make its financing more equitable and cost-effective, so that primary and secondary education can receive increased attention at the margin.

(World Bank 1994: 85)

Bank strategies for the reform of higher education revolved around four fundamental concerns, and although the authors were insistent that no single blueprint was being put forward for all borrowers, they cautioned that in no country would the package of reforms escape face an easy political passage. At the same time, country-by-country variations in implementing the package were likely to be ones of timing and degree:

- encouraging greater differentiation of institutions, including the development of private institutions;
- providing incentives for public institutions to diversify sources of funding, including cost-sharing with students, and linking government funding closely to performance;
- redefining the role of government in higher education; and
- introducing policies explicitly designed to give priority to quality and equity objectives.

(World Bank 1994: 4)

As far as Bank support for higher education was concerned, the paper made much of the historical tendency for Bank lending to support free-standing institutions, or parts of institutions. These, then, tended to become well-resourced "oases," with little bearing on the higher education system as a whole (World Bank 1994: 82). Rather, the authors contended that the Bank should focus more systematically on national capacity building through higher education as a whole, as it had done with such borrowers as Korea and China. In other words, a project emphasis should give way to a program emphasis, in line with general operational trends then underway across the Bank as a whole.

The institutional basis of the 1994 higher education policy paper can be seen in the reorganizations of Bank structure in 1987 and 1992. A central Vice Presidency for Human Resources Development and Operations Policy had been established, partly in order to speed up loan approval processes and to reduce the long-standing gap between officially stated Bank policies and actual lending practices. It is highly significant that this Vice Presidency, responsible for Bank education policy, was held by the ideologically driven Armeane Choksi, a strident proponent of "Washington consensus" policies that gathered around him political and methodological allies. It was also highly significant that his main education policy adviser was George Psacharopoulos, transferred from the Latin America and Caribbean Regional Department. In this move, Choksi was able to ensure the structural dominance of the education reform movement ushered in over the preceding decade by Aklilu, Haddad, and Psacharopoulos. As Psacharopoulos himself reminisced:

> [In this reorganization] the central education staff was reshuffled to include analytically trained economists moving to the center from other parts of the Bank, and the outside. As a result, another effort was made to define education policy. Naturally, the team again brought to the surface the messages of the white paper *Financing Education in Developing Countries* [World Bank 1986b]. Again, the team failed to sell internally a new policy paper on education because of extreme resistance from the regions and senior management.
>
> (Psacharopoulos 2006: 334)

What Psacharopoulos was referring to was the production of a new Bank paper on overall education policy, to be published in 1995. As a lead-in exercise, the 1994 higher education paper was a portent of the dramas that were to unfold a year later. Former Bank staffer Stephen Heyneman reflected on the fundamental stance concerning the higher education policy, the statement cited earlier that "primary and secondary education will continue to be the highest-priority subsectors in the Bank's lending to countries that have not yet achieved universal literacy and adequate access, equity, and quality at the primary and secondary levels" (World Bank 1994: 85). Such lines of thinking had led to unprecedented levels of debate and even protest inside the Bank, especially in the Regional Divisions which saw threats to their historical levels and patterns of lending to higher education. Heyneman commented:

> Within the Bank, this statement raised concerns among the operations staff that the short policy menu might be forced on the countries around the world regardless of the consequences. It raised the specter of having arbitrary authority within the Bank's structure, which might work against the interests of education sector [*sic*]. Staff suspicions laid the groundwork for the confrontation over the next policy paper, *Strategies and Priorities for Education* . . . .
>
> What the outside world did not know was that this statement itself had been inserted within the Office of the Senior Vice President [*sic*] after the final draft without approval of the regional division chiefs. Even the authors of the paper did not see the statement until after the paper had been published.
>
> (Heyneman 2003: 327)

It had now been 15 years since the Bank had last published a comprehensive policy statement on education, the *Education Sector Policy Paper* of 1980 that had followed relatively quickly from its 1971 and 1974 predecessors. Psacharopoulos had been constantly strident in his critique of that paper, referring to it as no policy at all, with nothing in it to drive Bank or borrower operations forward with purpose thereby preventing discriminating choices among options and competing priorities. The failure in 1986 to have *Financing Education in Developing Countries* elevated to formal policy status was felt keenly by Psacharopoulos who identified strongly with the paper as a principal co-author. The new structural arrangements, with a sympathetic Vice President, afforded opportunity for Psacharopoulos to shore up his view of core principles and priorities.

The historical significance of the 1995 policy on education is interesting. It stems only in part from its content. More telling was the bruising disputation that swirled throughout the Bank before and after its publication, the wounds taking years to heal. Attempts to heal those wounds were the key driver of World Bank education policy construction in the years 1996–2006. The relatively bland, unfocussed, and even innocuous character of Bank education policies over that period derived squarely from attempts to avoid any rerun of 1994 and 1995.

As stated so often throughout this book, interpreting World Bank policies in education is far from straightforward. More than this, any construction of official Bank policies for education is a complex undertaking. From 1971 onwards, central education policy staff were obliged to consider the lending experience and emerging priorities of an increasing number of borrowers, whose diversity was increasing also. Their proponents within the Bank, the regional lending Divisions, had the daunting task of summarizing policy matters on a regional level as well as shoring up their prime *raison d'être* – lending levels. On one level, the Bank's policy agenda as formulated through the 1980s had been in response to the twin crises of debt and recession. But on another, Bank crisis prescriptions were none other than "Washington consensus" requirements for comprehensive economic and policy reform, formulated as a universal recipe for the governance and management of national economies (Williamson 1990, 1993, 2000).

The historical pattern had been to achieve a degree of compromise between country- and region-specific policy requirements and global assessments of Bank education policy. Either the compromise was forged through narrow arbitrariness (as in 1971) or in broad policy looseness (as in 1980). This tension was all too apparent in 1994–5, but it was far more than the conventional divide between policy flexibility and a "one size fits all" or "cookie cutter" policy stance as Bank staffers were frequently prone to put it. This time, it was a fundamental dispute over ideology. At issue was the rise within the World Bank of uncompromising neoliberal advocates of uniform policy prescriptions for economic decision-making. Williamson had summed up the complex and interrelated program for reform: state fiscal discipline, restraint, and prioritization; financial liberalization; stabilization of interest rates and exchange rates; trade liberalization; foreign direct investment; privatization of state enterprises and services; deregulation of economic behavior; and state enforcement of law and order, of property rights, and of contractual agreements (Williamson 1993).

In other words, the technical challenge of constructing a revised statement of Bank education policy in 1995 was considerable, given enormous geopolitical changes since 1989, ongoing problems of debt and recession in sub-Saharan Africa and parts of Latin America, as well as the substantial economic and educational progress of many middle-income borrowers. The World Bank itself needed to learn, from a policy as much as an operational standpoint, how to remain globally relevant. The easy pathways were the ones adopted – strident policy uniformity as in 1995, and bland policy looseness as in the subsequent decade 1996–2006. In matters of policy, the Bank proved itself to be organizationally and institutionally incapable of taking on board the complexities of diversity and adjustment it was advocating to its clients.

A series of interviews conducted with some twenty five Bank officials reveals much about the unprecedented collapse of internal discipline in the processes whereby the 1995 policy paper was written and forwarded to Bank President Preston and the Executive Directors (in May 1995). Experience with the 1994 higher education policy revealed the policy rift between central and operational Divisions; that experience counted for little in 1995, except to strengthen resolve on each side. For example, an early draft led to deep concerns among regional staff, whose careers depended on keeping the flow of loan funds moving, that lending in education would dry up in countries with priority concerns other than UPE. One regional staffer, after rejecting the draft's exclusive dependence on rate-of-return analysis, commented in November 1994:

> The paper draws upon the same rate of return evidence to guide policy and future investment priorities, and that leads to catastrophe. The evidence is faulty; drawn from a few traditional borrowers; only provides a backward explanation of trends and only refers to the most simple of educational categories – primary, secondary, and higher. Because the paper relies exclusively on rates of return, it excludes other possible justifications for allocations of public finance: national interest, market failure, and equity.
>
> (cited in Heyneman 2003: 328)

In December, education staffers in five of the Bank's six Regional Divisions forwarded protest notes to their respective Vice Presidents over the contents of the latest draft. Among their objections was the failure of the production team to take prior objections into account, that successive drafts were barely changing. On February 2, 1995, in a move unprecedented in the education history of the World Bank, 20 of the 26 education Division Chiefs forwarded a joint memorandum to the President requesting that the paper not be forwarded to the Executive Directors. According to Heyneman, of the remaining six, two agreed with the objections but did not wish to sign, one disagreed with them, and three were away from the Bank at the time: "The Bank's education sector was in revolt" (Heyneman 2003: 328).

The 1995 paper was prepared by a team led by Nicholas Burnett, with Tom Eisemon, Kari Marble, and Harry Patrinos. In a formal sense, the group was required to report to Peter Moock, the current director of the Education and Social Policy Department. In reality, the processes of consultation, negotiation, and drafting were largely driven by Vice President Choksi's office, and notably George Psacharopoulos within it. Given the considerable data collection and analytic work that had gone into the three subsectoral papers in 1990, 1991, and 1994, the decision was taken to adopt a relatively brisk schedule for completing the paper, from January 1994 to Board presentation in May 1995 and publication in August 1995. This, in fact, suited the authors' intention to focus on general economic and policy principles rather than on detailed education matters. They opted to paint on the policy canvas with broad brushstrokes. A consultation meeting was conducted in September with ministers, senior officials, and academics from twelve borrowers (Armenia, Colombia, Guinea, India, Mexico, Nigeria, Pakistan, the Philippines, the Russian Federation, the Slovak Republic, Thailand, and Uganda), along with France, Jordan, and the United Kingdom. Discussions were held with UNESCO and UNICEF, and with the UNESCO Commission on Education for the Twenty-First Century, chaired by Jacques Delors. Bilateral agencies consulted included the Canadian (CIDA), Swedish (SIDA), and US (USAID). Despite Burnett's claim to the contrary, the consultation process led to only minor adjustments to the drafts, mainly recognition of some of the risks associated with the six key policy reforms advocated (Burnett 1996: 217).

Priorities and Strategies for Education: A World Bank Review (World Bank 1995) was presented to the Executive Directors in May 1995, but not for explicit endorsement, unsurprising given the storm swirling around it. The paper itself was principally concerned with the policy preconditions for efficient and effective spending on education, having little to say about educational processes themselves (on the somewhat shaky grounds that the 1990, 1991, and 1994 subsectoral papers had addressed them adequately). At heart, the paper depicted a neoliberal view of the ideal economy, one that can at best tolerate public education. State involvement in education was classed as an "intervention," justifiable on the grounds of reducing inequality, opening opportunities for the poor and disadvantaged, compensating for market failures, and disseminating information for the benefit of consumers (World Bank 1995: 3). Having noted that public spending on education is frequently "inefficient and inequitable," the authors argued that the main functions for governments were to set standards, to support inputs known to improve learning achievement, and to monitor performance (World Bank 1995: 6).

From the baseline of an uncompromising commitment to rate-of-return methods (with their focus on wages as indicators of labor productivity), the paper identified as priorities for public investment "those investments for which the social rate of return is highest and the level of public subsidization is lowest" (World Bank 1995: 8). Accordingly, much room was provided for "household involvement" in the financing of education and in educational decision-making. The extent and scale of what the paper envisaged was revealed in its assessment of the risks involved:

- Implementation of systemwide education policies can be more difficult.
- Enforcement of broader national objectives can be hampered.
- Social segregation may increase if schools become polarized between élite academies and schools for the children of the poor and uneducated.
- Equity may be reduced if schools and institutions accept students on the basis of their ability to pay rather than on academic entrance qualifications.
- Parents may lack the information they need to make judgments about quality.

(World Bank 1995: 12)

Such admissions about risk were nevertheless underplayed in the ensuing discussion. Emphasis was placed on the willingness of communities and households to pay the costs of education: "Even very poor communities are often willing to contribute toward the cost of education, especially at the primary level" (World Bank 1995: 105). Moreover:

> Since upper-secondary-school graduates will have higher earnings than those who leave school earlier, selectively charging fees for public secondary school can help to increase enrollments. Cost-sharing with communities can be encouraged at the secondary, as well as the primary, level. Fees can usually be charged without affecting overall enrollments ....
>
> The charging of fees at one level can affect enrollments by other family members at other levels. A poor family that has to pay fees for an upper-secondary student may not be able to enroll other children in primary school because the younger children's work is needed to generate the income from which the fees are to be paid.

(World Bank 1995: 106)

The authors' generally relaxed tone about the need for publicly funded stipends for children from poor families was in stark contrast to their concerns about the overall management capacity of public education systems, making the administration of such compensatory measures as stipends illusory. In similar vein, decentralization emerged as a major theme, not only in terms of breaking down national financing and management structures in education systems, but also breaking down the influence of centralized teachers' unions, whose existence was seen as a natural consequence of national administration of education (World Bank 1995: 137). Even the national profile of university student protests and unrest was interpreted as a consequence of the national public financing of higher education (World Bank 1995: 138). And at least in urban areas, a far from trivial qualification, decentralization "can be enhanced by the use of market mechanisms that increase accountability and choice" (World Bank 1995: 140).

The internal storm was matched by hitherto unprecedented levels of criticism of the Bank's education sector policies. Although by the mid-1990s the Bank was becoming used to strident external criticism, education had generally escaped the worst of it. The explicitness of the paper's ideological content and tone, however, changed the apparent innocence of the education sector. At one level, nothing fundamental had changed, the 1995 paper doing little more than codifying the cumulative policies of the past decade (with the soft shift of emphasis from *primary* education to *basic* education, less a matter of encouraging out-of-school basic education than lower secondary education as an extension of primary schooling). Its directness and starkness, however, shook the complacency of many participants and observers of Bank operations in education. No longer could education be seen merely as a "soft," social overheads sector: rather, its place as an expression of long-standing Bank orthodoxy was simply in clearer view (for a discussion see the special issue of the *International Journal of Educational Development*, especially Lauglo 1996; Bennell 1996; Samoff 1996b; also commentary by Burnett 1996; Burnett and Patrinos 1996; Psacharopoulos 1996a).

Conclusion

Tables 6.1 to 6.6 sum up the lending patterns in education in and leading up to 1990, and through to 1995. From the pronounced slump in lending in 1987, some recovery was evident by 1990, driven in large measure by Asian borrowers, not least China for higher education. Overall, the recovery in education lending levels was sustained through to 1995.

In the education sector, there was greater evidence of new thinking than was apparent elsewhere in the Bank. In particular, an impressive amount of research and policy analysis upset much conventional thinking about the effectiveness of Bank projects in education and, to a lesser extent, the role of education in development. But again, there was too tight a connection between these two areas of concern, the Bank assuming a centrality in the development process which dismayed borrowers, subjected as they were to an omniscience and assertiveness not usually found among multilateral agencies. Because the Bank assumed its role in educational development was greater than it was in reality, much Bank research and policy analysis in education failed to make an adequate distinction between factors working for successful Bank lending in education and those working for successful implementation of national policies in education. And as Bank education staff began to learn about the most basic of process issues in education, not least matters to do with the effectiveness of teaching and learning, borrowers could only react with wry smiles as they watched assertive self-confidence connect with innocence.

Table 6.2 World Bank education financing, by region, FY 1988–90

Region	Year	$US m	Percentage of lending	Number projects	Percentage of projects
Africa	1988	178	21	8	42
	1989	88	9	4	20
	1990	351	24	9	41
Asia	1988	356	41	5	26
	1989	484	50	10	50
	1990	903	61	10	45
LAC[a]	1988	88	10	2	11
	1989	140	15	3	15
	1990	—	—	—	—
EMENA[b]	1988	242	28	4	21
	1989	251	26	3	15
	1990	233	16	3	14

Source: World Bank Education Sector.

Notes
a LAC Latin America and Caribbean.
b EMENA Europe, Middle East, and North Africa.

Table 6.3 World Bank distribution of regional project investments, by education subsector, FY 1990 ($US m)

	Total	Africa	Asia	EMENA[a]
General education	1,222	280	669	275
Primary	456	83	201	172
Secondary	163	24	122	18
Non-formal (literacy)	—	—	—	—
Post-secondary	302	126	182	16
Teacher education	280	47	164	69
Vocational education and training	489	33	441	16
Secondary	69	20	49	—
Post-secondary	302	12	290	—
Non-formal	45	1	44	—
Teacher education	73	—	57	16
Non-allocated	207	70	100	38
Total project costs	1,918	383	1,209	329
World Bank share of total project costs	1,487	351	903	233

Source: World Bank Education Sector.

Notes
a EMENA Europe, Middle East, and North Africa.
There were no education loans or credits to Latin America and the Caribbean in FY 1990.

Table 6.4 World Bank distribution of regional project investments, by education subsector, FY 1990 (percentages)

	Total	*Africa*	*Asia*	*EMENA*[a]
General education	63	73	55	84
Primary	23	22	17	52
Secondary	9	6	10	5
Non-formal (literacy)	—	—	—	—
Post-secondary	17	33	15	5
Teacher education	15	12	14	21
Vocational education and training	26	9	37	5
Secondary	4	5	4	—
Post-secondary	16	3	24	—
Non-formal	2	—	4	—
Teacher education	4	—	5	5
Non-allocated	11	18	8	12
World Bank share of total project costs	65	75	65	57

Source: World Bank Education Sector.

Notes
a EMENA Europe, Middle East, and North Africa.
There were no education loans or credits to Latin America and the Caribbean in FY 1990.

Table 6.5 World Bank education financing, new commitments by region, FY 1990–5 ($US m)

FY	*Africa*	*East Asia and Pacific*	*Europe and Central Asia*	*Latin America and Caribbean*	*Middle East and North Africa*	*South Asia*	*Total*
1990	310	371	77	61	30	555	1,404
1991	221	566	198	534	240	278	2,037
1992	324	391	8	406	72	131	1,332
1993	364	461	10	480	108	431	1,854
1994	268	329	65	919	30	135	1,746
1995	175	277	63	1,058	152	417	2,142
Total	1,662	2,395	421	3,458	632	1,947	10,515

Source: World Bank Education Sector.

The problematic connections between policy and lending were well summed up in the much-cited 1992 report on World Bank project effectiveness (the so-called Wapenhaus Report, after its team leader – see World Bank 1992). Reporting that the proportion of Bank projects deemed "unsatisfactory" had risen from 11 percent in the early 1980s to 37.5 percent by 1991, the

Table 6.6 World Bank education financing, by region and subsector, FY 1990–5 ($US m)

	1990	1991	1992	1993	1994	1995	Total
AFR	310.2	220.9	324.1	364.4	268.5	175.0	1,663.1
Adult literacy/non-formal	—	2.4	9.2	—	—	—	11.6
General education support	58.0	9.4	0.9	2.5	18.0	18.1	106.9
Pre-primary education	—	—	—	8.0	—	—	8.0
Primary education	90.7	153.3	82.7	184.4	99.4	104.5	715.0
Secondary education	38.6	18.5	40.2	32.2	25.7	12.3	167.5
Tertiary education	119.7	30.7	163.7	131.0	69.9	30.2	545.2
Vocational training	3.1	6.7	27.4	6.3	55.4	10.0	108.9
EAP	371.3	565.6	390.9	461.4	329.3	277.3	2,395.8
Adult literacy/non-formal	—	2.0	22.9	3.5	—	—	28.4
General education support	—	26.9	1.4	7.2	2.1	35.5	73.1
Pre-primary education	—	—	—	5.6	—	—	5.6
Primary education	98.7	194.0	75.4	60.1	66.5	107.3	602.0
Secondary education	—	—	16.1	89.0	—	106.3	211.4
Tertiary education	212.7	307.0	217.0	292.6	228.8	28.2	1,286.3
Vocational training	59.9	35.6	58.2	3.5	31.9	—	189.1
ECA	76.7	198.0	8.0	9.8	65.4	63.2	421.1
Adult literacy/non-formal	—	—	—	—	—	—	—
General education support	—	—	8.0	—	11.2	—	19.2
Pre-primary education	—	—	—	—	0.5	12.3	12.8
Primary education	19.8	—	—	—	24.6	—	44.4
Secondary education	18.9	34.5	—	—	24.5	—	77.9
Tertiary education	32.5	88.5	—	—	4.5	12.8	138.3
Vocational training	5.4	75.0	—	9.8	—	38.1	128.3

LCR	60.6	534.2	405.9	479.7	918.9	1,058.2	3,457.5
Adult literacy/non-formal	2.0	2.1	—	27.1	—	—	31.2
General education support	22.3	79.8	47.4	18.7	6.6	140.1	314.9
Pre-primary education	25.5	44.2	28.9	34.1	6.6	6.9	146.2
Primary education	10.8	179.6	272.0	178.1	739.6	286.1	1,666.2
Secondary education	—	15.0	2.4	22.4	62.1	179.2	281.1
Tertiary education	—	78.5	55.3	35.6	98.0	35.6	303.0
Vocational training	—	135.0	—	163.7	6.0	410.2	714.9
MNA	30.3	239.6	72.0	107.8	29.8	151.8	631.3
Adult literacy/non-formal	—	—	—	—	0.7	—	0.7
General education support	1.3	12.5	—	—	—	—	13.8
Pre-primary education	—	—	—	—	—	—	—
Primary education	—	139.2	—	55.6	—	74.8	269.6
Secondary education	—	—	—	40.2	18.5	74.8	133.5
Tertiary education	29.0	82.4	72.0	12.0	10.6	2.2	208.2
Vocational training	—	5.5	—	—	—	—	5.5
SAR	555.0	278.2	130.9	431.3	134.7	417.4	1,947.5
Adult literacy/non-formal	—	—	0.3	—	—	—	0.3
General education support	—	1.8	—	15.0	34.4	—	50.2
Pre-primary education	—	—	—	21.3	—	23.4	44.7
Primary education	197.5	—	119.2	326.0	80.0	304.0	1,026.7
Secondary education	90.2	—	—	58.5	1.4	3.2	153.3
Tertiary education	158.0	138.2	8.3	8.5	17.8	86.1	416.9
Vocational training	109.2	138.2	3.2	2.0	1.0	0.7	254.3

Source: World Bank Education Sector.

Notes

AFR Africa; EAP East Asia and the Pacific; ECA Europe and Central Asia; LCR Latin America and the Caribbean; MNA Middle East and North Africa; SAR South Asia. Some totals are rounded.

Wapenhaus team placed considerable emphasis on the overly complex constructions of both policies and project designs, especially in the social sectors. As the Bank's official historians noted, the shift of emphasis in Bank operations to upstream macropolicy reform, with ministers of finance the principal counterparts for Bank staff, "it was harder to sustain the quality of relations in depth with the technical ministries and agencies with which Bank projects were lodged. The critiques of declining Bank project work and diminishing technical capacity in the 1980s were written by and large by Bank staff.... Certainly what became the familiar Wapenhaus Report complaint of excessive attention to loan making, not enough to implementation and 'supervision,' was consistent with the Bank's preoccupation with policy-based lending" (Kapur *et al.* vol. 1 1997: 588). Further:

> The oversophistication in social sector lending was symptomatic of a Bank-wide problem. As criticisms of the institution's lending record mounted, particularly following the release of the Wapenhaus Report in 1992, the Bank responded in the classic manner of a bureaucracy under siege: it became ever more meticulous, elaborate, and detailed in the design of its loans. Every virtuous goal of development was sought in the project design stage.... There was little recognition that the best could well be the enemy of the good; that indeed expecting very high average rates of project performance was naive. In the end, such projects rolled out Rolls-Royces where Model T-s would have served. Long-term sustainability of such projects was improbable, and they did little to enhance self-reliance. Governments have committed to primary education without the help of tens of millions of dollars of studies, analysis, and vehicles.... Indeed, if primary education was such a basic need, surely a basic function of the government was to provide it. And if governments could not discharge such a basic responsibility on their own accord, what else could they do? There could be no doubt of the importance of primary education, and the Bank's bully pulpit role was laudable. Yet egged on by a belief and pressures that wherever it saw important issues, meticulously engineered Bank lending was needed, the institution did not seek recourse to alternatives such as adjusting its overall lending volumes to some agreed-upon government effort and borrower self-help.
>
> (Kapur *et al.* vol. 1 1997: 796–7)

There developed throughout the 1980s and 1990s the tightest of linkages between the Bank's approach to banking and its policy work in education. The former dictated the latter. The Bank over this period determined that its education policies could actively support its macroeconomic objectives of global structural reform. Furthermore, it formed a clear view on which were the "bankable" aspects of education, and concentrated on these. Most certainly, they were not the products of free and wide-ranging educational research and analysis. Such work would have produced a far different set of concerns, principles, and priorities. Again, it is as a bank that the World Bank – and its work in education – needs to be understood. The Bank's protestations about developing broad and dispassionate concerns about education (particularly about the finer points of teaching and learning) simply do not ring true. That possibility is not in the overall scheme of things.

Notes

Of particular importance for Chapter 6 were interviews with Barber Conable, Aklilu Habte, George Psacharopoulos, Wadi Haddad, Federico Mayor, Colin Power, Adriaan Verspoor, Ralph Romain, Marlaine Lockheed, and Peter Moock.

By the mid-1990s, the Bank was increasingly prone to publishing its working documents and staff papers. Important unpublished reports include: *Update on Implementation of the World Bank Policy Study: Education Policies in Sub-Saharan Africa* (report to the Executive Directors, mimeo, April 1990). The *Annual Operational Review* for each financial year contains highly significant data on project implementation, cumulative data on lending, and analyses of policy trends. The review for FY 1990 contains a detailed analysis of impact on project lending of three major policy papers prepared in the 1980s: *Education Policies for Sub-Saharan Africa: Adjustment, Revitalization, and Expansion* (1988), *Primary Education: A World Bank Policy Paper* (1990), and *Skills for Productivity: Policies for Technical and Vocational Education and Training in Developing Countries* (1990c). Similarly, the *Annual Operational Review* for fiscal 1988 contained a detailed analysis of policy-oriented lending and its impact. The Wapenhaus Report on project effectiveness, dated September 1, 1992, was submitted to the Executive Directors in December 1992, and remains unpublished: *Effective Implementation: Key to Development Impact*, Portfolio Management Task Force Report R92–195.

7   From Wolfensohn to Wolfowitz

From the outset, the presidency of New York investment banker James Wolfensohn was overshadowed by the stridency and reach of a global campaign that gained momentum through the new medium of the internet. "Fifty years is enough" echoed around the world as the Bank and IMF marked their first half-century, the campaign slogan appealing to many in the resurgent non-governmental organization (NGO) movement so visible at the time. Bound up with the anti-Bretton Woods campaign was a broader "anti-globalization" offensive, with such events as the annual meetings of the World Trade Organization (WTO) providing location and opportunity for frequently violent protest. The 1994 annual meeting of the Bank and Fund (marking the half-century since Bretton Woods) ushered in new challenges for their external relations. Throughout its history, the Bank would have had little difficulty in shrugging off such nuisances. The mood had shifted somewhat by 1994, however, when questions concerning the Bank's role, relevance, and even legitimacy were being taken seriously, and on a wide front. Intense political scrutiny within the United States, the Bank's largest shareholder, was a sign that the times were changing.

Reclaiming legitimacy

It was a moment of considerable irony. On the one hand, the Bank was struggling to maintain its historical position as the world's preeminent development organization. Its position stemmed from the capacity to raise and lend out considerable sums to assist governments construct and maintain not only the material infrastructure of development but also the underlying economic and social policy framework for development. That function rested upon grand Keynesian assumptions, ones that looked not only to the centrality of governments in building up public infrastructure and policies for development, but also to the legitimacy of large-scale government borrowing for these purposes. By 1995, a time of resurgent neoliberalism that was shaking Keynesianism to its very core, the legitimacy of a Keynesian World Bank was under serious threat. Thus the Bank was itself a potential victim of the neoliberalism that was now questioning its future.

On the other hand, the populist campaign against the Bank had in its sights the Bank as a champion of neoliberalism, relentlessly promoting global capitalism through economic globalization. As mediated through structural adjustment lending and austerity measures, the Bank's program of neoliberal reform was an easy target for the "fifty years is enough" campaigners, who in calling for the demise of the World Bank found themselves in uncomfortable alignment with influential conservative opinion in, for example, the US Congress. At heart was the tension between the conventional view of the Bank as a development agency (chiefly through its lending) and the Bank as a promoter of fiscal conservatism and policy reform (chiefly through its loan conditions).

This general external environment dominated and shaped the presidency of James Wolfensohn, an Australian-born investment banker who had taken on US citizenship in 1980 in the hope that the Carter administration would appoint him as Robert McNamara's successor at the Bank. Wolfensohn's disappointment at that rejection was only matched by the zeal of his second campaign, a zeal that spilled over into the hothouse atmosphere of his two terms in office. His term was notable for the expansive view of Bank responsibilities and functions he adopted, nothing declared off-limits if it could be justified in terms of an assault on poverty. After her departure from the Bank, Wolfensohn's Managing Director Jessica Einhorn wrote of the Bank's "mission creep" under the energetic President: "Words like 'comprehensive' and 'holistic' have come into common use as the Bank struggles to encompass all agendas" (Einhorn 2001: 32). It was, in essence, Wolfensohn's way of transcending those tensions between the development and reform functions of the Bank, and of restoring confidence in the Bank, inside as well as beyond its walls.

Much was undoubtedly a matter of style, tactics, and external relations. Wolfensohn literally embraced his harshest NGO critics, inviting them to the policy table and ensuring for them a voice within the Bank. Such measures were part of a concerted effort to open up the Bank to external view, seen most easily in the capacity of the Bank's rapidly expanding website to host thousands of internal Bank documents that previously were either "for official use only" or otherwise difficult to obtain. Project documents and OED reports, for example, cascaded into the public domain under Wolfensohn, along with vast quantities of data, discussion papers that appeared on a daily basis, and general information about the Bank. Both tactics – greater engagement with NGOs and greater transparency and openness in Bank operations – were part of a more general push for the Bank to be seen as totally committed to the eradication of poverty, as being in constant dialogue with all relevant partners and stakeholders, and as being a "listening," "responsive," and even "humble" Bank, an organization that had learned from its critics the dangers of absolutism, overconfidence, and arrogance.

What remained in no doubt were the fundamentals of Bank policies and operations. Despite all the external relations pressures on Wolfensohn, the Bank continued to function along traditional lines. In many senses, the major pressures upon Wolfensohn were actually time-honored ones, involving the tension within the Bank between a limited and an expansive view of its role. Partly dictated by the external environment and the availability of loan capital, partly dictated by internal dynamics determining the flow of funds to borrowers (and how the pace could be justified), and partly dictated by the only-temporary resolution of competing internal views about the Bank's role, the ways in which the Bank has managed debate on the "expansive" versus "contained" view of its role are important features of its history. Wolfensohn's predecessor, Lewis Preston, through conviction, personality, and declining health had adopted a constrained view of the Bank's role, a view reinforced by serious limits on loanable capital in the early 1990s. By contrast, in thinking about economic management, poverty reduction, and public policy, Wolfensohn had embraced a broad view of *governance*, one that moved well beyond the traditional and privileged view of governments and their functional role (what has been termed *governmentalism*, in itself a reflection of wide-ranging Keynesianism). This, for Wolfensohn, implied an equally expansive role for the Bank, now to deal with a larger and more diverse range of stakeholders and partners, while at the same time recognizing limits on governments' own economic interventions. Early in his term, Wolfensohn adopted for the Bank a high profile in the aftermath of the Bosnian crisis, claiming for the Bank key responsibilities in postwar reconstruction and in the building of new political, economic, and social institutions. This, according to biographer Sebastian Mallaby, set the scene for the entire Wolfensohn presidency (Mallaby 2004: 116–44).

Organizing the Bank's new poverty focus

The turbulence marking the Bank's external relations was matched by unprecedented internal dissention and upheaval. It would be too extreme to see inside the Wolfensohn Bank a crisis of legitimacy. Nevertheless, the collapse of certainty and confidence so widespread among Bank staff collided head-on with a long-standing internal culture of a self-conferred supremacy and easy superiority. For Bank staff, there was widespread acceptance that to keep its traditional banking and policy functions intact, internal change was inevitable. In other words, the maintenance of business as usual would require new functions and style. The challenge for Wolfensohn was to keep the fundamentals intact while at the same time undertaking sweeping internal reforms. This was especially pertinent given the Bank's own assessments that its strict regime of imposing loan conditionalities in order to bring about policy reforms had not been particularly effective (see World Bank 1996).

To restore productive and efficient relationships with borrowers, with key western governments and with other stakeholders, and to restore productive and efficient working conditions within the Bank, Wolfensohn adopted a fresh assault on poverty as his key organizing theme. That assault, he declared, would require a new vision, as well as hardheaded commitments to increased operational effectiveness. Using his first address to an annual meeting (September 1995), Wolfensohn laid the foundations of his presidency through six key actions:

- bringing the eleventh replenishment of IDA to a successful conclusion
- addressing the debt problems of the poorest countries
- building and expanding partnerships
- accelerating private sector development
- doing more to help in post-conflict situations
- creating a "results culture" within the Bank.

(summarized from Wolfensohn 1996: 3)

In that month, Wolfensohn established two task forces, one to work on strategies to shore up the "professional excellence" of Bank staff, the other to develop a culture of "client responsiveness, results and accountability." Wolfensohn justified them by referring to a range of threats to the Bank: greater competition from other providers of development finance and assistance; increasing scepticism in donor countries about aid effectiveness; an eroding internal skills base; low staff morale; and internal resistance to change. Wolfensohn minced no words when he informed Bank staff in December 1995 of his initial conclusions about the organization: it was "a Bank faced with decay."

A year later, in the context of a bruising clash with the Executive Directors to gain a marked increase in the Bank's administrative budget (in contrast with the cutbacks effected by Preston), Wolfensohn outlined the details of two management principles that would dominate his presidency – the Strategic Compact and the Knowledge Bank (Wolfensohn 1996). Both principles were governed, in Wolfensohn's stated view, by the need to give effect to fresh commitments to the alleviation of poverty, what he termed a "new paradigm" that saw poverty reduction remaining "at the heart of everything we do":

Reducing poverty clearly involves the interplay of a number of issues: macroeconomic policy, private sector development, environmental sustainability, and investments in human capital, especially girls' education and early childhood development. All these elements are important.

(Wolfensohn 1996: 12)

This simple statement reeked with implications. It was a decisive moment, with Wolfensohn declaring his adherence to the expansive role of the Bank, one that not only tolerated but placed some emphasis on such "social overheads" areas as education.

The lesson is clear: for economic advance, you need social advance – and without social development, economic development cannot take root.

For the Bank, this means that we need to make sure that the programs and projects we support have adequate social foundations:

- By designing more participatory country strategies and programs – reflecting discussions not only with governments but also with community groups, NGOs, and private businesses
- By putting more emphasis on social, cultural, and institutional issues, and their interplay with economic issues...
- By learning more about how the changing dynamics between public institutions, markets, and civil society affect economic and social development.

(Wolfensohn 1996: 13)

Here was an attempt to shore up the President's market credentials, by rejecting narrow governmentalism in favor of a broader view of governance and participation. More than that, it was a strong signal that the Wolfensohn presidency would side with those that promoted an expansive rather than constrained view of the Bank's role and work. But to bring about his vision of an expanded Bank, Wolfensohn had much internal housekeeping to attend to.

The Strategic Compact was a principle designed to dampen internal disillusion and escalating morale problems. Wolfensohn's aspirations to strengthen the Bank, shore up its global standing, and increase its lending depended, as was evident through his repeated insistence, on nothing less than a decisive shift in the internal culture of the Bank. His language was peppered with references not only to poverty alleviation, but also to inclusiveness, humility, and responsiveness. Yet at its heart was the need to give effect to a trade-off between staff cuts and workplace reform, and Wolfensohn's tactic was to forge an accommodation between the Bank's conventional pro-growth and pro-reform concerns with fresh commitments to address poverty and inequality. Considerable sums were spent on modernizing the Bank's information technology systems, and hundreds of staffers went to Harvard and Stanford universities for several weeks' training on the poverty focus, capped off by a week in a borrowing country, ideally at village level. To compound the complexity and uncertainties of internal change, a kind of internal marketplace was established within the Bank, whereby staffers with expertise required by a Bank unit would be "purchased" to provide that expertise. The excessive costs, the staff distraction and the disruption to normal appraisal and lending operations were "transition costs...larger than they had to be.... [They] showed he had no feel for public institutions and no sense of the Bank's history" (Mallaby 2004: 169).

Equally ineffectual was the Knowledge Bank principle, a concept that had been previously promoted inside the Bank by staffer Stephen Denning, without apparent impact, but which was speedily embraced by

Wolfensohn when it was put to him a few days before the October 1996 speech (Mallaby 2004: 159–60):

> Development knowledge is part of the "global commons": it belongs to everyone, and everyone should benefit from it. But a global partnership is required to cultivate and disseminate it. The Bank Group's relationships with governments and institutions all over the world, and our unique reservoir of development experience across sectors and countries, position us to play a leading role in this new global knowledge partnership.
>
> We have been in the business of researching and disseminating the lessons of development for a long time. But the revolution in information technology increases the potential value of these efforts by vastly extending their reach . . . to gather development information and experience and share it with our clients. We need to become, in effect, the Knowledge Bank.
>
> (Wolfensohn 1996: 14)

Knowledge Bank strategies were placed under Denning's management, outlined in a paper (Denning 1998) anticipating Wolfensohn's 2000 target for attaining his Knowledge Bank objectives, reported also in the Bank's flagship World Development Report *Knowledge for Development* (World Bank 1999e). "Its objective is to make know-how and experience accessible not only internally, to World Bank staff, but externally to clients, partners and stake-holders around the world – and in the process to reach many who now have little or no access to its expertise" (World Bank 1999e: 139).

In such a way, the Knowledge Bank was a reflection of Wolfensohn's more open, communicative, and sharing Bank. It is possible to interpret the Bank's organizational knowledge management principles along three lines. First, the Bank can be understood as having accumulated – notably through its policy and lending operations – an enormous reservoir of knowledge about the global economy and development strategies. That reservoir can be said to give the Bank something of a distinct "competitive" advantage over other development agencies. Second, shifting views of the Bank's role demand of it greater sophistication in its use of information, especially given its emerging focus on policy (rather than project) lending, human capacity building, and promoting among borrowers "knowledge economy" aspirations. Thus, the Bank needs to be a generator of knowledge as much as an accumulator and disseminator of knowledge. Third, Wolfensohn recognized the need for the Bank to improve by a significant margin its internal knowledge management systems, aspiring to improve internal efficiency through greater knowledge sharing. It was all rather orthodox, by the standards of contemporary organization theory and practice, but for a public institution as large, complex, and cumbersome as the World Bank, Knowledge Bank principles were potentially upsetting.

Yet appraisals of Knowledge Bank in practice pointed to something of a victory of style over substance, of past practice over innovation. Kenneth King's assessment pointed to combinations of long-standing and new approaches to the generation, application, and dissemination of Bank knowledge, much conventional work (not least country and sectoral analysis, research, operations evaluations, and training) being co-opted into the framework (King 2002; see also King and McGrath 2003; McGrath and King 2004).

While Wolfensohn's Strategic Compact and Knowledge Bank principles were primarily felt inside the Bank, two other related principles had considerable potential to impact on Bank policies and lending operations as they were experienced by borrowers. The Comprehensive Development Framework (CDF) and the Poverty Reduction Strategy Papers (PRSP) were attempts to inform how the fresh poverty focus might give added impetus to the quality, scope, and impact of Bank lending. As reflections of the external pressures swirling around the Bank, however, the initiatives were more a matter of process than substance: their content had much more to do with the manner whereby Bank and borrower would negotiate policy and loans rather than with any new thinking about poverty, development, or growth. At the same time, a basic requirement of CDF and PRSP approaches was that poverty reduction would become a core focus of both Bank and borrower concerns, not generally subsumed as a hoped-for by-product of growth.

In this vein, at the heart of CDF were principles of inclusion. Indeed, Wolfensohn's September 1997 annual address was titled *The Challenge of Inclusion* (Wolfensohn 1997; see also Wolfensohn 1999). CDF reflected the pressures imposed on the Bank by the "small government" emphasis in neoliberalism, putting behind it to the extent possible the centrality of narrow state-centered governmentalism in favor of governance through broader participation. The principles of inclusion espoused by Wolfensohn indicated that national development policy frameworks, as well as the programs and projects financed by the Bank, needed to be the product of planning and negotiation conducted at far more than the national governmental level. Local community representatives, civil society, and non-governmental organizations, and the private sector were prominent in Wolfensohn's mind as he advocated full participation by local stakeholders. It was a partial response to the critique of the Bank as an essentially "pro government, big government" Keynesian organization. Yet what Wolfensohn set out to achieve, and to considerable effect, was a greater place for social development objectives within broader economic reform packages, integrating "Washington consensus" aspirations with hitherto separate "social overhead" concerns. It was a means of bringing closer together the Bank's traditional development and reform concerns, conventionally seen as being in exquisite tension.

A further dimension of the inclusive CDF concerned the rest of the international development assistance industry. Inclusion was to shape the Bank's working relations with bilateral agencies, other UN development bodies, regional development banks and organizations, international labor, the private sector, and NGOs. It was, on the surface, all about working together more intentionally and collaboratively at country level, so that the collective aid effort reinforced a country's singular development path and strategy rather than multiple ones (on CDF see Dollar 1999; Hanna and Agarwala 2000).

There had been considerable background to this second aspect of the CDF, launched by Wolfensohn in 1999. The mid-1990s had seen cumulative forces building up for reform of the entire UN system. At the heart of matters was the system's centerpiece, the Security Council, with many member states highly critical of the ongoing veto powers exercised by the five foundation powers. At the time, however, reform of the Security Council was seen as too difficult, and UN Secretary General Boutros Boutros-Ghali turned rather to the system's development cooperation efforts in a preliminary attempt to indicate progress on UN reform. Since 1994, the United Nation's development reforms were most in evidence at country level. In most, the UNDP Resident Representative had assumed the role of UN "country coordinator," responsible for ensuring the "harmonization" of UN development efforts, bringing the planning and budget cycles of the many UN agencies operating at country level together, and fostering greater sharing of resources, expertise, and common programming. It gave UNDP an acknowledged role as the United Nation's lead agency in development cooperation, a role that increasingly involved in the harmonization process the private sector and local NGOs. A central New York-based United Nations Development Group (UNDG) was established to oversee the effort, again chaired by the Administrator (i.e. executive head) of UNDP. It was an arrangement that sat very uneasily with both Wolfensohn and the Bank. As a UN Specialized Agency, the Bank could not remain aloof, yet it refused to join the UNDG as a full member. Rather, the principle of inclusion that underpinned the CDF was used to shore up the Bank's image of development supremacy and its role as self-appointed leader in development assistance and policy work. Thus while the UNDG was constructing – along the lines of inclusiveness – national level planning bodies to drive development coordination, the Bank set out on a parallel course, using its financial clout to ensure compliance in a group of thirteen carefully selected countries that had little option but to conform.

In a sense, what the CDF approach meant for a borrowing country was to expand and diversify the actors involved in development planning, that is in the construction of economic and social policy. Opposition parties, local NGOs, religious groups, and private sector organizations were all to be actively engaged. The CDF required this of borrowers, just as it required them to arrange for close collaboration between bilateral donors, the multilaterals, and international NGOs. Part of the requirement was to foster a broader conception of national development, so that macroeconomic issues would be informed by a range of social, governance, and environmental concerns. This aspect of CDF approaches reflected the import of Wolfensohn's appointment in February 1997 of Nobel laureate Joseph Stiglitz as Chief Economist.

Stiglitz, a declared supporter of core "Washington consensus" principles, had become increasingly strident in his criticism of the inflexible ways in which they were being promoted and imposed, particularly in the transition and East Asian economies (Stiglitz 2002). For Stiglitz, the impact of neoliberal reforms would be shaped through careful attention to their timing and sequence, requiring careful and detailed analysis of local conditions. At country level, the political and structural dimensions of reform, the impact of local conditions, prospects for building consensus and greater participation in reform, and detailed understandings of the impact of reform measures on the poor were all necessary for the successful promotion of change along neoliberal lines. This required of the Bank not only an expanded analytic capacity, but also a willingness to tolerate diversity. And it required of the Bank an insistence that borrowers behave accordingly in constructing policy and negotiating loans from the Bank (see also Stiglitz 1998a,b; for commentary see Cammack 2004).

This line of thinking, for Stiglitz, was particularly important given the diversity of the Bank's borrowers. Dogmatism would mean, in effect, that borrowers not able or willing to embrace Bank policy demands would turn elsewhere for finance that was, as the decade progressed, more readily obtainable from both the private and the regional development banks. The strident Bank would become increasingly sidelined as a source of loanable capital and thus as a source of ideas. Stiglitz also took up a keen interest in the indebtedness of the very poorest countries and more generally in the impact of reform measures on the poor. The long-standing squeamishness of the Bank concerning debt relief appeared to be easing as the decade progressed, and Stiglitz took a leading role in producing justifications for it. The Highly Indebted Poor Country (HIPC) initiative, in fact, became bound up with CDF in a process whereby CDF principles were mandated for countries seeking debt relief. For each of them, a PRSP needed to be prepared, along CDF lines, as a precondition to any approval for debt relief. This mandated status for the weakest borrowers enhanced considerably the take-up rate of CDF and PRSP procedures at country level as reported by the Bank (World Bank 2000a; see also World Bank 2004a). The price for borrowers was no option but to accept Bank prescriptions for macroeconomic reform. More generally, however, Bank conditionality reflected the accelerating trend across the donor community through the 1990s to insist on "results-oriented" aid programs; the Bank was far from alone in demanding policy changes in program countries and greater impact from aid programs as a precondition for more.

These developments were keenly felt in how the Bank dealt with the surging NGO movement having such an impact across the UN system at the time. First, Wolfensohn's expanded view of governance implied the participation of "civil society" in country-level and local-level decisions about development and poverty reduction strategies. The CDF and PRSP each imposed obligations for governments to broaden their consultations in formulating development policies, entirely consistent with Wolfensohn's broad view of governance. Second, as noted, Wolfensohn adopted the strategy of appeasement concerning his own dealings with NGOs, seeking to soften and blunt their hostility towards the Bank by inviting them to the policy table, part of a broader public relations offensive to promote the Bank as a consultative, responsive, and flexible organization. Third, the Wolfensohn years saw a concerted effort to include the NGO sector as a key partner in the delivery of Bank projects and programs, part of a broader offensive to reduce the focus on government-led implementation in favor of private sector and community-based delivery. Finally, Bank dealings with the NGO sector remained very much on the Bank's terms, the Bank's own governance and decision-making processes in no way reflecting Bank insistence that civil society play an ample role in country-level policy determination.

On the one hand, the World Bank under James Wolfensohn opened out the boundaries of operations. The Bank became increasingly expansive in its thinking, embracing a wider set of concerns deemed to be of relevance to its mission and objectives. Both Bank scrutiny and Bank lending proceeded on a broader front, the Bank seeking to shore up its relevance and even survival by including a growing number of subsectors in its portfolio and involving a broader constituency in the construction of funded interventions. The new poverty focus provided a rationale for all manner of shifts in both Bank substance and Bank style. A good example is the Bank's discovery in the 1990s of microfinancing, hitherto regarded as being of passing rather than mainstream interest, being small-scale and focussed on local communities unlike conventional operations. Relations with NGOs, too, were designed not only to stave off the venomous critiques of the Bank, but also to give the Bank a softer, more consultative and inclusive image. By insisting that borrowing governments tailor their governance so that markets and civil society could find their place, the Wolfensohn Bank could claim to be insistent in requiring of its borrowers the focus on poverty and on inclusive processes that it itself had embraced.

On the other hand, the Wolfensohn Bank was a Bank attempting to conduct business as usual. The general parameters of its mission and operations remained intact, even if its dominance in the world of public sector finance was declining. Equally relevant today is a portrayal of the Bank in the 1940s and 1950s as a champion of neoliberal macroeconomic policy and governance:

> In the period before the 1950s ... even a relatively small flow of funds could be justified as a contribution to development only if borrowing countries adopted sensible development policies. This meant in general settling outstanding external debt obligations, pursuing conservative monetary and fiscal policies, generating enough public savings to cover the local currency costs of necessary capital infrastructure, providing a hospitable climate for foreign and domestic private investment, and recognizing the management's boundary line between activities appropriate to the public sector and those appropriate to the private sector.
>
> (Mason and Asher 1973: 464)

The significance of Einhorn's view of mission creep becomes apparent when the view is adopted of a Bank attempting to shore up its conventional role through a diversification of its work. That is a time-honored practice for the World Bank, ever with an eye on its survival in the marketplace of borrowing and lending.

Education in the Wolfensohn Bank

The decade after 1995 saw the gulf between formal Bank education policy and its actual lending practices grow ever wider. For structural reasons, the Regional Divisions (and their Country Departments) were able to head off in their own directions, essentially in a quest to keep loan funds flowing, and so were increasingly flexible in accommodating borrower interests and preferences. Beginning at a time of central education policy stridency and dogmatism, the decade saw feeble attempts by the education policy core to keep up with Bank operations as they evolved in practice. This required the adoption of a new language and style, those of responsiveness and flexibility. The reality within the Bank's operations Divisions, however, was that attempts to formulate central policy positions were ignored to the extent that they could be.

The central policy tilt at flexibility was buttressed by a collapse in the education sector's central policy capacity to formulate anything new. Its research and analytic capacity declined rapidly, its influence dwindling as a shaper of Bank and borrower behavior. It was as if the central education sector, having dramatically overplayed its policy hand up to 1995, had lost the capacity to restore its reputation for decisive leadership and influence. For borrowers, that might amount to a good outcome, the Bank emerging in the opening years of the new century as merely one of a range of influential actors in educational development and assistance. The Bank's capacity to impose its ideas essentially through the weight of its lending and the quality of its analytical work had undergone considerable diminution. At the same time, country-level "education sector work" – the analysis of educational needs from which lending operations might be derived – continued on as before, driven by the Regional and Country Divisions' need to keep the pipeline well filled with potential lending operations. The overall policy picture was of the Bank wanting, yet struggling, to catch up with approaches to education policy that prevailed elsewhere. Although its stature remained intact as a champion of neoliberal reform in education, nothing in its specifically educational thought and practice made Bank stances particularly noteworthy.

Elusive credibility – education under O'Rourke

The minor internal reorganizations of Bank structures in 1992 and 1995 had resulted in somewhat flatter hierarchies. Of critical importance for the education sector in the second half of the 1990s was the establishment of a matrix system, whereby a Country Director would have two reporting lines – to a regional Vice President (e.g. for East Asia and the Pacific) and to a thematic Vice President, the head of a "network." For education, its network – Human Development – was led by Vice President David de Ferranti, a fervent advocate of education, who had joined the Bank following a period as chief administrator of the large United States food stamp program. His Human Development Network covered five sectors – education, health, nutrition, population, and social protection. Ferranti was keenly interested in education, and indeed one aspect of his work was often commented upon in interviews conducted for this book. A degree of protection for the education sector, exceptionally vulnerable within a sceptical World Bank, was perceived by many as deriving from de Ferranti's frequent meetings with Wolfensohn's spouse Elaine, education being a passionate and professional concern of Mrs Wolfensohn. As de Ferranti's Education Director put it, "you always felt like being in the laser beam."

That Education Director was Maris O'Rourke, who had been appointed by de Ferranti in September 1995. This was just four months after the Executive Directors had received the contentious *Priorities and Strategies for Education*, a policy publication whose parlous reputation both inside and outside the Bank was to shape O'Rourke's time as Director until her premature departure in 2000. For seven years, O'Rourke had been Secretary of the New Zealand Ministry of Education, managing the extensive neoliberal reform movement that had transformed education in that country. That experience was clearly the attraction for de Ferranti and the Bank, given O'Rourke's pronounced lack of experience in developing countries (she had been Secretary of the NZ National Commission for UNESCO and had extensive contact with OECD education policy work). Many of those interviewed for this book preferred to insist instead on the influence of O'Rourke's background as a kindergarten teacher and motel proprietor. O'Rourke herself would refer to a management style that insisted on a quick and extensive turnover of staff, their location in open-plan offices, and the requirement that her new staff leave all books, papers, and working documents behind when joining her Department. Staff "retreats" were styled "advances" on her insistence, and she proclaimed the virtues of establishing an "education family" within the Bank.

O'Rourke's lack of experience in the educational development of low- and middle-income countries was especially apparent in her neglect of devising substantive policy content and priorities. Rather, O'Rourke placed a premium on process. If the attempt was made to formulate policy stances and priorities, it remained well hidden from view. O'Rourke had warmed – even prior to her arrival – to the manner in which Wolfensohn was seeking to engender broad and deep cultural change within the Bank. While being wooed by de Ferranti, O'Rourke would listen spellbound to the new President's exhortations to staff, declaring that she "wanted to be a part of it." Thus O'Rourke, the self-styled change agent, embarked on a process of clearing out the old, insisting on new methods of working, but with very little of substance in view.

One aspect of the Wolfensohn internal strategy to which O'Rourke was strongly attracted was the "Knowledge Bank" ideal. In July 1996 O'Rourke received de Ferranti's blessing to have the education sector designated as the lead, or pilot, sector within his network for applying Knowledge Bank principles. In September the Education Knowledge Management System (EKMS) was established for "facilitating knowledge synthesis, stimulating discussion, and identifying areas that need attention" (Currie 1997: 5). Under the management of Bruno Laporte, O'Rourke's office roommate, the attempt was made to mold the 250 or so education specialists scattered across the Bank into a single "knowledge community." In principle, nine "thematic groups" were established, designed to share content, apply it to Bank and borrower operations, and to build broader contacts with research communities. In reality, it was the first two only that made much progress:

- economics of education
- early child development
- access and equity in basic education
- strategies for educational change
- post-basic education and training
- project design and implementation
- private investments in education
- effective schools and teachers
- educational technology.

The banality with which most thematic groups went about their work might be explained through the deliberate playing out of scepticism, if not outright cynicism and resistance, concerning Knowledge Bank principles and how they were imposed on the education sector (that banality also typifies a Bank-published report on the process – see Carayannis and Laporte 2002). Yet each group received an average budget in 1998 of $250,000, in order to develop "customized knowledge products" (Carayannis and Laporte 2002: 13). Some groups collapsed. Others emerged later with new titles, including tertiary education (which gathered around the preparation of a major report in 2002), adult outreach education, school health, and education reform and management. Overall, the attempt was made to assemble items that ranged from "informal tips and ideas, to key readings and Bank reports, to directories of internal and external experts on education issues" (Carayannis and Laporte 2002: 4). Many academic researchers and learned societies, especially in the United States, received pleas to submit reading lists and bibliographies to the groups. To greater effect, an Education Advisory Service (EAS) was established in November 1996 as a front-of-house information clearing house that provided information to both internal and external inquirers. *EdStats* was also established, a database with country-level data and information organized around themes, along with information on Bank lending patterns in education. These two services were far happier expressions of Knowledge Bank principles.

Yet knowledge has to be grounded in content, and has to be generally accepted as valid, credible, and relevant. For education, Knowledge Bank was a house built on sand. In a deliberate move, O'Rourke succeeded in shedding nearly every long-standing education researcher and analyst, including not a few who were prominent in the scholarly research literature on educational development and the economics of education. Their replacements, far fewer in number and of more junior standing, failed during her term of office to achieve anything like that prominence, policy influence, and professional engagement with external research and policy communities. Thus despite being an enthusiastic participant, the education sector was severely constrained in its application of Knowledge Bank principles. The caliber of its staff and the quality of their thinking ran counter to proclamations about leadership.

The shadow of the 1995 policy row cast a pall over O'Rourke's early years in the Bank. The deep wounds needed time to heal, and O'Rourke saw herself as something of a healer. For her, internal processes of policy formation were as important as content. By effectively dismantling the extant central policy department and starting from scratch, O'Rourke failed to grasp the importance of quality in analytical work. The price paid was a heavy one: by 2000 the Bank had given up its reputation as a recognized leader in educational policy analysis and development. This only widened the gap between central policy formation and operational practice in the Regional Divisions. The matter was urgent: borrowers were overtly bypassing education as a Bank sector of relevance to them.

On December 20, 1996, de Ferranti forwarded a memorandum to Wolfensohn's office headed "Decline in education lending." Its purpose appeared to be threefold: to raise issues that de Ferranti saw as of escalating urgency; to ensure that the President and Executive Directors were not caught by surprise at the steep decline in education lending; and to propose an "external communications strategy to deal with the situation – outsiders think that we are increasing lending for education, especially for basic education and for girls." De Ferranti presented an analysis prepared by Nicholas Burnett: from FY 1994 to 1997, lending had halved, from an all-time high of $2.2 billion to $1 billion. For the period 1993–6, only ten borrowers accounted for two-thirds of loans. Jomtien expectations seemed a distant memory, the analysis seeing the decline as particularly acute in Latin America, in postsecondary education, and among the Bank's traditional heavy borrowers for education. While speculating on borrower reasoning, de Ferranti was more precise on internal Bank factors: a trend to consolidate potential loans and to opt for pilot approaches rather than the large-scale; the perception (within the Bank) that lending was discouraged for post-basic education; limited analytical work at country level leading to fewer loan proposals; the relative inflexibility of Bank lending instruments and procedures; and relative shortages of Bank education experts. Of greatest significance, however, was de Ferranti's recognition that as a provider of external education finance the Bank was no longer dominant in most regions. For example, in Latin America and the Caribbean, Bank lending was eclipsed by the Inter-American Bank. The European Union and the Asian Development Bank had emerged as major providers, with Japan a significant bilateral. "We are losing regional market shares not only because of others [*sic*] financial terms (grants vs loans) but also because of the transaction costs that go with our lending (procedures, conditionality, etc.)."

Steps needed to be taken by O'Rourke to correct the dysfunctional nature of the education sector she had inherited, especially in terms of the working relations between the central policy group and regional operations staff (the latter accounting for about 80 percent of the Bank education staff total of just under 250). Of importance was the establishment of the Education Sector Board (ESB), bringing representatives of the two groups together on a fort-nightly basis. Over her five-year term, the ESB routinely addressed such issues as: trends in the external "education and development" environment, especially issues confronting borrowers and how other agencies were perceiving and addressing them; formulating key development objectives for the education sector and packaging them in terms of medium-range strategies; crucially, the review of Bank operations in education, including lending levels and trends, project and program performance, and target setting for future lending; and identification of sector risks and management issues requiring attention at senior levels within the Bank.

Also put in place by O'Rourke in 1996 was a standing External Advisory Panel on Education, to meet occasionally in order to provide comment on Bank education strategies. Chaired by Jo Ritzen (Netherlands Minister for Education, Culture and Science), its members consisted of Diallo Aicha-Bah (UNESCO Division of Basic Education), Vaidyanatha Ayyar (Indian Ministry of Human Resource Development), José Brunner (Chilean Ministro Secretario General del Gobierno), Fay Chung (UNICEF Education Chief), Mary Futtrel (George Washington University), and Quentin Thompson (Coopers and Lybrand, London). Meetings were polite exchanges of views, O'Rourke receiving nothing by way of rigorous or robust feedback. In March 1997, the Panel provided words of comfort: "It is the Panel's conviction that the World Bank's future is in education. Without proper education, the investments in infrastructure and technology won't last. Moreover in the field of loans for infrastructure projects the World Bank will be confronted with increasing competition of private banks. In the field of education however there is no alternative for the World Bank." Such a statement came at a time of falling education sector lending, and was accompanied by appeals for the Bank to be more involved in pilot projects, small-scale technical assistance lending, and to understand better the "socio-psychological and cultural aspects of education." It was not a recipe for expanded lending, and indeed failed dismally to engage with pre-vailing scepticism within the Bank concerning education.

With considerable rhetorical flourish, an *Education Action Plan* was released in 1997 (World Bank 1997), announcing "a new beginning, a commitment to a higher level of effectiveness and impact, and a fundamental shift away from old approaches and ways of thinking" (World Bank 1997: 1). It was vintage O'Rourke, dismissive of the old, trumpeting the new, but short on detail about what "the new" was to be. With studied intentionality, the Plan avoided any reference to the 1995 *Priorities and Strategies for Education*, and set aside any universal ideals, goals, or prescriptions. Rather, its focus was declining lending, and its business language addressed country-specific feasibilities and targets. Knowledge Bank rhetoric permeated the whole, the notion that a more knowledge-intensive Bank sector would result in borrowers being persuaded to take on higher levels of education lending.

In FY 1997, the Plan noted, 135 potential Bank borrowers had taken on education loans in a grossly uneven pattern of borrowing: 17 countries had borrowed 70 percent of the education total; 52 countries (27 percent of the total); and 66 countries (3 percent). The ailments of the World Bank in the early Wolfensohn years are all too evident in the Plan's response: to target vigorously the known major borrowers in education as a hard commercial line of attack, and to afford lesser priority to reluctant borrowers and to small economies. Although the Plan in no sense sought to abandon the poor, its effect did not bode well for EFA targets, already languishing. It failed to provide realistic Bank strategies for them, in favor of pursuing the best commercial prospects. The Plan was, at heart, a survival strategy for the education sector, faced with the prospect of fading away as a sector relevant to core Bank lending operations. Table 7.1 provides an overview of education lending for FY 1996–2000.

The policy highpoint of O'Rourke's tenure was the publication in 1999 of an *Education Sector Strategy* (World Bank 1999d). Summing up as it did the O'Rourke period's emphasis on process over content, the paper's importance as an actual or potential driver of policy or operations should not be overemphasized. Couched as much to an internal Bank audience as to those outside, the paper married two fundamental principles: that national education systems need to develop in a balanced manner, each subsector or component being important for the health of the others; and that the Bank needed to deal with its clients on a country-by-country basis, constructing particular operational interventions for each. What was most significant was the formal abandonment of the short policy menu that had triumphed over the 1980–95 period. While nothing by way of policy prescription replaced it, of potential importance were the new spaces opened up for policy flexibility and diversity.

Coordinated by a junior New Zealand Treasury official recruited by O'Rourke for the purpose, Jeffrey Waite, the *Strategy* was assembled almost exclusively through consultations within the Bank (although advice was sought and received from the External Advisory Panel). This unusual lack of systematic reference to external constituencies was justified in terms of the paper's focus on the Bank's own role in educational development and its immediate task to shore up lending, and hence the sector's survival within the Bank. Of considerable importance, however, were accompanying education policy and

Table 7.1 World Bank education financing, by region and subsector, FY 1996–2000 ($US m)

	1996	1997	1998	1999	2000	Total
AFR	194.6	115.2	400.0	208.8	189.8	1,108.4
Adult literacy/nonformal	10.2	—	—	30.5	6.1	46.8
General education support	36.8	56.5	27.4	11.0	92.9	224.6
Pre-primary education	—	8.3	—	0.4	—	8.7
Primary education	95.5	15.4	226.1	126.5	57.3	520.8
Secondary education	—	19.0	98.2	10.9	13.7	141.8
Tertiary education	41.8	11.6	46.0	24.7	14.0	138.1
Vocational training	10.5	4.4	2.4	4.9	5.9	28.1
EAP	444.3	619.8	184.6	638.7	84.4	1,971.8
Adult literacy/nonformal	—	—	—	4.2	—	4.2
General education support	1.0	16.2	99.8	58.8	4.0	179.8
Pre-primary education	—	—	1.0	10.0	—	11.0
Primary education	46.3	114.3	36.2	104.1	76.4	377.3
Secondary education	213.2	162.1	47.6	44.4	—	467.3
Tertiary education	135.9	298.7	—	387.2	4.0	825.8
Vocational training	47.9	28.5	—	30.0	—	106.4
ECA	89.3	126.0	544.1	54.3	22.7	836.4
Adult literacy/nonformal	—	5.0	—	—	—	5.0
General education support	64.0	—	19.2	18.1	10.3	111.6
Pre-primary education	0.5	—	22.4	—	—	22.9
Primary education	4.6	7.1	294.0	12.1	8.1	325.9
Secondary education	—	31.2	45.6	12.1	0.6	89.5
Tertiary education	20.3	80.2	151.0	7.2	3.7	262.4
Vocational training	—	2.6	12.0	4.7	—	19.3

LCR	474.0	76.3	857.8	461.8	62.8	1,932.7
Adult literacy/nonformal	—	—	7.0	7.0	—	7.0
General education support	64.7	16.4	103.7	140.3	5.3	330.4
Pre-primary education	8.4	3.7	29.5	11.8	13.1	66.5
Primary education	105.5	19.2	220.4	160.4	21.5	527.0
Secondary education	121.0	1.1	146.9	—	20.7	269.0
Tertiary education	174.3	35.9	356.7	130.7	20.7	718.3
Vocational training	—	—	0.6	11.6	2.2	14.4
MNA	97.2	99.6	129.0	59.4	197.1	582.3
Adult literacy/nonformal	5.1	—	—	—	—	5.1
General education support	—	7.6	—	16.9	71.6	96.1
Pre-primary education	—	—	—	—	—	—
Primary education	32.4	42.0	—	—	85.3	159.7
Secondary education	—	—	—	40.0	—	40.0
Tertiary education	5.4	30.0	77.4	2.5	39.2	154.5
Vocational training	54.2	20.0	51.6	—	1.0	126.8
SAR	420.4	—	705.7	64.5	171.4	1,362.0
Adult literacy/nonformal	30.8	—	—	—	—	30.8
General education support	—	—	2.5	—	32.2	34.7
Pre-primary education	—	—	24.2	9.0	—	33.2
Primary education	284.9	—	634.0	45.4	113.6	1,077.9
Secondary education	—	—	18.3	—	7.6	25.9
Tertiary education	104.7	—	26.6	10.1	16.2	157.6
Vocational training	—	—	0.1	—	1.8	1.9

Source: World Bank Education Sector.

Notes

AFR Africa; EAP East Asia and the Pacific; ECA Europe and Central Asia; LCR Latin America and the Caribbean; MNA Middle East and North Africa; SAR South Asia. Some totals are rounded.

strategy papers prepared in three of the Regional Divisions – Latin America and the Caribbean (World Bank 1999a), East Asia and the Pacific (World Bank 1999b), and the Middle East and North Africa (World Bank 1999c). These assessments of education and training issues reflected in large measure the emerging policy freedoms made possible by the collapse of the short policy menu and the abandonment of strong central constructions of World Bank education policy. While they upset no fundamentals, not least the commitment to public provision of primary education, as a set the papers reflected the realities of regional diversity, especially in East Asia. Counterpart papers were to follow in 2000 for the transition economies (World Bank 2000b) and sub-Saharan Africa (World Bank 2001), with South Asia noticeably absent.

At the same time, the cumulative effect could only be imprecise, the language of Knowledge Bank and of CDF–PRSP principles permeating. For the authors, global education trends were being driven by five major forces – democratization, market economies, globalization, technological innovation, and changing public–private roles. The "world of education" in fact comprised different worlds – one (involving two-thirds of the global population) still struggling with fundamental issues of access and quality, another world resisting changes to the educational *status quo*, another in the richer countries where education was being "rapidly reinvented," and yet another whereby education was transcending its traditional forms. The paper affirmed the Bank's long celebration of human capital theory:

> While human capital ideas focus on links among education, productivity, and economic growth, other disciplines have emphasized additional reasons why education is important. These further reasons stress education's contribution to building social cohesion. They note that education transmits values, beliefs, and traditions. It shapes attitudes and aspirations, and the skills it develops include crucial inter- and intra-personal capabilities. It empowers people. It frees them to learn and think for themselves. It has benefits for health and the environment.
>
> The more rapidly the world changes and the more complex it becomes, the more important are the skills that a good quality education can provide.... All countries need educated and skilled citizens who can operate in a democratic society, workers who can meet changing labor market needs and compete in global markets, learners capable of benefiting from the technology revolution, and policies capable of harnessing the evolving public/private interface.... Education is a key component of the Bank's "Social Agenda" or "Comprehensive Development Framework," which encompasses all these other elements. They include strong participatory democracy and competent and clean governance, an effective judicial and legal system, good financial systems, social services and safety nets, social and economic infrastructure and protection of the environment and national culture, many of which depend in part on the educational system.
>
> (World Bank 1999d: 6)

Such a sales pitch was directed to readers within the Bank as much as to those outside. Indeed, its reliance on assertion contrasted markedly with Bank attempts to ground previous policy declarations in research evidence. The sales pitch continued in conventional manner, however, with details provided on faltering progress on access to education, inequitable access, lack of relevance and quality in much teaching, and weak institutional capacities across education systems. Great store, in assessing ways forward, was placed on the construction of partnerships between and among governments, parents, communities, NGOs, foundations, the private sector, teachers, teacher organizations, and aid organizations at international, regional, and bilateral level. Overt recognition was afforded the decline in the Bank's dominance of the educational development sector:

> The challenge for the Bank for the years ahead is to respond effectively to the implications of partnership and, in doing so, to achieve the best impact possible on the people that development aims to serve. This will necessarily involve good communication between the Bank and its partners, at the country level, the regional level and at headquarters – along with a sense of openness to new possibilities and different points of view, an acknowledgment of one's own strengths and weaknesses, a willingness to compromise, and above all else, an enthusiasm for the many tasks ahead.
> (World Bank 1999d: 21)

With the short policy menu dead in the water, there was little sense of emerging priorities, except to get loan funds flowing again. Thus, the paper reflected lines of argument that had emerged 40 years previously in other mainstream circles:

> Staff now look at education as an integrated system, one part of which cannot function well if another is ailing. The emphasis on basic education, for instance, does not mean that nothing should be done in tertiary education: the role of tertiary institutions as centers of excellence, research hubs and training grounds for tomorrow's teachers and leaders is critical.
> (World Bank 1999d: 24)

It was a reasonable stance, to be sure. Yet its damning import was clear to all who wished to recognize it, that of a Bank that for decades had, for reasons of its own, contributed to uneven rather than balanced educational development. Equally damning was another set of admissions:

> Good analysis of issues and options is the foundation for effective project lending and sound policy advice. Reviews of the education portfolio find a consistent link between good analytic work and high quality projects. In education as in other sectors ... analytic work is being crowded out ....

The recent decline in the Bank's role in research in education is inconsistent with the Bank's quest to become a "knowledge bank" and with improving the impact of education operations. Research has had an important impact on priorities and strategies in education; for example, in making clear the broad benefits to [*sic*] investing in primary and girls' education, the role of textbooks in promoting school quality, and the potential importance of the private sector in financing and provision....

Operational relevance is now the main criterion for choosing new research topics in education. Most recent research aims at evaluating rigorously the impact of investments and policy changes that the Bank is supporting, in order to determine the preconditions and circumstances needed to maximize the chances of success of a project, program, or reform process.

(World Bank 1999d: 27)

O'Rouke's stewardship of Bank work in education is well-reflected in the paper's conclusions about how the Bank should tackle its work. They go some distance in explaining the protracted decline in lending, the parlous standing of the sector in its relations both inside and outside the Bank, and its dwindling policy influence and reputation:

If the relationship between the client and the Bank is characterized by mutual respect, careful listening, openness to new ideas and responsiveness to new challenges, the Bank and client should reach a common position on what the best strategy is for the country's development and what role the country can best play in its implementation. On occasion however, the Bank and the client government may disagree on priorities. Then the Bank will need to reassess its own analysis in light of a client viewpoint that might not have been adequately taken into account, try to convince the client that the Bank analysis has greater benefits than other options, or withdraw from the particular intervention the client wishes to embark upon.

(World Bank 1999d: 35)

This statement bears eloquent testimony to the first five years of educational policy development in the Wolfensohn Bank, its focus on process rather than policy substance looming large. Strategically, the paper made clear distinctions between Bank strategies at global, regional, and country level; in terms of global priorities, four themes were highlighted:

- basic education (especially for girls and for the poorest)
- early interventions (especially early childhood education and school health programs)
- innovative delivery (especially through distance education, open learning, and the use of new technologies)

- systemic reform (addressing "standards, curriculum and assessment; governance and decentralization; and providers and financiers outside of government").

(summarized from World Bank 1999d: 30)

It was a weak set of policy directions: EFA principles were affirmed, as were the Bank's neoliberal reforms in education. "Outcome indicators" set by the Bank were equally weak; for example: "learning improved in target countries," "worldwide knowledge of distance education enhanced," or "education systems operating more efficiently and more equitably." The Bank's Executive Directors were spared the task of formally endorsing the *Strategy* as policy, presumably to relief all round. Predictably, the Regional Divisions moved apace to capitalize on their affirmed freedom to devise local emphases in lending operations.

In a closely associated development, the Bank's Regional Divisions assumed a greater research profile than at any time previously in Bank history. Together with the small group at the center, they produced a useful and diverse range of studies, intended to inform local rather than global policies. From time to time, collaboration with researchers in borrowing countries was apparent, but there was little by way of systematic partnerships or research capacity building in borrowing countries. Both the center and the regions displayed a keen research interest in educational financing (Alderman *et al.* 1998; Kim *et al.* 1998; King *et al.* 1998; King and Orazem 1999). The Bank's private investment arm, the International Finance Corporation (IFC), emerged over this period as a significant supplier of loans for the development of private education institutions and systems, ending a decades-long silence on educational matters not only through financing but also through analytical work (Karmokolias and Maas 1997; Glewwe and Patrinos 1998; IFC 1999; Sosale 1999). Research themes pursued showed a degree of diversification, made possible by the breakdown within the Bank of the research–policy nexus. Rather, operations staff were boosted in their capacity to make use of recent analysis on themes of local interest especially: adult literacy (Lauglo 2000), violence, democracy, and education (Salmi 2000), education and child labor (Fallon and Tzannatos 1998; Cahagarajah and Nielson 1999), and decentralization and related reforms (Patrinos and Ariasingam 1997; Gaynor 1998; Corrales 1999).

If any concern could be regarded as a touchstone over this period (1995–9), it would be "education for all." As noted, the 1997 *Education Action Plan* indicated the reluctance of borrowers (most of all the low-income countries) to embrace either the Jomtien Declaration's "expanded concept" of basic education or the Bank's more confined version of primary education as top public sector priority in education. By the time of the April 2000 World Education Forum (in Dakar, Senegal) it was clear that any reliance on Bank financing as the centerpiece of EFA strategies was a forlorn hope. The parlous state of the Bank's education sector and the sluggish rates of borrowing for EFA were prominent factors in the rapid decline of the World Bank as the global leader in educational development, even if that leadership was largely self-proclaimed. By 2000, a broader coalition of western bilateral donors and NGOs had formed to take the reins of the EFA movement. At Dakar, they were prominent, while the original UN Jomtien sponsors were considerably less assertive. Such a condition was all too evident in the collapse in FY 2000 in World Bank education lending, falling to 4.8 percent of total Bank disbursements in that year. This, despite Clinton administration is insistence that the Bank play a more assertive role in EFA (Mallaby 2005: 84).

The major legacy of Dakar, and more precisely of the coalition-building that had preceded it, was the inclusion of core EFA objectives in the Millennium Development Goals (MDGs) for 2015 adopted by the United Nations General Assembly at its Millennium Summit in September 2000. Of only limited significance was the World Bank's own response – its "Fast-track Initiative" (FTI) – promoted by Wolfensohn to ensure that any borrower desirous of taking on loans for EFA would not be denied credit. The FTI was a Bank-sponsored attempt to ensure that lack of finance could be excluded as a prohibitive factor in achieving the education MDGs. Hosted by the Bank, FTI nevertheless involved (through shared governance and financing) partnerships with, as of 2006, more than thirty collaborating organizations (World Bank 2006a; see also Bruns *et al.* 2003). Of very great significance for FTI was its integration with development cooperation principles adopted at the United Nations Conference on Financing for Development (Monterrey, Mexico in 2002) whose "Consensus" looked to increased levels of ODA in return for greater country-level accountability for results.

Fully participating countries, of which there were twenty by 2006, were required to have highly developed education sector plans in place, and to have integrated them into their Poverty Reduction Strategy Papers (PRSPs). Such requirements were justified by the Bank and its FTI partners as feasible and transparent means of speeding up disbursements while ensuring that plans and accountability measures were in place. An additional set of countries (twenty-five in 2006) were classed as "analytical" FTI members, those that had still to finalize their education sector plans and/or PRSPs. These included the large South Asian countries (Bangladesh, India, and Pakistan) so central to any process of reducing global rates of nonparticipation in basic education. In addition to Bank lending and direct assistance from other donors, the FTI was supported by two relatively modest global funds. First, the Catalytic Fund provided direct financial assistance to full FTI participants. By 2006, $445 million had been pledged by nine donors for 2003–7, with $75 million actually dispersed (by 2006) to nine countries. Second, an Education Program Development Fund (EPDF) was established to provide technical assistance for countries requiring greater technical capacity in putting education sector plans into place. By 2006, five donors had pledged $30 million for the period 2005–7.

Repairing the policy–lending nexus: education under Kagia

A second outcome from Dakar, given effect in September 2000, was the sidelining of O'Rourke from her core education policy directorship to a "special" EFA unit, an essentially unfunded and barely visible unit which survived only a matter of weeks before O'Rourke's indignant resignation from the Bank. Despite a global search among key education leaders and officials, O'Rourke's successor as education policy Director was appointed from within – Ruth Kagia, a career official who in recent years had been Sector Manager (Human Development) for the sub-Saharan African region.

What such an appointment made possible was a greater synergy between the central policy group and the operations departments responsible for lending programs at regional and country level. Kagia, thoroughly in tune with the dynamics of regional operations, was well-placed to restore the internal credibility of the Bank's central education policy group through a careful strategy of integrating "lessons" learned at regional and country level with central policy formation. This approach energized the sense that the research and analytical work conducted by the Bank at regional and country level would have potential for mainstream policy impact. Further, it provided scope to dwell less on internal process matters in favor of policy revision of a substantive kind. Abandoning the short policy menu while at the same time keeping core human capital assumptions intact, Kagia trod a difficult policy path, determined to avoid the policy constraints dictated by undue reliance on rate-of-return analysis of wage differentials among various categories of both educated and noneducated persons. For the macroeconomic determinants of World Bank education policy, nothing changed. If anything, neoliberal policy demands made on borrowers' management of their education systems were promoted with increasing vigor and confidence. But as far as the fine details of specifically *educational* matters were concerned, the Bank under Kagia opted to stand for very little.

Three fundamental analytical reviews were of key significance as Kagia set about her task to ensure a better fit between Bank policy preferences and the realities of Bank lending for education: (1) the matter of user fees for primary schooling, (2) policies for higher education, and (3) policies for secondary education. By 2005, the basic work had been done in each of the three in a way that permitted a comprehensive "update" of the 1999 *Education Sector Strategy*, presented to the Executive Directors in November 2005 and published in mid-2006 (World Bank 2006b).

User fees for primary education

Since publication in 1986 of *Financing Education in Developing Countries*, the Bank had steered an uneasy course between two strategies of considerable policy significance. On the one hand, it was encouraging the privatization of education systems at all levels and expanded recourse to user fees and charges in public systems (especially for technical and higher education). On the other hand, it was promoting primary education and its expansion as the top priority for government expenditure on education. Given its assertiveness on these two policy prescriptions, the Bank since 1986 was cautious about two potential elaborations of them.

First, the Bank was shy about advocating fees for primary education. In a formal sense, the Bank had never advocated primary level fees to meet tuition costs. At the same time, it appeared tolerant of increasing household and community participation in resourcing primary education, which inevitably involved meeting some or all of the costs of textbooks, uniforms, and special purpose levies. Realities were that in many borrowing countries, the other-than-tuition costs of primary education were frequently higher and more burdensome than those for tuition, placing disproportionate burdens on the children of the poorest. Second, the Bank avoided calling for universal primary education as something to be achieved immediately, as if it were a basic human right. Rather, its stance was more patient, advocating education for all as soon as countries could afford it.

Although there is no evidence that the Bank had ever advocated primary school tuition fees, readers of its 1995 *Priorities and Strategies for Education*, as an example, could be forgiven for being a little confused: "Even at the primary level, the charging of fees need not be incompatible with the principle of free primary education, so long as those fees are regulated and are met by parents out of vouchers financed by the state" (World Bank 1995: 132). The issue of tuition charges, in other words, was inevitably bound up with Bank support for more extensive privatization of education. For low-income borrowers especially, quarantining primary education from tuition fee regimes was not altogether practicable.

The years after 1995 saw the emergence of hard-line donor positions concerning tuition fees and other charges at primary school level. A regional conference involving seventeen sub-Saharan African countries at Addis Ababa in 1997 had reached the so-called "Addis Ababa Consensus" on principles governing user charges ("cost-sharing") in both education and health (UNICEF 1998). UNICEF was a major broker of the consensus, actively campaigning across the subcontinent for the elimination of all primary level fees and charges, a position subsequently adopted by, *inter alia*, the UK Department for International Development (DFID 1999), the Asian Development Bank (ADB 2002), and, importantly, USAID (Mundy 2002).

Bank analysis showed remarkable increases in enrolment figures in selected countries that had abolished tuition fees in primary education: Malawi (51 percent), Uganda (70 percent), and Tanzania (50 percent). In Kenya, an additional 1.2 million children had entered the system (Bentaouert-Kattan and Burnett 2004: 8). That report showed a remarkable diversity in the user charges levied on households. While tuition fees were charged in some

40 percent of the 79 countries surveyed, all but two reported extensive recourse to user charges for other purposes, including many unofficial monies collected at local level. Significant burdens were reported in households, impacting severely on the poorest. The Bank had little option but to assert more boldly its opposition to tuition fees at primary level, as well as to modify its support of other charges. Free provision of textbooks in Africa, for example, was embraced (Bentaouert-Kattan and Burnett 2004: 25–6).

The Bentaouert-Kattan and Burnett report drew an interesting distinction between Bank policy and the Bank's public position. It recommended accordingly:

1. The World Bank should develop an explicit policy on user fees in primary education, taking account of their impact on enrollment and learning and of their major importance in total educational spending. This policy should be based on the premise that no child should be excluded from primary education on the basis of inability to pay. It should assume that the Bank will work actively with governments to find alternatives to existing fees, paying particular attention to revenue replacement.

2. The World Bank should develop a clearer and shorter public position on user fees in primary education. The current position, while reasonable, is cautiously worded.... A clearer position should note the Bank's active opposition to fees, rather than its current passive "does not support" statement. It should also reiterate the Bank's opposition to other obstacles (principally indirect costs) to enrollment and learning at the primary level.

3. The World Bank should review the determinants of enrollment in all countries that are unlikely to achieve the education Millennium Development Goals....

4. The World Bank should examine the effectiveness of textbook charging schemes it has supported and of accompanying fee mitigation measures for those unable to pay for books....

5. The World Bank should analyze the effectiveness of targeted fee waiver schemes in primary education....

(Bentaouert-Kattan and Burnett 2004: 25–6)

Kagia's subsequent endorsement of the recommended position enabled the Bank's Regional Departments to open up richer dialogue with borrowers on obstacles to expanding primary education enrollments. As at so many other moments in Bank history, the process involved correcting earlier Bank arbitrariness and inflexibility. While the Bank sought to project imagery of responsiveness and liberality, the reality was rather that it was dealing with the harsh after-effects of earlier stances, frequently adopted over the objections of borrowers, other donors, NGOs, and not a few voices from within.

Policies for higher education

While Bank clarification of user fees in primary education was an important policy matter (given the increasing likelihood that the 2015 Millennium Development Goals for education could not reasonably be met), of far greater overarching policy significance was the Bank's review of higher education. Having the potential to upset and lay to rest the short policy menu, this work had precisely that outcome. From 1980 onwards, the Bank had been engaged on nothing less than a crusade to shift public monies from higher education to primary education, a position that inevitably clashed with political realities in most borrowing countries. It was a matter of priority, to be sure, and the Bank had remained firm over the years that the greater social returns were to be derived from primary level public investments. A major UNESCO conference in 1998 opened up avenues for assessing such a stance. The World Conference on Higher Education, typical of UNESCO in its breadth of representation and participation, permitted a diversity of viewpoints and perspectives to be aired, especially concerning the role and outcomes of higher education in a range of economic and cultural contexts.

In a highly unusual move, the Bank agreed to participate with UNESCO in a joint Task Force on Higher Education and Society (TFHES), to work independently of both the Bank and UNESCO. Working closely with viewpoints outlined in both the Bank's World Development Report in 1999 *Knowledge for Development* and the OECD's 2000 report *Knowledge Management in the Learning Society*, the Task Force applied forcefully the logic of "knowledge economy" and "knowledge society" arguments to forge a view of the social benefits of higher education. Its report *Higher Education in Developing Countries: Peril and Promise* (TFHES 2000) was enthusiastically taken up and promoted by Wolfensohn. More than that, he quickly wooed to the Bank the Task Force's co-Chair, Mamphela Ramphele, a South African university Vice-Chancellor, to occupy the Bank's second most senior staff position, that of Managing Director for Human Development. For these and associated reasons, the Task Force's report enjoyed considerable status within the Bank, a trifle unsettling for the Bank's central education policy group who had been sidelined in its preparation and whose policy stances on higher education were very publicly being blown out of the water:

> The Task Force believes that traditional economic arguments are based on a limited understanding of what higher education institutions contribute. Rate of return studies treat educated people as valuable only through their higher earnings and greater tax revenues extracted by society. But educated people clearly have many other effects on society: educated people are well positioned to be economic and social entrepreneurs, having a far-reaching impact on economic and social well being of their communities. They are also vital to creating an environment in which economic development is possible. Good governance, strong institutions,

and a developed infrastructure are all needed if business is to thrive – and none of these is possible without highly educated people. Finally, rate of return analyses entirely misses the impact of university based research on the economy – a far-reaching social benefit that is at the heart of any argument for developing strong higher education systems.

(TFHES 2000: 39)

By now retired from the Bank and a member of the Greek Parliament, George Psacharopoulos was quick to see the damage that such a line of argument could do to his policy legacy within the Bank and among many borrowing countries. Invited to comment by the US–Canadian journal *Comparative Education Review*, Psacharopoulos was scathing in his attack on the report's technical credibility and its abandonment of his short policy menu (*Comparative Education Review* 2004). In terms of the technical assessments of rate-of-return analyses at stake, the stoush was essentially a rerun of a much earlier debate between Psacharopoulos and former Bank economist Nancy Birdsall, the latter having called into question the education sector's uncompromising reliance on Psacharopoulos' numbers (Birdsall 1996; Psacharopoulos 1996b).

Psacharopoulos' public intervention was insufficient to stave off the decisive shift in the Bank's position, its emerging policy stance becoming a clear echo of the Task Force position. The Bank's own report *Constructing Knowledge Societies: New Challenges for Tertiary Education* (World Bank 2002a) provided an even more detailed assessment of higher education as both public and private good and as a legitimate avenue for both Bank financing and for blends of public and private financing. Prepared by a team led by Jamil Salmi, the new higher education policy report was notable in that it was the first major Bank statement on education policy for some twenty-five years to bear no mention of the name or work of George Psacharopoulos. For his part, Salmi had undertaken considerable analytic work in the Latin America and Caribbean Regional Division on the impact of student loans (Salmi 2000), had conducted an extensive investigation of higher education published by the OECD (Salmi 2001), and would go on under Kagia's general direction to lead preparations for the 2006 education sector strategy update.

In a crucial sense, the report stopped far short of upsetting the notion of primary education being the top priority for government expenditures on education, that primary education should be universal as quickly as possible, and that primary education should be freely available. Rather, it justified a blend of financing sources for higher education – public and private – on the grounds of strong mutual benefits. The argument rested on clear assessments of *externalities*:

Despite the methodological difficulties involved in measuring externalities, it can be shown that tertiary education produces an array of important economic and social benefits. Public economic benefits reflect the overall contribution of tertiary education institutions and graduates to economic growth beyond the income and employment gains accruing to individuals . . . .

. . . tertiary education promotes nation building through its contributions to increased social cohesion, trust in social institutions, democratic participation and open debate, and appreciation of diversity in gender, ethnicity, religion, and social class. Pluralistic and democratic societies need the kinds of research and analysis that are fostered through social science and humanities programs. Tertiary education may contribute to reduced crime rates and corruption and to an increased community service orientation, as manifested in philanthropic donations, support for NGOs, and charity work. There are also strong social benefits from tertiary education associated with improved health behaviors and outcomes.

(World Bank 2002a: 76–7)

Very importantly for the Bank's overall policy position on education, the report was unambiguous in asserting that tertiary institutions "play a key role in support of basic and secondary education, and there is a need for more effective links among all levels of education" (World Bank 2002a: 79). The MDGs, for example, were not achievable without the strong involvement of higher education institutions and their graduates. More tellingly, the begrudging recognition so evident in the 1999 *Education Sector Strategy* that the components of education systems were mutually dependent was now a staple ingredient in Bank thinking, even if the principle had been so plainly self-evident to policy-makers for decades.

In addition to affirming the Bank's generic shift of support in higher education from free-standing institutional development to system-wide reform at the national level, the report opened up consideration of Bank support for higher education as a "global public good." Of concern here were several dimensions of higher education policy and practice, frequently intersecting with other dimensions of economic and social policy frameworks: brain drain, quality assurance, trade barriers, intellectual property rights, and bridging the digital gap (World Bank 2002a: 122–7). The report had nothing of substance to say how the Bank could be involved, except to "facilitate" a group of other international agencies and actors, the World Trade Organization being noticeable in its exclusion from the list. In its analysis of the impact of globalization on higher education, notably the demands of knowledge intensity worldwide, the report drew heavily on a more generic Bank report (*Globalization, Growth, and Poverty: Building an Inclusive World Economy*) extolling the economic benefits of economic integration (Dollar and Collier 2001), perhaps the most influential internal report circulating in the Bank at the time apart from the annual issues of the World Development Report.

The report on higher education sent powerful signals to both the Bank's Regional Divisions and to borrowers, that Bank policy assertions since 1999 on flexibility could be taken at face value. While the Bank remained wedded to its reformist agenda concerning the financing and operation of national education systems, and while the bulk of loans were programmatically oriented to boost reform processes, nevertheless borrowers – especially in middle-income countries – could be assured that they were free to formulate genuine subsectoral priorities for Bank financing.

This was especially significant for borrowers for which the universal coverage of primary education was no longer a challenge. Given that Bank stubbornness was now focused on publicly funded technical and vocational education, it was clearly secondary education and higher education that provided scope for expanded Bank lending. That is why "clarification" of Bank policy stances was so significant in the years immediately following the 1999 *Education Sector Strategy*. With higher education policies now in place, the Bank turned to the more troubled matter of secondary education.

Policies for secondary education

Throughout the twentieth century, the role of secondary education has been difficult to pin down. In the West, as mass education became increasingly feasible, tensions were clearly apparent between two fundamental ways of regarding the work of the secondary school. Was it there, most importantly, to identify the best and the brightest of students, grooming them for entry into higher education and thereby into the professions, academia, and the public service? Or, by contrast, was the secondary school there to extend the provision of basic education, building on and strengthening the work of primary education, and on a universal basis as part of a broader quest to raise educational and cultural levels throughout society as a whole? In Western countries, the latter view came to be associated with US progressive educational thought, with such apologists as John Dewey advocating the egalitarian approach to secondary education as a necessary step in the construction of democratic societies (Dewey 1916; see also Connell 1980). Such thinking, by the time of the Second World War, came to permeate official US foreign policy objectives concerning education and culture, the United States being scathingly critical of what it saw as hopelessly elitist and old-fashioned patterns of restricted secondary schooling in Europe and the United Kingdom. Promoting education on a "mass" rather than elitist basis was, for example, a major plank in US policies at the establishment of UNESCO in 1945 (Ninkovich 1981).

Between these two positions there had emerged a third emphasis, that the secondary school could provide vocational knowledge, skills, and experience of direct relevance to labor-market needs. This emphasis, more common in developing countries than in the West, came to be strongly connected with modernization and human capital perspectives on the connections between schooling, labor productivity, and economic growth. Given the World Bank's absolute ban on involvement in primary education in the 1960s and 1970s, borrowers understandably saw in the Bank a means to support the rapid development of secondary school systems. For its part, the Bank developed a deep unease about their rapid expansion along basic education lines. Rather, and Bank education chief Duncan Ballantine and his deputy Mats Hultin were of critical importance here, the Bank developed a concept of "diversified" secondary curriculum that saw a combining of general and vocational content, so that Bank-supported secondary schools could produce graduates immediately able to contribute to overall labor productivity. It will be recalled that the early 1980s saw an about face that had two principal effects for Bank secondary schools' policy: first, diversified curriculum was ditched in favor of general curriculum and, second, primary education emerged as the Bank's absolute lending priority. As with higher education, this presented problems in Bank–borrower relations with countries for which achieving UPE was not a significant issue.

Over the period 1963–2003, two sets of borrowers interested in secondary education had been ill-served by the Bank. First were those that had not warmed to the diversified curriculum, preferring the general. Second were those that preferred the American rationale for expansion and democratization, but whose aspirations collided with overwhelming Bank preference for primary education lending after 1980. A prominent factor in the collapse of Bank lending for education in the mid-1990s was undoubtedly confusion over the place of secondary education in the Bank's scheme of things, secondary education being noticeably absent in the 1990–4 period that saw the completion of primary, technical and vocational, and higher education policy positions. With the 1999 *Education Sector Strategy* setting the scene, and with the 2002 higher education report showing the extent to which the short policy menu could be discarded, the Bank set to work to correct its policy-level neglect of secondary education.

Kagia moved with considerable emphasis to ensure that the secondary education policy gap was filled, and filled credibly. Appointing a team led by Ernesto Cuadra and Juan Manuel Moreno, what emerged in 2005 was one of the Bank's more thoughtful and considered policy discussions in education (World Bank 2005b). Importantly, *Expanding Opportunities and Building Competencies for Young People: A New Agenda for Secondary Education* was utterly respectful of the historical dilemmas facing secondary schooling and how the dilemmas that had surfaced in the West had been reflected in developing countries. At the same time, what appeared as reasonable policy stances concerning secondary education were little more than statements of long-standing and prevailing policy wisdom and the correction of previous Bank inflexibility and narrowness.

Importantly, the report was constructed on several years' internal analysis, including the Regional Divisions' various education strategy papers, an influential review of secondary education in Africa (World Bank 2002b), and a comprehensive OED review of Bank lending in secondary education conducted by Gillian Perkins (World Bank 2004b). The Perkins review, on the surface, was especially influential, although it may be said to have accurately summed up much opinion already prevailing within the education sector. Reviewing project experience in secondary education from 1990 to 2001, Perkins found a highly uneven spread of successes: project components emphasizing civil works and physical infrastructure had much higher chances of attaining overall effectiveness than those addressing quality or reform concerns, such as efficiency, financing, planning, and management (World Bank 2004b: viii–ix, 16). As ever, the successful projects were those displaying "strong national ownership" and "government commitment," Bank-speak for projects that borrowers actually wanted, as distinct from those "sold" to them through Bank assertiveness. Overly complex project design was deemed responsible for the majority of ineffective projects, especially when they simultaneously addressed primary, secondary, higher, and even other education subsectors in a single project intervention.

Perkins' review highlighted confused rationales for secondary education lending. Middle-income borrowers tended to focus on increasing the employability and productivity of secondary school graduates, frequently favoring vocational curricula despite Bank objections. Also important in these countries were parallel commitments to national economic competitiveness, seen as achievable through improving the quality and reach of general secondary provision in the name of knowledge intensity. By contrast, rationales in countries with relatively low participation rates in secondary education placed greater emphasis on preparing graduates for public sector employment, and for meeting poverty reduction and equity objectives (World Bank 2004b: 12–13). Most glaring, however, was Perkins' conclusion that project rationales, objectives, and performance indicators tended to focus on the dynamics of education systems themselves. She regarded this lack of wider appreciation and concern as significant in the weak links apparent between education, labor-force dynamics, and meeting poverty reduction and equity objectives. Thus project objectives tended to be anchored within education systems themselves, rather than in "broader analysis of country economic, financial, institutional, social and labor market conditions" (World Bank 2004b: 27). In other words, Bank interventions in secondary education – and most likely in education projects as a whole – tended to neglect the key issues at stake when defending Bank lending in education at all. These issues were about "relating structural, curriculum, financing and governance options to specific development objectives – human, social, or economic – in different country contexts" (World Bank 2004b: 4). This was a powerful conclusion at a time of increasing scepticism across the Bank about the essential capacity of education to stimulate economic growth. Coupled with the finding that only one-third of projects were effective in achieving the educational reform measures intended, Perkins had produced a worrying report.

At heart, the Perkins review had highlighted the impact in lending operations of two decades of neglect of thoughtful policy attention to secondary education. Her report had identified four major areas requiring close attention in future project design: more precise identification of project objectives, benefits, and indicators; stronger secondary education project rationales in low-income countries; recognition that project complexity produces high risks of project failure; and more attention to management and efficiency concerns (World Bank 2004b: 25). These concerns fed directly into Bank preparation of its 2005 secondary education report.

Even with its reflective style, and its ready admission of two decades of World Bank neglect of secondary education policy concern, *Expanding Opportunities and Building Competencies: A New Agenda for Secondary Education* in 2005 was very much a report whereby the Bank sought to "catch up" with mainstream borrower and donor sentiments. Much was made in the report that 1995 had seen a shift of Bank emphasis from "primary" education to "basic" education, thereby capturing lower secondary schooling as an extension of primary provision. In practice, by contrast, borrowers (especially in other than low-income countries) tended to view their secondary school systems holistically, even if retention rates and curriculum objectives changed dramatically as students progressed from lower to upper stages. The key trends underscored in the report were threefold:

- Secondary education has become more and more coupled with primary and basic education.
- The curriculum is less specialized and evolves toward arrangements closer to those in primary schools.
- Teachers in secondary education tend to be trained and recruited in the same way as primary school teachers; and pedagogical practices are converging as participation rates in secondary education increase.

(World Bank 2005b: xvii)

For the authors, these key trends were a direct result of the "democratization" of education. This is a highly significant conclusion, for it takes the Bank to the conclusion that, in the most fundamental sense, the historical development of secondary education has it bound up with "education for all." It was not a huge leap, then, for the authors to interpret, worldwide, secondary education reform as "an integral part of EFA efforts" (World Bank 2005b: xvii). For various reasons, this is precisely how the Bank would prefer its borrowers to regard secondary education futures.

First, such a stance reinforces the Bank's absolute priority for EFA and achieving the MDGs. Even for those countries no longer challenged by universal primary participation and completion, the extension of the notion of a "basic education for all" keeps up the historical momentum for the continuous expansion of formal education. Placing secondary education policies in EFA context permits the Bank to maintain its stance that basic education is a public good – once UPE is achieved, countries that can afford to do so have the credible option of extending public provision in lower secondary schooling. For countries with less than UPE coverage or less able to fund it, the Bank would invoke its cost-sharing financing regime, that is, user charges for tuition and other costs. In this way, the Bank is able to maintain its insistence that public financing of education be kept to the lower levels of education only, and with universal coverage.

Second, the link with EFA reinforced the other time-honored Bank stance, that in favor of a general, academic curriculum at secondary level. It will be recalled that, around 1980, the Bank shifted its support dramatically, away from a secondary curriculum that combined general content with vocational knowledge and skills, in the name of producing graduates able to commence productive work in industrial and agricultural settings without delay. What the Perkins report had made clear, however, was that many Bank-supported projects in secondary education had retained the vocational emphasis, despite Bank preferences. Drawing heavily on a robust report on secondary education curriculum trends prepared by sociologist Aaron Benavot for the Bank and for UNESCO's International Bureau of Education (Benavot 2004), the Bank's authors were able to highlight a breakdown of the rigid distinction between general and vocational content. Subjects traditionally seen as general – "science, mathematics, English, philosophy – are in increasing demand because of their career and work relevance .... The critical dilemma and the traditionally hard-to-strike balance between vocational and general education at the secondary level are coming to a point of compromise and, in a way, are being superseded" (World Bank 2005b: 85).

Third, in another blow to the Psacharopoulos legacy, rate-of-return estimates of the relative returns from general versus vocational curriculum instruction were deemed to be inconsistent and ungeneralizable (World Bank 2005b: 86):

> In short, evidence from rates of return is contradictory. One can truly speak of the dialectics of general and vocational education at the secondary level, as the balance ... is a moving target within and across countries. The key appears to be that demand for vocational education and the market value of the credentials gained through it also depend on public and labor market perceptions of its quality. Most of all, they depend on the extent to which students, families, and employers no longer feel that vocational education is a second-class, dead-end, low-status option for working-class children and for those who fail at school.
>
> (World Bank 2005b: 86–7)

Interestingly, the report declared there to be a "policy vacuum around secondary education" – one that could in large part be the product of Bank perceptions given its own historical neglect, unlike its borrowers. At the same time, the authors summed up the historical policy paradoxes so evident throughout the twentieth-century history of secondary education:

- terminal and preparatory
- compulsory and postcompulsory

- uniform and diverse
- meritocratic and compensatory
- geared to serving both individual needs and interests and societal and labor market needs
- involved in integrating students with and offsetting disadvantages but also, within the same institution, in selecting and screening students according to academic ability
- charged with offering a common curriculum for all students and a specialized curriculum for some.

Secondary education thus features a double discourse. To give just one example, secondary education is called on to integrate youngsters in order to prevent social exclusion and achieve greater social equality and, at the same time, to stream, track, and label them, sometimes at an early age, thus introducing a powerful source of inequality and irreversibly determining their future life chances.

(World Bank 2005b: 14–15)

With the historically troublesome Bank legacies dealt with (of links with EFA, of curriculum focus, and of rate-of-return evidence), the report was able to move on to conventional Bank concerns – for expanding access, improving quality and relevance, teaching, financing, governance, and management. While most dimensions were summaries of Bank policy orthodoxies for the financing and management of education systems, some lines of argument were relatively new for the Bank, not least the significance of the international movement for the comparative study of student achievement, and the connections between secondary education and knowledge economy demands. In these ways the report straddled each of the twin policy emphases of the education portfolio under Kagia: (1) education for all and (2) gearing education for the demands of the knowledge economy. Overall, the message to borrowers was clear: should they be committed to overarching education sector reforms along the lines prescribed by the Bank, then they were free to engage the Bank in relatively flexible terms concerning the precise shape and orientation of their secondary school systems (Bank preference for a general secondary curriculum as an extension of basic education notwithstanding).

The consolidation of education reform agenda

In November 2005 the Executive Directors received, following consideration by the Bank's Committee on Development Effectiveness, the latest in the series (1971, 1974, 1980, 1995, and 1999) of education sector policy and strategy statements: *Education Sector Strategy Update: Achieving Education for All, Broadening our Perspective, Maximizing our Effectiveness* (World Bank 2006b). This update of the 1999 *Education Sector Strategy* was an institutional necessity, given the banality of the 1999 document, its lack of relevance to the education portfolio as a whole, and the subsequent progress made by the central policy

Department both to "catch up" with prevailing operational realities in the Regional Divisions and to reflect mainstream educational development thinking outside the Bank. The strategy paper, prepared by a team led by Jamil Salmi, was noteworthy for its breadth of strategic perspective.

Of particular significance for Salmi's team were numerous sets of findings concerning Bank performance in education. In particular, project reports from the Independent Evaluation Group (formerly OED) were drawn upon heavily. Especially significant were the OED report on secondary education prepared by Gillian Perkins discussed above (World Bank 2004b) and a parallel report of equal scope on primary education prepared by a team led by Dean Nielson *From Schooling Access to Learning Outcomes: An Unfinished Agenda: An Evaluation of World Bank Support to Primary Education* (World Bank 2006c; see also World Bank 2003). Nielson's group had drawn similar conclusions to Perkins in pointing to project design that was too ambitious and complex, an underestimation by the Bank of political and institutional constraints to achieving project objectives, and an overall lack of practicable indicators to monitor and indicate impact of project and program work on attaining national objectives. Of particular importance was the Nielson group's conclusion that the Bank and its borrowers were missing out on numerous opportunities to reinforce their commitments to primary education coverage and quality by failing to ensure that primary school support had been inadequately incorporated into noneducation Bank projects. Placing more emphasis on the scope and effectiveness of educational components of noneducation Bank interventions was seen as a potentially significant opportunity for the sector, requiring a shift in outlook and operational style. Further, the primary education report called for greater focus in Bank work on the quality of learning outcomes, on the monitoring and evaluation of Bank interventions, and on overall institutional development. Overall, three broad-ranging recommendations of the primary education report helped shape the thrust of the subsequent *Education Sector Strategy Update*: (1) that primary education efforts needed to adopt a fresh focus on improving learning outcomes, rather than relying on improved enrollment and retention rates; (2) that the Bank needed urgently to improve its own sector management performance in support of learning outcomes; and (3) that the Bank needed to work with its development partners to ensure that the Fast-track Initiative was reoriented in support of improved learning outcomes (World Bank 2006c: xiii).

As in 1999, the *Education Sector Strategy Update* was conceived primarily with a Bank internal audience in mind, so that Bank operations might be shaped by it. As before, much was in effect a matter of catching up with prevailing trends in the Regional Divisions and codifying them. Nevertheless, the strategy did this comprehensively and credibly. Three broad strategic themes emerged:

1   Education is central to developing dynamic economies and reducing poverty and must be actively integrated into a country-wide perspective. Education strategies must be part of any comprehensive

approach for putting developing countries on the path to economic competitiveness and social cohesion.... Participation in country assistance strategies and preparation of public expenditure reviews are key obligations of education sector staff, as articulation of these linkages in country assistance strategies is vital to ensuring that education interventions are adequately resourced and embedded in broader policy dialogue.

2   The Bank is broadening its strategic agenda for education and adopting a systemwide approach that looks at all aspects of education sector development. Significant progress has been achieved in support of primary education and it is critical to maintain that momentum.... At the same time, strategic dialogue is expected to increasingly include post-basic education... to help countries design and implement secondary education strategies tailored to their particular needs and to deepen the dialogue in support of tertiary education programs.

3   To maximize the effectiveness of Bank support, education interventions must be results oriented. Given weak data on learning outcomes, education strategies have been often driven by inputs rather than outcomes – and silent on how to improve learning consistently over time. It is essential to identify and understand indicators of progress, with monitoring and evaluation systems that support knowledge-driven reform. Resources need to be channeled, moreover, to where they can have the largest impact, i.e., the school and classroom level. Such a commitment will require a major shift in donor support.

(World Bank 2006b: 26–7)

It is noteworthy that, as an essentially internal sector strategy, the first line of emphasis gave considerable weight to the integration of education with Bank interventions across as many other relevant sectors as possible. Unlike earlier Bank strategies in education, where rhetoric was notable, the 2006 approach was to provoke the sector into active linkages and partnerships with other Bank sectors including health, social protection, water and sanitation, transport, energy, public sector management, private sector development, social development, agriculture, rural development, and environment. In many senses, such an approach was entirely consistent with integrated approaches to poverty reduction, as embedded in CDF and PRSP principles, hitherto applied by the education sector across other sectors very unevenly. Ensuring that the voice of the sector was heard was deemed important when the Bank was to consider core development objectives for particular countries, labor-market strategies, identifying and developing skills for the global economy, country-level fiscal policies (e.g. financing education services, user charges and access, taxation incentives and decentralization policies), governance, privatization and increasing the role of the private sector, public administration policies, country-wide policies for ICTs, tackling corruption, responding to HIV–AIDS, and fostering social cohesion.

The second strategic theme placed no particular obligation or expectation on borrowers to mold their education systems according to Bank-determined subsectoral priorities. Primary (and preferably lower secondary) education was to be free to households, even if provided by private means; upper-secondary, technical and vocational, and higher education were to be financed through blends of public support and user fees and charges. The Bank, how-ever, was not to insist on any one particular subsector over another, but rather called for dialogue on achieving balanced and well-performing national sys-tems of education. Thus the report reiterated the Bank's dual tack that had prevailed for several years: (1) attaining the EFA and MDG goals and (2) strengthening education to serve dynamic economies, by building the higher-level skills and knowledge needed to compete in global markets and foster economic growth and cooperation. Concerning the former, the paper noted that 2005 had passed without the second MDG being achieved, that is gender parity in basic education participation. Considerable emphasis was placed on resource mobilization as the answer to the paper's predictions that as many as 75 countries (52 of which were IDA-eligible) were likely to miss out on achieving the MDG education targets set for 2015.

Concerning "education to build knowledge economies," the report argued that once the "critical milestone" of UPE had been reached there was a no less vital need for education to "equip a nation to grow economically, keep up with changes in the global environment, and protect itself from obsolescence" (World Bank 2006b: 56). What followed was the conventional range of "knowl-edge society" and "knowledge economy" arguments that had gained currency over the past decade in OECD and many economic development circles, with the Bank's packaging placing emphasis on "education for knowledge economies" (EKE). "The broadening of the World Bank's agenda for education as a stan-dard feature of analytical work, policy dialogue and lending operations will require that country teams consistently apply a sector-wide perspective. This will allow for informed decisions regarding the appropriate mix of interven-tions designed to achieve Education for All and education for the knowledge economy in a given country" (World Bank 2006b: 62).

The third broad strategic theme of the paper involved conferring a "results orientation" on Bank operations in education, in line with prevailing trends across the entire development assistance community. The Bank's evaluations of its education projects "point to inadequate attention to learn-ing outcomes in adjustment operations and project objectives, activities, and monitoring and evaluation systems; insufficient inclusion of poverty and equity objectives in secondary education projects; and a weak monitoring and evaluation culture. Although a results orientation is needed at all levels of education systems, the specific indicators and outcome measures needed are currently more available at the primary level" (World Bank 2006b: 66). This was a major conclusion with highly significant policy implications for the

Bank, even if by its own admission it lacked the in-house knowledge and resources to embark speedily on such a course.

Of significance was the paper's acceptance of a line of argument that had been developing among Bank researchers concerning literacy (and especially reading) achievement, much stemming from staffer Helen Abadzi's work on the cognitive dimensions of reading (Abadzi 2003a,b). The argument was clear: that increases in education participation rates were meaningless if confined to school attendance. Learning achievement, rather, was the relevant yardstick, and so the paper moved to report in warm tones on the development in the West of the international learning achievement movement. Further:

> There is need for a global partnership to develop appropriate measures of reading literacy at the primary-school level in developing countries and to build capacity and secure country commitment for assessment of learning outcomes at all levels. The Bank should play a lead role in establishing such a partnership and in ensuring global consensus on appropriate indicators. The indicators developed for primary and secondary education should be adopted as part of ongoing monitoring of progress towards the Millennium Development Goals for education.
>
> (World Bank 2006b: 67–8)

While this was a starting point, the Strategy Update moved on to outline elaborate approaches and systems for monitoring the effectiveness of education expenditures, urging the donor community to work closely with it to develop and give effect to them. To be sure, for decades the Bank had expressed concerns about and commitments to the quality ("internal efficiency") of education. By 2006, it was poised to design and put its weight behind systematic means of monitoring effectiveness, an approach tightly bound up with its broader program of education system reform.

The Bank's proposed implementation strategy covered the conventional ground of "maximizing aid effectiveness," placing emphasis on an improved knowledge base, institutional capacity building, close partnerships with other donors, and mobilizing additional resources. These approaches concerned the Bank's internal processes as much as its dealings with borrowers. Of standout importance, when compared with earlier Bank policy and strategy stances, was the call for close collaboration with the International Finance Corporation (IFC): "Given the importance of mobilizing additional resources and building public sector capacity, efforts to engage the private sector in the provision and funding of education, particularly post-basic education, are imperative.... An important aspect of the World Bank Group's comparative advantage in this area relates to the role of the International Finance Corporation (IFC), in facilitating links with the private sector" (World Bank 2006b: 80).

Such an emphasis was part of a wider recognition in the Strategy Update that the Bank's education staff would be doing more of some things and less of others. Increasing in scale would be the inclusion of education issues in CASs and PRSPs, providing greater support to decentralized local authorities and at school level, targeting support for explicit poverty reduction strategies, fostering public–private partnerships, increased commitment to country-specific education sector analysis, harmonization of donor activities, increased commitment to "results-oriented" programming, and regional capacity building. Bank staff, by contrast, would scale back other kinds of activities: fewer activities that were unaligned with CASs, PRSPs, and the *Education Sector Strategy Update* itself, fewer projects without clear equity objectives, less exclusive reliance on public partners, less reliance on IDA-only support for primary education, less work in adult literacy, less educational research not prioritized in the *Education Sector Strategy Update*, less country-by-country capacity building in favor of region-wide efforts, and less support for quality improvement and for several of the sector's thematic groups (e.g. adult literacy and post-conflict education).

The Strategy Update placed some emphasis on reorienting the Bank's own research and analytical work in education, as well as assisting the strengthening of research capacity at country and regional level, this latter objective being an area of historical neglect. Internally, greater momentum was envisaged for the Bank's country and regional groups to be drivers of research, policy analysis, and impact evaluation. Priority areas for research were described weakly as "impact evaluation, the quality of education service delivery, and aspects related to poverty and equity." Broad research themes to "be considered" for 2006–9 included: "what works, when and why?," education and labor markets, human resource policies, civil service reform issues, alternative and innovative ways of funding secondary and tertiary education, and the use of ICTs to strengthen education outcomes.

The Update reported an overall decrease in Bank education sector staff since 1999, from 228 to an estimated 187 for FY2005, having bottomed out at 171 in 2002 and well down from 250 in the mid-1990s. Also acknowledged was the relatively high turnover of education staffers currently being experienced and expected to continue (with less explicit acknowledgment of the numbers arriving without previous experience or qualifications in education). Their work was not so much to provide leadership on narrowly *educational process* matters as on the broader macroeconomic policy framework in which national education efforts – public and private – would be located.

Overall, the *Education Sector Strategy Update* of 2006 looked to a bank that was intent on consolidating its education reform agenda. Moving away from free-standing and nonsystemic interventions was a hallmark of the paper, retaining a range of priorities (including those of the 1999 strategy) but placing them in the context of more wide-ranging Bank interventions. In its own words, the Update "offers guidance not only on the 'what' of the strategy but also the 'how,' by calling for attention to macroeconomic and cross-sectoral linkages, intrasectoral tradeoffs and opportunities, and a systematic focus on results and learning outcomes" (World Bank 2006b: 20).

Conclusion

As the Wolfowitz presidency progressed, it was clear (despite some initial speculation to the contrary) that the "education consensus" within the Bank would be maintained. That is to say, despite the lack of convincing evidence that education was an active contributor to economic growth and poverty reduction, the Bank was nevertheless content to include this component of "social overheads" lending in order to shore up its poverty fighting credentials.

Very early in his term which began in May 2005, Paul Wolfowitz made it clear that he was in no hurry to streamline Bank operations. His first address to the Board of Governors in September 2005 made pointed reference to education, as well as health, infrastructure, energy, sustainable development, and agriculture – all significant Bank concerns in promoting growth and poverty reduction. Also marked were Wolfowitz's references to the 1 billion persons in middle-income countries living in poverty, a strong signal to those borrowers to remain active Bank clients. The private sector, civil society engagement, and women in development also received endorsement, as were fighting corruption and promoting the rule of law (Wolfowitz 2005).

Highlighting the significance of the "education consensus" was former Bank staffer William Easterly who gained prominence after his departure with a series of arguments questioning – *inter alia* – the assumptions that educational expansion contributed to growth and that educational aid was an effective growth strategy (Easterly 2001, 2006). Easterly had been only one of an army of sceptics inside the Bank openly critical of the easy assumptions about education rate-of-return calculations and other dimensions of human capital thinking about the consequences of education. In the words of the Bank's official historians, "the argument that education, health and other social spending had impressive rates of return was in the end a highly intuitive and speculative proposition.... 'Softness' or nonmeasurability, which in earlier times had damned certain types of lending, now became a plus" (Kapur *et al.* vol. 1 1997: 370–1).

The maintenance of the "education consensus" as embodied in the 2006 *Education Sector Strategy Update* pushed the Bank's thinking about its education financing operations in two broad directions. First, it was clear that education would not escape the trend so evident in other development assistance agencies, that much education programming would become subsumed under and integrated with other sectoral commitments. The final years of the Wolfensohn presidency had seen a series of OED and other internal thematic assessments of Bank operations that addressed their effectiveness and impact (e.g. Crawford *et al.* 2006 on science and technology; World Bank 2002c and 2005a on gender; World Bank 2005d on social development; and World Bank 2005c on overall development effectiveness), as well as the usual spread of country impact assessments. Of some note in each of these was the relative neglect of education, whether in the original conceptualization of generic development and poverty strategies or in the willingness of education sector

Table 7.2 World Bank education financing, by region and subsector, FY 2001–5 ($US m)

	2001	2002	2003	2004	2005	Total
AFR	209.5	472.6	423.6	362.9	369.1	1,837.7
Adult literacy/nonformal	—	13.5	0.7	4.6	—	18.8
General education support	89.2	128.3	128.9	79.9	174.8	601.1
Pre-primary education	9.2	—	—	—	—	9.2
Primary education	59.9	214.2	237.9	91.8	106.1	709.9
Secondary education	14.4	—	53.9	124.2	11.2	203.7
Tertiary education	17.0	69.5	—	45.9	61.2	193.6
Vocational training	19.8	47.1	2.1	16.5	15.8	101.3
EAP	14.8	134.6	225.7	118.6	228.0	721.7
Adult literacy/nonformal	1.2	—	—	—	—	1.2
General education support	8.4	113.4	35.0	15.2	57.6	229.6
Pre-primary education	0.6	—	2.8	—	—	3.4
Primary education	3.9	11.3	172.1	102.0	75.4	364.7
Secondary education	0.6	—	—	—	12.9	13.5
Tertiary education	0.1	9.9	15.8	1.4	82.1	109.3
Vocational training	—	—	—	—	—	—
ECA	62.6	83.2	395.0	164.0	263.8	968.6
Adult literacy/nonformal	—	—	—	—	—	—
General education support	17.5	76.8	11.5	22.5	106.8	235.1
Pre-primary education	—	—	15.0	—	—	15.0
Primary education	16.1	3.2	248.4	33.6	11.1	312.4
Secondary education	7.3	3.2	118.3	29.1	107.5	265.4
Tertiary education	9.2	—	1.8	6.8	4.1	21.9
Vocational training	12.5	—	—	72.0	34.3	118.8

(Table 7.2 continued)

Table 7.2 Continued

	2001	2002	2003	2004	2005	Total
LCR	529.2	560.4	785.4	218.3	679.8	2,773.1
Adult literacy/nonformal	5.5	—	—	6.0	—	11.5
General education support	301.9	115.0	376.9	147.6	88.5	1,029.9
Pre-primary education	18.9	32.4	48.3	—	60.0	159.6
Primary education	96.5	177.3	58.5	30.9	254.8	618.0
Secondary education	102.0	58.4	70.3	26.4	101.5	358.6
Tertiary education	4.4	148.5	227.2	1.8	175.0	556.9
Vocational training	—	28.8	4.2	5.6	—	38.6
MNA	72.3	38.0	154.3	154.8	124.0	543.4
Adult literacy/nonformal	—	—	3.3	—	—	3.3
General education support	17.8	1.1	18.0	13.5	1.3	51.7
Pre-primary education	—	—	36.0	—	22.8	58.8
Primary education	48.4	—	43.0	85.1	58.3	234.8
Secondary education	—	—	42.0	52.1	41.6	135.7
Tertiary education	6.1	27.9	12.0	—	—	46.0
Vocational training	—	9.0	—	4.1	—	13.1
SAR	206.4	95.9	364.6	665.8	286.3	1,619.0
Adult literacy/nonformal	49.4	5.0	0	0	5.0	59.4
General education support	0	7.5	68.9	76.2	77.5	230.1
Pre-primary education	3.7	0	0	25.0	5.0	33.7
Primary education	90.4	0	20.0	539.8	59.5	709.7
Secondary education	0	71.3	0	18.6	100.9	190.8
Tertiary education	4.5	12.1	267.5	6.2	38.4	328.7
Vocational training	58.4	0	8.2	0	0	66.6

Source: World Bank Education Sector.

Notes

AFR Africa; EAP East Asia and the Pacific; ECA Europe and Central Asia; LCR Latin America and the Caribbean; MNA Middle East and North Africa; SAR South Asia. Some totals are rounded.

Table 7.3 World Bank lending to education by IBRD and IDA as percentage of total World Bank lending, FY 1963–2005 (in current $US m)

	IBRD education new commitments	*IDA education new commitments*	*Total education new commitments*	*World Bank total new commitments*	*Education as % of World Bank total*
1963	0	5	5	709	0.7
1964	0	18	18	1,086	1.6
1965	6	24	30	1,332	2.2
1966	3	31	34	1,124	3.0
1967	16	36	52	1,131	4.6
1968	11	14	25	954	2.5
1969	57	25	82	1,784	4.6
1970	52	28	80	2,187	3.7
1971	68	40	108	2,505	4.3
1972	134	47	180	2,966	6.1
1973	162	111	273	3,369	8.1
1974	134	19	153	4,314	3.5
1975	127	97	224	5,887	3.8
1976	245	76	321	6,632	4.8
1977	210	79	289	7,050	4.1
1978	269	83	352	8,411	4.2
1979	246	251	496	10,011	5.0
1980	360	80	440	11,514	3.8
1981	375	372	747	12,291	6.1
1982	428	98	526	13,016	4.0
1983	296	249	545	14,477	3.8
1984	491	211	702	15,522	4.5
1985	515	422	937	14,384	6.5
1986	578	258	836	16,399	5.1
1987	168	284	451	17,674	2.6
1988	672	195	867	19,221	4.5
1989	550	473	1,023	21,367	4.8
1990	504	900	1,404	20,702	6.8
1991	1,345	692	2,036	22,686	9.0
1992	822	509	1,332	21,706	6.1
1993	868	987	1,854	23,696	7.8
1994	1,232	514	1,746	20,836	8.4
1995	1,346	797	2,143	22,522	9.5
1996	933	787	1,720	21,352	8.1
1997	721	316	1,037	19,147	5.4
1998	1,683	1,138	2,821	28,667	9.8
1999	859	629	1,487	29,148	5.1
2000	273	455	728	15,276	4.8
2001	517	578	1,095	17,251	6.3
2002	753	632	1,385	19,519	7.1
2003	1,325	1,023	2,349	18,513	12.7
2004	524	1,160	1,684	20,080	8.4
2005	1,066	885	1,951	21,893	8.9
Totals	20,942	15,625	36,567	560,311	6.5

Source: World Bank Education Sector (some totals rounded).

staff to engage actively with Bank staff responsible for them in other sectors. What the Update made clear was that the survival of education as a viable Bank sector would depend on far tighter integration with cross-sectoral policy and lending strategies. As in many other agencies, this would lead to a certain reduction in organizational visibility and independence, with the actual rates of educational lending becoming harder to quantify.

The second direction was that education sector activity would be pushed further outwards and downwards, so that Bank policies and strategies at country level could be precisely determined. As so forcefully argued by such observers as Joel Samoff (1996a, 1999a,b) and Stephen Klees (2001), it has been Bank work in country-level analysis that has determined the precise pattern of priorities, programs, projects, and, of course, impact. Frequently appearing to be the result of external assessment, and only very slowly becoming a process of both partnership and local capacity building, education sector work is the process whereby countries "receive" a detailed platform or blueprint to shape their borrowings from the Bank. Increasingly, then, any assessment of World Bank financing of education needs to include both Washington-centered and country-level analysis.

Table 7.2 provides an overview of education lending for FY 2001–5, with Table 7.3 providing a general summary FY 1963–2005.

Notes

The assistance in the preparation of this chapter of Maris O'Rourke, Ruth Kagia, David Coleman, and the Australian Research Council is acknowledged with appreciation.

Among many interviews conducted were those with David de Ferranti, Maris O'Rourke, Ruth Kagia, George Psacharopoulos, Bruno Laporte, Peter Moock, Marlaine Lockheed, Stephen Heyneman, Alan Ruby, Jeffrey Waite, Jochen Kraske, Michael Potashnik, Sverrir Sigurdson, Daniel Viens, Paul Cadario, Anjimile Mtila Doka, Jeffrey Thindwa, Philip Twyford, Michael Drabble, Annette Dixon, Sheldon Shaeffer, Colin Power, John Daniel, and Richard Webb.

Scholars have benefited enormously from the Bank's willingness under James Wolfensohn to place a great deal of previously classified documentation on its impressive website: <http://www.worldbank.org>. Easily reached are sections devoted to the conventional lending sectors and other thematic or topical areas. Project and program loan data is also readily accessible, as well as country loan data. Also easily reached are sections devoted to such operational concerns as CAS, CDF, PRSP, HIPC, and Knowledge Bank. The annual World Development Report continues to provide broad indications of basic Bank concerns and stances. Importantly, the Operations Evaluation Department, recently renamed the Independent Evaluation Group, routinely places its reports and thematic studies on the Bank website.

For this period, the *International Journal of Educational Development* has periodically published special issues on Bank policy developments in education (1996 and 1999); Mundy (2002), Heyneman (2003), and Psacharopoulos (2006) provide useful documentation and commentary.

At the time of going to press, the key 2006 policy document *Education Sector Strategy Update: Achieving Education For All, Broadening our Perspective, Maximizing our Effectiveness* (World Bank 2006b) was still circulating within the Bank and development assistance circles in draft form, awaiting its official release. Use made in this chapter was accordingly of the final draft version of December 22, 2005.

8   World Bank priorities for educational financing

World Bank policies in education have never been static. Time and experience have subjected many to refinement, although in several major respects the pattern of evolution has been displaced by more fundamental change. The financing priorities and policy stances adopted in 1963 differed from some anticipated just a year earlier. Within a decade, policies expressed uncompromisingly at the beginning had been discarded, with equal vigor. The parallel processes of evolution and change have continued ever since and, in some key areas, yesterday's heresies have become today's orthodoxies. Yet the overall picture is one of conventionality and sobriety. Despite its proven dexterity, the World Bank functions within relatively firm parameters, the institution's banking character being their most powerful determinant. Where dramatic change in educational policy has occurred, it has more often resulted from the need to correct earlier arbitrariness or policy recklessness than from a change in fundamentals.

To only a limited extent have new approaches resulted from shifts in how education is seen to relate to development. Of far greater significance have been shifts in how the Bank has seen its own role in educational development. Many of today's policies, for example, were actively considered and rejected by the Bank in the 1960s, yet were adopted at that time in other education development circles. The Bank's current (and long-awaited) concern to encourage borrowers to view their education systems as a whole, without placing a premium on any particular subsector, is strongly reminiscent of UNESCO stances in the 1960s and 1970s in favor of comprehensive development and balanced performance of national education systems. Each time a new policy emphasis has been finalized, the Bank has tended to declare it in absolute terms, as if its correctness were as clear as day. The assertive Bank has tended to be a simplistic Bank.

Understanding Bank constructions of policy

The most powerful force for change in policy has been the desire to keep the Bank functioning as a bank. Its borrowers need to be confronted with new reasons for borrowing, whether on commercial or concessional terms. It is simply not in the scheme of things for Bank officers to promote a fresh view about education and development if it did not have possibilities for opening up new patterns of lending. The discovery of textbooks is an example, embraced through their potential to expand lending levels; other equally significant but less "bankable" aspects of pedagogy have had less success in gaining the Bank's attention. Such aspects are often dismissed as relatively insignificant "cultural" aspects of education, better left to less well-resourced agencies. Such a perspective can distort Bank views of educational development. It is not the case at all that the Bank is concerned with the "macro" questions only; relatively minor matters, because they are bankable, can assume prominence from the Bank's perspective. Therefore, the dangers are considerable for borrowers who look to the Bank for a balanced and comprehensive view of educational development. For institutional reasons, the Bank has had to be selective in its views, a factor perhaps least understood within the Bank itself. It is for this reason that Chapter 1 of this book opened with the assertion that the Bank, despite the complexity and diversity of much of its work, needs to be understood primarily as a bank.

In their daily work, loan officers are driven by (and to an extent their careers are dependent upon) their success in negotiating large numbers of sizeable loans and in encouraging quick disbursements for each stage of projects. This latter aspect, encouraging as it does superficial evaluation so as not to slow down the rate of disbursements during a project, helps explain the relative lack of interest displayed by the Bank in matters of educational detail, especially in the classroom. Loan officers, but also research and policy analysts in education, display – as a group – a certain naivety about process matters in education, not least the practical dimensions of teaching and learning, the processes of constructing policy and putting it into practice, encouraging community participation, and assessing householders' capacities and willingness to pay tuition fees. Their view retains its yearning for the ideal, in which the realities of human behavior fail to disturb models of education that read well on paper in Washington. Exceptions are to be found among Bank staff, naturally enough, but their relative rarity causes them to stand out and thereby cloud the more typical style of Bank education staff, especially the less visible army of loan officers who are the drivers of Bank operations.

Identifying Bank policies in education is problematic. The relatively few examples of formal policy statements produced since 1963 only go so far in revealing Bank policy stances. There are, perhaps, two broad ways of discerning Bank policies. One is to discover them through the loan negotiation and approval process, Bank policies perhaps best reflected in what the Bank is prepared to lend for and on what terms. Accordingly, Bank policy in a *de facto* sense is seen in the accumulation of project approvals and covenants. This model perhaps suits the early years, but with time the Bank accepted the relative weakness of free-standing projects – and of leverage exercised through covenants – in influencing the overall shape and quality of national education, especially in terms of its relationship with a national economy.

Thus a second model emerges, whereby Bank policies in education are also seen in that body of rhetoric, policy analysis, research, and publications through which the Bank has attempted to influence and shape prevailing climates of opinion about educational development. In this manner, it has attempted to move beyond the boundaries of free-standing projects, and even beyond the limitations of program loans for adjustment and sectoral reform, attempting to influence national policies overall, and even international climates of opinion about educational development. Given the growing significance of this second pattern of activity, Bank lending activity constitutes only a part of the institution's work.

Both approaches need to be recognized by those seeking to identify Bank education policies. In bureaucratic terms, their relative points of reference inside the Bank differ, and in a significant way. The first tends to find expression in the Bank's regional operations Divisions, those units directly responsible for lending but having little need publicly to expound Bank policy. The second pattern of policy formulation is found more easily in the work of the central policy analysis and research Department, whose public face is usually better known. The institutional priorities and objectives of these two groups within the Bank are not identical. Further, each in its work seeks to exert an influence on the other, as well as on borrowers, who can receive conflicting signals from these two institutional elements within the Bank.

Two examples might illustrate this last point. First, after its many years of economic and educational isolation, China in the early 1980s began an active program of substantial educational borrowing from the Bank, placing absolute priority on its high-level scientific and technological objectives, to be achieved in particular through the revitalization of its university system. Bank operations staff supported such moves with enthusiasm, not surprisingly given the size of the loans envisaged. This came at precisely the time the central policy analysis and research staff were promoting a shift in public expenditures on education away from higher education, in favor of basic education, a subsector in which the Chinese claimed they had a proud record. Tensions between the two Bank groups were not inconsiderable and continued through the 1990s, the size of the Chinese higher education loans distorting overall Bank figures which were supposed to be displaying borrower sentiment that favored primary education. It was not until the Bank resolved its ambivalence over higher education in its 2002 policy that matters were put to rest.

Second, there were the high expectations surrounding post-Jomtien lending for basic education. By the mid-1990s, it was clear that Bank education lending levels were in steep decline, threatening in fact the very survival of the Bank's education portfolio. Much, of course, had to do with country-level capacity and willingness to borrow for education, but nevertheless for the financial years 1993–6 only ten countries accounted for two-thirds of Bank education lending. Internal Bank assessments pointed to a decline in Bank expertise in education, both in Washington but also crucially at country level (de Ferranti 1996: 2).Other providers of finance were raising their profile and funding levels, threatening the Bank's "market share." The internal memorandum put it bluntly: "outsiders think that we are increasing lending for education, especially for basic education and for girls." The poorest countries, especially, were not participating to any great extent in the Jomtien vision of a basic education for all. In short, the Bank's lending patterns failed to reflect its stated priorities.

The complexities facing the World Bank's policy and financial commitments in education compounded as the years progressed. Conventional project lending was seen to be of declining relevance as an instrument for effecting qualitative and lasting educational reforms, and was customarily organized around projects that were too large and expensive for many borrowers. The economic situation facing borrowers was not only becoming generally more serious, but more complex, with an increasingly diverse set of factors upsetting traditional approaches to the economics of education and development. Internal divisions and inconsistencies served to limit the efficiency with which the Bank interacted with education borrowers, not least because of intensifying differences between its lending operations, sector policy work, and research, in addition to tensions between project and program lending. If anything, the education sector was faced with the need for a flexible and context-driven dialogue with each borrower. The Bank in its public pronouncements will state that this was encouraged and achieved. The reality is that the Bank failed to respect borrower differences (with the exception of some loan officers in the Regional Divisions), mounting an agenda for worldwide educational renewal over the past twenty years that, while not prescriptive, nevertheless projected vigorously a narrow set of policy options and recommendations. If by 2000 the official policy line had changed, it was in terms of a radical swing towards standing for not much at all, a rejection of any kind of priority-setting *within* the education sector. The years since 2000 have seen a sharp divide – between absolute Bank insistence on the neoliberal groundings of educational reform, and Bank disengagement from policy prescription on matters of specifically educational detail.

For a period, especially through the 1980s, it was research that had emerged as the engine of formally declared Bank educational policy. The educational work of the Bank in that decade cannot be understood without direct reference to it. Research was a commitment that gradually began to lose institutional power by the later years of the decade, mainly because the Bank's researchers in education tended to follow policy changes rather than provoke them. The institutional zenith of the Bank's educational researchers was the set of policy papers from 1990 to 1995, with their narrow view of priorities and stunted recipes for change. From that point, institutional capacity to maintain a strong connection between research and policy fell dramatically, although interesting papers continued to flow, especially concerning educational phenomena at country level.

This chapter presents, selectively, an analysis of the major policy matters to have exercised the World Bank down the years and how the Bank has attempted to resolve the dilemmas presented by them. Again, bold assertions are difficult given the varying locales for Bank policy formulation, the Bank's variable emphases on project and sectoral adjustment activity, and the shadowy nature of its discussions with individual governments. To repeat, however, Bank concerns are relatively narrow, shaped as they are by the banking character of the institution. This is in stark contrast with such other agencies as UNESCO, whose educational concerns remain conceptually broad, even if operational capacity is more limited. Accordingly, it can be constructive also to ponder those matters fundamental to educational development that have failed to emerge as priority concerns for the Bank.

Bank stances on educational priorities

In this and preceding chapters, difficulties in identifying World Bank policies in education have been described. Policies intended to drive the Bank lending process forward are not identical to policies designed as advice to borrowing governments. Nevertheless, down the years a solid body of Bank project documents, evaluations, research projects, policy explorations, and education sector reviews have accumulated. Their combined effect is to make possible some tentative generalizations about preferred Bank positions in several key areas to do with educational development. Often, aspects of these preferred positions are as much a matter of institutional culture as they are of stated policy or carefully formulated lending criteria. They frequently permeate Bank policy and practice in shadowy form.

Identifying Bank policy stances is highly complex, given the divide between Bank policy rhetoric and actual lending practice, the varying lending priorities displayed by the Regional Divisions of the Bank, and the varying purposes of Bank lending (which have seen differential emphases placed on expansion, innovation, reform, and structural change – all in contrasting contexts, some experiencing economic growth, others recession). Also to be acknowledged are the differing patterns of Bank–borrower dialogue, some instances revealing an assertive and strong-willed borrower, other occasions seeing a transfer of these attributes to the Bank. The result has been a far from even application of the Bank's preferred policy positions.

To come down to detail, the following areas sum up the major educational research, policy, and lending concerns of the World Bank. It can be instructive to ponder upon the many key aspects of education which have *not* been embraced by the Bank as being fundamental. It is also helpful to consider how flexibly each stance has been conceived, irrespective of Bank disclaimers about universal prescription, general or universal policies being as useful as they are flexible. At the same time, it should be noted that the following list reduces substantially a much larger number of policy concerns of interest to the Bank. At the heart of these concerns is a single question with which the Bank grapples unceasingly: how might education better contribute to poverty reduction and national development, especially by means of economic growth through increased productivity? The list, in fact, revolves around the standard set of "internal" and "external" efficiency in education questions grounded in the economics of education literature. These core concerns are:

- understanding education as a factor in development and poverty reduction;
- views of educational policy, management, and change;
- alternative policies for financing education;
- policies for enhancing the economic relevance of education, not least through increased efficiency and quality, and through more appropriate curriculum content; and
- policies for promoting equity, not least a basic education for all through primary schooling, and through particular emphasis on rural education and the education of girls and women.

Understanding education as a factor in development and poverty reduction

The World Bank's understanding of education's role in development is sur-prisingly straightforward. Its commitment to education has been no less than a celebration of human capital theory. This theory, above all, embodies a supreme expression of faith in the power of human knowledge, skill, and experience to transform individuals and societies. Its positive, optimistic assertions of human potential are partial reflections of the economic buoyancy and opti-mism seen in the levels of economic growth experienced when the theory was first expounded in the late 1950s and 1960s. Its origins, in fact, were an attempt to explain the high rates of postwar economic growth then being experienced in the United States and western Europe (Schultz 1961, 1963; Denison 1962, 1967). With that explanation in place, human capital theory underwent a rapid transformation, becoming a model for engineering eco-nomic growth in the future. In particular, the educational establishment was quick to grasp it as a justification for the rapid expansion of ("investment in") education. This, however, was undertaken uncritically, with educational plan-ners and economists both displaying imprecision about the kind of education most likely to produce the increases in productivity foreseen by the model.

In terms of its contribution to theory, this positive and optimistic view of education had run its course by the end of the 1960s. Its basic propositions were, in fact, extremely simple. Further, their validity rested upon applica-tion in favorable circumstances, namely, the context of an already expanding economy in which the fundamental educational requirements of efficiency and equity were securely in place. By 1970, theorists were turning their attention to the less favorable side of things, attempting to understand the interaction between education and development in the context of declining growth, imbalanced education systems, both gross and subtle inequalities in education and society, views of education that stressed its screening function, and declining public sector budgets for education. Education was seen not only in terms of its potential to produce and distribute knowledge and skills, it was also seen as a powerful allocator of economic and social roles, not always distributed equitably on a basis of merit. Human capital theory had very little to offer these considerations and, from the point of view of educational and economic theory, was poised in 1970 to be merely remembered as a product and reflection of its times.

Without the World Bank, this is how things would most likely have rested. The Bank, however, has clung to the model as if its pertinence and power were as clear as day. Right through periods of protracted recession, the Bank has invited adherence to a model explicitly conceived in and for contexts of economic expansion. Despite the model's silence on such key matters as equity – a key concern of the Bank's – human capital theory remains intact as the World Bank's major theoretical perspective on its work in education.

The flame of human capital theory has been kept alight in the corridors of the Bank partially through the devotion of those analysts committed to manifesting its pertinence through cost-benefit analyses of educational expenditures. A generation after the model ceased to say much that was new, they have persisted with demonstrating its soundness, despite the general acceptance outside the Bank that human capital perspectives are indeed useful when prevailing conditions are right. An additional function, moreover, has been to highlight the deficiencies of alternative and credible techniques of economic analysis and policy construction, such as growth accounting. Institutionally, this commitment needs to be appreciated in light of the Bank's tendency – as an international political bureaucracy – to seek overarching views on matters of policy, to promote models for universal application. Because such an institution warms to rhetoric that is positive and optimistic in tone, yet sufficiently bland and general in substance, human capital theory has served a useful institutional purpose, irrespective of its dated and limited theoretical character. Yet simply because the Bank prefers to keep things neat and tidy by adopting singular perspectives on things, the stakes are extremely high when it moves to adopt one theoretical perspective in favor of others. Internal debates over fundamentals have always been vigorous.

More fundamentally, the Bank's continuing adherence to human capital theory reveals something of its stances about the meaning of development. In particular, it reveals a Bank that asserts an interest in fundamentals but which in reality avoids them. The Bank has very little to say about just what education does to make people more productive. It is dismissive of the cultural foundations of education. It is a Bank that shows itself to be both structurally incapable and attitudinally unwilling to tackle the fundamental issue of economic power and distribution in borrowing countries. It ought to be self-evident that as both an international financial institution and as a Specialized Agency of the United Nations, there are limits to which the World Bank can tackle the harsh realities of economic and political corruption, as well as gross social inequity, so frequently seen in borrowing countries. To be sure, from 1995 (and as boldly reasserted by President Wolfowitz in 2006), corruption has been in the Bank's sights. Yet, for education, the Bank ought not to respond by asserting its adherence to models of education and development declared falsely to be sufficiently powerful to transcend the parlous moral state of many borrowers, not least the stark inequities in educational provision and outcome. It does not ring true, except to the uninformed, the naive, and the wilfully biased. And a focus on girls' education is beside the point. Even such a sober analysis as that provided by the Bank's own commissioned history concluded:

> As one reviews the history of the Bank, taking into account the predom-inant ideology of the directors representing countries having a majority of the votes (and . . . the ideology of management as well), one must in all fairness concede a measure of validity to the left-wing criticism [of the Bank]. The way in which this ideology has been shaped conforms in sig-nificant degree to the interests and conventional wisdom of its principal stockholders. International competitive bidding, reluctance to accord preferences to local suppliers, emphasis on financing foreign exchange costs, insistence on a predominant use of foreign consultants, attitudes toward public sector industries, assertion of the right to approve project managers – all proclaim the Bank to be a Western capitalist institution. Such an institution can contribute and, we believe, *has* contributed to the development of the less-developed world. But increasingly the Bank has found itself in conflict with its less developed member countries.
>
> (Mason and Asher 1973: 478–9)

It is best to interpret and evaluate the contribution of the World Bank to edu-cational development and poverty reduction on its own terms. Little of prac-tical benefit emerges from criticizing the Bank simply because it is a supreme example of capitalism applied to international finance and development. Its Articles of Agreement, its character as a bank, and its responsibilities as a UN Specialized Agency all combine to impose definable limitations to the scope and nature of its work. These parameters are more or less fixed, and for some it is surprising just how agile and flexible the Bank has proven to be.

Views of educational policy, management, and change

It is something of a myth that in its first two decades of educational financ-ing the Bank was a "bricks and mortar" institution interested only in educa-tional expansion through the construction of facilities. From the beginning, the Bank has displayed a keen interest in the qualitative aspects of educa-tional provision. Less apparent at the classroom level, this commitment has focussed primarily on the quality of educational management and leadership, especially its role in the planning and administration of education systems. As outlined in Chapters 3 and 4, the early years saw the Bank relying on pro-ject covenants – side-conditions – as the principal means of stimulating change in borrowing countries. Yet as the Bank's own reviews were highlighting by 1978, covenants were an extremely weak means of exerting influence if they were not backed up by the Bank in programmatic terms. This is contrary to much mythology about the Bank, that its use of covenants – leverage – provides evidence of a heavy-handed, manipulative, interfering institution, dictating education policies to borrowers. The reality is that borrowers, especially in the first two decades, could simply ignore the side-conditions attached to lending with relative impunity. It was only with moves in the 1980s and 1990s towards sector-wide program lending that the Bank put itself in a position to address more realistically the management capacities of borrowing countries. In fact, these capacities became a prime object of program loans.

A key issue arising from this analysis is the Bank's view – more a matter of unstated institutional culture and behavior than clearly articulated policy – of the process of educational policy formulation. The Bank's *de facto* model was one that put a premium in borrowing countries on the official determination of policy. This model, perhaps the most conventional, imposes a gulf between policy formation and implementation. Educational personnel "down the line" are not determiners or shapers of policy, but are assigned the role of passive implementers. Conventional models can only explain failures in educational change in two ways: either the formal policies were ill-advised or, more commonly, those responsible for implementing them behaved defectively. Alternative models place a far higher premium on the policy formulation role and potential of those more conventionally seen as passive. The classroom teacher interpreting a new curriculum document, for instance, or the school principal ignoring an administrative fiat, are as much involved in the actual process of policy formulation as their superiors. These more dynamic models, further, acknowledge the place of conflict and discourse as key components of policy formation, as actors at all levels seek to resolve their clashes of interest, perspective, or opinion. Ownership of educational policies, then, becomes a key ingredient for their acceptance and success in practice.

There can be no doubt that the Bank has gravitated – as part of its institutional culture and behavior – to conventional models of how education policy is conceived and implemented. This is perhaps seen no better than at loan negotiations when the Bank, insistent on certain policy reforms, receives ministerial assurances that such changes will be announced. Many early project covenants were of this type, the Bank displaying little if any interest in how change was to be implemented and providing little if any support for it. It employed a model of policy that saw the ministerial edict as the key to educational change. Subsequent project completion reports that complained about the seeming failure of borrowers to implement agreed-upon policy changes became painfully common in the Bank. Bank documents – not least policy papers and loan documents – inevitably reflect the combination of a managerial, imperative tone with a state-centred bias. To be sure, the Bank's shareholders are national governments and loan agreements are concluded with national governments, but it does not follow that an education system needs to be managed as the Bank itself is (by a few powerful, central officials) or that policies for effective educational change must issue from edicts of central government officials. Policy is not something the Bank would naturally see as best formulated and owned down the line, and its language sees a prevailing of the language of obedience rather than of motivation and incentive.

Yet a seemingly paradoxical position faces the Bank. Evidence accumulated by the Bank is overwhelming that its conventional projects were far too complex and ambitious, especially as far as educational change was concerned. Projects needed to become simpler and more realistic. However, the growth of program lending, not least structural adjustment lending, worked against any trend in favor of simpler projects, many program loans overshadowing conventional projects in their complexity. While on paper many loans boasted a "comprehensive" and "integrated" approach to mutually supportive change components, the reality more usually was one of continuing excess of aspiration and expectation.

One of the core tensions in Bank operations – to the point of being a contradiction – is the Bank's essentially Keynesian design. Governments, their management of economies and their use of loan monies to pursue their economic and social objectives lie at the heart of things for the World Bank. Yet the Bank is an institution that by nature is highly sceptical of the role of governments in economic and social life. The Keynesian Bank serves as a ready critic of Keynesianism. Increasingly, the Bank has lampooned government planning and management of national education systems. Governments confuse supply and demand; they are cumbersome, inflexible, and inefficient; they need to rely more on market forces in education, and to decentralize control and management. This presents an acute dilemma for a bank that is somewhat free in its critiques of government: to what extent does it attempt to assist governments, to strengthen their planning and management capacities, and to what extent does it tell them to let go?

From 1995 onwards, much of the Bank's rhetoric has seen centralized governmental control over education as a core problem. Their cumbersome bureaucracies are seen as obstacles to achieving the broad range of objectives set out for them. On one level, these diagnoses are not new. What is more apparent is the vigor with which the Bank has promoted the dismantling of many conventional national governmental responsibilities in education. In particular, decentralization and privatization have gone hand in hand. Every program loan since 1995 has placed emphasis on shifting the basis of governance in national education efforts. Mostly, it has been undertaken crudely, the Bank's blueprints being somewhat blunt instruments for promoting changes that will stick. What is sticking, however, are the effects of dismantling national capacities that have taken decades to build up. However fragile they were, however limited in strength and resources, however cumbersome and rigid, they nevertheless constituted an expression of state responsibility. Whether the Americanization of the world's education systems has been a rational and productive policy pathway for the World Bank will not take much time to become apparent.

Policies for the financing of education

A consistent line of argument emerging from the World Bank has been the need for developing countries to spend more on education and to spend more wisely on education. The former argument has been justified essentially on the basis of human capital theory's sunny optimism that education and training will make workers, and thereby entire economies, more productive. For a time, the planned expansion of formal education systems was supported, but the ascendancy of rate-of-return arguments provided greater weight to assertions about the handsome returns from investing in education. The "numbers" concerning education returns, in fact, remain almost unbelievably high when compared with other sectors. Many in the Bank would reject them outright, as they would reject cost-benefit analysis as an exclusive basis on which to construct policy. But the education sector's capacity to maintain lending and thus survive as a Bank sector has depended greatly upon the political skill of its education policy staff in "selling" education, both inside the Bank and to borrowers.

What upset things was the end of sustained economic growth, the bedrock of human capital assumptions. The education sector was not able to remain innocent of the Bank's overall responses to the twin crises of debt and recession, a major theme of Chapters 5 and 6. Bank and IMF austerity measures frequently targeted the government sector as that component of national economies most amenable to rapid alterations in policy, within the longer-term context of price reform and the liberalization of economic arrangements. For developing countries, IMF and World Bank strategies for economic reform and adjustment were challenging, not only in terms of the austerity measures put forward, but more fundamentally because they raised profound political questions, not least of the relationship between the public and private sectors in economic life. With developing countries' education sector budgets accounting for 10 to 30 percent of public sector outlays, the educational implications of austerity measures and reduced public spending were obvious. The Bank's education sector needed to devise ways, in particular, of responding to the educational challenges of declining public budgets for education and IMF and Bank preferences for user charges in the public arena.

The education sector's policy insistence on raising private capital for the financing of education in developing countries was fundamental to its survival as a sector within the Bank. Without it, the sector would have gone the way of other "social overheads" sectors, notably population, rural development, or urban poverty reduction, generally fading to inconsequential levels. Both education and health were tolerated during the period of austerity reforms in that they were part of a set of welfare, safety net, and social concerns able to ease the transition to full-blown neoliberal norms. In the context of the overt triumph of neoclassical orthodoxy over Keynesianism in the Bank, the Bank had found in them something of a political safety valve. These social areas of lending enabled the Bank to assert its commitment to poverty reduction and to equity, but only so long as the social sectors returned the favor by insisting on the application of neoliberal ideals within their own policy jurisdictions. The relationship is crucial. Without it, education would have ceased to be a "bankable" World Bank sector.

Changing the financial basis for national education systems across the developing and transition economies was a huge undertaking. Typically, those systems attracted large proportions of national budgets. On the one hand, the Bank had the challenge of effecting reductions in overall public sector budgets worldwide. On the other hand, the Bank's education sector was promoting the benefits of increased expenditures on education, whatever the source. The challenge for the education staff was to bring these two requirements together, and convincingly.

What provided the way forward were rate-of-return calculations that pointed to primary education as the best investment subsector in education (and indeed an excellent investment area over many others outside education). Because he regarded the social rates of return so highly, Psacharopoulos was able to construct a policy platform for governments, one that made inescapable for them the provision of primary education for all citizens. The financial trade-off was increasing revenues at higher levels of education from students and their families themselves. Technical and vocational education would be radically affected, one that the Bank regarded as economically fundamental but one that governments need not, in principle, finance. Similarly, higher education, despite all its claims as a public good, would recede in prominence as a recipient of public funding. The saga in the late 1990s over user fees for primary education illustrated the stark politics of such reform measures in many borrowing countries. Although never promoted by the Bank, primary level fees were not actively opposed by it either, requiring intervention by the US Congress to make clear the incompatibility of primary education as a fundamental public good and the charging of fees for it in developing and transition countries.

Thus, while the Bank continued to assert how important the various subsectors of education were for national development and poverty reduction, it nevertheless was uncompromising in lecturing governments about where their priorities should lie. Despite all manner of attempts to soften the blunt policies that were declared so unambiguously in 1995 and to mollify its critics, nothing fundamental has changed since, not even with the policy statements of 1999 and 2006.

Policies for enhancing the economic relevance of education

From the very beginning, the World Bank's commitment in education has rested on the assumption that some patterns of educational provision are more conducive to stimulating economic growth than others. Although its particular choices have been both arbitrary and subject to change, the Bank has never avoided declaring which approaches to education it considers most dynamic in economic terms. The issue is directly related to its view of development, one that places a premium on increased worker productivity. At the same time, the Bank has never displayed much concern about what it is about education that makes people more productive, reflecting a major gap in the development education literature as a whole (Foster 1985).

At the beginning, many projects rested on the assumption that they would contribute to development by producing estimated numbers of trained persons, these manpower projections providing the economic rationale for most Bank activity in education. It did not take long for disappointments to abound, and for manpower projections to become weak and very loosely stated elements of project justification and objectives. Further, until the mid-1980s, it was curriculum reform (favoring technical and work-related content) that lay at the heart of Bank concerns to make education economically relevant, and which has proven to be the element most subject to dramatic shifts in Bank policy. Allied to this has been the question of which levels of schooling deserve most emphasis. Most recently, the developmental impact of education has been scrutinized in terms of efficiency and quality, themes made necessary with declining public sector budgets for education and Bank strategies for structural adjustment, privatization, and reform. Together, these concerns provide a relatively clear, if changing, picture of Bank views on those approaches to education most capable of stimulating economic growth. In sum, the Bank has been explicit about the kinds of education it has been prepared to back with finance.

Much has been made of policy emphases in the 1960s, and the arbitrary lending conditions in education imposed by President Woods. The first policy emphasis reflected the Bank's economic analyses of the 1950s, which saw many large-scale capital investment projects jeopardized through borrower shortages of technical staff to design and maintain them. Accordingly, a subsectoral emphasis on technical education ensued. The Bank, however, could not confine this emphasis to traditional postsecondary technical training, given borrower and UNESCO support for comprehensive programs of educational expansion at all levels. What emerged was priority Bank support for technical education at both secondary and higher education levels.

Many borrowers and potential borrowers in the 1960s had been declaring the rapid expansion of secondary schooling as their absolute educational priority. The Bank's technical education emphasis, to a considerable extent, collided with such aspirations, and its solution was to discourage support for general "academic" secondary curricula in favor of "diversified" curricula, which saw some combination of general curricula with work-oriented technical content. Thus the orthodoxy of the 1960s emerged – massive Bank lending for the rapid expansion of secondary school systems with heavy emphasis placed on the diversification of the curriculum.

Two education staff members achieved prominence through their attempts to evaluate the Bank's commitments to diversified curricula, Wadi Haddad and George Psacharopoulos. Both were fully cognizant of the highly influential vocational school "fallacy" argument first expounded by Philip Foster (1965) and taken up by many others (for instance, Blaug 1973), that the mainstream school system in fact was not the optimum location for the teaching of job skills. Given the extent and depth of Bank commitments to diversified curriculum reform, Haddad's initial questioning of the Bank's record in the late 1970s was an act of conviction and professionalism not always apparent in the Bank. His 1979 analysis, which cut right against Bank conventional wisdom, the sector working papers, and the findings of the OED review of education lending in 1978, remained unpublished by the Bank until external pressure led to its release in 1987 (Haddad 1987).

By 1985, Aklilu Habte was sufficiently confident of the available research evidence to issue a policy note based upon it. In June he instructed the regional lending Divisions, on the basis of research findings from just Colombia and Tanzania, in uncompromising terms, imposing a fascinating procedural condition upon planners in scores of borrowing countries: "Given the results of the study, the Bank should not in principle promote diversified schools. Borrowers requesting a Bank loan for such purposes should satisfy us that diversification in their particular case would be a cost-effective way of raising the cognitive achievement of graduates, and that the latter would follow careers consistent with their prevocational training."

Running in parallel with the demise of secondary diversification was the "ruralization" of the curriculum in nonurban areas, especially in primary and secondary schools. The McNamara years, with their educational focus on redistribution of investments and basic human needs, had seen large increases in Bank support for educational expansion in the countryside, and Ballantine had made much of the need for appropriate curriculum content in these areas. By 1980, however, the tide had turned: "Attempts to 'ruralize' the primary school curriculum have proved difficult and have often tended to create a dual system of education . . . . Agricultural programs in secondary schools, set up to prepare prospective farmers, have generally had disappointing results" (World Bank 1980a: 50). The rationale was essentially the same as that for diversification, with the prior benefit of important research findings from Dean Jamison indicating strong links between basic, general education, and farmer productivity (subsequently published as Jamison and Lau 1982).

More generally, the Bank's education sector has, in recent years, adopted quality as one of its major concerns in education. It is important to appreciate the manner in which the term "quality" has been employed by the Bank. For the Bank, the quality or internal efficiency of education has to do with the relationship between inputs and outputs in educational systems or institutions, outputs being assessed in terms of the system or institution's own objectives, rather than those externally applied through social and political forces. Key measures come to include examination scores, cognitive achievement subject by subject, length of time students take to reach certain performance standards, and results of assessments in noncognitive areas (not least student attitudes and values). The central quality issue is how student and institutional performance interacts with determining variables, which can include home, cultural, and socioeconomic variables as well as in-school factors.

The potential breadth of these variables, naturally enough, is enormous, but it is of some importance to note that the Bank has maintained only a limited interest in them. The breadth of its interest has been shaped by its own project experience, the Bank acting upon the assumption that the dynamics of a World Bank education project mirror those of an education system as a whole. Thus it seeks to understand education systems through analyses of its own project experience: if projects improve, so too should education systems. Thus its interest in quality issues becomes constrained: the effects of preschool investments (for instance, maternal literacy), the use of capital facilities, examinations and selection, teacher education, textbooks, wastage and repetition, the quality of educational management, and the use of time in educational institutions. A large and generally impressive body of material on these and related issues has now been published by the Bank. Because such issues are of concern in Bank projects, and because they can be deemed as "bankable," they serve to shape Bank views on educational quality. Thus the application of such tangibles as textbooks, equipment, and physical plant assumes prominence, through their potential significance in Bank lending programs. The more subtle and less tangible aspects of teaching and learning might be subsumed under Bank support for teacher education, but again Bank support tends to be confined to the tangible – buildings, equipment, textbooks, library collections, and the like. Program lending has offered only a partial solution.

Such a point should not be construed as a criticism of the Bank and its concerns. As a banking institution, its finance presumably needs to be applied in tangible and visible ways. Areas of difficulty emerge, however, when the Bank seeks to give the impression that its view of education is a comprehensive one, or that the aspects of education beyond its interest are not important. A related point has been made in several earlier chapters, that in order to stay in business the Bank (especially the IBRD) has needed to broaden continually the areas eligible for lending. Otherwise, a successful bank would run dry of needs and clients.

If the early 1990s had seen some emphasis on project design as a key means for promoting educational quality, the latter part of the decade and the early years of the new century saw program loans take on deeper significance for attaining it. They constituted part of Bank strategies and initiatives to reduce public sector budgets, increase the effective use of remaining public commitments, and foster privatization. The agenda put forward tended to be couched in terms of policies for the enhancement of educational quality, when in reality the agenda was one of reform and adjustment – doing more with less. A more positive expression of the need for reform came with the Bank's adoption of much OECD rhetoric concerning "knowledge society" and "knowledge economy" imperatives. Even the poorest countries were encouraged to think competitively about their location in a rapidly globalizing world economy, and Bank reform prescriptions increasingly pushed them in the direction of reforming education and raising quality in the name of improving their performance relative to others.

Policies for promoting equity, not least a basic education for all

It was the McNamara focus on poverty alleviation that produced the initial commitments to equity in education. Redistribution of investments and meeting basic human needs led to a concern, in particular, for education in rural areas, stimulating in turn a series of analyses that questioned the efficiency of concentrating economic investments on urban, academically oriented educational elites. As indicated in Chapter 4, this concern with a more even distribution of educational investments had nothing to do with the outworking of radical politics; nor did it see a transfer of Bank investments away from the groups that had traditionally benefited from them. In a period of rapidly expanding lending, it was more straightforward for the Bank to extend additional loan monies to unconventional areas, especially to rural primary schools and nonformal adult education, rather than to question the nature of distributive justice in borrowing countries.

Two particular commitments remain well in place: primary education and the education of girls. It is a hallmark of the educational leaders in the World Bank that they have maintained their commitments to these expressions of equity through periods of economic decline and growth alike. Just as it was easy for the Bank to extend new patterns of lending during economic growth, so too it would have been easy to abandon commitments to equity during recession. Although periods of recession are ones of severe constraints on educational budgets and of structural reform in many countries, the Bank has not resiled from its insistence that equity commitments – as a matter of economics rather than ethics – remain intact. Much has been done to accumulate evidence – from cost-benefit analyses in particular – that such was a rational course of action for borrowers. Where conflict was apparent between equity and efficiency – in appraising Bank projects, for instance – the Bank's position has tended to be neutral, preferring political judgments to be made by borrowers for any resolution of normative conflicts or dilemmas. One result was that Bank concerns for efficiency and equity have tended to sit side-by-side, poorly integrated. The Bank, choosing as it does to remain aloof from fundamental issues in borrowing countries of political power and economic privilege, can do little more than to emphasize rhetorically the equity side of the planning equation when economic rationales are lacking.

It remains a matter for speculation whether the Bank would retain its equity commitments in the face of any evidence having them clash stridently with efficiency. To date, the Bank has remained aloof from the human rights and justice concerns prominent elsewhere in the UN system, avoiding any kind of explicit moral concern in its statements of policy. Its arguments remain firmly embedded in economics. Yet in attempting to shore up education's position within the Bank, senior education staff have consistently sought to demonstrate that economic rationality is sufficiently amenable to moral influence for equity commitments to remain intact. Sceptics would say that economic criteria cannot hope to remain free from such subjective, normative, and ideological influence.

At the same time, the equity commitment required a justification that appeared more hardheaded than heartfelt, and on cue the education researchers organized themselves to demonstrate the benefits of investing along the lines implied by equity. What emerged was a cascade of evidence that, on the whole, was convincing, about such matters as the impact of primary education on economic development; interactions between learning achievement and mothers' literacy; benefits of schooling for farmer productivity; distributional analyses of educational expenditures for geographical region, sex, and income; income benefits of schooling for disadvantaged groups; links between education, literacy, and women's health and fertility; and detailed cost-benefits analyses of educational investments among various socioeconomic groups and subsequent earnings. Much more troublesome has been the internal dynamics of making the case for education as an instrument for promoting equity. Down the decades, it has been hard enough for the "education believers" in the Bank to promote the sector as a ready means of stimulating growth, worthy of inclusion in the Bank's portfolio.

Conclusion

It is on its own terms as an international financial institution that the World Bank should primarily be assessed and its work in education interpreted. Borrowers and commentators alike need not dwell on comparisons with donor agencies or intellectual organizations. Conversely, in their rhetoric and organizational behavior, the Bank and its staff would do well to reflect the limits of the Bank's charter and the constraints on its thinking imposed by its banking character.

As a bank, there is considerable room for adjusting its style and improving its effectiveness. Explaining the size of World Bank lending to any particular country is only possible if understood in terms of international politics and those factors determining how much and how quickly the Executive Directors get loan monies out to borrowers. This constraint profoundly affects the technical credibility of its lending year by year. Such sectors as education cannot remain innocent of the major operational concern of the Bank – to set the pace of its foreign exchange disbursements to borrowers. The lack of Bank pretension that the pace of its disbursements has an underlying developmental or poverty reduction rationale (as far as sectoral work is concerned) indicates much about the Bank and its style. In particular, it points to the operational tensions between the Bank's core functions – banking, development assistance, and poverty reduction. There can be no doubt that banking shapes the other two, providing the institution with the considerable challenge of ensuring the availability of sectoral finance in ways consistent with its policy rhetoric. On a rolling five-year basis the Bank knows something of its lending intentions, intentions driven far more by the extent of available finance and the creditworthiness of individual borrowers than by any technical understanding of what, sector by sector, might be achieved in developmental terms through the activities to be financed by that lending. It is in the scheme of things that there is no effective contribution made by education sector staff to the extent and timing of Bank education loans and credits to borrowers.

This aspect of the Bank's character is further reflected once disbursements are flowing, seen in the almost absolute lack of interest in evaluating implementation of project and program work. Disbursements might be audited, but not much else. An education project cannot help but reflect this neglect of whether it is having the developmental impact described when justified to the Executive Directors, and whether its quality can be improved prior to completion. To the outsider, these two aspects – the apparently arbitrary way in which finance becomes available for a borrower's sectoral loans, and the neglect of formative, qualitative project evaluation – are among the most surprising features of the Bank. They are eminently capable of change.

Those Bank officers more interested in the pace of disbursements than in the quality of projects tend to be those who see in leverage – the covenants and side-conditions attached to projects – the best means for the Bank to make a difference in borrowing countries, addressing policy fundamentals rather than the confines of a single project and its institutions. In more recent years, they have seen similar possibilities in program lending. Yet World Bank instruments of leverage are far less powerful than some commentators and critics have suggested. Borrowers frequently take the opportunity to ignore covenants, often pleading changed circumstances, especially in terms of sectoral policy. Leverage, in effect, is a much less effective policy device for the Bank than is commonly supposed.

In terms of influence on borrowers, Bank lending (with its dual elements of project activity and policy advice) is perhaps eclipsed by the Bank's entry into the world of ideas. As a reflective organization committed to generating research-derived justifications for its policy stances, the Bank yearns for a deeper and more comprehensive impact through avenues of influence transcending both project and program loans. Not least in education, the World Bank is investing much in its quest to shape global opinion about economic, developmental, and social policy. Rather than imposing views through specific loan negotiations, Bank style is broadening in attempts to lead borrower country officials to its preferred way of thinking. The power and influence of global climates of opinion in matters of educational and development policy cannot be overstated, and the Bank is proving successful in its aspiration to shape important elements of global opinion. But again, there are clear limits in place as to the Bank's intellectual influence, given the policy-driven nature of its research and the lack of penetrating, critical, open-ended inquiry. For a time, roughly 1980–95, the focus and policy of the Bank's research and analytical work in education produced findings powerful enough to drive Bank and borrower policies alike, whatever might be said about the content of those policies. Since 1995, it has been the Bank's more basic stances on economic fundamentals and governance that has been the driver of its educational policies and influence. Its own research capacities collapsed, but nevertheless the Bank retained enormous influence over borrower education systems, policies, and outcomes. The strength and influence of the Bank is frequently derived from borrower perceptions of that strength. Those borrowers who have stood firm against the Bank's overbearing style and policy arbitrariness are those to have most effectively utilized the finance made available through it. Those who are intimidated by it appear most vulnerable to the impact of its collective operational elements – project and program activity, policy advice, and intellectual influence.

Nevertheless, it is proving difficult for the Bank to construct a fully comprehensive view of educational development, constrained as that view is by the banking character of the institution. Its view can only be determined by what it sees as the bankable aspects of education, given that it cannot afford too wide a gap between its policy rhetoric and what it is prepared – or able – to back with finance. More than that, the World Bank's experience in education reveals a difficulty in forging convincing links between economic rationality in educational policy and education's normative and cultural aspects. Not least, its commitments to efficiency and equity – both real – do not rest easily together, in no sense the product of an overriding perspective which demands such a dual commitment. There is nothing in the Bank's economic view of education which in itself imposes the concern for equity, which is no more than a concern about constrained access to formal education of girls, rural populations, and the urban poor. Underlying factors determining inequality have not, to date, interested the Bank's educational researchers and policy analysts.

Economic reasoning cannot remain a matter of mere technique. The subjective, the interpretive, the aesthetic, the normative, and the ideological all play their part in the resolution of economic problems, and in that prior questioning leading to the posing of economic questions. As in so many areas of public and private life in the contemporary world, forging an integration of the moral and the material is proving elusive. Public policy, business life, international relations, and development cooperation all tend to be forced into compromising stances through the dilemmas posed by the state of the world and by human nature. Even were the Bank more fully to reflect its stature as a United Nations Specialized Agency, given that system's evolving applications of normative principles to international life, it is doubtful if the necessary integration would take place. Both the Bank's financial basis and the normative limitations imposed by the United Nations political character combine to present limits to that possibility.

A starting point could involve fresh consideration of the humanistic and spiritual dimensions of development. The domain of the spirit, giving expression to the integrity of human and cultural values, might provide an adequate definition of development, one sufficiently powerful to inform the dilemmas facing the global community, not least those deriving from the divorce in contemporary affairs between the moral and the material. The complex and costly arrangements embodied in the work of the World Bank, more costly to borrowing governments and their peoples than to the immediate providers of Bank finance, might well enjoy invigoration and technical revitalization through fresh consideration of their underlying purposes – the promotion of peace, human dignity, well-being, and happiness – that collectively have come to be termed development. Such a foundation would provide the World Bank with an agenda in education capable of releasing the full potential of education to contribute to the Bank's development work. Any genuine commitment to poverty reduction, not to say poverty eradication, readily provides a moral signpost. To date, the Bank's vision of education has been a stunted one, unlikely to make much by way of contribution to that most fundamental of developmental requirements – freedom.

The world's steady realization of an adequate education for all owes much in the past generation to the Bank's faith in it. Over the next generation, its quantitative aspirations for universal access to education may or may not be realized. Even the Millennium Development Goals set for 2015 appear increasingly elusive. The challenge from now on is to discover a view of education that is sufficiently comprehensive and powerful to create the conditions conducive to individual, community, and national freedom. Any imposed and narrowly utilitarian view of education serves to hold those conditions at bay, constraining the potential capacities of education so to contribute to development. Whether the institutional factors determining the Bank's approach to education can permit such a possibility is entirely another question.

Bibliography

Abadzi, H. (2003a) *Adult Literacy: A Review of Implementation Experience*, Washington, DC: Operations Evaluation Department, World Bank.

———(2003b) *Improving Adult Literacy Outcomes: Lessons from Cognitive Research for Developing Countries*, Washington, DC: Operations Evaluation Department, World Bank.

Adler, J.H. (1972) "The World Bank's concept of development: an in-house Dogmengeschichte," in J.N. Bhagwati and R.S. Eckaus (eds), *Development and Planning: Essays in Honour of Paul Rosenstein-Rodan*, London: Allen and Unwin, pp. 30–50.

Akins, M.E. (1981) *United States Control over World Bank Group Decision-Making*, unpublished dissertation, University of Pennsylvania.

Aklilu, H. (1983) "Where the World Bank is going in education," *Canadian and International Education*, 12(1): 63–74.

Aklilu, H., Psacharopoulos, G., and Heyneman, S.P. (1983) *Education and Development: Views From the World Bank*, Washington, DC: World Bank.

Alderman, H., Orazem, P., and Paterno, E. (1998) *School Quality, School Cost, and the Public/Private School Choices of Low-Income Households in Pakistan*, Impact Evaluation of Education Reforms, Working Paper no. 2, Washington, DC: World Bank.

Alexander, N.C. (2001) "Paying for education: how the World Bank and the International Monetary Fund influence education in developing countries," *Peabody Journal of Education*, 76(3–4): 285–338.

Altbach, P.G. (ed.) (1989) "Symposium: World Bank Report on education in sub-Saharan Africa," *Comparative Education Review*, 33(1): 93–133.

Annis, S. (1986) "The shifting grounds of poverty lending at the World Bank," in R.E. Feinberg (ed.), *Between Two Worlds: The World Bank's Next Decade*, New Brunswick, NJ: Transaction Books for the Overseas Development Council, pp. 87–109.

Ansari, J. (1986) *The Political Economy of International Economic Organization*, Boulder, CO: Rienner.

Apter, D. (1965) *The Politics of Modernization*, Chicago, IL: University of Chicago Press.

Archer, C. (1983) *International Organizations*, London: George Allen & Unwin.

Arndt, H.W. (1987) *Economic Development: The History of an Idea*, Chicago, IL: University of Chicago Press.

Arnove, R. (1980) "Comparative education and world systems analysis," *Comparative Education Review*, 21(1): 48–62.

Ascher, W. (1983) "New development approaches and the adaptability of international agencies: the case of the World Bank," *International Organization*, 37(3): 415–39.

Asian Development Bank. (2002) *Education: Our Framework – Policies and Strategies*, Manila: ADB.

Ayres, R.L. (1983) *Banking on the Poor: The World Bank and World Poverty*, Cambridge, MA: MIT Press.

Baldwin, D.A. (1966) *Economic Development and American Foreign Policy*, Chicago, IL: University of Chicago Press.

Ballantine, D.S. (1976) "Is the cup half full or half empty?," *Prospects*, 6(2): 210–16.

Baum, W.C. (1982) *The Project Cycle*, rev. edn, Washington, DC: World Bank.

Baum, W.C. and Tolbert, S.M. (1985) *Investing in Development: Lessons from World Bank Experience*, New York: Oxford University Press for the World Bank.

Benavot, A. (2004) *Comparative Analysis of Secondary Education Curricula*. Paper prepared with the collaboration of Massimo Amadio. Washington, DC and Geneva: World Bank and the International Bureau of Education.

Bennell, P. (1996) "Using and abusing rates of return: a critique of the World Bank's 1995 education sector review," *International Journal of Educational Development*, 16(3): 235–48.

Bennell, P. and Segerstrom, J. (1998) "Vocational education and training in developing countries: has the World Bank got it right?," *International Journal of Educational Development*, 18(4): 271–87.

Bennett, A.L. (1984) *International Organizations: Principles and Issues*, Englewood Cliffs, NJ: Prentice-Hall.

Bentaouet-Kattan, R.B. and Burnett, N. (2004) *User Fees in Primary Education*, Washington, DC: World Bank.

Berg, R.J. and Whitaker, J.S. (eds) (1986) *Strategies for African Development*, Berkeley, CA: University of California Press.

Bergsten, C.F., Cline, W.R., and Williamson, J. (1985) *Bank Lending to Developing Countries: The Policy Alternatives*, Washington, DC: Institute For International Economics.

Berk, D. (2002) *Tertiary Education: Lessons From a Decade of Lending, FY 1990–2000*, Washington, DC: Operations Evaluation Department, World Bank.

Berman, E.H. (1979) "Foundations, United States foreign policy, and African education, 1945–1975," *Harvard Educational Review*, 49(2): 145–79.

Bird, G. (2003) *The IMF and the Future: Issues and Options Facing the Fund*, London and New York: Routledge.

Birdsall, N. (1996) "Public spending on higher education in developing countries: too much or too little?," *Economics of Education Review*, 15: 407–19.

Black, E.R. (1963) *The Diplomacy of Economic Development*, New York: Atheneum.

Blaug, M. (1967a) *A Cost-Benefit Approach to Educational Planning in Developing Countries*. Economics Department paper EC-157, December 20, 1967. Washington, DC: World Bank.

—— (1967b) "Approaches to educational planning," *Economic Journal*, 77: 262–87.

—— (1968) *Economics of Education: Selected Readings*, vol. 1, Harmondsworth: Penguin Books.

—— (1973) *Education and the Employment Problem in Developing Countries*, Geneva: International Labour Organisation.

Bleicher, S.A. (1970) "UN vs IBRD: a dilemma of functionalism," *International Organization*, 24(1): 31–47.

Bøås, M. and McNeill, D. (2003) *Multilateral Institutions: A Critical Introduction*, London: Pluto Press.

Botti, M., Carelli, M.D., and Saliba, M. (1978) *Basic Education in the Sahel Countries*, Hamburg: UNESCO Institute for Education.

Bruns, B., Mingat, A., and Rakotomalala, R. (2003) *Achieving Universal Primary Education by 2015: A Chance for Every Child*, Washington, DC: World Bank.

Bujazan, M., Hare, S.E., La Belle, T.J., and Stafford, L. (1987) "International agency assistance to education in Latin America and the Caribbean, 1970–1984: technical and political decision-making," *Comparative Education*, 23(2): 161–71.

Burnett, N. (1996) "Priorities and strategies for education – a World Bank review: the process and the key messages," *International Journal of Educational Development*, 16(3): 215–20.

Burnett, N. and Patrinos, H.A. (1996) "Response to critiques of priorities and strategies for education: a World Bank review," *International Journal of Educational Development*, 16(3): 273–6.

Cahagarajah, S. and Nielson, H. (1999) *Child Labor and Schooling in Africa: A Comparative Study*, School Protection Discussion Paper, Washington, DC: World Bank.

Cammack, P. (2004) "What the World Bank means by poverty reduction, and why it matters," *New Political Economy*, 9(2): 189–211.

Camps, M. (1981) *Collective Management: The Reform of Global Economic Organizations*, New York: McGraw-Hill for the Council on Foreign Relations.

Carayannis, E.G. and Laporte, B. (2002) *By Decree or By Choice? A Case Study: Implementing Knowledge Management and Sharing at the Education Sector of the World Bank Group*. World Bank Institute Discussion Paper. Washington, DC: World Bank.

Carnoy, M. (1980) "International institutions and educational policy: a review of education-sector policy," *Prospects*, 10(3): 265–83.

Cassen, R. (1986) *Does Aid Work? Report to an Inter-Governmental Task Force*, Oxford: Clarendon Press.

Chabbott, C. (2003) *Constructing Education for Development: International Organizations and Education for All*, New York and London: RoutledgeFalmer.

Chenery, H.B. and Syrquin, M. (1975) *Patterns of Development 1950–1970*, London: Oxford University Press.

Chenery, H., Ahluwalia, M.S., Bell, C.L.G., Duloy, J.H., and Jolly, R. (1974) *Redistribution with Growth: Policies to Improve Income Distribution in Developing Countries in the Context of Economic Growth*, London: Oxford University Press for the World Bank and the Institute of Development Studies, University of Sussex.

Clark, W. (1981) "Robert McNamara at the World Bank," *Foreign Affairs*, 60(1): 167–84.

Clausen, A.W. (1985) *Promoting the Private Sector in Developing Countries: A Multilateral Approach*. Address by the President of the World Bank (London, February 26, 1985). Washington, DC: World Bank.

Cochrane, S.H. (1986) *The Effects of Education on Fertility and Mortality*. EDT Discussion Paper 26. Washington, DC: World Bank.

Colclough, C. (1983) "The impact of primary schooling on economic development: a review of the evidence," *World Development*, 3: 167–85.

Commins, S.K. (ed.) (1988) *Africa's Development Challenges and the World Bank: Hard Questions, Costly Choices*, Boulder, CO: Rienner.

Commission on International Development. (1969) *Partners in Development*. Report of the Commission on International Development, chaired by Lester B. Pearson. New York: Praeger.

Comparative Education Review. (2004) "Moderated discussion: the Task Force on higher education and society," *Comparative Education Review*, 48(1): 70–88.

Connell, W.F. (1980) *A History of Education in the Twentieth Century World*, Canberra: Curriculum Development Centre.

Coombs, P.H. (1968) *The World Educational Crisis: A Systems Analysis*, New York: Oxford University Press.

——(1985) *The World Crisis in Education: The View From the Eighties*, New York: Oxford University Press.

Coombs, P.H. with Manzoor, A. (1974) *Attacking Rural Poverty: How Nonformal Education Can Help*, Baltimore, MD: Johns Hopkins University Press for the World Bank.

Copple, C. (1990) *Education and Employment Research and Policy Studies: Annotated Bibliography, 1987–1990*. PHREE Background Paper Series 90/26, Population and Human Resources Department. Washington, DC: World Bank.

Corrales, J. (1999) *The Politics of Education Reform: Bolstering the Supply and Demand – Overcoming Institutional Blocks*, Education Sector Report no. 22549, Education Reform and Management Series, Washington, DC: World Bank.

Cox, R.W. and Jacobson, H.K. (eds) (1973) *The Anatomy of Influence: Decision Making in International Organization*, New Haven, CT: Yale University Press.

Craig, J.E. (1987) *Implementing Educational Policies in Sub-Saharan Africa: A Review of the Literature*. EDT Discussion Paper 79. Washington, DC: World Bank.

Craig, D. and Porter, D. (2003) "Poverty Reduction Strategy Papers: a new convergence," *World Development*, 31(1): 53–69.

Crawford, M.F., Yammal, C.C., Yang, H.Y., and Brezenoff, R.L. (2006) *Review of World Bank Lending for Science and Technology 1980–2004*. Science, Technology, and Innovation Discussion Paper 1. Washington, DC: World Bank.

Currie, A.P. (1997) "World Bank sees value in becoming an internal, external 'Knowledge Bank'", *Knowledge Management in Practice*, American Productivity and Quality Center. Issue 7: 1–8.

David, W.L. (1985) *The IMF Policy Paradigm: The Macroeconomics of Stabilization, Structural Adjustment, and Economic Development*, New York: Praeger Publishers.

de Ferranti, D. (1996) *Decline in Education Lending*, internal memorandum 20 December 20, 1996. Washington, DC: World Bank.

Demery, L. and Addison, T. (1987) *The Alleviation of Poverty Under Structural Adjustment*, Washington, DC: World Bank.

Demuth, R.H. (1973) "Relations with other multilateral agencies," in J.P. Lewis and I. Kapur (eds), *The World Bank Group, Multilateral Aid and the 1970s*, Lexington: Heath and Company, pp. 133–8.

Denison, E.F. (1962) *The Sources of Economic Growth in the United States and the Alternatives before Us*, New York: Committee of Economic Development.

——(1967) *Why Growth Rates Differ: Postwar Experience in Nine Western Countries*, Washington, DC: Brookings Institution.

Denning, S. (1998) *What is Knowledge Management?*, Washington, DC: World Bank.

De Vries, B.A. (1987) *Remaking the World Bank*, Washington, DC: Seven Locks Press.

De Vries, M.G. (1976) *The International Monetary Fund, 1966–71*, vol. 1, Washington, DC: IMF.

——(1985) *The International Monetary Fund, 1972–78*, vol. 2, Washington, DC: IMF.

——(1986) *The IMF in a Changing World, 1944–85*, Washington, DC: IMF.

Dewey, J. (1916) *Democracy and Education: An Introduction to the Philosophy of Education*, New York: Macmillan.

DFID. (1999) *Learning Opportunities for All: A Policy Framework for Education*, London: UK Department for International Development.

Dollar, D. (1999) *The Comprehensive Development Framework and Recent Development Research*, Washington, DC: Development Economics Development Research Group, World Bank.

Dollar, D. and Collier, P. (2001) *Globalization, Growth, and Poverty: Building an Inclusive World Economy*, New York: Oxford University Press for the World Bank.

Dove, L.A. (1981) "How the World Bank can contribute to basic education given formal schooling will not go away," *Comparative Education*, 17(2): 173–83.

Drattell, A. (1986) "A.W. Clausen talks about the World Bank," *The Bank's World*, 5(6): 2–5.

Easterly, W. (2001) *The Elusive Quest for Growth: Economists' Adventures and Misadventures in the Tropics*, Cambridge, MA: MIT Press.

—— (2006) *The White Man's Burden: Why the West's Efforts to Aid the Rest Have Done So Much Ill and So Little Good*, London and New York: Penguin Books.

Einhorn, J. (2001) "The World Bank's mission creep," *Foreign Affairs*, 80(5): 22–35.

External Advisory Panel on Education ("Bell external panel"). (1978) *Report of the External Advisory Panel on Education to the World Bank*, mimeo, Washington, DC: World Bank.

Fagerlind, I. and Saha, L.J. (1989) *Education and National Development: A Comparative Perspective*, second edn, Oxford: Pergamon Press.

Fallon, P. and Tzannatos, Z. (1998) *Child Labor: Issues and Directions for the World Bank*, Social Protection Discussion Paper, Washington, DC: World Bank.

Farley, L.T. (1982) *Change Processes in International Organizations*, Cambridge, MA: Schenkman.

Farrell, J.P. and Heyneman, S.P. (eds) (1989) *Textbooks in the Developing World: Economic and Educational Choices*, Washington, DC: World Bank.

Faure, E. (1972) *Learning to Be: The World of Education Today and Tomorrow*, Paris/ London: UNESCO/Harrap.

Feinberg, R.E. (ed.) (1986) *Between Two Worlds: The World Bank's Next Decade*, New Brunswick, NJ: Transaction Books for the Overseas Development Council.

Feld, W.J. and Jordan, R.S. (1983) *International Organizations: A Comparative Approach*, New York: Praeger.

Fiala, R. and Lanford, A.G. (1987) "Educational ideology and the world educational revolution, 1950–1970," *Comparative Education Review*, 31(3): 315–32.

Fine, B. (2002) "The World Bank's speculation on social capital," in J.R. Pincus and Winters J.A. (eds), *Reinventing the World Bank*, Ithaca, NY and London: Cornell University Press, pp. 203–21.

Finkelstein, L.S. (ed.) (1988) *Politics in the United Nations System*, Durham, NC: Duke University Press.

Foster, P.J. (1965) "The vocational school fallacy in development planning," in C.A. Anderson and M.J. Bowman (eds), *Education and Economic Development*, Chicago, IL: Aldine Publishing Company, pp. 142–66.

—— (1984) *Issues in Curriculum Diversification and Some Commentary on the Colombian and Tanzanian Studies*, DiSCuS Background Document RPO 672–45, mimeo, Washington, DC: World Bank.

——— (1985) "Economic development and education," *The International Encyclopedia of Education*, Oxford: Pergamon Press, 1528–36.

——— (1989) "Some hard choices to be made," *Comparative Education Review*, 33(1): 104–10.

Fox, J.A. (2000) "The World Bank Inspection Panel: lessons from the first five years," *Global Governance*, 6: 279–318.

Fox, J.A. and Brown, L.D. (1998) *The Struggle for Accountability: The World Bank, NGOs and Grassroots Movements*, Cambridge, MA: MIT Press.

Fretwell, D.H. and Colombano, J.E. (2000) *Adult Continuing Education: An Integral Part of Lifelong Learning. Emerging Policies and Programs for the 21st Century in Upper and Middle Income Countries*, Washington, DC: World Bank.

Fry, G.W. and Thurber, C.E. (1989) *The International Education of the Development Consultant: Communication with Peasants and Princes*, Oxford: Pergamon Press.

Gaynor, C. (1998) *Decentralization of Education: Teacher Management*, Washington, DC: World Bank.

Gilbert, C.L. and Vines, D. (eds) (2000) *The World Bank: Structure and Policies*, Cambridge: Cambridge University Press.

Gilpin, C.W. (1979) *Issues in Non-formal Education and Training for Rural Development*, Education Department mimeo, Washington, DC: World Bank.

Ginsburg, M.B., Cooper, S., Raghu, R., and Zegarra, H. (1990) "National and world-system explanations of educational reform," *Comparative Education Review*, 34(4): 474–99.

Gittinger, P.J. (1972) *Economic Analysis of Agricultural Projects*, Baltimore, MD: Johns Hopkins University Press.

Glewwe, P. and Patrinos, H. (1998) *The Role of the Private Sector in Education in Vietnam: Evidence form the Vietnam Living Standards Survey*. Report no. LSM132, Washington, DC: World Bank.

Goode, R. (1985) *Economic Assistance to the Developing Countries Through the IMF*, Washington, DC: Brookings Institution.

Gradstein, M. (2003) *The Political Economy of Public Spending on Education, Inequality, and Growth*. World Bank Policy Research Working Paper 3162. Washington, DC: World Bank.

Haddad, W.D. (1985) *Teacher Training: A Review of World Bank Experience*. EDT Discussion Paper 21. Washington, DC: World Bank.

——— (1987) *Diversified Secondary Curriculum Projects: A Review of World Bank Experience 1963–1979*. EDT Discussion Paper 57. Washington, DC: World Bank.

Haddad, W.D., Carnoy, M., Rinaldi, R. and Regel, O. (1990) *Education and Development: Evidence for New Priorities*. World Bank Discussion Paper 95. Washington, DC: World Bank.

Hamadache, A. and Martin, D. (1986) *Theory and Practice of Literacy Work: Policies, Strategies and Examples*, Paris: UNESCO.

Hancock, G. (1989) *Lords of Poverty: The Power, Prestige, and Corruption of the International Aid Business*, New York: Atlantic Monthly Press.

Hanna, N. and Agarwala, R. (2000) *Toward a Comprehensive Development Strategy* OED Working Paper Series No. 16. Washington, DC: World Bank.

Harbison, F. (1965) *Manpower and Education: Country Studies in Economic Development*, New York: McGraw-Hill.

——— (1967) *Educational Planning and Human Resources Development*, Paris: International Institute for Educational Planning.

Harbison, F. and Meyers, C.A. (1964) *Education, Manpower and Economic Growth: Strategies of Human Resource Development*, New York: McGraw-Hill.

Harriss, J. (2002) *Depoliticizing Development: The World Bank and Social Capital*, London: Anthem Press.

Hawes, H. and Coombe, T. (eds) (1986) *Education Priorities and Aid Responses in Sub-Saharan Africa*, London: University of London Institute of Education.

Hayter, T. and Watson, C. (1985) *Aid: Rhetoric and Reality*, London: Pluto Press.

Helleiner, G.K. (1986) "Policy-based program lending: a look at the Bank's new role," in R.E. Feinberg (eds), *Between Two Worlds: The World Bank's Next Decade*, New Brunswick, NJ: Transaction Books for the Overseas Development Council, pp. 47–66.

Heneveld, W. and Craig, H. (1996) *Schools Count: World Bank Project Designs and the Quality of Primary Education in Sub-Saharan Africa*. World Bank Technical Paper 303, Africa Technical Department Series. Washington, DC: World Bank.

Heyneman, S.P. (guest ed.) (1983) "Education and the World Bank: special issue," *Canadian and International Education*, 12(1).

——(1985) "Diversifying secondary school curricula in developing countries: an implementation history and some policy options," *International Journal of Educational Development*, 5(4): 283–8.

——(2003) "The history and problems in the making of education policy at the World Bank 1960–2000," *International Journal of Educational Development*, 23(3): 315–37.

Heyneman, S.P., Jamison, D.T., and Montenegro, X. (1984) "Textbooks in the Philippines: evaluation of the pedagogical impact of a nationwide investment," *Educational Evaluation and Policy Analysis*, 6(2): 139–50.

Hinchcliffe, K. (1985) *Issues Related to Higher Education in Sub-Saharan Africa*. Staff Working Paper 780. Washington, DC: World Bank.

Hirosato, Y. (1987) *Organisational Ideology, Policy and Budgets: A Case Study of the Changing Policies of the World Bank for Educational Intervention: 1946–86*, unpublished dissertation, University of Pittsburgh.

Hirschman, A.O. (1967) *Development Projects Observed*, Washington, DC: Brookings Institution.

Hultin, M. (1984) "Researchers and policy makers in education: the World Bank as middleman in the developing countries," in T. Husen and M. Kogan (eds) *Educational Research and Policy: How Do They Relate?*, Oxford: Pergamon Press.

——(1987) *Vocational Education in Developing Countries*. Education Division Documents 34. Stockholm: Swedish International Development Authority.

Hunter, W. and Brown, D.S. (2000) "World Bank directives, domestic interests, and the politics of human capital investment in Latin America," *Comparative Political Studies*, 33(1): 113–43.

Hurni, B.S. (1980) *The Lending Policy of The World Bank in the 1970s: Analysis and Evaluation*, Boulder, CO: Westview Press.

Hurst, P. (guest ed.) (1981a) "Education and development in the third world: a critical analysis of aid policies (special issue)," *Comparative Education*, 17(2).

——(1981b) "Aid and educational development: rhetoric and reality," *Comparative Education*, 17(2): 117–25.

——(1981c) "Some issues in improving the quality of education," *Comparative Education*, 17(2): 185–93.

——(1983) "Key issues in the external financing of education," *Prospects*, 8(4): 429–38.

IFC (1999) *Investing in Private Education in Developing Countries*, Washington, DC: World Bank/IFC.

Independent Commission on International Development Issues ("Brandt Commission report"). (1983) *Common Crisis: North-South Cooperation for World Recovery*, London: Pan Books.

Inter-Agency Commission, WCEFA (UNDP, UNESCO, UNICEF, World Bank). (1990) *Meeting Basic Learning Needs: A Vision for the 1990s*. Background Document for the World Conference on Education for All. New York: IAC, WCEFA.

International Labour Organisation. (1976) *Employment, Growth, and Basic Needs*, Geneva: International Labour Organisation.

International Monetary Fund. (1985) *The Role and Function of the International Monetary Fund*, Washington, DC: IMF.

Jackson, R. (1969) *A Study of the Capacity of the United Nations Development System* ("Jackson capacity study") DP/5, 2 vols, Geneva: United Nations.

Jacobson, H.K. (1984) *Networks of Interdependence: International Organizations and the Global Political System*, second edn, New York: Knopf.

James, E. (1987a) *The Political Economy of Private Education in Developed and Developing Countries*. EDT Discussion Paper 71. Washington, DC: World Bank.

——(1987b) *Public Policies Toward Private Education*. EDT Discussion Paper 84. Washington, DC: World Bank.

Jamison, D.T. and Lau, L. (1982) *Farmer Education and Farm Efficiency*, Baltimore, MD: Johns Hopkins University Press for the World Bank.

Jamison, D.T. and McAnany, E.G. (1978) *Radio for Education and Development*, Beverley Hills, CA: SAGE Publications.

Johanson, R. (1985) *Sector Lending in Education*. EDT Discussion Paper 18. Washington, DC: World Bank.

Jones, P.W. (1988) *International Policies for Third World Education: UNESCO, Literacy and Development*, London: Routledge.

——(1990a) "UNESCO and the politics of global literacy," *Comparative Education Review*, 34(1): 41–60.

——(1990b) *Literacy and Basic Education for Adults and Young People: Review of Experience*. A special study for the World Conference on Education For All. Paris: UNESCO.

——(2005) *The United Nations and Education: Multilateralism, Development and Globalisation*, London and New York: RoutledgeFalmer.

Jordan, R.S. (1988) " 'Truly' international bureaucracies: real or imagined?," in L.S. Finkelstein (ed.) *Politics in the United Nations System*, Durham, NC: Duke University Press.

Kapur, D., Lewis, J.P., and Webb, R. (1997) *The World Bank: Its First Half-Century*, 2 vols, Washington, DC: Brookings Institution for the World Bank.

Karmokolias, Y. and Maas, J. (1997) *The Business of Education: A Look at Kenya's Private Education Sector*. Report no. IFD32, Washington, DC: International Finance Corporation, World Bank.

Kennedy, P. (2006) *The Parliament of Man: The United Nations and the Quest for World Government*, London: Allen Lane.

Kim, J., Alderman, H., and Orazem, P. (1998) *Can Private School Subsidies Increase Schooling for the Poor?*, Impact Evaluation of Education Reforms, Working Paper no. 11, Washington, DC: World Bank.

King, E. and Orazem, P. (1999) "Evaluating educational reforms: four cases in developing countries," *World Bank Economic Review*, 13(3): 409–15.

King, E., Orazem, P., and Wohlgemuth, D. (1998) *Central Mandates and Local Incentives: The Columbia Educational Voucher Program*, Impact Evaluation of Education Reforms, Working Paper no. 6, Washington, DC: World Bank.

King, J.A. (1967) *Economic Development Projects and Their Appraisal: Cases and Principles From the Experience of the World Bank*, Baltimore, MD: Johns Hopkins University Press.

King, K. (2002) "Banking on knowledge: the new knowledge projects of the World Bank," *Compare*, 32(3): 311–26.

King, K. and McGrath, S. (2003) *Knowledge for Development?*, London: Zed.

Klees, S. (2001) "World Bank development policy: a SAP in SWAPs clothing," *Current Issues in Comparative Education*, 3(2): <http://www.tc.columbia.edu/cice> accessed September 21, 2006.

Knight, W.A. (2000) *A Changing United Nations: Multilateral Evolution and the Quest for Global Governance*, New York: Palgrave.

Kollodge, R. and Horn, R. (1986) *Education Research and Policy Studies at the World Bank: A Bibliography*. EDT Discussion Paper 23. Washington, DC: World Bank.

Kreuger, A.O. (1982) *The Role of the World Bank as an International Institution*. Paper presented at the Carnegie-Rochester Public Policy Conference, University of Rochester, 16–17 April 1982.

Kuznets, S. (1966) *Economic Growth of Nations*, Cambridge, MA: Harvard University Press.

Lauglo, J. (1996) "Banking on education and the uses of research: A critique of World Bank Priorities and Strategies for Education," *International Journal of Educational Development*, 16(3): 221–33.

—— (2000) *Engaging with Adults: Should the World Bank Invest More in Adult Basic Education in Sub-Saharan Africa?*, AFTHD Discussion Paper, Washington, DC: World Bank.

Le Prestre, P.G. (1982) *The Ecology of the World Bank: Uncertainty Management and Environmental Policy*, unpublished dissertation, Indiana University.

—— (1989) *The World Bank and the Environmental Challenge*, Cranbery, NJ: Susquehanna University Press.

Little, I.M.D. and Mirrlees, J.A. (1974) *Project Appraisal and Planning for Developing Countries*, London: Heinemann.

Lockheed, M.E. and Longford, N.T. (1989) *A Multilevel Model of School Effectiveness in a Developing Country*. World Bank Discussion Papers 69. Washington, DC: World Bank.

Lockheed, M.E. and Verspoor, A.M. (1991) *Improving Primary Education in Developing Countries: A Review of Policy Options*, New York: Oxford University Press for the World Bank.

McGee, R. (2000) *Participation in Poverty Reduction Strategies: A Synthesis of Experience with Participatory Approaches to Policy Design, Implementation and Monitoring*. IDS Working Paper 109. Brighton: Institute of Development Studies, University of Sussex.

McGee, R., Levene, J., and Hughes, A. (2002) *Assessing Participation in Poverty Reduction Strategy Papers: A Desk-Based Synthesis of Experience in Sub-Saharan Africa*.

IDS Research Report 52. Brighton: Institute of Development Studies, University of Sussex.

McGrath, S. and King, K. (2004) "Knowledge-based aid: a four agency comparative study," *International Journal of Educational Development*, 24(2): 167–81.

McKitterick, N.M. (1986) "The World Bank and the McNamara legacy," *The National Interest*, Summer 1986: 45–52.

McLaren, R.I. (1980) *Civil Servants and Public Policy: A Comparative Study of International Secretariats*, Waterloo, Ont.: Wilfred Laurier University Press.

McLean, M. (1981) "The political context of educational development: a commentary on the theories of development underlying the World Bank Education Sector Policy Paper," *Comparative Education*, 17(2): 157–62.

McNamara, R.S. (1973) *Address to the Board of Governors, Nairobi, 24 September 1973*, Washington, DC: World Bank.

Maddux, J.L. (1981) *The Development Philosophy of Robert S. McNamara*, Washington, DC: World Bank.

Mallaby, S. (2004) *The World's Banker: A Story of Failed States, Financial Crises, and the Wealth and Poverty of Nations*, New York: Penguin Press.

—— (2005) "Saving the World Bank," *Foreign Affairs*, 84(3): 75–85.

Manzoor, A. and Coombs, P.H. (1975) *Education for Rural Development: Case Studies for Planners*, New York: Praeger Publishers.

Mason, E.S. and Asher, R.E. (1973) *The World Bank Since Bretton Woods*, Washington, DC: Brookings Institution.

Meisler, S. (1995) *United Nations: The First Fifty Years*, New York: Atlantic Monthly Press.

Middleton, J. and Demsky, T. (1989) *Vocational Education and Training: A Review of World Bank Investment*. World Bank Discussion Paper 51. Washington, DC: World Bank.

Middleton, J., Ziderman, A., and Van Adams, A. (1993) *Skills for Productivity: Vocational Education and Training in Developing Countries*, New York: Oxford University Press.

Morris, J. (1963) *The Road to Huddersfield: A Journey to Five Continents*, New York: Pantheon Books.

Mosley, P., Harrigan, J., and Toye, J. (1995) *Aid and Power: The World Bank and Policy Based Lending*, London and New York: Routledge.

Mundy, K. (2002) "Discussion: retrospect and prospect: education in a reforming World Bank," *International Journal of Educational Development*, 22(5): 483–508.

Nagel, J. and Snyder, C.W. (1989) "International funding and international development: external agencies and internal adaptations – the case of Liberia," *Comparative Education Review*, 33(1): 3–20.

Nelson, J.M. (1999) *Reforming Health and Education: The World Bank, the IDB, and Complex Institutional Change*, Baltimore, MD: Johns Hopkins University Press for the Overseas Development Council.

Nelson, P.J. (1995) *The World Bank and Non-governmental Organizations: The Limits of Apolitical Development*, New York: St Martin's Press.

Ninkovich, F.A. (1981) *The Diplomacy of Ideas: U.S. Foreign Policy and Cultural Relations, 1938–1950*, Cambridge: Cambridge University Press.

Noor, A. (1981) *Education and Basic Human Needs*. Staff Working Paper 450. Washington, DC: World Bank.

—— (1985) *Strengthening Educational Management: A Review of World Bank Assistance 1963–83*, Education and Training Department mimeo, Washington, DC: World Bank.

OECD. (2000) *Knowledge Management in the Learning Society*, Paris: OECD.

Oliver, R.W. (1959) *The Origins of the International Bank for Reconstruction and Development*, unpublished dissertation, Princeton University.

——(1975) *International Economic Co-operation and the World Bank*, London: Macmillan.

Patrinos, H. and Ariasingam, D.L. (1997) *Decentralization of Education: Demand-Side Financing*, Directions in Development Series Paper, Washington, DC: World Bank.

Payer, C. (1982) *The World Bank: A Critical Analysis*, New York: Monthly Review Press.

Peet, R. (2003) *Unholy Trinity: The IMF, World Bank and WTO*, London: Zed.

Pentland, C. (1981) "International organizations and their roles," in M. Smith, R. Little and M. Shackleton (eds), *Perspectives on World Politics*, London: Croom Helm for the Open University, pp. 226–32.

Pettman, R. (ed.) (1979) *Moral Claims in World Affairs*, Canberra: Australian National University Press.

Phaup, E.D. (1984) *The World Bank: How It Can Serve U.S. Interests*, Washington, DC: Heritage Foundation.

Phillips, H.M. (1987) *UNICEF in Education: A Historical Perspective*. UNICEF History Series Monograph 9. New York: UNICEF.

Pincus, J.R. and Winters, J.A. (eds) (2002) *Reinventing the World Bank*, Ithaca and London: Cornell University Press.

Please, S. (1984) *The Hobbled Giant: Essays on the World Bank*, Boulder, CO: Westview Press.

Psacharopoulos, G. (1973) *Returns to Education: An International Comparison*, Amsterdam: Elsevier Scientific Publishing Company.

——(1980) *Higher Education in Developing Countries: A Cost-Benefit Analysis*. Staff Working Paper 440. Washington, DC: World Bank.

——(1981) "Returns to education: an updated international comparison," *Comparative Education*, 17(3): 321–41.

——(1985a) "Curriculum diversification in Colombia and Tanzania: an evaluation," *Comparative Education Review*, 29(4): 507–25.

——(1985b) "Returns to education: a further international update and implications," *The Journal of Human Resources*, 20(4): 584–604.

——(1986) *To Vocationalize or Not To Vocationalize? That Is the Curriculum Question*. EDT Discussion Paper 31. Washington, DC: World Bank.

——(1987) *Critical Issues in Education: A World Agenda*. EDT Discussion Paper 96. Washington, DC: World Bank.

——(1990) "From theory to practice in comparative education," *Comparative Education Review*, 34(3): 369–8.

——(1996a) "Designing educational policy: a mini-primer on values, theories and tools," *International Journal of Educational Development*, 16(3): 277–9.

——(1996b) "Public spending on higher education in developing countries: too much rather than too little?," *Economics of Education Review*, 15: 421–22.

——(2006) "World Bank policy on education: A personal account," *International Journal of Educational Development*, 26(3): 329–38.

Psacharopoulos, G. and Loxley, W. (1985) *Diversified Secondary Education and Development: Evidence From Colombia and Tanzania*, Baltimore, MD: Johns Hopkins University Press for the World Bank.

Psacharopoulos, G. and Woodhall, M. (1985) *Education for Development: An Analysis of Investment Choices*, New York: Oxford University Press for the World Bank.

Psacharopoulos, G. and Zabalza, A. (1984) "The effect of diversified schools on employment status and earnings in Colombia," *Economics of Education Review*, 3(4): 315–31.

Reid, E. (1973) *Strengthening the World Bank*, Chicago, IL: Adlai Stevenson Institute.

Riggs, R.E. (1988) "The United Nations and the politics of law," in L.S. Finkelstein (ed.), *Politics in the United Nations System*, Durham, NC: Duke University Press, pp. 41–74.

Righter, R. (1995) *Utopia Lost: The United Nations and World Order*, New York: Twentieth Century Fund Press.

Romain, R. (1985) *Lending in Primary Education: Bank Performance Review, 1962–1983*. EDT Discussion Paper 20. Washington, DC: World Bank.

Romain, R.I. and Armstrong, L. (1987) *Review of World Bank Operations in Nonformal Education and Training*. EDT Discussion Paper 63. Washington, DC: World Bank.

Rondinelli, D.A., Middleton, J., and Verspoor, A.M. (1990) *Planning Education Reforms in Developing Countries*, Durham, NC: Duke University Press.

Rosenau, J.N. (1992) *The United Nations in a Turbulent World*, Boulder, CO: Lynne Rienner Publishers.

——— (1997) *Along the Domestic-Foreign Frontier: Exploring Governance in a Turbulent World*, Cambridge and New York: Cambridge University Press.

Rotberg, E.H. (1981) *The World Bank: A Financial Appraisal*, Washington, DC: World Bank.

Salmi, J. (2000) *Student Loans in an International Perspective: The World Bank Experience*. LCSHD Paper Series 44. Washington, DC: World Bank.

——— (2001) "Tertiary education in the 21st century: challenges and opportunities," *Higher Education Management*, 13(2): 5–130.

Samoff, J. (1996a) *Analyses, Agendas, and Priorities in African Education: A Review of Externally Initiated, Commissioned, and Supported Studies of Education in Africa, 1990–1994* (with N'Dri Thérèse Assié-Lumumba), Paris: UNESCO.

——— (1996b) "Which priorities and strategies for education?," *International Journal of Educational Development*, 16(3): 249–71.

——— (1999a) "Education sector analysis in Africa: limited national control and even less national ownership," *International Journal of Educational Development*, 19(4–5): 249–72.

——— (1999b) "Institutionalizing international influence," in R.F. Arnove and C.A. Torres (eds) *Comparative Education: The Dialectic of the Global and the Local*, Lanham, CO: Rowman and Littlefield pp. 51–89.

Saraf, S.N. (1980) *Education in the 1980s: World Bank Perspectives – the Myth and the Reality*. IIEP Occasional Paper 57. Paris: International Institute for Educational Planning.

Schultz, T.W. (1961) "Investment in human capital," *American Economic Review*, 51: 1–17.

——— (1963) *The Economic Value of Education*, New York: Columbia University Press.

Schwartz, A. and Sack, R. (1996) *Sector Work and Project Performance in Education: A Review of Bank Experience*, Washington, DC: World Bank.

Schwartz, A. and Stevenson, G. (1990) *Public Expenditure Reviews for Education: The Bank's Experience*. Policy, Research and External Affairs Working Paper 510. Washington, DC: World Bank.

Scott, A.M. (1982) *The Revolution in Statecraft: Intervention in an Age of Interdependence*, Durham, NC: Duke University Press.

Searle, B. (1985) *General Operational Review of Textbooks*. EDT Discussion Paper 1. Washington, DC: World Bank.

Searle, G. (1987) *Major World Bank Projects: Their Impact on People, Society and the Environment*, Camelford, Cornwall: Wadebridge Ecological Centre.

Sewell, J.P. (1966) *Functionalism and World Politics: A Study Based on United Nations Programs for Financing Economic Development*, Princeton, NJ: Princeton University Press.

——(1975) *UNESCO and World Politics: Engaging in International Politics*, Princeton, NJ: Princeton University Press.

Simmons, J. (ed.) (1980) *The Education Dilemma: Policy Issues for Developing Countries in the 1980s*, Oxford: Pergamon Press.

Smith, M., Little, R., and Shackleton, M. (eds) (1981) *Perspectives on World Politics*, London: Croom Helm for the Open University.

Smyth, J.A. (undated) *World Bank Lending to Education: An Inside View From the Outside*, unpublished mimeo.

Sosale, S. (1999) *Trends in Private Sector Development in World Bank Education Projects*. Policy Research Working Paper 2452. Washington, DC: World Bank.

Spaulding, S. (1981) "The impact of international assistance organizations on the development of education," *Prospects*, 9(4): 421–33.

Stephens, M.D. (ed.) (1988) *International Organizations in Education*, London: Routledge.

Stewart, F. and Wang, M. (2003) *Do PRSPs Empower Poor Countries and Disempower the World Bank, or is it the Other Way Round?* Queen Elizabeth House Working Paper. Oxford: Elizabeth House, University of Oxford.

Stiglitz, J.E. (1998a) *More Instruments and Broader Goals: Moving Towards the Post Washington Consensus*, WIDER Annual Lecture, January 7, 1998, Helsinki: WIDER.

——(1998b) *Towards a New Paradigm for Development Strategies, Policies and Processes*, The Prebisch Lecture, October 19, 1998, Geneva: UNCTAD.

——(2002) *Globalization and Its Discontents*, New York and London: Norton.

Street, B.V. (1984) *Literacy in Theory and Practice*, Cambridge: Cambridge University Press.

Taylor, P. and Gordon, A.J.R. (eds) (1978) *International Organisation: A Conceptual Approach*, London: Pinter.

TFHES. (2000) *Higher Education in Developing Countries: Peril and Promise*, Washington, DC: World Bank, for the Task Force on Higher Education and Society.

Thias, H.H. and Carnoy, M. (1972) *Cost-Benefit Analysis in Education: A Case Study of Kenya*, Baltimore, MD: Johns Hopkins University Press for the World Bank.

Tilak, J.B.G. (1989) *Education and Its Relation to Economic Growth, Poverty, and Income Distribution: Past Evidence and Further Analysis*. World Bank Discussion Paper 46. Washington, DC: World Bank.

Tinbergen, J. (1958) *The Design of Development*, Baltimore, MD: Johns Hopkins University Press.

UNESCO. (1987) *Education and Training Policies in Sub-Saharan Africa: Problems, Guidelines and Prospects*, Paris: UNESCO.

UNICEF. (1998) *Addis Ababa Consensus on Principles of Cost Sharing in Education and Health*, New York: UNICEF.

United Nations. (1952) *Agreements Between the United Nations and the Specialized Agencies*, New York: UN.

United Nations Department of Economic Affairs. (1951) *Measures for the Economic Development of Under-Developed Countries*, Report of a Group of Experts Appointed by the Secretary-General of the United Nations, E/1986.ST/ECA/10, May 3, 1951, New York: United Nations.

United Nations Development Programme. (1985) *Generation: Portrait of the United Nations Development Programme, 1950–1985*, New York: UNDP.

——— (1989) *Education and Training in the 1990s: Developing Countries' Needs and Strategies*. UNDP Policy Discussion Paper. New York: UNDP.

——— (1990) *Human Development Report*, New York: UNDP.

United Nations Monetary and Financial Conference, Bretton Woods, July 1–22, 1944. (1944) *Proceedings and Documents*, Washington, DC: United States Department of State.

Van De Laar, A. (1980) *The World Bank and the Poor*, Boston, MA: Martinus Nijhoff Publishing.

Van der Gaag, J. (1995) *Private and Public Initiatives: Working Together for Health and Education*, Washington, DC: World Bank.

Velez, E. and Psacharopoulos, G. (1987) *The External Efficiency of Diversified Secondary Schools in Colombia*. EDT Discussion Paper 59. Washington, DC: World Bank.

Verspoor, A. (1985) *Project Management for Educational Change*. EDT Discussion Paper 12. Washington, DC: World Bank.

——— (1986a) *Implementing Educational Change: The World Bank Experience: Overview and Cases*, Education and Training Department mimeo, Washington, DC: World Bank.

——— (1986b) *Implementing Educational Change: The World Bank Experience*. EDT Discussion Paper 44. Washington, DC: World Bank.

——— (1986c) *Textbooks as Instruments for the Improvement of the Quality of Education*. EDT Discussion Paper 50. Washington, DC: World Bank.

——— (1989) *Pathways to Change: Improving the Quality of Education in Developing Countries*. World Bank Discussion Paper 53. Washington, DC: World Bank.

Vincent, R.J. (1986) *Human Rights and International Relations*, Cambridge: Cambridge University Press.

Wagner, D. (ed.) (1987) *The Future of Literacy in a Changing World*, vol. 1, New York: Pergamon Press.

Watson, K. (1988) "Forty years of education and development: from optimism to uncertainty," *International Journal of Educational Development*, 8(2): 137–74.

Weiss, C. and Jequier, N. (eds) (1984) *Technology, Finance and Development: An Analysis of the World Bank as a Technological Institution*, Lexington, MA: Heath and Company.

Weiss, T.G., Forsythe, D.P., and Coate, R.A. (1997) *The United Nations and Changing World Politics*, second edn, Boulder, CO: Westview Press.

White, N.D. (2002) *The United Nations System: Toward International Justice*, Boulder, CO: Lynne Rienner Publishers.

Williams, P. (1975) "Education in developing countries: the view from Mount Olympus," *Prospects*, 5(4): 457–78.

——— (1981) "Education in developing countries: halfway to the Styx," *Comparative Education*, 17(2): 147–56.

Williamson, J. (1990) "What Washington means by policy reform," in J. Williamson (ed.), *Latin American Adjustment: How Much Has Happened?*, Washington, DC: Institute for International Economics.

Williamson, J. (1993) "Democracy and the "Washington Consensus," *World Development*, 21(8): 1329–36.

———(2000) "What should the World Bank think about the Washington consensus?," *The World Bank Research Observer*, 15(2): 251–64.

Wolfensohn, J.D. (1996) *People and Development: Address to the Board of Governors, 1 October 1996*, Washington, DC: World Bank.

———(1997) *The Challenge of Inclusion: Address to the Board of Governors, 23 September 1997*, Washington, DC: World Bank.

———(1999) *A Proposal for a Comprehensive Development Framework: A Discussion Draft*, Washington, DC: World Bank, Office of the President.

Wolfowitz, P. (2005) *Charting the Way Ahead: The Results Agenda*, 2005 Annual Meetings Address, September 24, Washington, DC: World Bank.

World Bank. (1970) *Lending in Education*, Document for the Board of Executive Directors R70–147, July 23, 1970, Washington, DC: World Bank.

———(1971) *Education Sector Working Paper*, Washington, DC: World Bank.

———(1974) *Education Sector Working Paper*, Washington, DC: World Bank.

———(1978) *Review of Bank Operations in the Education Sector* (the "Romain Report"), Washington, DC: Operations Evaluation Department, World Bank.

———(1980a) *Education Sector Policy Paper*, Washington, DC: World Bank.

———(1980b) *World Development Report 1980*, Washington, DC: World Bank.

———(1981) *The McNamara Years at the World Bank: Major Policy Addresses of Robert S. McNamara 1968–1981*, Baltimore, MD: Johns Hopkins University Press for the World Bank.

———(1982a) *IDA In Retrospect: The First Two Decades of the International Development Association*, Washington, DC: World Bank.

———(1982b) *Report of the Task Force on the Bank's Poverty Focus*, Policy Planning Division mimeo, Washington, DC: World Bank.

———(1983a) *Education and Development: Views From the World Bank*, Washington, DC: World Bank.

———(1983b) *Focus on Poverty: A Report on a Task Force of the World Bank*, Washington, DC: World Bank.

———(1986a) *Financing Adjustment with Growth in Sub-Saharan Africa*, Washington, DC: World Bank.

———(1986b) *Financing Education in Developing Countries: An Exploration of Policy Options*, Washington, DC: World Bank.

———(1986c) *Improving the Efficiency of Education in Developing Countries*, mimeo, Washington, DC: World Bank.

———(1986d) *Recovery in the Developing World: The London Symposium on the World Bank's Role*, Washington, DC: World Bank.

———(1986e) *The Effects of Education on Fertility and Mortality and the Effects of Education and Urbanisation on Fertility*. EDT Discussion Paper 26. Washington, DC: World Bank.

———(1988) *Education Policies for Sub-Saharan Africa: Adjustment, Revitalization, and Expansion*, Washington, DC: World Bank.

———(1990a) *Annual Operational Review: Fiscal 1990 Education and Training*, Education and Employment Division mimeo, Washington, DC: World Bank.

———(1990b) *Primary Education: A World Bank Policy Paper*, Washington, DC: World Bank.

——— (1990c) *Skills For Productivity: Policies for Vocational and Technical Education and Training in Developing Countries*, Washington, DC: World Bank.

——— (1990d) *The Dividends of Learning: World Bank Support for Education*, Washington, DC: World Bank.

——— (1990e) *World Development Report 1990*, Washington, DC: World Bank.

——— (1991) *Vocational and Technical Education and Training: A World Bank Policy Paper*, Washington, DC: World Bank.

——— (1992) *Effective Implementation: Key to Development Impact*, Portfolio Management Task Force Report (Wapenhaus Report) R92–195 unpublished report submitted to the Executive Directors, Washington, DC: World Bank.

——— (1993) *The East Asian Miracle: Economic Growth and Public Policy*, Oxford: Oxford University Press for the World Bank.

——— (1994) *Higher Education: The Lessons of Experience*, Washington, DC: World Bank.

——— (1995) *Priorities and Strategies for Education: A World Bank Review*, Washington, DC: World Bank.

——— (1996) *The Social Dimensions of Adjustment: The World Bank's Experience 1980–1993*, Washington, DC: World Bank.

——— (1997) *Education Action Plan*, Human Development Division, Education Directorate (HDDED), Washington, DC: World Bank.

——— (1999a) *Educational Change in Latin America and the Caribbean*, Human Development Network Latin America and the Caribbean Document, Washington, DC: World Bank.

——— (1999b) *Education and Training in the East Asia and Pacific Region*, Human Development Network East Asia and Pacific Document, Washington, DC: World Bank.

——— (1999c) *Education in the Middle East and North Africa: A Strategy Towards Learning for Development*, Human Development Network Middle East and North Africa Document, Washington, DC: World Bank.

——— (1999d) *Education Sector Strategy*, Washington, DC: World Bank.

——— (1999e) *World Development Report 1999: Knowledge for Development*, Washington, DC: World Bank.

——— (2000a) *Comprehensive Development Framework Country Experience, March 1999–July 2000*, Washington, DC: World Bank.

——— (2000b) *Hidden Challenges to Education Systems in Transition Economies*, Washington, DC: World Bank.

——— (2001) *A Chance to Learn: Knowledge and Finance for Education in Sub-Saharan Africa*, Washington, DC: World Bank.

——— (2002a) *Constructing Knowledge Societies: New Challenges for Higher Education*, Washington, DC: World Bank.

——— (2002b) *Secondary Education for Africa: Strategies for Renewal*, Washington, DC: Human Development Sector, Africa Region, World Bank.

——— (2002c) *The Gender Dimension of Bank Assistance: An Evaluation of Results*, Washington, DC: Operations Evaluation Department, World Bank.

——— (2003) *Evaluation of the World Bank's Support for Primary Education: Approach Paper*, Washington, DC: World Bank.

——— (2004a) *Overview of Poverty Reduction Strategies*, Washington, DC: World Bank: <http://www.worldbank.org/poverty/strategies/overview.htm> accessed January 4, 2006.

World Bank. (2004b) *Rationales and Results in Secondary Education Investments: A Review of the World Bank's Portfolio, 1990–2001* (by Gillian Perkins), Washington, DC: Operations Evaluation Department, World Bank.

———(2005a) *Evaluating a Decade of World Bank Gender Policy: 1990–99*, Washington, DC: Operations Evaluation Department, World Bank.

———(2005b) *Expanding Opportunities and Building Competencies for Young People: A New Agenda for Secondary Education*, Washington, DC: World Bank.

———(2005c) *Improving the World Bank's Development Effectiveness: What Does Evaluation Show?*, Washington, DC: World Bank.

———(2005d) *Putting Social Development to Work for the Poor: An OED Review of World Bank Activities*, Washington, DC: Operations Evaluation Department, World Bank.

———(2006a) *Education For All – Fact-Track Initiative (EFA–FTI) Informal Board Briefing, 2 February 2006*, Washington, DC: World Bank.

———(2006b) *Education Sector Strategy Update: Achieving Education For All, Broadening our Perspective, Maximizing our Effectiveness*, Washington, DC: World Bank.

———(2006c) *From Schooling Access to Learning Outcomes: An Unfinished Agenda: An Evaluation of World Bank Support to Primary Education*, Washington, DC: Independent Evaluation Group, World Bank.

World Bank/UNESCO. (1984a) *Joint Study of Technical Assistance in Bank-Financed Education Projects: Report of the Steering Committee to the President of the World Bank and the Director-General of UNESCO* mimeo, Washington, DC/Paris: World Bank/UNESCO.

———(1984b) *Joint Review of the UNESCO/World Bank Cooperative Program*, mimeo, Washington, DC/Paris: World Bank/UNESCO.

Zachariah, M. (1985) "Lumps of clay and growing plants: dominant metaphors of the role of education in the third world, 1950–1980," *Comparative Education Review*, 29(1): 1–21.

Zymelman, M. (1977) *Manpower Planning Methods*, Education Department mimeo, Washington, DC: World Bank.

———(1980) *Forecasting Manpower Demand*, Education Department mimeo, Washington, DC: World Bank.

Index

Note: Page numbers in italics indicate tables.